BRITAIN'S WONDERLAND OF NATURE

Frontispiece

BY THE SIDE OF THE LAKE

When the bell-like flowers of the foxglove are in full bloom, this beauty spot in Lakeland looks even more attractive. The banks yield soil that is kind to the flowers and myriads of them find homes there.

BRITAIN'S
WONDERLAND OF
NATURE

Edited by
JOHN R. CROSSLAND
and
J. M. PARRISH

With Contributions by
F. KINGDON WARD, F.R.G.S.,V.M.H.,F.L.S.
RICHARD ST. BARBE BAKER
OLIVER G. PIKE, F.Z.S.,M.B.O.U.,F.R.P.S.
DR. VAUGHAN CORNISH
HAROLD BASTIN
MARIAN H. CRAWFORD
and over 20 other specialists

Special Literary Articles by
E. ARNOT ROBERTSON
DOREEN WALLACE
LEO WALMSLEY

LONDON AND GLASGOW
COLLINS' CLEAR-TYPE PRESS

Printed in Great Britain

Among the many beauty spots in Westmorland is the above scene, which shows the river Lune, near Kirkby Lonsdale. The bridge dates from the fourteenth century. This district is the scene of Charlotte Brontë's *Jane Eyre*.

INTRODUCTION

By JOHN R. CROSSLAND

"THIS other Eden, demi-Paradise," so sang Shakespeare as he spoke of England. Had he set his eyes on the northern borders and beyond, or cast them across the sea to the fair green isle to the west he would probably have held to his words and included the whole of our islands in his loving description.

In each land we have our dismal places, in every case made harsh and unsightly by the hand of man, in his struggle for existence in the grip of industry and commerce. The cities and towns of our island home have their sordid corners, and the natural glories of the countryside have given way unwillingly to the march of human progress. Still, through the very cracks in the brick-covered back-yards and along the wall-sides of factory, warehouse, and flat the blades of verdant grass throw up their spears to the sunlight. Balsam blooms in mill-yard amid the bales of cotton or wool, and the modest flowers of meadow and hedgerow launch their seeds in the breeze or fasten them to the birds and insects, to be carried and set in the midst of urban brick and stonework.

The countryside dies hard. In the dark hours the Mouse and Rat slip back and forth in our very habitations. In our parks the Squirrels dart about our trees in spite of our civilisation. The Sparrows come to our doors for crumbs, while the Starlings drive all before them to scavenge the edible matter we discard in garden or yard. Timid and alert, the Thrush visits our garden plot, while a piece of fat will tempt the Tit to most unlikely places.

The Blackbird sings on our chimney stacks, while in the fall of the year the welcome, solitary Robin cheers us with his audacity and sprightly self-confidence. Keats spoke but sober truth when he told us that " the poetry of earth is never dead." The drone of the willing Bee, the crazy flight of the Butterfly and the insistent hum of the Gnat all tell us that the countryside is never far from any one of us. The child who brings home his little gallipot complete with Stickleback or Bull-head, or who cheerfully hunts out for teacher his meed of Frog-spawn or couple of Common Newts reminds us mutely that even the ponds in our quarries teem with life that the industrialising of Britain cannot entirely drive from our midst.

To our suburban Hen-roosts creeps the stealthy Fox, most ingenious and knowing of all our wild creatures, while the Stoat and Weasel run across the roads in front of our cars before we leave the houses well behind us. Trees flourish in our roadsides, and even persist in the heart of the Metropolis, lending shade, colour and a sense of coolness to an otherwise purely geometrical scene.

BUT what of the land we inhabit? The rocks and the soil that has crumbled from them, the high hills and the valleys filled with verdure or water ; these are but the background for a teeming life that knows no human law. Wander where we will outside our human communities there is glory before our eyes. Perhaps the sweetest description of England is that of Elizabeth Barrett Browning when she speaks of " the ground's most gentle dimplement

(As if God's finger touched but did not press
In making England) such an up and down
Of verdure—nothing too much up and down,
A ripple of land ; such little hills, the sky
Can stoop to tenderly and the wheatfields climb."

Scott's description of " Caledonia stern and wild " fits well the mountain fastnesses, but there are softer glories unexcelled anywhere on earth, where the hills come down in more gentle slope to wooded loch or waving field of grain. There are river valleys where the Bees labour amid the luscious fruit, and moors clad in heather that are a feast to eye and heart. " God did not press " in making parts of Scotland, but when He laid a heavier hand on its rocks there came forth the noble mountains, with their laced caps of scudding cloud. Here are the noble Eagle, the magnificent Deer and the untameable Wild Cat, while on the moors Grouse, Partridge, and Capercailzie camouflage themselves from their enemies.

The nature-playground of Wales, with its towering mountain and rushing waterfall, that country spoken of by the Briton as " the Land of my Fathers," shows forth our trees and flowers at their best, the Ireland of Tom Hood and William Butler Yeats shines back to the heavens the reflected glory from its placid lakes, its hills and its verdant valleys. We must know more of the trees and the star-spattered meadows, more of the wild dwellers within its hills and vales.

A SCENE ON ELTERWATER.   [Will F. Taylor.

This picture illustrates the calm beauty of the English lakes. Shrouded with trees and guarded by the mountains that send their reflection into its depth, Elterwater is a spot admired by all lovers of beauty.

NATURE IN THE RAW. [*John R. Crossland.*
This Highland Cow was eager enough to pose for her photograph, but the Calf, being more diffident, turned tail. The mother, showing a fine pair of horns, looks ready to use them if the photographer should prove antagonistic.

THE ENCHANTED PATHWAY.   [*John R. Crossland.*

Stretching through woods blazing with warm colour from the Rhododendron bushes, the winding path gives promise of greater glories round each bend. The variety of rich shades on all sides enchants and delights the eye.

Photo : J. P. Taylor.]   OUTLAWS OF THE WOOD.   *[Mallinson.*

Fox cubs, gambolling as light-heartedly as only young puppies can, add a touch of colour and gaiety to the woods, and we cannot help admiring them in spite of the thought of the destruction they are likely to cause later on.

"The bold, majestic downs" of the southern land, the moors and fragrant vales of the north of England have each their beauties and their wild inhabitants. In the river plains and the broad acres of Yorkshire and East Anglia the corn waves its myriad golden heads, while through the rich red soil of Devon grows a harvest of good things for our daily need. In the Lake District we have a pocket world ; hill and scree, rock and fell, deep lake, and whispering forest. Forests? What of Robin's legendary home in Sherwood, the New Forest with its ponies and its avenues steeped in witchery? Epping and Hainault, Savernake—the list might go on and take in lesser woods. The old Oak built our ships of old as to-day the Willow helps our cricketers.

NATURE breathes history as it breathes life and movement. It tells of scientific truth, that matter cannot be destroyed. Year by year the buds appear and the trees increase their girth and size. The flowers shed their petals and scatter their seeds.

Young Fox-cubs are trained by their parents to carry on the work of depredation, while in the ponds and hedgerows the smaller life gives birth and dies. We may not have our Lions and our Crocodiles, Pythons may not crush our Pigs and Sheep in their coils, but we have a wonderland of Nature's wild things about us all the same, and we would not be without them if we could.

Our hills would be bare without their coats of verdure and the protecting trees to hold their moisture and keep their surface soil in place. Imagine our meadows without the star-like maze of flowers, or our hedgerows robbed of the scent of Honeysuckle, Hawthorn Blossom, and Meadowsweet. Our ponds would be filthy quagmires shorn of their busy inhabitants, and our gardens would suffer had we no cheery, persistent birds to take their toll on Worms, Slugs and injurious insect life.

Think of your home with all its clocks for ever silent, and you have a sense of the countryside without its wild life. The call of the Cuckoo, the rattle of the elusive Corncrake, the joyous song of the Lark in the sky above the Corn, and the cheep, cheep of the ubiquitous Sparrow even at our doorstep. Would you care to see these disappear from your homeland?

The story here told brings home to its readers the multifarious activities of Britain's wild life. It attempts to make that life live before the reader's eyes, and to encourage insight and desire to know more of the busy

AT THE END OF THE DAY.   [*Robert McLeod.*

The husbandman, rolling the seed into the ground, is one of Nature's most valued servants. His work in tilling the soil and giving it a chance to yield a fruitful store gives her a chance of displaying her talents of reproduction.

wonderland of Nature that lies about us. Flowers, shrubs, trees, and grasses are described. Not only are they enumerated and their characteristics set down, but the artist and the litterateur both come to the aid of the naturalist. Folk-tales, old superstitions and medicinal lore are all given a place, and the individual growths become more interesting when these varied lights are thrown upon them.

The busy life of pond and stream is carefully unfolded, while the creatures that contribute to the music and motion of field and hedgerows are drawn in word and picture. The animals that steal furtively beneath the trees by night, the nimble Squirrel and the crazy-flying Bat; the Badger, cleanest of animals; the Otter in his watery lair; all these and many more have their life story set out in an engrossing manner.

THE birds of woodland and mountain, the lonely and the social, the waders and those that live on the sea, are all given their proper place and their habits faithfully described by those who have made a first-hand lifetime study of the beautiful creatures in their native haunts.

Fishes of stream, lake, river and coastal waters are included, as are such marvellous sea-creatures as the Eel and the Salmon. Even the Molluscs and the small life of the seashore are described, for there is wonder in the smallest, least assuming inhabitants of the great outdoors.

In the insect world we read of the industrious Ant, the never-resting Bee, the Wasp, Hornet and Dragonfly. This vastly-populated world of insect life is thoroughly

dealt with, and facts set down that only experts studying the actual creatures in their native haunts can tell. Butterflies and Moths, Cockroaches and Earwigs are given their proper place, and the marvels of these small creatures' instinct intimately described.

The few remaining descendants of our larger wild animals are included, in the chapters on our Deer, Wild Ponies and Wild Cattle. The Wild Cat, Polecat, Weasel, Stoat and Pine Marten are shown in their daily and nightly hunt for prey. The Eagles from the mountain peaks, the Owls and Hawks of our islands, the Ravens, Carrion Crows and other destroyers are dealt with in their proper place.

Did you know that the Cormorant and the Kingfisher vied with each other for the filthiest home, while that of the Badger is the cleanest of all? Did you know that Ants kept their own Cows, that Newts shed their skins and left each foot and leg as a perfect glove? Is it news that the Hare begins his journey from home with a huge jump, and do you know why? Are you aware that some of our flowers eat insects, and that no vegetation will grow under a Beech Tree? If these facts are news to you, this volume will prove of great interest, for it tells of these and many more intensely interesting wonders of our wild world out of doors.

The writers are people of personal research into the wonderland of the wild. They have hunted with camera and keen eye, and written with a love of their subject. Their object has been to place before their readers a cinema film, if such can be done in words and " still " pictures, of our homeland's outdoor life. Our combined object has been to interest and amuse, and at the same time to assist those who love the country and know little in detail of its wonders to look with keener insight and more loving enthusiasm at the many marvellous and beauteous things around their feet.

Photographs have been carefully selected from thousands submitted to the editors, and every effort has been made to include in one handy volume something of the thriving and fascinating world outdoors. It is hoped that this will be a book to assist the reader in ramble and holiday expedition, teach the younger members of the family to love Nature and be kind to its smallest creatures, and furnish a work of easy reference to those who would know details of any of our wild creatures, trees, or flowers.

Nature is all about us, if we have eyes to see. But we need more than eyes. A trained intelligence that seeks to find out more than meets the eye at first glance is required. It is essential that the explorer in the realm of Nature shall study his subject carefully, with sympathy and insight. The life story of the flower, plant, tree, or moving creature should be traced. The childhood and growth of even our smallest creatures is a fascinating study, for Nature has given certain instincts to each type of wild creature, instincts that are faithfully followed without the slightest deviation by countless generations of those creatures. The Moth will always trace his mate by her scent, the Bee will ever gather honey for the cells in the hive, the Mole will burrow and construct his chambers to the set pattern of his ancestors, the Gull will find her own nest among the hundreds clustered around.

It is fascinating to go out into the woods, meadows, hedgerows or marshes, or to ramble over moor or seashore with one topic in mind all the time. It may be you study Nature's methods of camouflage for her less militant creatures. You may trace out the family life of a bird, animal or insect. Again, your interest may lie in the method of building a home, of snaring prey or of defending the home against invasion. Whatever your study, if you have a definite topic, it will be engrossing. There is still much to learn about even the smallest of Nature's children; the experts have not exhausted the tale of wonder.

WHY and how does such and such a thing happen? For what reason does this bird or that reptile perform certain evolutions? Why are some seeds winged and others attached to a parachute or armed with barbs? These are intriguing questions, and Nature study, wholeheartedly taken in a questing spirit, will furnish answers to all these and countless more inquiries.

You may not attain to the heights that Wordsworth attained, for he tells us that:

" The meanest flower that blows can give
    Thoughts that do often lie too deep for
        tears."

But if you go out into the open air to learn, to enjoy and to be in tune with Nature in all her moods, you will at least be able to say with the poet Keats:

" The poetry of earth is never dead."

EVENING ON THE HILL-TOP.   [Robert McLeod.
Silhouetted against the sky, man and horses plough their last furrow before the deepening shadows send them home to rest. A steady hand and eye is required in the man, and dogged strength in the beasts.

A SURREY LANDSCAPE.

[J. Dixon-Scott.

The beauty of Surrey is difficult to surpass. This picture gives a view as enchanting as any to be seen in the country. Taken from Crooksbury Hill, it looks toward Frensham Common and the Devil's Punch Bowl at Hindhead.

Loch Lomond, with Ben Lomond on guard in the distance, is a gem of Scottish scenery whose lure attracts many.

CONTENTS

CONTENTS

When the river Ure is in spate the falls at Aysgarth, in Yorkshire, present a magnificent appearance. The river descends a series of step-like rocks, spreading out and forming deep pools under the rocky banks.

[Photo: John R. Crossland.

BRITAIN'S NATURAL SCENERY

By Dr. VAUGHAN CORNISH

BRITAIN'S beauty spots are enumerated below for the benefit of the Nature lover who can admire a purple-carpeted sweep of moorland or the gentle ripple of an inland lake. This trip round Great Britain, picking out the gems of scenery, will prove refreshing and will act as a tonic to those who find it a relief to " get back to Nature."

THE troubled times in which we live are no mere state of tribulation, but equally a kind of stirring, as expressed in the phrase " troubled waters," a stirring of the spirit of Man. Indeed, throughout the world to-day mankind is engaged in a re-valuation of his possessions. Of the revaluations which show the character of permanence none contains greater promise for the welfare of mankind than the general recognition that a closer communion with Nature is not only a means for physical recuperation, but for that development and enrichment of the human personality upon which the future of the Human Race principally depends.

In Victorian times the devotees of Natural Scenery were wont, as far as opportunity allowed, to travel abroad in search of the spectacular forms of the world's landscape. Not the least interesting development of the newer outlook is the almost passionate devo-tion to the scenery of our native land which has sprung up since the Great War. Patriot-ism apart, it is a geographical fact that the

scenery of Great Britain presents an immense variety of natural beauties. For their full appreciation close observation is required and will certainly be repaid, for the beauties of our landscape are largely of a kind that may escape the careless passers-by but which, once recognised, are good to live with and never pall upon the sight.

The regional variety of our landscape is due to the circumstance that the whole geological sequence of rocks crops out on the surface as we pass from the south and east to the north and west of the island. Beginning in East Anglia with the more recent strata, soft and easily worn down, it continues through the chalk and oolite limestone and ends in the Devonian peninsula, Wales, the Lake District and the Highlands of Scotland with lofty, rugged and irregular masses of volcanic rock and ancient sediments compacted by the pressure of strata now stripped away.

In the corn lands of East Anglia the whole landscape is cultivated, nothing of the wild remaining, nevertheless to the discriminating nature-lover this countryside has both pic-torial charm and poetic appeal, for it is typical of the Arcadian world (the world which began in the Garden of Eden) where Nature is cared for and tended by the hand of Man. Moreover, the wild life of this countryside has not been unduly impoverished for, while the predatory species of mammals and birds have almost vanished, the copses and quickset hedges (an essentially English feature) provide nesting-places for innumer-able song-birds whose music is so important an element in the æsthetic aspect of Nature.

Where Nature is untamed.

East Anglia has no uncultivated heights of land, but in the marshes, lagoons and river channels of the Norfolk and Suffolk Broads, Nature is untamed, the landscape and the sky impress the sense of freedom and space, golden reed-beds beside the blue waters fill even the winter landscape with colour, and all manner of waterfowl delight the eye with dainty movement and decorative plumage.

In the South-Eastern counties we come to an older geological formation than that of East Anglia, the chalk, which provides a more perfect example of undulating country than any other kind of rock. Compact, yet both friable and soluble, it has weathered in the form of a succession of downs and coombs whose sweeping curves are continuous as those of the crest and trough of the ocean swell. Enfolded between the North and South Downs of the chalk lies the fertile plain of the Wealden clay in Kent, Surrey and Sussex where the oak tree flourishes, and is permitted to grow in its proper spreading habit, thereby decorating the landscape with a restful pattern of rounded shapes. It is however, farther west, in Hampshire, that we find the best remaining example of the characteristic English woodland with its end-less succession of billowy tree tops, for here the New Forest is maintained under laws and regulations which approximate to those which Nature-lovers hope to see applied in an Act of Parliament for the constitution of the national parks which are needed for the preservation of typical landscapes of wild Britain.

In Western Somerset, Devon and Cornwall we find the southernmost example of the spectacular hills which have been formed by the weathering of hard rocks. In the South-Eastern and Midland counties the hills,

whether of gravel, chalk or oolite limestone (as the Cotswolds) provide admirable view-points for spacious panoramas of the smiling plain but are seldom of striking appearance as viewed from below. It is otherwise with the great, rounded boss of Dartmoor capped by granite tors, a massif of true mountain form which dominates the landscape of Devon.

The rounded heights of Exmoor are less spectacular, but this delectable country of heathery hill and grassy coomb has its own special charms. It is still a riding country, after the fashion which was general through-out England before Macadam's time. More-over, the recesses of this open " forest " still harbour the wild red deer.

There is something singularly appropriate in the circumstance that the Land's End, the Atlantic outpost of England, should be buttressed with cliffs of granite, the primeval rock. The visual character of the coast also fully satisfies the demands of association, for the cliffs, which rise sheer from the waves, are made of great jointed blocks and look like cyclopean masonry piled up by giant hands as a bulwark of the land.

Returning from the Devonian peninsula, let us glance at the landscape of the Western counties of England bordering on Wales. Where the lonely height of Malvern is viewed across the golden harvest fields of Gloucester or Hereford we have a picture of agricultural England with a background of mountainous forms. As we follow the valleys of the Wye, the Severn or the Dee, which link the two national regions of South Britain, the colour scheme changes, for we have left the plough lands of England for the green, upland pas-tures of Wales. Following the valleys upwards to the recesses of the hills, the traveller who comes from the English plain finds a new delight in the swift-flowing waters of the mountain stream, clear as crystal, coloured as the Cairngorm, flashing back the light from the ripples in the shallows, and making gentle music as it courses round the bend.

A shrine of beauty.

The chief shrine of natural beauty in Wales is Snowdonia, a land still called by a medieval Latin name. Its most characteristic aspect is from the west, whence the whole chain of peaks is visible, the most perfect example of a mountain range in Great Britain. In the recesses of its rocky heights some of the rarer wild mammals breed and the larger hawks

PISTYLL CAIN.

[*G. P. Abraham*

In Wales there are many scenes so beautiful that they look almost like glimpses of fairyland. Pistyll Cain, in North Wales, is one of these picturesque spots that has a great appeal to all lovers of natural scenery.

3

A GEM OF SCOTTISH SCENERY.   [*Photo : Donald McLeish*

Here is a glimpse of Loch Lomond from one of its many wooded islands. Beyond can be seen the noble form of Ben Lomond, rising to a height of 3192 feet, and still snow-capped even in the early summer days.

GOAT FELL.

[*Photo : W. S. Thomson.*

This view from Cirmhor, in Arran, looking towards Goat Fell, shows the rugged grandeur of the Scottish hills. Though bare and bleak, they have a beauty that surpasses the " prettiness " of lowland scenery.

find nesting-places, which are not, however, perfectly secure.

The Shropshire Highlands, a promontory of the Cambrian heights projecting into historic England, combine the beauty of the Welsh hills with the charm of English medieval architecture. Thence, crossing the Severn at its northern bend, we reach by a low divide the winding Trent, the arterial river of the Midland Plain. Following either of its left-bank tributaries, the Dove or Derwent, we enter the mountain limestone of Derbyshire, a formation which is soluble as chalk but hard as granite, and has so weathered that the conspicuous features of the scenery are not the broad uplands, but the narrow gorges called "dales," with precipitous, turreted cliffs overhanging level pastures through which winds the swift current of a stream of perfect clearness.

So we come to the Peak country, where at Kinder Scout the limestone is capped with millstone grit, whose outcrop in abrupt "edges" marks the transition from the scenery of the Midlands to that of the Northern counties. Thenceforward across Yorkshire and as far as the Tyne Gap in Northumberland stretch the broad heights of the Pennine Chain, bleak in winter but in late summer clothed in purple heather which imparts a soothing fragrance to the strong moorland air and makes the shadows of the hill harmonious in colour with the blue spaces of the sky, and so unites the whole environment in one chromatic scheme.

In the Valley of the Eden.

The Midland route of the L.M.S. Railway affords fine views of Pennine scenery, and in particular of Ingleborough, the best example of a four-square mountain capped with the stubborn millstone grit. Later, the train glides down into the fertile Eden valley. On the right stands Cross Fell, the immensely long straight-edged escarpment of the Pennine Moors, but the eye of the traveller is more strongly attracted by the mountain peaks on the left which crown the Lake District. This country, being almost circular in plan, and attaining its greatest height near the centre, has been geographically defined as the Cumbrian Dome. In form, in substance and in geological antiquity this country resembles the most mountainous parts of Wales, but in the valleys which radiate from the central nucleus lie beautiful lakes, a

AN OLD-WORLD VILLAGE.   *[Mondiale.*

A most picturesque village in Devon with its thatched roofs, cob-wall, and quaint street is Cockington, near Torquay. This corner attracts many thousands of tourists eager to recapture the old-world atmosphere.

A GLIMPSE OF STRATFORD-ON-AVON.   [*Mondiale.*
The spire of Holy Trinity Church rises majestically from the wooded banks of the Avon near whose quiet waters Shakespeare was born. Here is found his monument, and the American window erected in his honour.

feature not found in the valleys of Snowdonia. They owe their charm in some measure to a fortunate proportion between the expanse of their waters and the height of the surrounding land. A lake among mountains is one of the most precious things in scenery in whatever part of the world it may be found. In traversing the length of Britain we first find this desirable feature in the northern counties of England about half-way between Cornwall and Caithness. In Scotland, however, the numerous mountain lochs or lakes are a principal and characteristic feature of the landscape. The English Lake District, combining some of the finest features of Wales and Scotland, presents also in its valleys certain qualities of Arcadian charm which are specially characteristic of the English scene.

All the upper levels of the central mass, the " Fells," remain entirely wild. The rocky summits are no mean test for the true mountain-climber. The surrounding slopes, grassy not heathery, are sheep walks, and therefore free from the restrictions which hamper the enjoyment of the Rambler on the Pennine grouse moors.

Crossing from the Lake District to the western entrance of the Tyne Gap, we soon encounter a feature which is novel to the traveller from the south : the outcrop of the Great Whin Sill, a line of volcanic crags extending diagonally across Northumberland from Thirwall (near Gilsland on he Cumberland border) to Dunstanborough on the east coast. The Romans took advantage of these crags by carrying the Hadrian Wall along their steep north-facing edge. The vast prospect thence across the country of the Pictish tribes is a moorland of sedge and grass, unlike the purple moors of Yorkshire, a foretaste of the Southern Uplands of Scotland.

Fortresses that face the Sea.

Further east, on isolated outcrops of the Great Whin Sill overlooking the North Sea, stand the castles of Dunstanborough and Bamburgh. The site of these medieval fortresses so different from those of Arundel and Windsor, is similar to that of the castles of Edinburgh and Stirling, which also crown intrusions of volcanic rock. Taking into account the two important features, lakes and volcanic crags, I suggest that we may properly divide the scenic geography of Great Britain by a line following the River

7

IN THE LAKE DISTRICT.

[*G. P. Abraham*

On the east side of Derwentwater, near Keswick, is found this beautiful spot, Friar's Crag. This picture, taken in springtime, shows the calm serenity of the lake under the shadow of the snow-capped hills.

A WELSH WATERFALL.

[*G. P. Abraham*

One of the most beautiful scenes in Wales, which attracts tourists to linger in admiration, is the Swallow Falls near Bettws-y-coed. The sweeping journey over the rocks has crested the rushing water with white foam.

9

Kent from its mouth at Morecambe Bay, Cross Fell, and the Great Whin Sill from the Tyne Gap to Dunstanborough. This leaves the mountains and lakes of ancient Cumbria and the whole of the Cheviots in North Britain. The line differs both from the short defensive frontier of the Roman garrison and from that ultimately determined by the contest of two nations for the good farm lands of the Border, but is perfectly in accordance with the structural features of the land itself, for although the island stretches north and south, the lie of the rocks of which it is composed is diagonal thereto, running from south-west to north-west; thus a division which places the whole of the Pennines in South Britain while leaving the Lake District in North Britain is entirely in accordance with the facts of nature as represented on both the geological and the orographical (or relief) map. North of the national frontier the valley of the Tweed has the verdant fertility of the Eden to the south, and the rugged mountains of Galloway, facing the English Lake District of ancient Cumbria across the Solway Firth, are also diversified by

numerous lakes, although these are of a smaller size.

The Southern Uplands sink somewhat rapidly to the Central Lowlands, where the population of Scotland is mainly concentrated. The Central Plain of Scotland is in fact a Rift Valley, let down by subsidence of the earth between the fault-lines of the Southern Uplands and the Highlands. The coal measures and sedimentary rocks which provide a fertile soil have been preserved from denudation in the central lowlands, but entirely stripped from the Highlands, where a huge area (as areas are reckoned in Britain) is entirely composed of ancient rocks remoulded by heat and pressure to the crystalline condition of gneiss and schists. These " metamorphic " rocks, running in folds from south-west to north-east, cover something like one-half of Scotland, an area much greater than the whole of Wales. The scenic features of the gneiss and schists are in fact not upstanding but incised, glens with corries (half-cauldron-shaped crags); swift burns with clear water brown from the peat; and lakes, called lochs, which often lie in

BURNHAM BEECHES. [J. Dixon-Scott.

This famous tract of forest lies in the heart of Buckinghamshire. Some of the Beeches are very old. The picture above gives an idea of their beauty and the marvellous play of light and shade among their branches.

DAFFODILS AT ULLSWATER.   [Photo: G. P. Abraham

When Wordsworth, wandering on the flower-clad banks of Ullswater in the Lake District, suddenly came upon this beautiful scene, it is little wonder that he was inspired to write his famous poem, " The Daffodils."

long fingers in the furrows of the folds. The landscape is brightened by the watery expanse, but lochs which lie thus longitudinally have a monotonous outline, and so we find that the Highland lochs most celebrated for beauty are those which lie in the transverse valleys which cut across the grain of the the country, and so have variety of outline and of slope of shore, as well as being often diversified by islands. Such are Loch Katrine and the great Loch Lomond.

THE western coast of the Highlands is deeply indented with long narrow arms of the sea which have all the characters of the glen lochs, except that they are open at one end, and it is evident that here the former glen lochs have been converted to inlets of the sea by the sinking of the western shore. The "sea lochs" of Scotland are a unique contribution to the scenic features of Britain, and these long lanes of water, flanked by mountains and with a distant prospect across the sea to the setting sun, have a great appeal to the emotions.

It is in the Western Highlands that the glens are diversified by lakes. East of a line from Perth to Inverness they are absent. Here the most striking feature of the scenery is a great boss of granite which has withstood the weathering of the ages and stands out boldly above the less resistant schistose rock. This is the Cairngorm group, the greatest mountain block in Britain.

With a much drier climate than that of the Western Highlands, the Cairngorms provide a summer recreation ground which is unsurpassed for the ramblers and campers who take their summer holiday socially in groups. Moreover, the snow, which lies deeply in winter, is drier and firmer than that on the hills near the Atlantic, and is often in good condition for ski-ing and other winter sports.

The uninhabited spaces of the Highlands are so large that it is easy to find places which are suitable for Nature Sanctuaries. The best situations are thought to be certain promontories on the west coast opposite to the Isle of Skye, both on account of their inherent advantages for the preservation of rare

A SYLVAN SCENE. [G. P. Abraham.
Firs and Birches are the outstanding features of this lovely Scottish scene, the entrance to the Trossachs at the foot of Loch Katrine. Bold, heather-fringed rocks make a foil for the delicate beauty of the trees.

MATLOCK HIGH TOR. [*Mondiale.*

There are steep crags, leafy dells and peaceful waters to be seen from Matlock High Tor, a centre of the beautiful Peak District. The Nature lover can always find plenty to satisfy him amid such varied scenery.

species and because the continuously rainy character of the climate makes the district relatively unattractive for general recreation.

In the Isle of Skye itself the mountain climber finds a suitable field for his activities on the Cuillin Hills of the rugged volcanic gabbro rock, but of all Nature Lovers, it is the landscape painter to whom the island is most important. There is probably no part of Great Britain where the pictorial effect of the blue distance is so remarkable. The air is free from smoke and dust, the comparatively high temperature serves to hold in clear solution a great charge of moisture, and the volcanic rock provides an exceptionally dark background.

THE scenic resorts which I have mentioned occupy a very small proportion of the Highlands. The greater part is indeed not spectacular, and in the northern portion the winter day is distressingly short. During the summer, however, all parts of the Highlands exhibit certain characters which have a strong appeal to the Nature-lover. The long day is associated with a comparatively low altitude of sun which softens the light and emphasises the modelling of the landscape. The colour of the heathery hills is sober but rich, the

birch and pine are seen in greater perfection than in the climate and surroundings of Southern England, and the sound of running waters contributes to the peaceful charm of the surroundings. There are those among the devotees of natural beauty for whom solitude is necessary if they are to receive the revelation which comes from communion with Nature. This need for solitude by no means implies a lack of social sympathy or indifference to human needs, for was it not in the wilderness that the great prophets of old time sought and received that revelation of the Divine which they passed on to later generations?

I have dealt so far only with the forms of the land and of its clothing of forest. It is the inherent deficiency of such geographical description that it represents scenery as if devoid of light and shadow. The features of landscape are however but the warp of the World's garment of beauty, across which the shuttle of the light weaves the most various patterns. The play of light and shadow depends upon the climate of the country, which is determined partly by latitude, partly by situation relatively to the ocean. These jointly constitute the conditions of illumination and the character of the sky whose domed space of cloud and blue ether canopies the landscape. Apart from visual appearances, the climate has an aesthetic appeal to other senses, both in the briskness of frosty air and the soothing warmth of summer ; and the round of the seasons brings a periodic change of that fragrance of the atmosphere which we associate with " country air." All these things should be closely observed and noted by those who wish to enjoy to the full the pleasures of scenery, for " scenery " is the aspect which the natural world presents to all the senses, not to the sense of sight alone.

In the gentle South, where Nature is kind.

With these considerations in mind let us now retrace our steps from the Northern Highlands to the South Coast of England. As we go southward the forms of the land become less bold and the spaces of wild landscape are narrowed by the encroachment of town and suburb. But against these drawbacks the discriminating student of Nature will not fail to recognise the gain which results from a more favourable apportionment of the seasons. Winter is shorter, summer longer ;

and a more fertile soil, co-operating with milder climate clothes the land with a finer forest. In connection with the seasonal aspects of our landscape it should be remembered that Britain, owing to its oceanic situation off the west coast of a continent, has a great scenic advantage in the lengthening of both spring and autumn, the seasons of opening blossom and the golden leaf.

In regard to the scenic advantages of the South we must also bear in mind the importance of ready access to climatic resorts where outdoor life can be enjoyed during the brief holiday of Christmas. In this respect the South and South-Western coasts of England and Wales are pre-eminent. Here sunshine, length of day and a mild air make outdoor life enjoyable in winter, whether we be upon the cliff path looking away to the distant horizon of the sea or on the beach where the waves make ever-changing music as the tide advances and recedes. This wonderful scene, the priceless heritage of an island people, is unsurpassed in plentitude of space and in charming harmony of tone and colour. Moreover the mighty ocean, breathing even in its sleep and yet untouched by time, is the image of Eternal Life.

A SNOWY SCENE.   [Photo : G. P. Abraham.

The glory of winter-time is illustrated in this beautiful scene taken from Friar's Crag, in the ever beautiful Lake District, showing Derwentwater and the surrounding country brooding under a snowy sky.

Photo : Ernst Krause]

[Mondiale.

The Primula, a species of Primrose found growing wild in Britain has also its home in many foreign lands. Here it is seen growing on the heights of Tibet. The leaves sometimes produce a nasty rash on the skin.

WHERE OUR FLOWERS COME FROM

By F. KINGDON-WARD, F.R.G.S., V.M.H., F.L.S.

MR. KINGDON-WARD, the famous traveller and botanist, who has made a life study of the origins of plants, here shows how various types of flowers which we call our own have descended from the wild flowers of other lands. Below he tells how even our well-known Horse Chestnut is a native of the Near East, and that nearly every country of the world has sent its offering to make our island fragrant.

WE all love flowers. Births, marriages, and deaths are occasions for floral displays ; and few gifts are more appreciated when one is sick ; a bunch of flowers from a friend is more appreciated than a bottle of medicine. I doubt whether there is a country in the world where so many flowers can be seen as in England, or in such infinite variety. That is, of course, partly because we are not plagued with a climate, we have just seasonable weather instead.

When you look round the English country-side you see a great many trees, shrubs and wild flowers which are natives of this country. For instance, you see Dog Roses, and Travellers' Joy, Meadowsweet, Cowslips and Buttercups. You notice, too, how certain plants grow together under certain conditions. Thus you all know the bare, windy chalk downs covered with crisp turf and strewn with stunted flowers at midsummer, or the Norfolk Broads, where tall flowers line the banks of the lodes, and wade knee-deep in the mahogany-coloured water ; or the woods, carpeted in spring with Anemones and Primroses ; or the red Devon lanes spicy with the scent of Honeysuckle ; or the grey, breezy fells of Cumberland and Yorkshire ; or the moors, hot with the liquid gold of Gorse.

We all recognise these flowers as English because they grow wild in typically English surroundings ; and we would not exchange these gems of English scenery for all the alleged glories of the Tropics. Indeed the Tropics are sadly disappointing. No tropical land is, as you might suppose, gorgeous with brilliant flowers. It is either closely cultivated, or bare looking, or it is swamped beneath a dead weight of impenetrable and sombre jungle, completely lacking the varied greens which give charm to an English sylvan scene ; and flowers in the jungle are hard to find.

Now, suppose I asked you to name a dozen familiar English trees ! Wouldn't you, who live in the towns almost certainly include the Horse-chestnut and the Plane, and you who live in the country the Larch and Fir ? What would be more natural ! And yet all four are aliens, deliberately introduced into Britain, as so many of our trees have been ! To most of us at any rate, Laburnum and Lilac, Crocus, Wallflower, Hollyhock, Sunflower, and a score of others are so familiar that we regard them as more English than the English. And yet if we think about it, we have to admit that common as they are, they are confined more or less to parks and gardens, and are not usually seen growing wild ; though even that hardly applies to the ordinary Rhododendron. Therefore, they must have been introduced from abroad.

These, however, are not a tithe of the plants commonly grown in this country. If you visit Kew Gardens, or any of the great private gardens thrown open to the public, from time to time, or the parks, you will notice hosts of unfamiliar looking plants growing quite happily ; and you have only to read the labels to see that they come from every country. In fact, the world has been, and is being, ransacked for hardy plants to beautify England.

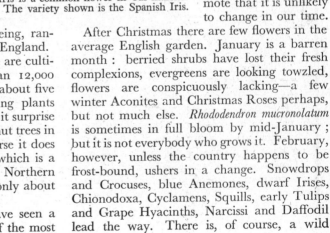

Harold Bastin] **THE EXOTIC IRIS.** *[Mondiale.*

The Yellow Iris is a common flower in our marshes and ditches. The variety shown is the Spanish Iris.

But apart from wild flowers, there are cultivated in this country not less than 12,000 species of foreign plants ; which is about five times the total number of flowering plants growing wild in these islands. Does it surprise us to go out and see the Horse-chestnut trees in bloom along the roadside ? Of course it does not. And yet the Horse-chestnut, which is a native of the Near East, Persia and Northern India, was introduced into Britain only about four hundred years ago.

Queen Elizabeth could never have seen a Horse-chestnut. To-day it is one of the most familiar trees in the country, and has been so far woven into our national tradition, that the popular press has dedicated a day in the calendar—Chestnut Sunday—to it. No wonder we are apt to regard it as a native tree, as we do also a host of familiar garden trees and flowers such as Lilac, Laburnum, Chrysanthemum, Crocus, Michaelmas Daisies, and Irises, to mention a few.

OF the 12,000 species of alien plants cultivated in Great Britain, it is hardly possible to state explicitly, in a short work, whence each is derived. But I propose to indicate briefly firstly where some of our commoner flowers come from, and conversely the plants which some of the more familiar places have contributed. To begin gently then, let us start in the New Year (Western Calendar) since some quite arbitrary point must be selected. We will avoid the lunar calendar of the East, whose New Year may fall on any date between January and March, necessitating elaborate adjustment later in the season. The virtue of January 1, as we celebrate it, is that at least the date is determined by an event calculated by the stars and so remote that it is unlikely to change in our time.

After Christmas there are few flowers in the average English garden. January is a barren month : berried shrubs have lost their fresh complexions, evergreens are looking towzled, flowers are conspicuously lacking—a few winter Aconites and Christmas Roses perhaps, but not much else. *Rhododendron mucronolatum* is sometimes in full bloom by mid-January ; but it is not everybody who grows it. February, however, unless the country happens to be frost-bound, ushers in a change. Snowdrops and Crocuses, blue Anemones, dwarf Irises, Chionodoxa, Cyclamens, Squills, early Tulips and Grape Hyacinths, Narcissi and Daffodil lead the way. There is, of course, a wild

Photo: Harold Bastin]   MEDITERRANEAN HEATH.   [Mondiale.

Altogether there are about five hundred different varieties of Heath, some bearing flowers of brilliant colours. The Mediterranean Heath, pictured above, is a plant of a particularly striking appearance.

Photo: F. Kingdon-Ward] THE FRAGRANT MAGNOLIA. [Mondiale.

The Magnolia is seen growing on the Burma-Tibet frontier, The flowers, which might be white, yellow, rose, or purple, measure from five to eight inches across. This shrub was named after a French botanist, Pierre Magnol.

18

Photo: F. Kingdon-Ward]   THE RHODODENDRON IN BLOOM.   [Mondiale.

The Rhododendron, a hardy, evergreen shrub, is found flowering in a great variety of tints, varying from white to purple.   In the mountain districts of Tibet, where this picture was taken, it is found growing in profusion.

Photo : *Harold Bastin*]   [*Mondiale.*

JAPANESE HONEYSUCKLE.

Honeysuckle is found growing in all parts of Great Britain. The Japanese species is a hardy creeper.

English Snowdrop, but other species from South-east Europe are also cultivated.

Crocuses are amongst the most familiar spring flowers, but we have no native Crocus ; the cultivated species, both spring and autumn flowering, hail from Asia Minor and the Balkan Peninsula. Forsythias and Witch Hazel from Japan are also early on the scene, shaking and shivering in the draughty month of March. The Wind Flowers bloom under leafless trees ; *Anemone blanda*, and *A. apennina*, also from Southern Europe, together with the more robust Narcissi and Daffodils.

Early Spring blossoms.

Most of our spring plants are bulbous, and live normally in dry, waterless regions round the shores of the Mediterranean ; yet they thrive happily in England. Many of these plants are so familiar, coming at a lean season, that they deceive the thoughtless into believing them to be true natives of Britain. They are not ; yet how poorly off we should be without these blithe first-comers ! Throughout the late spring and early summer (April, May)

Chinese and Himalayan Rhododendrons and other familiar plants, such as Primulas, mainly Himalayan and Chinese, Tulips from the Mediterranean lands and Asia Minor, and Alpines from the mountains of Europe are blooming. By June the garden is a molten sea of colour, chopping and changing with the ever-rising flood— Irises, Lilac, Laburnum, Sweet Peas, Azaleas, Magnolias, Barberries, and dozens of other plants, a roaring tumult of blossom.

Flower visitors from all over the World

The whole world has sent its quota to swell the amazing pageant. There are Irises from Northern Asia, Azaleas from China, Magnolias from North America, Escallonias and Calceolarias from South America, Cinerarias from South Africa, Lilac and Laburnum from Southern Europe, Cenotheras (Evening Primrose) from Central America, Heaths from the Mediterranean, Begonias from Peru, Clarkias from the Pacific coast, European Hollyhocks, Japanese Maples, and so on. By August the flood has spent itself somewhat, and exhausted with the violence of adolescence, the garden settles down to a sedate middle age.

Many plants from the southern hemisphere flower now, the Eucryphias, *Plagianthus Lyallii*, Embothrium, Desfontania spinosa, Fuchsias, and rarer plants ; followed in September by the Africa Gladioli, and the autumnal Gentians and Asters, which come mainly from temperate or alpine Asia.

Japan, pre-eminently, has given us our finest Cherries, Japanese Anemones, the exquisite *Magnolia stellata*, *Primula japonica*, the Golden-rayed Lily, the Clematis-flowered *Iris kaempferi*, the Maidenhair tree or Ginkgo and the Umbrella Pine.

No single country has contributed more to our gardens than China, although perhaps three-quarters of her contribution dates only from the beginning of the century. It will be enough to mention here the China Asters, Chrysanthemum, Tree Paeony, Camellia, funereal Cypress, *Acer griseum*, and *Davidia involucrata*. In spite of the traffic in alpines of late years, it is chiefly for her trees and shrubs that we are grateful to China.

Coming now to the Himalayas, we find that their influence on English gardens has been scarcely less than that of China. Moreover, although the recent exploration of Western China has temporarily eclipsed the Himalayas, it is the latter region which is again coming to the front, thanks to the exploration of Nepal and Tibet. *Meconopsis wallichii*, Giant Lily, Mountain Clematis, *Buddleia colvillii*, and *Magnolia campbellii* are worthy representatives of this region ; while the Sikkim Rhododendrons, if less numerous than those of China, have not been surpassed, and the Himalayan Primulas hold up their heads with the best.

Treasures for the Plant Collector.

Farther north, in Tibet itself, some beautiful plants are found, several of which—for instance the wonderful Tibetan Blue Poppy, *Primula florindae*, *Gentiana waltonii*, and many fine Rhododendrons—have been introduced. It may be pointed out, however, that there are few genera found in the Himalayas which were not subsequently discovered to be represented by other and more numerous species in Western China ; so that it is difficult to think of them as separate regions. Rather are China and the Himalayas one great reservoir of hardy plants, although particular species may be confined to one or other region.

Going farther west into the drier country of Persia, Asia Minor and Greece, typical garden plants are the Acantholimons, Cistuses, *Medicago arborea*, *Crepis incana*, *Onosma tauricum*, and *Campanula rupestris*. Our Horse-chestnut, too, comes from Persia. Then the Balkans, Caucasus and Carpathians have each added something—*Primula grandis* (which does not look so grand as it sounds), *Gillenia trifoliata*, *Ranunculus pilostachys*, and plenty more, though probably not so much as they could. But now that we are on home ground, it is hardly necessary to say anything, since most people realise the debt we owe to the Continent. The sunny Riviera, for instance, has given us Lavender, Rosemary, and other aromatic shrubs ; Switzerland contributed our first alpine plants, before the richer mountains of Asia were explored—summer flowering Gentians, Saxifrages, and Campanulas.

It is a curious fact that although the alpine plants of the Himalayas are, broadly speaking, an expansion of the Swiss flora, yet there are hardly any Himalayan Campanulas, and none worth growing. Even China has submitted only one to our inspection—*C. calciphila*—and it disliked Britain so much than it pined away within a few years of its introduction. Southern Europe in general has given us many of our most familiar and popular flowers such as Aubretias, Foxgloves, Pinks and Wallflowers.

Continuing westwards across the Atlantic, we come to North America, home of many plants widely different from those of Western Europe, though strangely enough, there is a closer connection between the Chinese and North American floras.

Amongst adopted North American plants we find Swamp Honeysuckles (species of Azalea), the popular " flowering " Currant, Mariposa Lily, Kalmias, and most of our finest Conifers. The scented Musk, too, came originally from British Columbia. Even Central America, and particularly Mexico, rich in gorgeous tropical plants, have given us a few hardy ones such as *Abelia floribunda* and *Choisya ternata*.

THE South American continent has attracted collectors from Europe for over a century, yet it is impossible to believe that it has yielded up its last treasures. The Chilian and Peruvian Andes and the highlands of Brazil especially, have sent offerings. *Berberis Darwinii*, *Embothrium coccineum*, *Abutilon vitifolium*, *Lapageria rosea*, *Ourisia coccinea*, and the Monkey Puzzle are all Chilian plants ; Hippeastrums come from Peru ; *Abutilon megapotamicum* is Brazilian,

Photo : Harold Bastin]   *[Mondiale.*

AN OPIUM POPPY.

From the seeds of this flower poppy-oil is obtained, and also a juice, which, when dried, yields opium.

as also is Bougainvillea, a flamboyant climber, better known in the East than in Britain.

In passing, I may note that many tropical African, South American, and Central American plants, little known in this country, where they dwell in glass houses, are as commonly grown in India as Roses are in Britain. Turning eastwards again, we reach South Africa, famous for its Heaths, Ice-plants, and Clivias. Here, too, grows the Arum Lily and Sparaxis, the Wand-Flower, and hosts of beautiful composites like Gazania and the Red Hot Pokers.

The land where the Heather blooms.

From the African highlands come thousands of bulbous plants, daisy-like flowers, and Heather. It is a strange fact that there are only two regions in the world where Heather grows, Europe, including Scotland, but more particularly the Mediterranean coast, and the Cape of Good Hope ; and these regions are separated by the whole bulk of Africa, where no heather grows.

New Zealand has long been known as the home of beautiful flowers, many of which have come to us, in return for English plants sent to the Antipodes. Our Olearias and shrubby Veronicas, *Clianthus puniceus*, *Pittosporum tenuifolium*, and *Phormium tenax* come from New Zealand. On the other hand, for its size, Australia has made only a small contribution, and Australian plants are hardy only in the warmer parts of Britain. Nevertheless the Wattles, Bottle-Brushes, Grevilleas, and *Ratas* (Metrosideros) with dazzling scarlet flowers, make up in quality something of what they lack in quantity. The Blue Gum (Eucalyptus) is hardy in the south-west, and is seen in India, where the Silky Oak is equally at home.

Those who hanker for the tropics might pause to remember the deadly monotony of the magnificent and exuberant vegetation. It palls on the senses far more quickly than does our changeful flora.

If you wonder why we English encourage these aliens in our midst, the answer is easy. England would be a poorer and duller place without them, especially in the winter. But the plants didn't fly here. Men went overseas to find them and bring them home. There is ample scope for the future, and plant hunting is a fascinating game. But no one ought to undertake it unless he loves it, and likes his own company, and can do without that of other people ; because all the populated parts of the world have been thoroughly combed out, leaving only the trackless, uninhabited and uninhabitable waste places to me and to the next generation of plant hunters.

Photo : Harold Bastin] BEAUTIES OF THE MARSH. *[Mondiale.*

A patch of Marsh Marigolds in bloom is a pleasant sight in early Spring. These large buttercups blossom from March till July, the deep golden yellow flowers contrasting gracefully with their dark green leaves.

Photo : Harold Bastin]   *[Mondiale.*

One of the sweetest of our wayside flowers is the Wild Rose, which brightens up the hedgerows of many a country lane and perfumes the air with fragrance.   The blossoms are followed in autumn by bright scarlet " hips."

WILD FLOWERS AT HOME

By HAROLD BASTIN

NO matter how many exotic and carefully-cultivated flowers we have in our gardens, we find an added touch of grace in the wild blossoms that owe their beauty solely to the gentle touch of Nature.   They are all worthy of note, and it is interesting to learn their characteristics in the chapter below before seeking them out.

THE systematic study of plants in relation to their surroundings (including other kinds of plants which happen to be their neighbours) is a comparatively recent branch of botany, called " ecology," from the Greek word signifying " home." Of course it was recognised long ago that plants tend to form associations or communities of species, and that these are characteristic of localities which provide certain definite conditions of soil, aspect, climate, and so forth. When we speak of " wayside and woodland blossoms " we have in mind a particular type of vegetation quite distinct from that which we should expect to see growing on a moor, or in a marsh ; while every rustic urchin knows that he will not find Wild Hyacinths and King-cups flourishing in close proximity, or Blackberry Brambles in a peat bog.

But it was not until some time after Charles Darwin's work and discoveries had galvanised students of natural history into renewed and enthusiastic activity that serious attention was paid to these matters. Then, quite quickly, a

host of fascinating facts concerning the home-life of plants came to light—how they make terms with their neighbours, oust undesirable upstarts, form intimate friendships, and generally contrive to live and let live in a world where all things are said to come to those who can wait. A plant community has been likened to a city within whose boundaries there is scope for the exercise of many profitable activities, but where too many of the same trade cannot be tolerated.

In a thickly populated country like England, where agriculture has been practised for centuries, the flora—or wild vegetation—in many localities must have changed completely since the husbandman—to say nothing of the industrialist and the speculative builder—first got to work. Extensive upland areas, once clothed with dense beech forests, are now covered with short, thyme-scented turf on which sheep graze. Acres upon acres of land are parcelled out as rectangular plots devoted to the cultivation of all manner of crops from which " weeds " — or " wild flowers," as some prefer to call them—are excluded by every means that scientific technique can devise.

During the past century, the steady growth of the large towns has wiped out many a happy hunting-ground which botanists of an earlier generation knew and loved. We have it on good authority that the London bird-catchers used to spread their nets for goldfinches " behind a hedge which then existed on the present site of the Great Western Railway at Paddington " ; and where goldfinches came, there must have been great thickets of Thistle and Ragwort and Knapweed, and other rural delights too numerous to catalogue.

How Nature fights the Builder.

Our modern habit of erecting bungalows and petrol stations, apparently without rhyme or reason, on every available plot of land which happens to be in easy reach of a high-road, has been responsible for evicting many rare plants from the nooks and corners in which, for many a year, they had tenaciously contrived to hold their own. Still, as the Roman poet Horace said, " You may drive out Nature with a pitchfork, but she will return through the back-door." As soon as a plot of land goes out of cultivation—always provided that it is not actually built over, wild plants of one kind or another reappear on it as if by magic.

This process of reclamation is very interesting to observe, as may sometimes be done when ploughed land near a town is sold for building, and then allowed to lie idle for several years. A definite series of happenings will be seen to take place. First, the ground will be appropriated by a variety of plants whose seeds were already present in the soil, or were brought there from a distance by the wind, or carried by birds and beasts on their feet, or attached to their fur or feathers.

Vampire plants that live by strangling.

There will not be serious competition to begin with, because the individual plants will be scattered at fairly wide intervals over the surface ; but before long the stronger, quick-growing plants—assuming that the locality is agreeable to their inherent requirements—gain upon the weaker, less assertive sorts, and in the end literally crowd them out of existence. One of the ways in which they do this is by spreading out their lower leaves in rosettes just above the surface of the soil, and thus preventing any seedlings in their immediate vicinity from obtaining a share of sunlight.

Many climbing plants, such as the pretty field Bindweed, behave like thugs, and ruthlessly strangle their competitors in the struggle for existence. Others play the part of vampires, robbing their neighbours of the life juices which they have elaborated for their own maintenance. Among these, some—like the Broomrapes, which infest clover—are wholly parasitic and dependent on their victims for support. Others, such as the Eyebright and the yellow Rattle, are quite well able to feed themselves, but when opportunity occurs " tap " the roots of plants growing conveniently near, and thus add clandestinely to their legitimate resources.

Probably the worst of all the parasites are the Dodders, whose victims are Clover, Heath, Vetch, Gorse, and a variety of other plants, including some garden species. The Dodder has neither roots nor leaves in the ordinary senses of these terms, although it produces in due season numerous tufts of small, flesh-pink flowers, and, eventually, enormous quantities of minute seeds. When one of these germinates in early summer, a red, thread-like stem protrudes from the ruptured seed-coat, and feels round in all directions.

The insidious Dodder.

If its quest is in vain, it perishes soon after the supply of nourishment contained in the seed is exhausted. Usually, however, its tip comes into contact with the stem of a suitable " host," into whose living tissues it insinuates a sucker—or, more accurately, a group of suckers ; and thereafter all is merry as a marriage bell—for the Dodder. Not so for the attacked plant ! Its enemy soon develops into a tangled mass of stems, sending out sucker-discs at every point of contact, so that the miserable sufferer is soon reduced to a dry and shrivelled corpse. Observation on cultivated land has shown that a single Dodder plant is capable of killing all the Clover or Lucerne on an area of about thirty square yards in the short space of three months !

Fortunately " the balance of Nature " is more than a figure of speech. It operates as a principle in every combination of circumstances, and with peculiar appropriateness in the case of hard-bitten parasites, which—if they prosecute their vocation too successfully, so as to kill off all their victims—must themselves perish from lack of food. So that the upshot of

Photo: Harold Bastin]   THE FLOWERING RUSH.   *[Mondiale.*

The rosy pink blossoms of the Flowering Rush, each one inch in diameter, grow in clusters in ditches on marshy ground. This water-loving plant is common in Southern England, but rarely found growing farther north.

25

Photo: *Harold Bastin*]   [*Mondiale.*
THE DEADLY DODDER.
Twining its stem round the nettle, and clinging with a deadly grip, the Dodder extracts its nourishment.

Photo: *Harold Bastin*]   [*Mondiale.*
THE PURPLE LOOSESTRIFE.
This tall plant with its reddish-purple flowers, looks imposing when seen rising to a height of four feet.

Photo: *Harold Bastin*]   [*Mondiale.*
THE DANDELION.
The root of this familiar plant is often used in making medicine.   In France the leaves are used in salads.

Photo: *Harold Bastin*]   [*Mondiale.*
CORNISH HEATH.
Heath is often confused with heather or ling, but though they belong to the same family they are distinct.

this struggle, in all its phases, is that every plot of land, left to itself, eventually gets exactly the plant population which is not only best suited to the conditions of soil and aspect, but of which the idiosyncrasies and interests of the various members are least likely to clash. For those that are fit, and can fit in, persist ; while the rest perish, or migrate to " fresh woods and pastures new."

HENCE, in the same coppice or meadow, we see strongly contrasted—but always complementary—differences of habit. Some plants favour shade, others full sunshine. For this kind the soil can hardly be too wet, for that the " perfect drainage " which is the gardener's ideal seems all but indispensable. Obviously such diversities of requirement open the way to mutual accommodation. The sun-loving species provide shade beneath their branches for such as like it ; the hard drinkers render the soil more tolerable to those plants that are of temperate habit. One might almost say that a plant is known by the company it keeps. Certainly it is possible confidently to predicate many things concerning its tastes and disposition when one has found out the particular community or association to which it naturally belongs.

The direct influence of the soil in determining, in the first instance, what plants shall grow in it is very marked. On a newly made embankment consisting mainly of stiff clay we should expect to find little besides Coltsfoot and Couch-grass, with perhaps some clumps of Rock and Stinging-nettle. Dandelions, Daisies and Buttercups are fairly catholic in their tastes, though they flourish best on grassland where the soil is rather poor from neglect. In damp meadows the lovely Cuckoo Flower, or Lady's-smock, is often the prevailing " weed " ; whereas on higher and drier

situations the Ox-eye Daisy frequently runs riot, to the detriment of the more tender pasture grasses.

Rhododendrons and Heaths are lime-haters. The latter are happiest on arid hillsides with their roots in a mixture of sandy gravel and peat—all except the Cross-leaved Heather, which prefers the vicinity of a bog, where the ground in winter is spongy with moisture, or even inundated. Unfortunately for the farmer, the kind of soil which suits his cereal crops makes also a strong appeal to the Scarlet Poppy, the Blue-bottle and the Corn-cockle— not to mention a score or so of lesser invaders, all intent upon securing places in the sun. If, as sometimes happens, the Corn Marigold adds itself to the trio just specified, a truly gorgeous display of colour results—scarlet, bright blue, brilliant yellow, and (for the Corn-cockle) a particularly striking shade of purple.

For continuous sheets of pure colour, however, nothing can excel the Charlock, or Wild Mustard—perhaps the most troublesome weed with which the cultivator of arable land has to contend. Its seeds are endowed with extraordinary vitality, and are capable of lying dormant for a considerable number of years until a chance to germinate presents itself. Deep ploughing sometimes brings them to the surface in such numbers that the resulting riot of young seedlings filches every inch of standing room from the legitimate crop.

Parcels of waste land, and the margins of cultivated fields, provide many opportunities for observing the home-life of our native plants. So, too, the great hedgerows of our countryside —which, alas, become fewer as each year passes—are veritable theatres wherein both tragedies and comedies are enacted, especially in springtime and the early summer, when newcomers are manœuvring to place old-

Photo : Harold Bastin]   *[Mondiale.*

A PREYING PLANT.

The Dodder, seen here on Heath, gets its food from the plants to which its clings. This parasite has no leaves.

stagers at a disadvantage. To see some of the most interesting plant communities in a state of stable equilibrium, however, one must needs visit the woods, the moors, the waterside, and the seashore. Three particularly well-marked varieties of woodland formation may be noted, viz., those in which respectively the dominant tree is the Oak, the Beech and the Scots Pine. Oaks are best suited by a fairly heavy soil, and their spread of foliage is seldom so dense as to preclude the growth of humbler plants beneath their branches. Also, in spring, before the oak leaves expand, the shrubby and herbaceous vegetation has ample time to make full use of the life-giving property of the sunlight, so large a share of which is subsequently appropriated by the big trees.

The first Spring blooms.

Primroses, Anemones, Dog Violets, and so forth, are early bloomers which get the best of the light when they most need it. At the same time the summer-flowering species are busily engaged in storing up food material for future use ; so that later we get Foxgloves and Thistles, Hawkweed and Golden-rod, Betony and Rose-hay Willow-herb. Brambles, Briers and Bracken flourish in the glades, and at the sides of the footpaths ; while here and there we see young Birches and bushes of Hazel, Dogwood or Buckthorn.

At the outskirts of the wood the Crab-apple, the Hawthorn and the Holly will fairly certainly be represented ; and every square foot of surface beneath the trees will have its carpet of Grass and Moss, with here and there, in due season, groups of Toadstools—gaily attractive or forbidding, as the case may be— to vary the monotony.

By contrast with all this, the undergrowth of a pine wood is scanty or non-existent. The well-nigh continuous canopy of evergreen foliage above allows little of the sun's radiant energy to penetrate to the ground below, most of which is, in consequence, devoid of vegetation ; while even the lower branches of the trees themselves, being unable to function in the unending twilight, die back and are eventually discarded ; so that the great holes rise up sheer and rugged, like pillars supporting the roof of a vast cathedral.

Several kinds of Moss grow sparingly, and towards the fringe of the wood Bracken is often abundant, where also occasional patches of Bilberry, and tufts of Ling and Cross-leaved Heath, are likely to be seen. In some of the

THE MAY IN BLOOM.

The Hawthorn, which is sometimes called May because its bloom is at its height in May, shows a sweet-scented white, pink or scarlet blossom. Though quite a small tree. the Hawthorn may live as long as 250 years.

Photo : Harold Bastin] THE PURPLE HEATHER. [Mondiale.

Ling, or Scottish Heather, grows profusely on dry moors where its purple flowers appear in late summer. It may vary in size from a tiny shrub to a large bush of over two feet, the pure white variety being very rare.

pine woods of Scotland grows that dainty little plant which the Swedish botanist Linnæus made his namesake—*Linnæa borealis*, with trailing stems and flesh-pink, bell-shaped flowers. Toad-stools, of course, are well represented in every pine wood, including—especially when silver birches mingle with the pines—the spectacular scarlet-and-white "Fly Agaric," which is very poisonous.

ABSENCE of undergrowth is also a marked feature of the typical beech wood, partly because the soils favoured by this tree are less suited to the requirements of our woodland flora—such as Primroses, Dog Violets, Stitchwort and Dead-nettle, still more because the leaf canopy of the Beech has far fewer gaps in it than that of the Oak, and so absorbs most of the light. The Bluebell, or Wild Hyacinth, is the spring flower *par excellence* under the Beeches, where it spreads itself out in great sheets of colour like patches of summer sky brought down to earth. With it you will sometimes find the Wood Anemone or Windflower, the Lesser Celandine, and the Dog-mercury ; also, perhaps, the Wild Raspberry and the Dewberry, where the trees are not too thickly massed.

But in summer, when the Beech leaves are fully expanded, there is hardly any herbaceous undergrowth ; while only those shrubby plants can succeed whose demand for direct sunlight has been reduced almost to zero. Perhaps the most curious associate of the Beech tree is the Bird's-nest Orchis. It has no true leaves—only brown scales and pale reddish-brown flower spikes ; but it forms in the soft leaf mould a tangled mass of roots and underground stems which resemble a bird's nest—whence its popular name. At one time it was believed to be parasitic on the roots of the Beech ; but it is now recognised as a saprophyte : that is to say, it draws its food supply from the humus, or decaying organic matter, in which it grows.

Plants of the wild moorland.

The plant associations characteristic of moors varies considerably according to the nature of the soil and the height above sea-level. Frequently, however, the dominant plants are Ling (" the bonny purple heather " of Scotland), two or more kinds of Heath, Gorse—the early-flowering kind, as well as the " petty whin " which flowers later, Bilberry, Cowberry, and the conspicuous Cotton-grass, which is really a sedge. In hollows, and on the slopes of hillsides where the drainage is slow and water accumulates, Sphagnum, or Bog-moss, flourishes, as well as a variety of other plants which find these conditions to their liking. Among these may be mentioned the Bog-asphodel, the Grass of Parnassus, the Bog-pimpernel, and Sundew—the latter frequently growing *on* the moss, among the fronds of which its roots ramify.

These notes refer to what is known as a " peat bog "—where, too, that charming little shrub, the Bog-myrtle, may be looked for. In districts where peat is absent the marshy patches will have a different plant population, which may include the Bog-bean, Marsh Violet, Lesser Spearwort, Ragged-robin, Sedges and Rushes.

The Plant that is bigger than a Man.

Several of these marsh plants occur commonly at the margins of ponds and meres, where they link up, so to speak, with the many interesting species which root in the wet mud with the water " well above their ankles," as a friend of the writer's used to say. As one might expect, most of these " aquatics " are tall growers with long, sword-like leaves and lusty flower spikes ; for they rarely suffer detriment from drought. Conspicuous among these water-side dwellers are the Reed-maces or Cat's-tails—" greater " and " lesser "—of which the former sometimes attain a height of fully eight feet. These are commonly known as " Bulrushes," a name more properly applied to the Giant Sedge, the *Scirpus lacustris* of systematic botany, which sends up equally tall, but cylindrical and rush-like stems, bearing brown flower-tufts.

" Flowering rush " is also a misnomer, since the delightful plant for which this name is used has no affinity with the true rushes. Indeed, the folk-names of most of our water-plants prove misleading if we accept them as guides to natural relationship. The Bur-reeds —" branched " and " unbranched "—are, in fact, allied to the Cat's-tails ; the " Common Reed," which often flourishes in the brackish backwaters of tidal estuaries, is really a gigantic, moisture-loving grass ; while the Water-plantain is first cousin to the Arrow-head—that dainty naiad of the mud-banks, whose presence still graces Thames-side, even in the heart of London-town.

From careless usage, " flag " and " sedge " have become words of almost unexampled vagueness, and are now employed quite indiscriminately to denote any one of a variety of plants " with bladed leaves, growing on moist soil." Probably the best known of these is the Yellow Iris, or fleur-de-lis (perhaps the prototype of the Prince of Wales's " feathers "), whose handsome blooms, followed in autumn by gaping capsules of large, orange-coloured seeds, are conspicuously ornamental.

The foliage of the so-called Sweet-flag (*alias* Sweet-sedge) resembles that of the Iris, except for the strong fragrance of cinnamon that it exhales when bruised or broken. This plant, though of no great beauty, has points of considerable interest. Its flower-spike resembles nothing on earth more closely than a large, round—or " rat's tail "—file. It is the kind of inflorescence, or compound flower-cluster, known to botanists as a " spadix." In the swamps, and by the rivers of Eastern Asia, whence this plant has wandered, the spikes develop in due course into cone-shaped clusters of berries ; but throughout Western Europe, the flowers are invariably sterile, presumably because the right kind of insect does not visit them ; so that no berries appear on the plant.

Nevertheless, the Sweet-flag prospers, and continues to spread ; for bits of its creeping stems, or rhizones, which get detached and washed away by floods, readily root when they come to rest on mud-banks where the water is shallow. In this manner, we must suppose, it contrived in the passage of centuries to work its way across Siberia and through Central Europe ; so that now it traffics with our aborigines as if it were one of them. How it managed to cross the ocean we are left to speculate, but cross it certainly did.

How Plants can alter their surroundings.

Waterside vegetation, of which not more than a tithe of even the more conspicuous species has been mentioned, provides an interesting object lesson of the way in which plants slowly but surely change the character of the localities in which they grow. The large, robust plants, by dying down each autumn, tend gradually to raise the level of the submerged mud, thus making the margin of the pool shallower, and enabling a score or more of shore-hugging species to take root. Year by year, as more and more refuse accumulates, the mud rises nearer to the surface of the water, and Kingcups, Water-mint, Brooklime, Forget-me-not, and Dropwort press forward, to be followed soon afterwards by the smaller

THE WILD CRANESBILL.

[Photo: R. McLeod.

This meadow flower is a type of wild Geranium, with a blue-purple flower and long, pointed seed-vessels from which it has derived its name. It is common all over England and also in Southern Scotland.

sedges, rushes, moisture-loving grasses, Willow-herb and Meadow-sweet.

If space permitted, each of these names should be supplemented by at least a dozen others—the idea being to supply the reader with a word-picture of the way in which one community of plants is succeeded by another, until at length what was once water is transformed into marshy land. Of all trees, the Alder is probably the most efficient drainer of the soil ; and when it has gained a foot-hold, all excess of moisture will soon disappear, leaving the land fit for invasion by plants from the woodland and the meadow.

Building the Sand-dunes.

The same process of reclamation is proceeding on many parts of our coast-line—although here, of course, the " enemy " to be overcome is not superfluous water, but the menace of banked up shingle and shifting sand. Two or three pertinacious sedges and grasses flourish in sand, which their spreading and fibrous roots bind together and hold securely in place. Of these the Marram is the sand-lover *par excellence*. When it and its industrious companions have done their work, they are followed by such plants as the

Thrift, Tree-mallow, Sea-buckthorn and Eryngium or Sea-holly, which

Sits like a queen among the scanty tribes
Of vegetable race.

A little later Gorse, Broom, Creeping Willow, and perhaps here and there a Dwarf Pine, will take root ; so that in the end the barren dune is converted into a thriving thicket.

Among the most conspicuous of our seaside plants is the Yellow-Horned poppy—a biennial which loves coarse shingle, through which it sends down its roots to the subsoil, perhaps many feet below. A well-established colony in its second season makes a brave show, with its greyish green leaves and large, four-petalled flowers whose clustered stamens are bright orange. As in the case of other poppies, the two-piece calyx is shed when the flower opens, while the petals are unsubstantial, and soon fall away. But the pistil behaves in a surprising manner. Instead of developing into an urn-shaped seed-vessel, as one might readily anticipate, it grows with a downward curve into a pod which is often seven or eight inches — sometimes as much as a foot — in length. These are the " horns " from which the plant gets its popular name !

Photo : Harold Bastin]   THE SAVIOUR OF THE SAND.   *[Mondiale.*

Marram Grass serves the useful purpose of binding the shifting sand and shingle which the sea is trying to lure away from the shore. So persistently does this plant spread its roots that it acts as an efficient barrier.

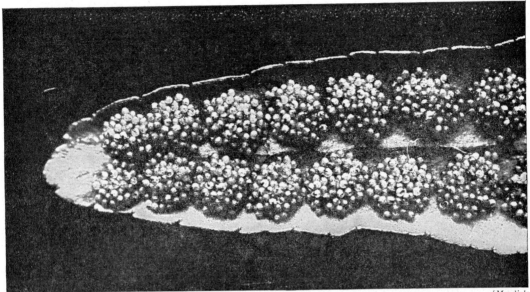

Photo: Harold Bastin]
[Mondiale.

The underside of the fern leaflet bears the *sporangia* which, when ripe, produce the "fern-seeds" which are carried away by the wind to germinate if they settle on moist soil. Above is the underside of a male fern.

"FERN-SEED" AND FRUIT

By HAROLD BASTIN

IT is interesting to learn how a new generation of plants and flowers arises and how, in such a subtle way, Nature induces the honey-seeking insects to help in the process of reproduction. This chapter sets out in detail the wonderful reproductive process of Nature in plant life. It will be seen that some plants reproduce themselves, while others depend on wind, or on the visits of insects for the fertilisation of their "seeds."

IN the earlier stages of their history, no plants bore flowers. This much is vouched for with certainty by geological experts who have examined the records of the rocks, and traced them backwards into the remote past. Deduction, based upon observation of what is actually taking place to-day, suggests that the primitive plants—each of which presumably consisted of a single, minute but self-sufficing "cell"—reproduced themselves by "fission": that is to say, when one of them attained to a specific size-limit, it thereupon divided itself into equal halves, and became two.

But even in these far-off times it seems probable that a principle analogous with that which we now term "sex" had begun to operate. Individual cells probably came into contact on occasion, and "paired," uniting their substance in intimate association, and effecting a mutual exchange of certain vital properties.

We cannot tell to what extent this process was originally bound up with that of repro-duction. In its simplest form it is called *isogamy* (literally, "equal marriage"), be-cause, although a temporary coherence between two separate individuals takes place, neither of them is sexually distinguishable from the other. We do know, however, that each of the parties to isogamous intercourse derives immediate benefit therefrom. It evidently experiences some kind of rejuvenation, whereby its vigour as an individual is increased; and we may assume that the stamina of the race is also enhanced, since after isogamy multiplication by fission usually goes on more briskly.

With these considerations in mind, it is not very surprising to discover that reproduction and isogamy have tended, in the course of evolution, to draw together and eventually to merge as two aspects of the same process. This state of things did not come to pass suddenly; and even at the present time we find highly organised plants which reproduce themselves by two different methods in alternation: first, asexually by *spores*—which are really little bits separated off from the parent organism—then sexually through the union of two germ cells (called " gametes ") to form a single *zygote* (*i.e.*, joined together) capable of developing into a new individual of the species concerned.

Strictly speaking, the term *conjugation* should be reserved for these sexual unions in which " male " and " female " entities are distinguishable, and from which reproduction ensues as a matter of course ; then we can use " isogamy " to describe the temporary coalescence of two mutually undifferentiated cells, resulting in immediate revivification for both, and often, though not necessarily, followed by fission.

How the Fern family grows up.

The most highly developed of all plants—*i.e.*, those which produce conspicuous " flowers "— appear to be predominantly sexual in their reproductive activities ; but they still perpetuate the spore-producing generation, only in a disguised and abbreviated form. We shall gain at least an inkling of how this has come to pass if we trace, first, the life-cycle of a Fern. In this instance the conspicuous plant to which we give the name " fern " is the spore-bearing generation. If we examine the under surface of its leaflets, especially in the late summer, or the autumn, we shall find small, kidney-shaped structures. These cover the *sporangia*, which, as they ripen, produce enormous quantities of dust-like spores—the so-called " fern seed."

When the sporangia rupture, the spores escape, and are carried about by the wind. If one of them chances to fall on moist soil in a shady position, it starts to germinate, putting forth first a delicate, root-like process, and eventually developing by cell-division into a single, more or less heart-shaped leaf, lying prone upon the soil, to which it becomes attached by a number of filaments. This is the *prothallus*, the inconspicuous plant whose duty it is to produce and foster the *gametes*, or sexual cells, destined by their union and subsequent growth to complete the life-cycle of the Fern.

If we carefully remove a mature prothallus from the soil, and examine its lower surface through a sufficiently powerful lens, we shall be able to locate the male and female organs. The former appear as tiny knobs or pustules, usually situated among the root-filaments ; the latter are flask-shaped, with a swollen base embedded among the cells of the pro-

thallus, and a curved neck—rather like the spout of an old-fashioned pump—pointing towards its hinder end, where the male organs are.

The sex-cells from the ripe male organs eventually burst, thus liberating immense numbers of extremely minute, lash-tailed bodies called *sperms*, which swim freely in the film of water on the under side of the prothallus, or on wet soil. These are the active male elements. They make their way to a female organ, and several of them may enter its curved neck ; but only one succeeds in penetrating to the contained egg-cell, with which it fuses. Following this act of " fertilisation," the egg-cell becomes a *zygote* which develops into a baby fern-plant, sending down a root into the soil and tiny leaves upwards into the free air.

For some considerable time the little plant remains attached to the parent organism— the prothallus ; but eventually the latter dies away, while the young fern grows to maturity, produces spores on its own account, and so completes the life-cycle of its species. Then this roundabout method of asexual followed by sexual reproduction is enacted all over again, before we get the next generation of ferns.

How another generation of Mosses arises.

Somewhat similar processes characterise the life-histories of Mosses, Horsetails and Club-mosses ; but there are important differences in detail which, when they are compared one with the other, seem to show pretty clearly that the evolutionary tendency among land plants has been to curtail the independence of the sexual generation. In the case of the Club-Mosses, for example, which represent a decisive step in advance of the Ferns and Horsetails, the prothallus does not make its appearance as a distinct and separate individual, but only as a phase in spore-development. Already among the Horsetails we find that large and small spores, producing large and small prothalli, have become the vogue, and that these give rise respectively to " female " and " male " reproductive organs —not to both on the same prothallus, as is the habit with ferns.

But a Club-moss produces both kinds of spores between the overlapping scales of a modified shoot called a " cone " ; and in these sheltered retreats the nuptials of the plant are accomplished. What happens is

FERNY FOLIAGE.   [*Photo: G. P. Abraham.*

Ferns grow in great profusion in humid, temperate regions. In the Tropics, a species called the tree-fern rivals the palm in magnificence. The British specimens, though pygmies in comparison, are equally graceful.

this. The large "female" spore-cases ("macrosporangia") burst open, but without immediately scattering the four large spores which they contain. The small "male" spore-cases ("microsporangia") on the contrary, shed their very numerous minute spores in the usual way, and some of these—the lucky ones—drift into the gaping cases where the large spores lie waiting for them.

HERE they germinate, producing a rudimentary prothallus represented by a single cell bearing one solitary male organ which eventually ejects a number of sperms. The latter fertilise the egg-cells which the developing prothalli of the "female" spores have by this time produced ; so that when the embryos —i.e., of the next spore-bearing generation— finally fall to the ground to begin life on their own account, they carry with them the remains of a prothallus whose main business has already been transacted, since it has nothing more to do but help the young plants to make a good start, and is thus comparable with the "endosperm," or stored-up nutrient substance, found within the true seeds of the higher plants.

Additional technical details would be out of place here. Enough have been given to indicate that while the earlier, less specialised plants practised quite openly, two alternating methods of reproduction—one by spores, the other by sperms and egg-cells (or ova), the trend of evolutionary development has been in the direction of suppressing the prothallus, as a distinct and self-supporting entity.

Among the highest groups, the plant which produces the spores is a still conspicuous organism with roots, stems and leaves, while that which by derivation counts as the prothallus has dwindled away in dimensions until it no longer has an existence apart from the spore itself. This is the case with all seed-bearing plants. The spore is retained on the spore-producing generation throughout the whole development of the gamete-producing generation, and even until the next spore-producing generation has appeared in embryo, wrapped up in the seed coat, along with the endosperm or food-store which gives it its start in life.

True seeds, therefore, are very different from the dust-like spores scattered by ferns, to which the term "seed" is popularly applied. When ripe and ready to germinate, each one really comprises in itself parts of three generations, thus : (1) the seed-coat, or testa, is

THE FRUIT OF THE BRYONY.
The Black Bryony, that twines through the hedges by means of its long stem, has an oval berry for fruit. This grows in clusters and when ripe is of a bright crimson hue. It is found chiefly in the south of England.

36

Photo: Harold Bastin]   THE FRUIT OF THE SPRUCE.   *[Mondiale.*

The cones of the Spruce Fir are, on an average, about five inches long. They hang downwards, and their brown scales overlap loosely. There are two seeds under each scale provided with transparent brown wings.

provided by the original spore-producing parent; (2) the endosperm, or food-store, represents the disguised prothallus; while (3) the embryo *is* the next spore bearing generation in immature form.

All this, of course, refers to the *macrospore*, or female element. But the *microscpore*, or male element, has undergone no less remarkable transformations which have fitted it to perform its task of fertilising the egg-cell without recourse to the method of free-swimming sperms, which are obviously capable of operating only in water, or on very moist surfaces. In a word, the microscores of the higher plants are the *pollen*, which has a characteristic method of germination quite distinct from that of its prototype, the fern seed. The essentials of this method consist in the development of the individual pollen-grain to form a structure, called the pollen-tube, by way of which the sperms (now reduced to two in number) are conveyed to the waiting ovum.

Seed-bearing plants constitute two major groups, viz., (1) the Pine-trees, or Conifers, and their allies, and (2) the flowering plants *par excellence*, comprising a vast number of very dissimilar species, ranging from the humble Buttercup to the lordly Oak. The Conifers are typically cone-bearing plants—a cone being essentially a terminal shoot having numerous scale-like leaves which produce either pollen-sacs or ovules, as the case may be. Each leaf of a "male" cone bears two pollen-sacs on its back, or outer aspect; whereas the corresponding leaf of a "female" cone carries its two ovules on its inner face, on a flattened outgrowth called the *ovuliferous scale.*

The pollen that is provided with wings.

The reader may readily verify these descriptions by examining—through a pocket-lens—the cones of such a tree as the Scots Pine during May and June. This species, like other conifers, is wind-pollinated, and each of the pollen-grains is provided with a pair of minute "wings," which add to their buoyancy; so that they are often carried to great distances by air-currents. On a fine day when the atmosphere is dry, the male cones shed their pollen in clouds, like puffs of Flowers-of-sulphur. Most of it is wasted; but here and there a few grains fall through the gaps between the scales of the female cones, thus reaching the ovules, into which their pollen tubes are thrust, and fertilisation is effected.

Among the flowering plants proper this uncertain and wasteful method of pollination has been largely superseded by the intervention of insects, and a few other creatures (e.g., humming-birds and water-snails), which carry the potent dust from one blossom to another. We have reason to suppose that insects, in particular, have been closely associated with plants from very remote times, probably before flowers as we know them to-day came into existence. Indeed, the colour, fragrance and other attractive features of flowers, as well as many of their structural peculiarities, would be inexplicable, save on the grounds that they serve to attract special kinds of insects, and to render their visitations efficacious in this matter of pollen-transference.

IT seems likely that insects first began to frequent flowers for the sake of the pollen, which they used as food. Later, when certain flowers started to secrete nectar, this sweet substance served as a counter-attraction to the insects, which were thus induced to devour less of the valuable pollen, though they must still have carried off stray grains of it among the hairs of their legs and bodies. As a matter of fact, many present-day insects—such as butterflies—pay no attention to the pollen of the flowers that they visit.

Bees, on the other hand, take both pollen and nectar, collecting large quantities of the former to feed their brood, and of the latter to make honey. Even so, bees are so numerous and so active, that they easily rank first in importance among those agents which secure the effective pollination of flowers, both in the wild state and in our fields and gardens.

Though repeated elsewhere in this book, it will not be out of place here to enumerate the parts of a flower. The essential parts of a flower adapted for fertilisation by insects are :

(1) the stamens, or male element, and (2) the pistil, or female element. A stamen is simply a spore-bearing leaf, more highly specialised than that of the pine-tree, and has normally a stalk carrying at its summit a two-lobed head called the *anther*, which contains the pollen. Similarly, the pistil consists of one or more modified leaves which produce ovules on their inner faces ; but unlike the corresponding female spore-bearing leaf (or *sporophyll*) of the Pine, this one is folded inwards on its middle line, so that its edges meet and become united, thus forming a cavity or chamber, known as the *ovary*.

When the pistil consists of only one such leaf, as is the case with flowers of the Pea and Bean tribe, it is usually spoken of as a *carpel* ; but frequently a number of carpels are united together to form a large, compound structure divided interiorly into several chambers, for instance, the pistil of the Poppy.

Another type of pistil is exemplified by the Buttercup, which has a central group of disunited carpels mounted on the receptacle at the pot of the flower-stalk. It is worth while studying the topography of a few common flowers, the better to understand the marvellous special contrivances which have been brought into play, to the end that the visits of the insects shall be turned to good account. What is needed is to bring the pollen into contact with the sticky apex, or *stigma*, of the pistil. When this has been achieved, the grains germinate, and form tubes which grow downwards into the ovary, thus conveying the sperms to the ovules.

A kind of race takes place between the individual pollen-tubes, because normally only one is needed to fertilise each ovule, and the winner gains the prize. The ovules of many kinds of flowers are capable of developing into seed after fertilisation by their own pollen, or

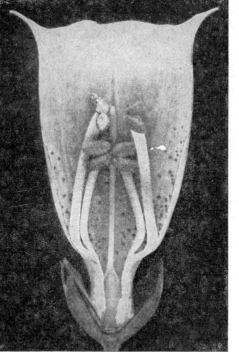

Photo : Harold Bastin]   *[Mondiale.*

THE FOXGLOVE'S COROLLA.

The corolla of the Foxglove split open to show the arrangement of the essential organs of reproduction.

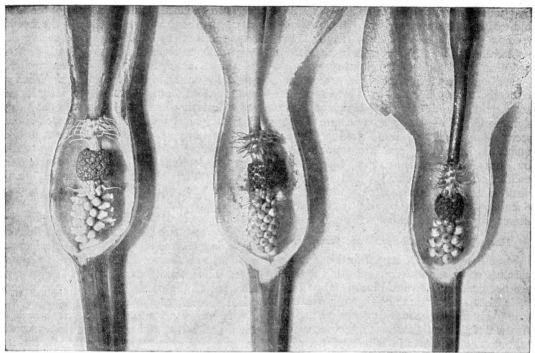

Photo: Harold Bastin] HOW THE ARUM-LILY GROWS. [Mondiale.

These three pictures show the details of inflorescence of the Arum Lily in successive stages. The fertilising pollen has been brought by an insect to the leaf-like sheath and the process of growth is now advancing.

Photo: Harold Bastin] THE PRIMROSE FROM INSIDE. [Mondiale.

The Primrose can be found in two different styles, the thrum-eyed and the pin-eyed. Here are magnified half-sections of the thrum (left) and the pin-eyed (right), showing the arrangement of the stamens and pistils.

by pollen conveyed from a neighbouring blossom born of the same plant. But generally speaking better seed results from cross-pollination : *i.e.*, when pollen is brought from a distinct individual of the same species.

Bearing these facts in mind, let us now look critically at some common flowers of the countryside, and try to interpret their significance. The Dog-rose and the Poppy secrete no nectar, but produce great quantities of pollen, and are much visited by bees and pollen-eating flies. Self-pollination often occurs ; but since the pistil offers a convenient alighting place, a pollen-dusted insect coming from another flower is likely to effect cross-pollination.

How " spinster " flowers have families.

Some flowers cannot be self-fertilised in the absolute sense of the term, because the sexes are not combined as one bloom. The Vegetable Marrow is a case in point, easy to investigate ; so is that beautiful water plant, the Arrow-head. The flowers of the latter are arranged on the stems in whorls of three, the lower whorls being female, the upper male ; and since the flowers of a given stem open from below upwards, self-pollination is clearly impossible. This plant also affords an interesting example of what is called "isolation by water." Insects which come through the air for nectar and pollen are welcome visitors, but creeping insects, which would be of little service, cannot reach the stems—unless they are swimmers !

The Foxglove bloom is a kind of tunnel, into which the big, hairy bumble-bee creeps with avidity in order to reach the nectar which is secreted at the far end. The stamens and stigma lie pressed against the roof, so that the bee cannot fail to rub his broad back against them. As the pollen matures before the stigma becomes receptive, a bee, passing from a newly opened bloom to one in a more advanced stage of development, is almost certain to effect cross-pollination. Should it fail to do this, however, the flower's own pollen would be applied to its stigma when the tunnel-like corolla finally falls off. This explains the fact that every flower carried by the long stem invariably produces abundant seed, even when humble-bees are scarce.

The flowers of the Honeysuckle are visited chiefly by hawk-moths, which are attracted after dusk by their strong perfume. In the newly-opened flower, the pollen-covered anthers are bunched together in front of the tube which gives access to the nectar. In the second stage the stamens bend downward, while the long, delicate style of the pistil, with its terminal stigmatic knob, is in the position originally occupied by the anthers. When a pollen-dusted moth, poised on the wing in the act of inserting its long tongue into the tube, brushes against the essential organs, it either takes up more pollen from the anthers, or else deposits some on the stigma, according to the stage of development which the flower has reached. Thus, while self-pollination occasionally occurs, all the adaptations favour cross-pollination.

Primroses and Cowslips are dimorphous— that is to say, two structurally distinct flowers occur on the same plant. In one form, known popularly as *thrum-eyed*, the pistil has a short style, while the stamens are visible at the entrance of the corolla tube ; in the other, called *pin-eyed*, the style is long, bringing its stigma into view, while the anthers are low down and out of sight. Consequently, when an insect visits a " thrum-eyed " flower its proboscis is dusted with pollen at a point which—if it subsequently flies to a " pin-eyed " one—comes into contact with the stigma ; and *vice versa*.

That charming riverside plant, the Purple Loosestrife, is trimorphous : by ringing the changes on three forms of flowers, always on separate plants respectively, a possibility of self-pollination has been eliminated. Darwin proved by experiment that no seeds are set if the visits of insects are prevented ; and further, that perfect fertility results only when the pistil receives pollen from stamens of a corresponding length.

How the Orchis deals with its visitors.

Another interesting flower is the early purple Orchis. The arrangements of its parts is a little puzzling to the beginner, but its method of dealing with an insect visitor may easily be demonstrated by poking the pointed end of a lead-pencil into the flower's throat. When withdrawn, the pencil carries away a pair of tiny stalked masses of pollen. A bee does the same when it leaves an Orchis bloom after rifling its store of nectar ! Moreover, the sticky discs which adhere to the insect's head contract unequally when drying, with the result that the pollen-masses are bent forward, and at the same time splayed out somewhat to right and left. Thus, when the bee visits

Photo: Harold Bastin]   [*Mondiale.*

SOME WAYSIDE FRUITS.

Top, Woody Nightshade; below, Wild Rose; r. Honey-suckle; l. Wild Arum; middle, Hawthorn; r. Yew.

Photo: Harold Bastin]   [*Mondiale.*

TREE FRUITS.

On the left is the fruit of the Acorn; right, Birch; bottom left, Lime; middle, Alder; and right, Ash.

Photo: Harold Bastin]   [*Mondiale.*

CHESTNUTS.

The prickly case which holds the fruit of the Horse Chestnut reaches full size in October, when it splits open and reveals two or three nuts inside. This tree, however, does not yield fruit until it is twenty years old.

another flower, they are in exactly the right position to strike the sticky stigmatic surfaces, which lie just within the flower's throat, into which the insect thrusts its head in order to reach the nectar.

Some of our familiar wild flowers are really co-operative associations which contrive to do big business with a minimum of expenditure on advertisement. Flowers of the Daisy type are of this kind. In these instances the association—or *inflorescence*, as the botanist calls it—consists of many small, bi-sexual yellow florets grouped closely together to form a central disc, surrounded by a smaller number of female florets, with white strap-like corollas pointing outward. At maturity, the tube of each tiny floret contains much nectar, which is eagerly sought after by short-tongued insects; and as these fly constantly from one Daisy bloom to another, exchanges of pollen are frequent.

ANOTHER kind of co-operative association is exemplified by the Wild Arum or Cuckoo-pint—the Lords-and-Ladies of country children. Here, the conspicuous part is a leaf-like sheath, called the *spathe*, with a purple club (the *spadix*) standing up centrally. Insects are attracted by this display, and by the odour given off by the club. They pass into the hollow, bulbous part of the spathe, where the small and simple flowers are arranged in groups round the stem of the spadix—first, hair-like organs, which seem to have been flowers originally, but are now " neuters " in so far as any direct connection with reproduction is concerned ; then staminal flowers ; then pistillate ones. The hair-like flowers radiate downwards, and allow the insects to creep into, but not to escape from, the chambered portion of the spathe. The lowest—female—flowers mature first, and receive any

pollen which the midges may have brought with them from another Arum.

Later, the male flowers mature, and shed their pollen, which falls to the bottom of the chamber, where the midges get thoroughly dusted with it. Eventually the hair-like flowers shrivel up, and allow the insects to escape, which they are ready enough to do. This is the way in which the Wild Arum contrives to get its pollen carried about !

These are only a very few examples of the manner in which our British wild flowers press insects into their service. The object is always the same, namely, to achieve that union of sexually dissimilar bodies which is the indispensable preliminary to seed-production. After fertilisation, the ovule and its immediate surroundings enter on a period of growth and development the outcome of which is the structure known as the " fruit."

To the botanist, this term has a perfectly definite meaning. It is generally applied to the whole result of fertilisation, and in particular to the development of the pistil after this event has taken place. Obviously, the name covers a multitude of forms so varied that even to catalogue the more distinctive would call for many pages of description. Think, for instance, of a pod of Peas, an Acorn, an Orange, a Horse-chestnut in its prickly husk, the winged contrivance of the Ash or Sycamore, and the dainty parachute of the Dandelion—all fruits, judged by the botanist's standard. Like the carpel, so the fruit may be simple or multiple, and may contain from one up to an enormous number of seeds.

The seed itself, as distinct from the fruit, consists simply of an embryo plant, together with its store of nourishment (the free gift of the parent) and its outer skin, or " testa."

Photo: Harold Bastin]   *[Mondiale.*

TALL FOXGLOVE.

The large Humble-Bee finds the tunnel-like bloom of the Foxglove a good hunting-ground for nectar.

The common Daisy which flourishes in meadows and by the roadside is one of the humbler of wild flowers, yet it is none the less beautiful. Almost any kind of soil provides a suitable home for this hardy plant.

HOW PLANTS FEED

By HAROLD BASTIN

IT is every bit as necessary for a plant as for a human to have nourishment to assist growth. In the plant world, as we are told below, there is an active army at work to provide the necessary supply of sustenance. This food which they concoct nourishes not only themselves, but provides feeding for the animals as well. You will learn here how leaves provide starch for their plants and why they drink so much water.

ONE sometimes hears it said that plants, unlike animals, manufacture the food which they eat. In so far as green plants are concerned, this is strictly true, although " concoct " would, perhaps, be a better word to use than " manufacture," since plants have no hands. But the bald statement, however we phrase it, fails to convey an adequate impression of the marvellous powers which plants are able to exercise. When, in ordinary conversation, we talk about manufacturing food, we usually mean that certain kinds of existing food are converted, by a process of mixing, grinding, cooking, and so forth, into other foods which are more palatable and digestible, or in some other manner made more acceptable to those who eventually eat them.

But when plants manufacture the food which they need for their maintenance and growth, the raw materials which they use are not such that they could be eaten and digested, at a pinch, without more ado—as a hungry man might stave off starvation by devouring will berries or uncooked turnips. No ; the stuffs which the plants work with are simple chemical substances taken from the atmosphere, and from the water sucked in by their roots ; and from these, by an intricate process which is not yet completely understood by man, they produce food, not only for themselves, but incidentally for the whole animal population of the world as well.

We may express what has just been said in different words by saying that neither the plant nor the animal is able to feed directly on inorganic substances, but that green plants are vested with the ability to transform these substances into organic compounds, or foods, capable of sustaining life.

One of the commonest foodstuffs found in the tissues of plants after a hard day's work is starch. The chemist can prove, by a simple test, that a green leaf which has been functioning for some hours in full sunlight contains large numbers of starch granules ; whereas the same leaf, examined in the morning soon after sunrise, would contain little or no starch.

43

Now starch is not a simple or " elemental " substance, but an organic compound having food-value, which is not present in the soil or the atmosphere. We conclude, therefore, that the leaf, aided in some mysterious way by sunlight, plays a supremely important part in the formation of starch ; and we want to know what this part is, as well as what happens to the starch when it can no longer be found in the leaf.

Why Leaves are green.

In the first place, it is important to realise that the *greenness* of leaves is essential to their starch-compounding capacity. Non-green leaves do not contain starch, even in full sunlight. The greenness is due to the presence in the leaf tissues of numerous minute bodies, called *chloroplastids*, which are produced as need arises by the living jelly, or *protoplasm*, that constitutes the basis of the plant's physical being.

A series of experiments has shown that these chloroplastids, in the presence of sunlight, take up carbon from the carbon dioxide gas which is normally diffused in atmospheric air. They do this to some extent even in the artificial light of a gas or oil-lamp ; but they need sunlight to work at full capacity. We conclude, therefore, that plants get one of the elements that they need for starch-production—namely, carbon—from the air around them ; but that they can do this only when they are illuminated, preferably by the sun's rays. That they really need carbon for their activities can be demonstrated experimentally by supplying a plant with air out of which all carbon dioxide gas has been filtered. A plant so treated concocts no starch, and in consequence soon ceases to grow.

Carbon dioxide gas (known to the chemist as CO_2) is given off, and mixes with the atmosphere, whenever what we call combustion takes place—whether it be the rapid combustion of coals or wood burning, or the slow combustion which goes on in our bodies as we draw breath.

Nevertheless, under normal conditions the proportion of this gas in atmospheric air rarely exceeds 4 in every 10,000 parts—so greedily do the plants suck it up ! It should be noted, too, that with every unit of carbon which the plants obtain in this way, they get *two* units of oxygen, one of which they eventually discard, thus purifying the air from the standpoint of animals, which use it only for breathing

But plants cannot build up starchy compounds from carbon and oxygen alone. They need also a third element, namely, hydrogen, which they take from water. Water consists of two gases in the proportion, by volume, of two parts of hydrogen to one part of oxygen. But these are not merely mixed in stable proportions as oxygen and nitrogen are mixed to form pure air. On the contrary, they are " chemically combined," in the same way that carbon and oxygen are intimately united to form CO_2. Hence, when we say that plants get their supply of hydrogen from water, and carbon from CO_2, we imply that they liberate a considerable quantity of oxygen.

In point of fact, when leaves are actively engaged in taking carbon from CO_2 and hydrogen from H_2O (or water) they do turn adrift a lot of oxygen into the atmosphere—
—as the botanist can easily show by experiment in the laboratory. This is the explanation of the erroneous statement which is sometimes made that plants do not " breathe " or use up oxygen. Actually, they need oxygen for the performance of their vital processes, just as animals do. Only, when they are busily employed in breaking down the chemical unions referred to above, they give off far more oxygen than they use. After dark, the reverse is true ; so that, after all, there is good sense in the old wives' injunction not to keep pot-plants in your bedroom at night because they " spoil the air."

How the Plant makes its food.

We may say, therefore, that the green plant makes its own food and eats with its leaves. The chloroplastids, energised by the sunlight, take carbon from CO_2 and hydrogen from H_2O, and mysteriously combine these elements with a certain proportion of oxygen to form sugary or starchy compounds—carbohydrates, as they are called. The whole process is termed *photosynthesis*—literally, a building up through the agency of light. It is probable that one form or another of sugar is the immediate outcome of the green plant's activity, a percentage of which is used up there and then by the leaves, while some is passed along from cell to cell through the tissues to nourish other parts of the plant. But in full sunlight the activity of the leaves is greatly in excess of the facilities for transport, so that much of their output is locked up temporarily in the compact form of insoluble starch.

Then, at night, when the work of the leaves

Photo: *Harold Bastin*]   A COLONY OF PLANTS.   [*Mondiale.*

These plants, growing in great profusion on the outskirts of an oakwood, find their surroundings suitable for healthy growth.   They take care to extract enough sustenance from the starch which is stored up in their leaves.

as at a standstill, the starch is reconverted into sugar, which is passed into circulation. If it is not needed at once for nutritive or respiratory purposes it may be changed to starch for convenient storage in roots, and tubers.

IT is time now to consider in detail the leaves and the roots—the organs by which a plant feeds and grows. If we examine through the microscope a very thin slice cut transversely from a leaf, we see (1) the outer skin or "epidermis"; (2) the main mass of the leaf substance, termed the *mesophyll*; and (3) the so-called veins, or supports, which have been cut across at various angles. The epidermis is composed chiefly of close-fitting cells devoid of chloroplastids, which are continuous over the whole upper surface of the leaf. But on the lower surface the regular mosaic of epidermal cells is interrupted at frequent intervals by pairs of smaller cells with a minute gap between them. These are the so-called *guard-cells*, while the gaps between them are named *stomata*, and are, in effect, the plant's mouths. It has been estimated that you might count several hundreds of thousands of stomata on the underside of a leaf of medium size; there are usually from 300 to 350 of them found to every square millimetre of the leaf surface.

Photo : *Harold Bastin*]   [*Mondiale.*

GROWTH OF RUNNER BEAN.
The seed-coat of this young plant has been discarded, but the cotyledons still contain much food material.

The mesophyll, with which the gaps between th guard-cells communicate, consists of an upper part composed of one or two layers of sausage-shaped cells, set vertically close together, and a lower mass of smaller cells, loosely arranged, with many air-spaces between them. All the cells of the mesophyll contain chloroplastids, which—when the leaf is actively working in sunshine—instantly seize upon any carbonic acid gas that happens to be carried by the atmosphere through the stomata into the inter-cellular spaces. The stomata, however, serve a dual office. Besides admitting atmospheric air, they permit the escape of water vapour.

A wonderful water system.

To appreciate the importance of this from the standpoint of the plant, we must remember that the "veins" of the leaf contain the final ramifications of an elaborate water-conveying system which begins in the roots far below the surface of the soil. The roots are covered with delicate hairs, the cells of which absorb moisture and pass it inwards to the main aqueducts of the stem, by way of which it eventually reaches the leaves.

It is said that a fair-sized oak tree, the number of whose leaves will be in the neighbourhood of 700,000, raises 226 times its own weight of water during the five months from June to October. A large proportion of this water evaporates from the mesophyll into the air-spaces, and thence through the stomata into the atmosphere. A small quantity, however, is needed by the plant; and the outward flow of water vapour is subject to control, according to the state of the atmosphere.

When this is well charged with moisture, as is usually the case at night and in dull weather, the guard-cells become turgid, curve somewhat, and so separate from each other along the middle line, thus opening the stomata; whereas in full sunlight when the air is dry, and the guard-cells are flaccid, their free surfaces come into close contact, and the stomata close. In this way the transpiration current of the plant is retarded or accelerated in exact proportion to its needs, as determined by the activities of the leaves.

The question now arises : Why does the plant absorb so much more water through its roots than it appears to need ? The answer is that the water contains, in solution, small quantities of "salts," such as sulphates, nitrates, phosphates of lime, magnesia and

Photo : Harold Bastin] THE OPIUM POPPY. [*Mondiale.*

The most important of the Poppy family is the Opium Poppy from the seeds of which poppy-oil is extracted. From the seed capsules, seen above, a juice is obtained which, when dried, is known as opium and is used as medicine.

potash ; and it is for the sake of these that the plant imbibes so freely. They are employed in the factories of the leaves to elaborate food substances—far more complex than sugar or starch—which the plant requires for its maintenance and growth. For the photo-synthesis of carbohydrates is only a first step in the marvellous feats of bio-chemistry which the plant is capable of performing.

How Plants find nitrogen.

Of all these " salts " which the plant derives from the soil, the nitrates are the most im-portant. If you attempt to cultivate a plant in soil from which all nitrates have been excluded, it rapidly pines away and dies. There is an inexhaustible supply of " free " nitrogen in the atmosphere, but the plant is quite unable to make use of it. Why this should be, we do not know ; but the fact remains that green plants must, so to say, be spoon-fed with nitrogen in the form of those simple compounds which are produced in the course of decay and putrefaction. These are continuous processes, due to the activities of minute organisms called *bacteria*, which resolve the complex chemical compounds of dead

Photo: *Harold Bastin*]   [*Mondiale.*
THE LESSER CELANDINE.
This picture shows the flower-stalk and the leaf-stalk of this plant, whose roots carry a store of food.

bodies, and of effete organic substances, by ordered stages, into their simple components.

Thus, as putrefaction proceeds, nitrogen is eventually liberated, and escapes into the air —but not all of it, because plants manage to secure some of the intermediate compounds before the nitrogen is finally set free. Still, there is normally a considerable leakage of nitrogen from the organic to the inorganic world ; and cultivated land must be con-stantly replenished by the addition of nitro-genous matter—or manure—of the kind best suited to the requirements of the particular crop which is to be sown.

Under natural conditions, the droppings of animals, and the decay of both animal and plant bodies after death, usually effect the restoration of nitrates to the soil in sufficient quantities. But " combined nitrogen " is never any too plentiful or easy to come by. Accordingly, it is much sought after, and highly prized ; and some plants have evolved special devices for obtaining it in larger quantities than would be possible by the ordinary method of root-absorption.

The leaves of some are modified to act as fly-papers, and traps of various kinds, which serve to capture insect prey. Others enter into a kind of partnership with nitrogen-fixing organisms, such as bacteria and fungi. For example, when the roots of certain trees are examined, they are found to be covered with a network composed of the *mycelium* (the thread-like, vegetative body) of a specific fungus. Microscopic investigation shows that this net-work takes the place of the usual root-hairs, and has established a vital connection with the tree by sending strands, or processes, through the outermost skin of the roots.

The explanation seems to be that the fungus-threads actually perform the function of root-hairs by absorbing water and dissolved salts, and passing them on to the tree in consideration of a small dole of organic sub-stance which the latter can well afford to give. Furthermore, since the fungus almost certainly has the power to " fix " free nitrogen, it is also able to supply the tree with a much larger quantity of the coveted " salts " than could be obtained from the soil by ordinary means.

Similar relationships exist between legu-minous plants—Peas, Beans, Clovers, and so forth—and soil-frequenting micro-organisms. In these cases the roots swell locally, and form characteristic nodules, or " galls," and carry on their beneficent, nitrogen-fixing activities.

Photo : Harold Bastin]
[Mondiale.

The Pyrethrum, a daisy-like flower, is seen displaying its different types of florets—the " ray " and " disc." A good view of the "pincushion" in the centre is seen and also the "receptacle" (top left).

THE PARTS OF A FLOWER

By C. E. HUBBARD

THE aspiring botanist will find this chapter very helpful in showing him the different sections of his specimens. The diagrams tell at a glance every detail of the flowers, and it is interesting to learn their wonderful construction and to find that Nature has fashioned even the humblest of plants with infinite care. This section also tells among many other interesting things how flowers attract bees to visit them and how their pollen is stored away.

A BRIEF examination of some of the innumerable flowers of our countryside and gardens will be sufficient to reveal the wonderful variety of floral structure which has been evolved by each plant. In many cases the tendency has been towards producing a highly-attractive and conspicuous flower, whilst in others the reverse has taken place. Corresponding parts of a flower may be somewhat similar in different plants ; on the other hand these same parts may be considerably altered, or in some plants may be entirely absent. It is in such cases that a difficulty may arise in deciding what organ a certain portion of the flower may represent.

In order to obtain a clear idea of each part of a flower, it is necessary to examine one in which all organs are represented, and which at the same time has a simple structure. The Common Buttercup of our meadows is a good example for this purpose. The flowers are borne singly at the tip of a slender stalk. When some of the parts of the flower are removed from one side, the summit of the stalk is seen to be cylindrical or conical, and slightly swollen. The thickened portion is conveniently termed the *receptacle*. It bears the parts of the flower in a regular and close sequence.

The lowest and outermost organs are green, somewhat boat-shaped, and are arranged around the receptacle in a ring of five. They are termed *sepals*, and collectively form the *calyx*. Immediately above them is a ring of five bright yellow *petals*, which constitute the *corolla*. The next layer is composed of a large number of stalked bodies known as the *stamens*. These are tightly packed together. Each consists of a thread-like stalk (the filament), which is terminated by a swollen yellow tip (the *anther*). This collection of *stamens* is the male portion of the flower.

49

The summit and upper portion of the receptacle is occupied by a number of small green, flask-shaped bodies, each of which is called a *carpel* or simple *pistil*. If an individual carpel be closely examined, it will be found to consist of three parts : a broad basal portion termed the *ovary*, terminated by a narrow beak, the *style*, the latter bearing at its apex a sticky surface, the *stigma*. The carpels collectively represent the female part of the flower. Thus a flower in its complete state consists of four series of organs—Sepals, petals, stamens and pistil.

The flower is really a leafy branch in which the ordinary leaves have become modified to serve special functions. Thus the sepals and petals protect the flower when it is in bud, or close over the open flower during bad weather. When brightly coloured, they attract insect visitors to assist in pollination. In double flowers, such as some kinds of Roses and Tulips, the stamens assume the leaf-like form of petals, whilst in other double flowers even the carpels may become petal-like.

The perfect flower of the Buttercup.

The Buttercup has a perfect type of flower, as both male and female organs are present in each individual. This is not the case, however, with all flowers. There are quite a number in which either the male or the female organs may be missing. Such flowers are termed imperfect. The flowers of the Vegetable Marrow are male or female, both sexes being found on the same plant. This is also the case with the Hazel, the female flowers being very small and inconspicuous, whilst the male are borne in the familiar pendulous catkins. On the other hand, the

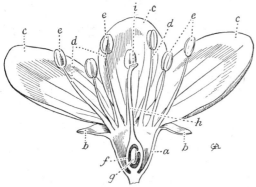

PLUM BLOSSOM.
Above is the vertical section through flower of the Plum : *a.* receptacle ; *b.* sepals ; *c.* petals ; *d.* filaments ; *e.* anthers ; *f.* ovary· *g.* ovule ; *h.* style ; *i.* stigma.

Willow has the male and female flowers in catkins on different plants. We will now consider the varied modifications of each part of the flower which may be met with in our more common wild and garden plants.

The Receptacle and its uses.

The *receptacle* is of considerable importance in classifying plants. It is not always like that of the Buttercup, but shows a remarkable diversity of form. It is situated at the summit of the flower stalk, and varies in shape from a minute, knob-like tip to an elongated, thickened axis, or it may be flattened, or hollowed out. In the Buttercup, as we have seen, it is a short cylindrical or conical axis bearing at its summit the pistils, with the stamens, petals and sepals successively below them. Such a flower is said to have *hypogynous* petals and stamens. Other examples which possess this type of flower are met with in the Poppy, Chickweed and Tulip. In some flowers the receptacle becomes more or less flattened or saucer-shaped as in the Spiræa of our gardens, but here the pistils are situated on a slight outgrowth from the centre of the receptacle, and are above the other parts of the flower.

A further stage in the modification of the receptacle is reached in the flowers of the Plum and Rose. Here it has become hollowed out and more or less cup- or flask-shaped. The pistil or pistils are to be found inside, and are quite free from the sides of the receptacle. The stamens, petals and sepals are produced from the margins of the latter and are above the female part of the flower. This type of flower is described as having *perigynous* petals and stamens.

In the flowers of the Daffodil, Carrot and Daisy, the pistils, except for the styles and stigmas, are completely enclosed by and joined to the receptacle, and the stamens, petals and sepals are borne at the top. In this case the petals and stamens are termed *epigynous*.

In many cases the receptacle merely affords support to the various parts of the flower, but in others, such, for example, the Apple and the Rose, it gives additional protection to the ovules, and at maturity, by means of its bright colour or fleshy texture, attracts birds to assist in the dispersal of the seed.

The calyx and corolla are frequently termed the *perianth* and constitute the non-essential

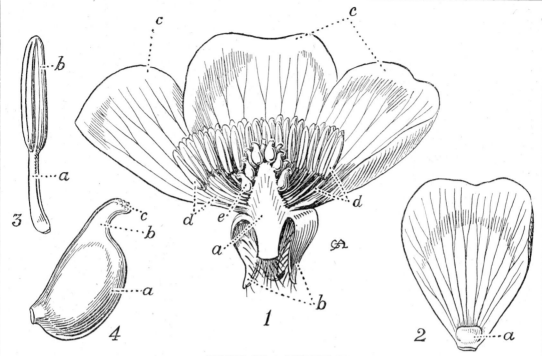

PARTS OF A BUTTERCUP.

1. Vertical section through flower : *a.* receptacle ; *b.* sepals ; *d.* stamens ; *e.* pistils. 2. petal : *a.* nectary.
3. stamen : *a.* filament ; *b.* anther. 4. pistil : *a.* ovary ; *b.* style ; *c.* stigma.

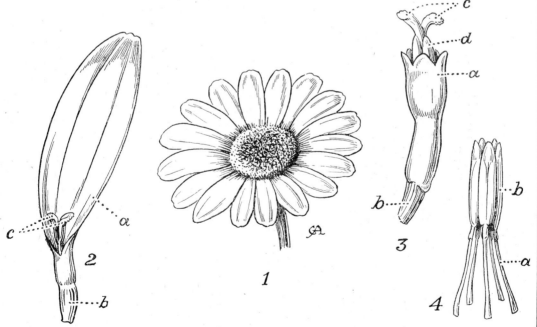

SECTIONS OF A DAISY.

1. Flower-head. 2. Outer flower : *a.* corolla ; *b.* ovary ; *c.* stigmas. 3. Inner flower : *a.* tubular corolla ;
b. ovary ; *c.* stigmas ; *d.* stamens. 4. Stamens from inner flower : *a.* filaments ; *b.* anthers.

parts of the flower. When both are present the flower is said to be *complete* ; if one or both are absent, then the flower is spoken of as *incomplete*. In the Stinging Nettle the calyx alone is present, whilst in the Ash and Willow both calyx and corolla are suppressed and the flower is quite *naked*. The term perianth is very convenient for describing such flowers as the Tulip, where it is difficult to distinguish between calyx and corolla, as both are brightly coloured and similar.

The parts of the perianth, when present, vary greatly in size. They are extremely small in grasses, but in most flowers are usually larger than the stamens and pistils. The sepals and petals are usually arranged in the flower-bud in one of three different ways. They may have their margins touch-

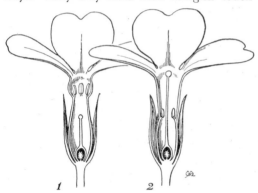

SECTIONS OF PRIMROSE.

Figure 1 above shows the short-styled form of primrose as contrasted with the long-styled beside it.

ing, as in the sepals of Clematis, of overlapping, as in the petals of the Buttercup ; or they may be twisted, as in the petals of the Mallow. Sepals and petals usually occur in rings or whorls of a regular number. In many flowers they are in threes, fours or fives ; frequently they are very numerous. This is especially the case with the petals.

How Sepals are placed.

The *sepals* are usually green and smaller than the petals. Occasionally they are white or coloured, common examples being the Fuchsia, Marsh Marigold, and Wood Anemone, in which they are petal-like. When in bud they fit tightly over and completely envelope the other parts of the flower. The Poppy is a familiar example of a flower in which they fall off as it begins to open. In others they may become erect like those of the Cabbage, or spread, or finally become

reflexed, as in those of the Bulbous Buttercup. Usually they persist for some time after the flower has opened, and frequently remain long after the petals and stamens have withered. Occasionally the calyx becomes much enlarged, and completely encloses the fruit ; an example of this type of calyx is seen in the Winter Cherry or Physalis.

Inferior and superior Sepals.

Sepals are without stalks. Their position on the receptacle is of some importance. When they are situated below the pistils, as in the Buttercup, they are *inferior*. If they are placed on top of the receptacle above the ovary, as in the Hemlock, then they are termed *superior*. Each sepal may be quite free and distinct, or it may be more or less joined by its margins to the adjacent sepals. The margins may be united only at the base or high up, and in the latter case form a cup, leaving only the tips free.

The Buttercup, Rose and Wallflower are examples with free sepals. Here the calyx is termed *polysepalous*. In the Sweet Pea, Primrose, and Carnation the sepals are united, and the calyx is said to be *gamosepalous*. The gamosepalous calyx varies much in shape. It may be tubular like that of the Primrose, urn-shaped as in the Henbane, or bell-shaped as in the Dead Nettle. Individual sepals are usually alike in shape and size, but one or more may be dissimilar. For example, in the Rock Rose, the two outer sepals are much smaller than the other three. Modifications of the calyx are seen in the Larkspur, where the sepals are spurred at the base, whilst in the Sage the calyx is two-lipped. In many flowers the calyx is composed of one row of sepals. Occasionally there may be two or more rows, or sometimes a large number of sepals, in which case they merge downwards into ordinary leaves and upwards into petals.

In the Dandelion family, where the flowers are crowded into a head, and where there is consequently less need for protection, the calyx is represented by a ring of hairs or bristles at the top of the ovary. This crown, or *pappus*, as it is usually called, often enlarges and spreads at maturity, assisting in the dispersal of the seed, as in the Dandelion and Grounsel. Occasionally in other cases, where the flowers are densely crowded, such as in the Hemlock family, the calyx is often greatly reduced, and appears simply as a green rim.

The petals are often referred to as the flower, and are usually brightly coloured. They are often more delicate than the sepals, and alternate with them, so that the back of a petal fits over the margins of the two sepals

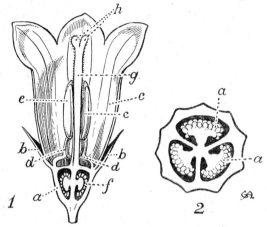

HAREBELL.

1. Vertical section through flower: *a.* receptacle; *b.* sepals; *c.* corolla tube; *d.* filaments; *e.* anthers; *f.* ovary; *g.* style; *h.* stigma.
2. Transverse section of ovary: *a.* ovules.

below it. Like the sepals, they have become modified in various ways, but usually more so. In some flowers the petals are quite distinct from one another, and are said to be *polypetalous*. Examples of this type are met with in the Rose and Carnation. In these cases the petals are attached to the receptacle by a narrow base or stalk, and have a broader upper part or limb.

The Harebell is an example of a flower in which the petals are joined along their margins. Such a flower is said to be *gamopetalous*. A gamopetalous corolla may be bell-shaped as in the Canterbury Bell, barrel-shaped, like that of the Heather, funnel-shaped, as in the Bind Weed, two-lipped, as in the Dead Nettle, or tubular and mask-like as in the Snapdragon. There are a number of other shapes, but those mentioned will suffice to illustrate some of the variations commonly encountered. The limb of a petal, or the free portions at the tip of a gamopetalous corolla, may have an entire margin, or be variously cut or divided like those of the Ragged Robin and some of the garden Pinks. In flowers of the Buttercup, Wild Rose, and Wallflower, the petals are similar in shape, but there are many flowers in which they differ considerably.

In the Sweet Pea there are five petals. One of these is broader than the others and stands erect. It is called the Standard. On either side are two smaller petals known as the wings, whilst the remaining two at the bottom form a kind of keel and enclose the stamens and pistil. The corolla of the Snapdragon is somewhat pouched at the base, and in the Violet and Toadflax is produced downwards into a spur. After fertilisation has taken place the corolla usually shrivels or falls away; in some cases, however, it persists, as in the Heather and Harebell.

In a number of flowers the sepals or petals may be altered to serve as nectaries for the secretion of honey. This is the case with the spurs of the corolla in the Violet and Larkspur. In the Buttercup a nectary is found on each petal, whilst in other flowers they occur between the petals and the stamens.

THE stamens and pistils are the essential organs of the flower, because they are necessary for the production of seed. When both are present the flowers are said to be bisexual; if the stamens alone are present the flowers are male, and with only the pistil they are female. In some cases the flowers are entirely barren, being without stamens or pistil. This is especially the case with the outer flowers of the Guelder Rose.

The stamens differ considerably from the

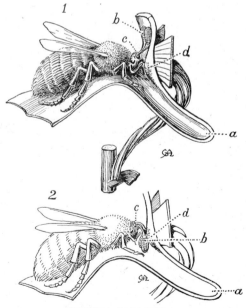

ORCHIS MASCULA.

1. Bee about to withdraw from the flower with pollen masses on head. *a.* spur; *b.* pollen masses; *c.* sticky dish; *d.* stigmatic surface.
2. Bee depositing pollen masses on flower.

MARSH MARIGOLD FLOWER.

This section of the Marsh Marigold illustrates the "regular" floral arrangement and also the "receptacle."

WILD ROSE.

Here is the Wild Rose stripped of some of its petals so that the student can examine its inner mysteries.

FLOWER OF MEDLAR.

Note the different arrangement of the internal "organs" of this flower, the Medlar blossom.

BRAMBLE FLOWER.

The essential organs of this flower are illustrated in the picture above, showing the petals and sepals.

Photos : Harold Bastin]

SWEET PEA.

The two united petals by which the essential organs of the Sweet Pea are usually enclosed are seen above.

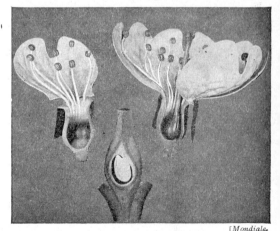

[*Mondiale.*

PEAR BLOSSOM.

These models, illustrating the structure of the Pear Blossom, show in detail the "make up" of the flower.

A BRANCH OF LABURNUM.

[*Mondiale.*

The flowers of the Yellow Laburnum grow in great profusion, hanging head-down in clusters. Above are seen :
a. the legitimate flowers of the Laburnum, and *b*, " hybrid " flowers growing together on the same branch.

55

sepals and petals, although in double flowers there may be a series showing a gradual transition from petal to stamen. A complete stamen consists of a slender stalk or *filament* which bears at its tip a swollen body or *anther*. Filaments are usually thread-like as in the flowers of grasses, or may be stiff and rigid like those of the Tulip, or considerably thickened as in the Water Lily. Occasionally the filament is absent and the anther may be borne directly on the corolla; this is found to be the case in the Lilac. Sometimes the anther is suppressed and only the filament remains. Most anthers have two cavities or cells joined by their backs. In the cells is found a fine, yellow dust, the grains of pollen. When mature, these cells mostly open by long slits in order to shed the pollen, but there are a few cases where they open by a valve (in the Barberry), or by a small hole at the tip (such as in the Potato).

How the Stamen grows.

The number of stamens varies from one to many. Frequently they are equal in number to the petals, and alternate with them, or they may be some multiple of that number. Thus a flower with five petals may have ten stamens. The latter may be quite separate from one another, or more or less united. In Flax the filaments are joined at the base to form a short tube, or they may be united for their whole length like those of the Gorse. The Fumitory has its filaments fused together

ANEMONE CORONARIA.

The single and double flowers of the Anemone, a member of the Buttercup family, are here shown.

into two groups, each of which has three anthers at the tip.

In the Dandelion and Daisy the filaments are quite free, whilst it is the anthers which are united. Stamens are normally borne on some part of the receptacle, but in the Cowslip they are produced on the corolla. Often they are similar in length, but there are many cases where they are unequal; for example in the Wallflower four are long and two are short.

How the Pollen Grains are caught.

The pistil or female portion of the flower is composed of one or more carpels. Its function is to produce ovules, which later develop into seeds. A simple carpel, as in the Buttercup, consists of ovary, style and stigma. In some flowers the style is absent and the stigma is placed directly on top of the ovary, as in the Wallflower or Poppy. The stigma is intended for catching the pollen grains, and, on this account, its surface is sticky, or it may be divided into teeth, or covered with hairs.

The Sweet Pea is an example of a flower with a single carpel, whilst the Buttercup has several which are free from one another. The latter are said to be *apocarpous*. In other flowers the carpels are united in various ways, and a pistil with one or more cavities is produced. Here the carpels are termed *syncarpous*, like those of the Hyacinth. The ovules are often small, delicate bodies and may be borne in rows on the walls of the ovary, or at the centre. There is only one in each ovary of the Buttercup, several in that of the Sweet Pea, whilst they are extremely numerous in Orchids.

In some groups of plants the flowers have a special clustered arrangement which is commonly referred to as the flower. In the Daisy family it takes the form of a flattened head, which may bear one or more different types of small flowers. Around the margin of the Daisy flower-head is a ring of female flowers, each with white petals united to form a spreading, strap-like portion, whilst the central yellow part is composed of yellowish flowers with a tubular corolla. In the Arum Lily again, the part spoken of as the flower is really a collection of minute, naked male and female flowers arranged around a central axis, and the whole is enclosed by a white, flower-like leaf. The catkins of Willows, Poplars and the Hazel are likewise densely clustered gatherings of small male or female flowers.

The large white flowers of this beautiful water plant appear on the surface in August, surrounded by great heart-shaped leaves that float around them. The plant roots in the mud, the stem growing to a length of many feet.

THE PLANT'S FIGHT FOR LIFE

By HAROLD BASTIN

NATURE has provided even the humblest of plants with efficient means of resisting the hostile influences that threaten to destroy them. Some have thorns to protect their flowers and fruit from destructive fingers ; others sting unwary intruders such as ants who come to destroy their carefully-hoarded store of nectar. Learn, in this chapter how the Virginia Creeper resists the gale, and why plants fold up their leaves and go to " sleep."

SELF-PRESERVATION—or, as the dictionary has it, " the instinct impelling living things to go on living and avoid injury "—is a profoundly significant fact of Nature. Indeed, when we come to think of it, the criterion by which we judge that any given object *is* alive amounts to this : we observe its ability to preserve independence in face of the inanimate forces to which it is exposed. It swims, for example, against the stream, or (still more wonderful !) absorbs and makes one with its own substance particles of extraneous matter, which thus serve it as " food."

Although plants are not the hopeless immobile organisms that many people imagine —witness their widespread distribution over the earth—the majority remain anchored to one spot during the whole of their adult life, and they have thus been forced to develop this power of adaptability along lines quite

different from those which animals have pursued. The typical animal, finding itself unsuited by the conditions prevailing in one locality, is able to " clear out," and try its luck in another. The plant, on the contrary, has little chance of escape, but is usually obliged to adapt itself to its surroundings, or it succumbs. How plants have succeeded in this enterprise is the subject of a profuse literature, to which the interested reader may refer at leisure. Here we have space to cite only a few instances.

Let us consider first the importance of hairs in plant life, and the varied ways in which they have been modified and pressed into service as aids to self-preservation. The term " hair " may be used to describe any structure that is developed from the outer skin of any part of the plant—root, stem or leaves. Root-hairs take up water from the soil, together with the dissolved mineral salts which it contains ; and this is conveyed by way of the stem and its offshoots to the leaves, where in sunny weather the business of food-production proceeds apace.

Hairs present on the leaves of certain insectivorous plants, such as the Sundew and the Butterwort, serve to entrap and digest their prey. In the case of the Butterwort—known also as the " Bog Violet "—the surface of one of the larger leaves is said to carry as many as 70,000 glandular hairs, which pour out a peptic mucilage when stimulated to activity by insects creeping among them.

Some botanists believe that the peculiar arrangement of hairs on the stems of such plants as the Common Chickweed serve to conduct water caught off the surface of the leaves down to the soil, where it becomes available for absorption by the roots. Again, the dense hairiness of many leaves, which is especially characteristic of plants (e.g., the Edelweiss and certain Hawkweeds) that grow in exposed or arid situations, undoubtedly prevents a too-rapid evaporation of moisture through the minute stomata, or " mouths "— a highly important function when water is scarce, or hard to come by, as may happen if the soil contains much brine.

It is interesting to note in this connection that the Restharrow, a pretty little shrub with pink-and-white " butterfly " flowers, is more hirsute near the sea than when growing inland. Extreme hairiness may also be turned to good account as a protection against cold. Many kinds of leaves are wrapped up in " warm woollies " during their tender youth, when they burst through the bud scales to keep them warm in early spring.

How Plants climb over the Hedgerow.

Climbing plants often depend mainly on hairs, especially when these are stiff and hooked at the tip, in order to hoist themselves up to points of vantage. Examine the stem of the Goose-grass or Cleavers through a lens, and you will understand how it manages to ascend so quickly through the dense tangle of a hedgerow, and why, when rubbed lightly against the lips or tongue, it draws blood.

The " prickles " or " thorns " of the Rose and the Bramble, which from the botanist's standpoint are hair-like outgrowths, also assist the plants in climbing by acting as grapples and holdfasts. Moreover, they no doubt serve, in part, as a protective device against the attacks of browsing animals—this duality of function being an example of the economy often observable in natural contrivances.

Likewise, the student should notice that prickles, thorns and spines are not always derived from the surface-layer of the stem or leaf-stalk. Those of the Holly are extensions of the veins of the leaves, and it is a significant fact that they are rarely produced by the foliage of the upper branches, beyond the reach of deer and cattle. Again, the protective prickles of the Blackthorn and the May-tree are modified branches — stiff and sharply pointed, somewhat resembling lances.

How Plants make use of their tendrils.

The various methods adopted by climbing plants in their efforts to gain a place in the sun for their leaves constitute a study of absorbing interest. As a result of his own investigations, Darwin proposed the following classification : (1) the twining of the whole plant round its support, e.g., the Hop and the Honeysuckle ; (2) the use of the leaf-stalk only, as seen in the Old-man's-beard, or Wild Clematis ; (3) the employment of specialised tendrils, as in the case of the Vetch Pea, Passion-flower and Vine ; and (4) climbing by means of hooks (to which we have already referred), or of clinging rootlets. An example of the last-named method is seen in the Ivy.

Tendrils are really prolongations of the stem ; but sticklers for accuracy point out that while some—such as those of the Vetch and the Pea—are denuded and highly sensitive leaf-veins, others—like those of the Vine—must be regarded as abortive flower-stems. The efficiency of plants in the use of these various contrivances is amazing. Darwin tells of a climbing Bignonia which ascended an upright stick by spirally twisting round it, and " seizing it alternately by two tendrils, like a sailor pulling himself up a rope hand over hand." Again, many of these arm-like shoots and tendrils develop an extraordinary revolving motion in search of supports. Thus, the Hop revolves with the sun's rays, the Garden Pea against it ; and as the growing stem rapidly elongates, sooner or later its tip is almost certain to discover what it seeks, although like a blind man its quest is wholly by touch.

A plant of outstanding interest is the well-known Ampelopsis, or Virginian Creeper. Each of its tendrils is divided into a number of tiny branches, like fingers, with hooked tips. These search everywhere for supports. Some are thrust into cracks, others twist round twigs.

Photo: *Harold Bastin*]   BRAMBLE FLOWERS AND FRUIT.   [*Mondiale.*
Here is the common Bramble or Blackberry, showing the shoot, flowers and fruit. If the pink flowers bloom at
the beginning of June it is thought a sign of early harvest. The fruit ripens in Autumn to a deep purple shade.

Then, when the fingers have taken hold, they swell out, wedging themselves into the cracks, or stiffening their hold on the twigs, as the case may be, until their weight-supporting capacity is increased to the utmost possible limit. This is why the Virginian Creeper, once firmly established, can successfully resist the rending force of a winter's gale !

Returning from this digression to the subject of hairs, we find that these structures occur frequently in association with flowers—either on the petals, the sepals, or the stems. They are often so arranged as to form a kind of *chevaux-de-frise* which keeps unwanted insects, such as ants, from gaining access to the nectar.

ANTS, and other small, wingless insects, are apt to make themselves a nuisance, because, while they are eager to plunder the flower's store of sweetness, if they can reach it, they are unfitted to effect the swift transfer of pollen from one bloom to another, which is the " payment " required. Hence plants use hairs to guard their treasure from undesirable guests.

As an instance the common White Dead-nettle may be cited. Here, both the hooded part of the corolla and the calyx are hairy,

Photo : Harold Bastin]   *[Mondiale.*

THE WILD CLEMATIS.
This plant has slender, wiry stalks which act as tendrils, and enable the Clematis to make its position secure.

making it difficult for a small insect to creep into the flower's interior, while the last line of defence consists of a ring of close-set hairs at the narrow, basal extremity of the tube, just above the nectary. Of course these arrangements in no way hamper the humble-bees, which are the welcomed visitors. They alight on the flower's lip, thrust their heads into the neck of the corolla to reach the nectar, and in so doing inevitably rub their backs against the essential organs—which is precisely what they are " meant " to do !

How to prevent the Nettle from stinging.

One more kind of hair is worthy of special remark, namely, the so-called " sting " found on the leaves of Nettles and some other plants. Fortunately, we have only two examples among our British flora—the " Great " and the " Small " Nettles, both common weeds. When one of these plants is touched with the bare hand, a painful, burning sensation is experienced, although many people know that if a Nettle is grasped boldly and held tightly, it does not " sting." It is also a fact that when a Nettle leaf is gently stroked in a particular way, its stinging propensities do not come into play.

The explanation is that the stinging hairs are hollow, brittle-walled, and equipped with a swollen, poison-filled base which is wedged among the ordinary small cells forming the surface skin of the leaf. Hence, when the hairs are carelessly handled, and pressed from above, the tips break off, and the sharp edges at the place of rupture penetrate one's flesh, with the result that poison is injected.

In short, the working of the Nettle's sting closely resembles that of a hypodermic syringe constructed to respond automatically to slight pressure. The hairs sting only when they are pressed gently and from above. Gentle pressure from one side causes them to lie close to the leaf surface ; and when the pressure is removed, they spring erect again.

The unavoidable inference that the Nettle's stinging-hairs are a protective device lends colour to the suggestion that this plant is " mimicked " by other species which have no such obvious means of defence—just as many inoffensive flies and moths, in all parts of the world, resemble bees and wasps in their colour-patterns and habits.

Certainly there are several native plants which look so much like Stinging Nettles, especially in the springtime before they come into bloom, that they are known popularly as " dead-nettles " ; and it is a fact that young white dead-nettles, for example, are frequently found growing in close association with " stingers," from which they are almost indistinguishable at first sight, although the two species are only very distantly related.

The movements of plants, usually so slow as to be scarcely noticeable, are nevertheless purposive in the sense that they serve the end of self-preservation by appropriate responses to stimuli received from the environment. The " sensitive plant," exceptionally, collapses quite suddenly when it is touched or shaken —as if it were the victim of fright ; but so far as the present writer is aware, no botanist has put forward a plausible theory to account for this astonishing behaviour. It is easier to understand why this plant and some of its relatives habitually fold together their leaflets, and droop their stalks, at the approach of dusk.

Not a few of our native wildlings " go to sleep " in this manner—for example, the Clovers and the Wood Sorrel. But we must not run away with the notion that this " sleep " of plants is identical with the slumber of animals. So far as can be discovered, the habit of folding up the leaves is an adaptation responding to the fall in temperature which takes place at eventide, or when heavy clouds obscure the sunlight. " It is just as though the plant turned up its collar and buttoned its coat more closely preparatory to a night's watch ; for scientific observation goes to show that it preserves a normally active power of assimilation during its periods of so-called ' sleep.' "

Why Plants go to sleep.

Many flowers open or close with remarkable regularity at definite hours of the day, or in accordance with the varying intensity of light, or of moisture in the air. The Mouse-ear Hawkweed, which blooms from mid-June onward on roadside banks and in dry pastures, is one of several plants to which the term " poor man's weather glass " has been applied, because its yellow flower-heads close up when rain is imminent. It is an infallible guide ; and when you are walking in the country, and notice that the Hawkweeds have shut their eyes, you do well to seek shelter, unless you are prepared to take a wetting !

So, too, with that quaint-looking plant, the Carline Thistle, which occurs on dry uplands, and may be known from all other British

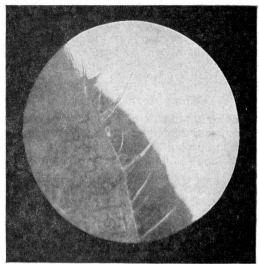

Photo : Harold Bastin]   [Mondiale.

THE NETTLE'S WEAPON.

When the stinging hairs are roughly handled, the sharp edges penetrate the skin and the poison is injected.

Thistles by the circle of ray-like bracts which surround the central cushion of tightly-packed florets. These bracts have remarkable hygroscopic properties. In dry weather they lie flat ; but when the atmosphere becomes charged with moisture, and rain is likely to fall, they turn inwards and form a kind of umbrella which keeps the wet off the florets.

In some continental districts, rustics in doubt about the weather consult the Carline Thistles as we consult a barometer. Indeed, sprays of these plants may often be seen fixed above cottage doors, where they do duty as weather guides.

Generally speaking, however, the opening and closing of flowers have reference to the visits of insects. Different kinds of insects are active at different periods during the twenty-four-hours ; and the flowers expand when the particular insects which they seek to attract are on the wing, and keep shut at other times in order to conserve their resources.

We are talking now as if the plant were a wise and prudent purveyor of high-class confectionery, careful to shut up shop when no customers are about the streets—for it is difficult, if one discards the trite jargon of science, not to fall back upon these homely modes of expression. But in all probability the plant has not the vaguest consciousness of what is taking place. Yet we cannot consistently speak of it as a cunningly wrought machine, because—in some instances, at least —it can be "taught" to alter its normal behaviour. Certain flowers which habitually close at a definite hour in the evening soon learn to "keep awake" all night if they are subjected continuously to brilliant artificial light.

Clocks made of flowers.

Taking advantage of the fact that almost every flower has its regular time for opening and shutting, the Swedish naturalist, Linnæus, constructed at Upsala what he called a *horologium floræ*—i.e., a floral clock. Many clocks of a similar kind have been arranged since, but at the present time they are out of fashion.

In a striking passage, Jean Paul Richter describes one that he was able constantly to observe from his chamber window, which also overlooked the palace grounds and the town market-place. "At three o'clock in the morning," he wrote, " the yellow goat's beard opens and the birds awake, and the stable boy begins to rattle and feed the horses beneath the lodge. At four o'clock the little hawkweed and the bakers awaken, and choristers, who are clocks with chimes, wend their way to the cathedral. At five, kitchenmaids, dairymaids, and buttercups awake. At six, the sowthistle and the cocks ; at seven o'clock many of the ladies'-maids are awake in the palace, the chicory in my botanical garden, and some tradesmen. At eight o'clock all the colleges awake, and the little yellow mouse-ear. At nine o'clock the female nobility already begin to stir ; the marigold, and even many young ladies, who have come from the country on visits, begin to look out of their windows. Between ten and eleven o'clock the court ladies and the whole staff of lords of the bedchamber, the green colewort and the alpine dandelion, and the princess's reader, rouse themselves out of their morning sleep, and the whole palace, as the morning sun gleams so brightly to-day from the lofty sky through the coloured silk curtains, curtails a little of its slumber."

The complete passage is too long to quote ; but he goes on in this strain through all the hours of the day, contrasting the periodic activities of the floral world with those of its human counterpart.

The self-preservation of plants reaches its climax at the period of fruitfulness, when the flowers have set their seeds and must needs

Photo: Harold Bastin]   A CLUMP OF NETTLES.   *[Mondiale.*
In this group stinging-nettles (right) and white dead-nettles are growing together. The hairs on the corolla of the white dead-nettle keep back unwanted insect visitors : stinging-nettles are well prepared to defend themselves.

Photo : Harold Bastin] CARLINE THISTLES. [*Mondiale.*

Carline Thistles, found growing in dry positions, bear purple flowers that are protected in dull weather by the straw-coloured bracts that cover them. These plants, common in Great Britain, flower from July to November.

disperse them. Very many seeds simply drop to the ground, when ripe, beneath the branches of the parent plant, and germinate where they fall. This is particularly the case with annual vegetation—plants that are dead and gone long before their progeny begin to flourish. But quite obviously plant life as a whole, and especially perennial plants, will benefit by any circumstances likely to remove seeds from the localities in which they are produced. AS a matter of fact, most plants have developed adaptive artifices for getting rid of their seeds, and giving them the chance of making a fresh start in life. The methods employed vary enormously, but most of them may be classed under one of the following heads, viz. : (1) the seeds are shot out from the fruit or capsule by an expulsive mechanism ; (2) they are dispersed by wind ; (3) by water ; or (4) through the agency of animals.

Expulsive mechanisms may be illustrated by the fruit of the well-known Balsam, or "Noli-me-tangerie," and the pods of the Pea tribe. The former, when ripe, bursts open at the least touch or vibration, and scatters its seeds over a wide area. So, too, the thoroughly dried valves of a pod suddenly split apart and twist spirally, jerking out the seeds to right and left, often to considerable distances. On a warm day in summer, if you stand to listen on a Gorse common, you may hear the tiny reports of the bursting pods in every direction !

Seeds carried away by parachute.

Many of the fruits and seeds destined for dispersal by the wind are very beautiful objects, for instance, those of the Wild Clematis and the Dandelion. The Dandelion's " clock " consists of numerous seeds, each with a parachute-like attachment ; and on a fine, dry day these sail away separately, sometimes floating for miles on an air-current before they finally come to earth. This is why Dandelions establish themselves on every suitable plot of uncultivated land throughout the country !

As an instance of water-conveyance, take the case of the common yellow Water-lily, whose flowers have the bouquet of old brandy, and are called " brandy bottles " by rustic lads and lasses. The seeds, when they escape from the capsule into the water, remain cohering in lumps, held together by a mass of sticky material which gradually dissolves away.

As the mass floats with the current, the seeds are liberated singly, but do not fall at once to the bottom, since they are buoyed up by air enclosed between the two layers of the seed-coat. Eventually, however, the latter decays, the air escapes, and the seed sinks to the mud and germinates. Hence, it is easy to understand how a single plant, growing in the upper reaches of a stream or river, is capable of stocking the whole of the water below with yellow Lilies.

How Birds are tempted to carry Seeds.

Beasts and birds are pressed into the service of plants as carriers of seeds in two ways : either they are hoodwinked, so to say, into performing this office, by being tempted to devour brightly coloured and luscious fruits ; or the fruits and seeds are furnished with hooked spines and get caught among the hair or wool of animals when they are pushing a way through rank vegetation. In this manner they are carried away and distributed by the unsuspecting animals. Doubtless many of the larger pips and stones of succulent fruits are never eaten at all, but discarded as soon as the delicious pulp has been consumed ; but even in those instances in which the seeds actually pass through the alimentary canal of a bird or a beast, their tough outer coats are usually capable of resisting the action of the digestive ferments to which for a time they are subjected.

Thus, it is evident that sweet and attractive fruits must exercise a direct influence upon the geographical distribution of the many kinds of plants which produce them. The same is true of the plants whose fruits are hooked or burred—like those of the Burdock, the Agrimony, the Common Avens and the Cleavers, to instance only a few out of many possible examples.

If you own a rough-haired dog, examine his coat after he has been enjoying himself in a meadow, or by a country roadside, and you will almost certainly find that he has collected a number of seeds of this kind. In countries, like Australia, where sheep roam vast areas of uncultivated land, it is found necessary to arrange that the time of shearing shall fall at a date preceding that at which the smaller kinds of hooked and burred seeds are known to ripen ; otherwise myriads of them will be found among the wool, greatly to its detriment.

Photo : Harold Bastin]   WATER BUTTERCUPS.   *[Mondiale.*

The Water Buttercup, shown above, is an extremely hardy plant, making its home readily in ditches or marshy ground. Its flowers are a deep golden yellow in colour and its dark-green leaves are heart-shaped.

THE MISTLETOE BOUGH.

The Mistletoe, which was held in great reverence by the Druids, was thought to possess the power of healing. Its leaves and young twigs were dried to be used for nervous disorders, epilepsy and internal bleeding.

PLANTS THAT CURE THE SICK

By J. H. TURNER

THE old herbalists who studied the medicinal value of plants made many valuable discoveries that were effective in curing ailments. Their knowledge is still put to use to-day, and in this chapter we are told of their experiments and how certain simple plants should be used to remedy ills. It shows us how much we owe to the humble wayside plants that we often trample heedlessly underfoot.

THE importance of plants to Mankind cannot be over-estimated. Our very lives depend on green plants in some form or other, not only because they purify the air, but because all our food is derived directly or indirectly from them. In the immensity of the oceans, life begins with the plant. Certain fishes feed on minute forms of floating plant life, and they in turn are eaten by larger fish. On the land, the flesh-eating animals prey on those which feed on grass and herbage, so that all life may be said to owe its existence to the plant.

We are apt to forget how great a part of our immediate surroundings, our houses, food and clothing, have their origin in the fields and forests of the world. The floor, its table and tablecloth, the linoleum, the bread we eat, the sugar, jam, pepper and mustard, were once part of the living plant. Our leather, wool and meat is obtained from animals which feed on plants. Our shoe-laces are plant products, and it is probable that our coat buttons are from the nuts of the vegetable Ivory Palm of the Amazon region. From the plantations of the tropical Malay Peninsula comes the rubber for mackintoshes, " Wellingtons " and fountain pens, and for the tyres of the million and one motor vehicles hurrying to and fro, some with newspapers printed on wood-pulp from the forests of Scandinavia and North America. The fuel which cooks our food, heats our dwellings and drives the machinery of factories, ships and locomotives, comes either from plants recently alive or from coal-plants which died long ago, and were buried in the earth. In sickness we turn to plants to make us well. In the museums of the Royal Botanic Gardens, Kew, are specimens of nearly one hundred thousand useful things obtained from plants. This gives some idea of how intimately our lives are bound up with theirs.

Man's knowledge of herbs for purposes of healing dates from the beginning of civilisation. Formerly almost every plant, however insignificant, was credited with some property such as that of warding off evil spirits, of curing human ailments, whether mental or physical, or of promoting love between the suitor and the object of his affection.

How Horehound cures a Cough.

A number of plants were known to the ancient Greeks, and it is probable that the bitter cup of Hemlock given to Socrates to drink was (*Conium maculatum*) which grows in this country on waste ground and on hedgebanks. The Greeks also used the castor-oil plant, and opium poppy, the *Artemisia*, and other plants which are still in constant use in modern medicine.

The Saxons had a wide knowledge of the healing plants of the countryside, and prescribed a remedy, largely compounded of herbs, for those who were in any way afflicted. Some of the concoctions advocated may appear rather amusing to us to-day, accompanied as they were with incantations and ritual, but nevertheless, some of them were quite sound. The translation of a Saxon manuscript, about the year A.D. 1040, gives the following : " For cough, take horehound, seethe (boil) in water, give it warm to the patient to drink." Horehound is still the most popular of remedies for coughs and chest complaints. Other remedies consisted of equal proportions of numerous plants, such as Parsley, Fennel, Dill, Rue, Colewort, Celandine, Feverfue, and so on, powdered together and administered in wine. " Wort " is the Saxon name for " plant " and survives in such names as Pennywort, Pillwort, Leadwort, Woundwort, Spearwort, Danewort, Squinancywort, (squinancy means quinsy), Ribwort, Spleenwort, and numerous others.

The Plant that had a human form.

In the Middle-Ages books, and especially references to plants, were rare. Herbs were endowed with all kinds of magical powers, and some of them were put to very different uses from what they are nowadays, showing that their real properties were only imperfectly understood. As there was then no means of identifying plants, a great deal of confusion must have existed, and the legendary attributes of the various herbs were implicitly believed. A good example of the mystery which the

early herbalists wove around their " simples " is shown by the Mandrake, which belongs to the potato tribe. The forked, parsnip-like root of the Mandrake was reputed to have the form of a man or woman. It was said to be death to dig up a root, which shrieked and groaned, and that none might hear it and live. As it was esteemed for its medicinal virtues, it was recommended that the plant should be loosened in the ground, and a dog tied to it. In attempting to get away, the dog would uproot the Mandrake, and fall dead. Once out of the ground, the Mandrake could be handled with safety.

Ancient herbals show a dog harnessed to this plant in the act of drawing it out, and depict the male mandrake as a bearded man, and the female as a woman with flowing hair. Apart from a tuft of leaves growing from the head of each, they have perfect human forms !

The first book on Herbs.

In 1516 the first English printed book about herbs appeared. This was the " Grete Herball," by an unknown author, " whiche geveth purfyt knowledge and understandying of all manner of Herbes." It was, however, full of inaccuracies and strange ideas of the time. At this period there were a few books on the subject in Latin, but " the apothecary for lack of knowledge of the Latin tongue is ignorant of herbes, and putteth either many a good man in jeopardy of his life or marreth good medicine." Thus wrote William Turner, Doctor of Physic. To him the need for a reliable treatise was very apparent, and in 1551 he published a " New Herball." This was a great advance on the " Grete Herball," for Turner did not take doubtful statements on trust.

Turner first gave names to many British plants, and his " New Herball " and other books marked the beginning of English Botany. He was followed by John Gerard, Herbalist to James I., who studied simples, and grew nearly 1,100 different plants in his garden at Holborn. Gerard's masterpiece, the " Herball, or General Historie of Plants," published in 1597, was the most important work on botany of its time. Thirty-two years later appeared the " Paradisus," by John Parkinson. Its full title is shown on the opposite page. The publication of these famous herbals did much to dispel popular superstition about plants, and to make available more accurate knowledge concerning them.

PARKINSON'S HERBAL. [Mondiale.

The title-page from the 1656 edition of Parkinson's *Paradisus* gives a graphic review of the "herbs"
therein described. The advertisement under the title sets out quaintly the purpose of the book.

At the present time many of the once renowned herbs have been displaced by drugs obtained from tropical plants, whilst the romance of the discovery of the Peruvian *Cinchona* tree which yields quinine, and its subsequent cultivation in the East, would require a chapter to itself.

Many herbs which are no longer considered of primary importance in diseases of mankind, are still cultivated for use in veterinary practice, or grown for their old-time associations, their flowers and aromatic leaves. The most important British medicinal plants range from Ferns, Mosses and the Sweet Flag by the waterside, to the Mistletoe on some lofty tree top. Some are good to eat, others are so poisonous that a very small quantity proves fatal, for example Monks-hood, which is grown in borders for its decorative leaves and dark-blue, helmet-shaped flowers. Monkshood now ranks as one of our most useful drugs for fevers, heart trouble, and in neuralgia. The extract is prepared from the leaves, stem and root.

HENBANE and Belladonna both belong to the same family as the potato and tomato, but, unlike them, all their parts are poisonous. Henbane is found on waste, sandy places, or on chalk slopes by the sea. The pale-green leaves are covered with soft, sticky hairs and the flowers have a hairy, pitcher-shaped calyx. The funnel-shaped corolla is a dingy yellow, marked with purple veins. A preparation from the leaves is frequently used in nervous affections, and in many children's complaints, such as whooping cough.

THE DISCOVERY OF THE MANDRAKE. [*Mondiale.*
In this ancient drawing the Goddess of Discovery is seen handing the root of the Mandrake to the famous Greek physician of the first century, Dioscorides. The plant must be pulled up by a dog, that thereupon dies.

CHAMOMILE IN BLOOM.
This plant has been cultivated for many hundred years.
Chamomile tea soothes the nerves and helps digestion.

THE AUTUMN CROCUS.
The roots and seeds of this plant are frequently
prescribed with success in the treatment of rheumatism.

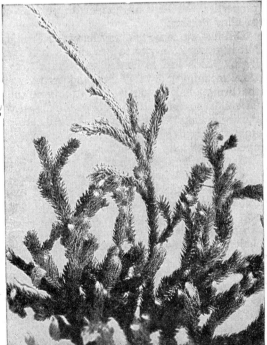

Harold Bastin]   CLUB MOSS.
When the spores of this moss are applied to inflamed
parts of the body, they are found to ease the pain.

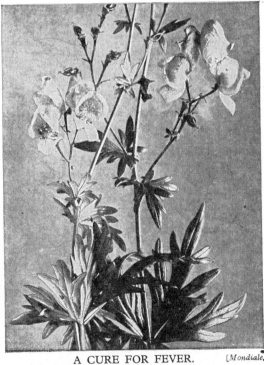

A CURE FOR FEVER.   [*Mondiale*.
An extract prepared from the leaves, stem and root
of Monkshood, is one of the best drugs for fever.

Belladonna, or Deadly Nightshade, with its dull-green, oval, unpleasant smelling leaves and purplish coloured stems is occasionally found wild on chalk or limestone. It grows from three to five feet high, and the hanging, dark-purplish flowers are bell-shaped and tinged with green. The shining black fruit, about as large as a cherry, ripens in September. Children are sometimes poisoned through eating them, as they are very sweet. Belladonna, prepared from the root, has the effect of dilating the pupil of the eye, and is most valuable in eye examination. It is also used in heart trouble and to lessen pain in many diseases.

Another poisonous drug is obtained from Hemlock, which belongs to the carrot and parsley family. In fact, the leaves have been mistaken for parsley and the root for parsnip, but they have a bitter taste. Hemlock grows from two to four feet high, with a bright green, hollow stem, mottled with small purplish spots. The leaves and fruits are gathered, as they are of service in all spasmodic affections, such as epilepsy.

Less poisonous is the purple Foxglove, with spikes of drooping, tubular flowers, beloved of the honey-bee. It is of great value in heart diseases; the leaves are collected before the flower spike has fully expanded.

The Plant that yields Laudanum.

From the capsules of the Opium Poppy, Laudanum is prepared. The half-ripened seed heads are scarified with small knives, and the milky juice which exudes is allowed to harden before removal. The flowers vary from pure white to a reddish purple. Those of the common Red Poppy are a rich scarlet. The Red Poppy grows in corn fields and the fresh petals are used in preparing a syrup.

Some plants are not only of importance in the kitchen for flavouring, but are of distinct medicinal use as well. It was formerly the practice to boil Fennel with fish, and Fennel is often found in kitchen gardens. It is an umbelliferous herb, from four to five feet high. The leaves are feathery, and the yellow flowers bloom in July and August. On account of their aromatic and warming properties, the seeds are used with purgatives to allay griping.

Dill has the same feathery leaves as Fennel, but it grows from two to two and a half feet high. Dill is said to be derived from a Norse word meaning " to lull," from the property of the drug. Dill Water is a popular medicine for children, and is obtained from the " seeds." Parsley belongs to the same family. An extract from the seeds and roots has a tonic and aperient action.

Garden Sage was held in the highest repute in the Middle-Ages. Gerard remarks, " Sage is singularly good for the head and brain, it quickeneth the senses and memory, strengtheneth the nerves, restoreth health to those that have the palsy, and taketh away shakey trembling of the members." It is a good blood purifier.

Common mint or Spearmint is of value in children's complaints. Spearmint Oil is added to many compounds for its warming and soothing properties, whilst an infusion of spearmint relieves stomach pains.

Peppermint is grown around Mitcham, in Surrey, at Hitchin in Herts, and in Lincolnshire, for its use in flavouring. The plants

HENBANE.   [Mondiale.
From the leaves of this plant a preparation is used for such children's complaints as whooping-cough.

are harvested before they flower, and distilled. The oil is stimulating, and is used as an infants' cordial.

Pennyroyal, the smallest of the mints, grows by streams and in damp places. The leaves are oval, greyish-green, with toothed edges ; the flowers are in whorled clusters, reddish purple to lilac blue. Pennyroyal is used in chills and colds, and affections of the stomach.

Fragrant Rosemary and Lavender are grown in almost every garden. Lavender is principally cultivated for perfume at Hitchin, Long Melford and Market Deeping, and is now seldom used in medicine. Spirit of Lavender is an admirable tonic against faintness. Rosemary was once used to flavour ale and wine, and burnt as incense. Oil of Rosemary is distilled from the flowering tops, leaves and stems and added to liniments. Rosemary tea is good for headaches and nervous ailments.

Herb of Grace or Rue is one of our oldest garden plants. It has bluish-green divided leaves, and gives off a powerful unpleasant smell. The greenish, yellow flowers appear from June to September, and the leaves have a bitter, nauseous taste. Rue was considered by the Greeks to ward off magic and contagion. Oil of Rue is distilled from the fresh herb, and the dried herb is used for making tea. It is good for coughs and affections of the stomach.

Cough mixture in the making.

Liquorice has been cultivated in England since 1562, and is grown commercially near Pontefract in the Vale of York. It is a graceful plant with leaves like an ash, and small blue and white, pea-like flowers. The roots, which go down to a depth of three to four feet, are dug up in autumn, then crushed and boiled. The evaporated extract is rolled out into various shapes. Liquorice is an ingredient in all popular cough medicines, whilst liquorice powder is well known as a children's medicine.

The " Marsh Mallows " sold by confectioners, however, do not contain any extract of mallow. Marsh Mallow is found in most of the sea-bordering counties in the south of England. It grows from three to four feet high with rounded, three to five lobed leaves, which are soft and velvety. The leaves, the bluish-white flowers and the thick, long roots furnish a popular remedy for whooping cough and chest complaints.

The handsome, purple-flowered Burdock grows by the wayside and is well known to children, who love to throw the ripe flower

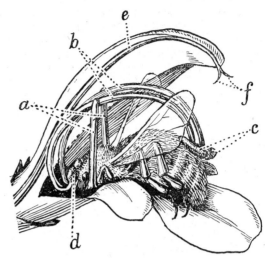

DETAILS OF SAGE.

In this picture are shown : *a.* filaments of stamens ; *b.* connectives ; *c.* fertile anther lobes ; *d.* barren anther lobes ; *e.* style ; *f.* stigmas.

heads or burrs at one another. The burrs are covered with hooked prickles, which cling to everything with which they come in contact. The seeds are thus carried long distances by the coats of animals. Burdock is one of the best blood purifiers, and the dried roots, leaves and shoots are a remedy in skin diseases.

Equally purifying are the roots of Dandelion, which are dug in autumn. Dandelion wine, prepared from the flowers, is an excellent tonic. Marigold, with deep orange flowers and pale green leaves, is employed in fevers. Marigold flowers are in demand for children's ailments, and also are used, both internally and externally, for ulcers and varicose veins.

The yellow flowers of Coltsfoot are a familiar sight along railway embankments in February. After the flowers have died down, the hoof-shaped, white-felted leaves appear. Both flowers and leaves are collected, for syrup of Coltsfoot is much recommended for use in chronic bronchitis. This property of Coltsfoot was known to the ancient Greeks.

Like Rue, the Chamomile has a great reputation, and has been cultivated for hundreds of years. It is a sun-loving plant, and seems to prefer sandy waste places. The feathery leaves and yellow, daisy-like flowers have stomachic and antispasmodic properties. Chamomile tea has a wonderful soothing effect on the nerves and aids digestion. German Chamomile has smaller flowers than the preceding, and is used in children's complaints.

Elecampane, with its enormous, toothed leaves and bright yellow, sunflower-like blooms is often to be found growing in borders. The roots are collected in autumn, and provide a favourite and effective remedy in bronchitis and lung trouble. It has been in general use since the time of the Romans.

The romance of the Mistletoe.

The Mistletoe was held in great reverence by the Druids, who gathered it from the Oak with a golden sickle, during their religious festivals. They sent round branches of Mistletoe to announce the New Year, and this custom probably survives in its use for Christmas decoration. The leaves and young twigs are dried and used in nervous disorders, epilepsy and internal bleeding.

The lowly growing Club Moss, common on moorland in the north of Britain, is no less useful. The spores of this moss are applied to inflamed surfaces of the body. A teaspoonful of the spores, thrown into a bowl of water, will float as a thin layer, and one's finger may be repeatedly thrust into the water without becoming wet.

Carragheen, or Irish Moss, is not a moss at all, but a seaweed. It is found on the shores of the North Atlantic, and contains a large percentage of mucilage and sulphur. It is made into jelly for lung complaints and kidney affections.

The Sweet Sedge or Flag grows by the margins of lakes and streams, and its leaf somewhat resembles the Yellow Flag or Iris. The whole plant is fragrant, and in olden days was strewn on floors instead of rushes. The rhizome or root has stimulant, tonic properties.

Lad's Love, or Southernwood, is also well known for its characteristic odour, and it is said that moths will not attack clothes upon which it is laid. It provides a good stimulant tonic, and is given to children for certain ailments.

Like Southernwood, the Male Fern is an important vermifuge. It is one of the commonest of our ferns, with fronds two to four feet long, and pinnæ or leaflets arranged alternately on the mid-rib. The rhizome is the part which furnishes the extract.

The Larch Agaric, a fungus which grows like a white, spongy mass on the trunks of larches, is used in the treatment of consumption, and is also found to be very effective in the checking of profuse perspiration.

Black Currant, occasionally found wild in damp woods in the north, is used in feverish complaints. The boiled juice is excellent for sore throats and colds.

Hops are usually associated with brewing, but the ripened female, cone-like catkins, are gathered and dried for their blood purifying and sleep producing properties.

Scurvygrass is employed in certain skin diseases. It is a tiny plant, with thick, fleshy, egg-shaped leaves and white, cross-shaped flowers, abundant on the Scottish shores. It flowers all the summer. In the days of sailing ships, when sea voyages occupied many months, this bitter tasting herb was taken to prevent scurvy, caused through lack of vegetables.

From the styles and stigmas of the Saffron Crocus, Tincture of Saffron is obtained. More than four thousand flowers are required to yield one ounce of saffron, which is used in various complaints. As a dye, it was highly prized in olden days, and the village of Saffron Walden in Essex commemorates the extensive fields of Saffron Crocus which flourished there during the Middle Ages. The list of important British medicinal plants is by no means complete, and we shall therefore have to be content with brief references to some of those that still remain to be mentioned.

When Roses are useful.

Four roses are recognised by British pharmaceutists—the Red Rose, the Cabbage Rose, the Damask Rose, from which rose water is distilled, and the common Dog Rose. Another extract is prepared from the flowering tops of the Broom.

The roots and seeds of the Meadow Saffron, or Autumn Crocus, the roots of Horseradish, and the bark, stem and berries of Mezereon, are prescribed in the treatment of rheumatism.

The Bearberry of the Scottish moors and the meadowland Valerian, whose name signifies " to make well," also contribute their part. Even the tiny sweet Violet lends its aid towards the alleviation of man's pain and illness.

These are but a few items out of the vast resources of nature, which is so lavish in our British fields, woods and gardens. Though a short outline, yet it will supply the answer to those who may question " But of what good are pretty flowers and weeds ? " Some are more vital to human life than we realise ; they are essential to our well-being, while in addition they add to the glory of our countryside.

Photo: Harold Bastin.] [*Mondiale.*
Animals are said to possess a keen instinct where poisonous plants are concerned and are careful to avoid the Yew, whose feathery leaves and seeds of the scarlet fruit should not be eaten because of the poison they contain.

DEATH IN THE HEDGEROWS

By E. D. RHODES

IN field and hedgerow there are enemies lurking unknown to the unwary. Brightly-coloured berries of enticing-looking promise may turn out to be dealers of destruction, and though the animals seem able instinctively to distinguish between good food and poison, many of us have still to learn the warning given below. Children especially, who are fond of conveying everything they see to their mouths, should be taught the lesson explained here.

MATTHEW ARNOLD has written of the never-idle workshop of Nature, and it is interesting to trace the very complete pharmacy that exists in the fields and hedgerows of these islands.

Those who rejoice in the warm brown soil and wealth of plant life which has made Great Britain a source of envy to visitors from lands covered with wide sun-bleached spaces and devoid of colour and life, may be a little shocked to realise the deadly nature of some of our best-known and loved wild flowers.

From the time when ancient Britons wore jerkins of Bear-skin and the fields were blue with Woad, there has been much legendary and folk-lore associated with the remedial and poisonous nature of plants. And even to this day in the untouched villages, something of the past still remains, and old customs prevail, whereby it is possible to drink Elderberry Wine and Sloe Gin, brewed in old copper pans, and far sweeter and more mellow than any synthetic drink bottled in the hideous factories that blotch the landscape. Here, too, recourse is made to Nature for simple remedies in sickness and injury, and herb teas are almost a commonplace. Among Highlanders the plantain was known as " the healing plant," because of its astringent value and the relief occasioned when a plantain leaf was applied to cuts and open sores, or the swelling caused by insect bites and stings. And what child does not run instantly for a Dock leaf after coming into contact with a Stinging Nettle ?

This is a side of natural history known and loved, but to those who, like Mary Webb, refuse to admit of a ruthless or destructive element in Nature and attribute these solely to human wickedness, to dwell on the death-dealing attributes of plants, must seem in the nature of a crime. From a sentimental point

73

of view it is pleasing to regard a flower as a thing of beauty and a joy for ever, but nevertheless it must be admitted that they are also dealers in destruction.

Even the greatest poets are aware that beauty is no guarantee of virtue, and Shakespeare's three witches in *Macbeth* make full use of poisonous plants in their bubbling cauldron. Among other unpleasant ingredients chosen for their magic qualities, were included a " root of Hemlock, digg'd i' the dark," and " slips of yew," all contributing to a " charm of powerful trouble." History tells us, moreover, that Socrates the Wise, and Phocion the Good, were both condemned to death by Hemlock juice in the fourth century B.C. And yet Hemlock is one of the commonest wild flowers to-day, and grows plentifully by the roadside and in fields and hedges all through the summer, and few people give a thought to its poisonous nature. The purple streaks on the stem of Water Hemlock are in older legends the marks put on Cain's brow when he murdered his brother. It is related to the Carrot, Parsnip, Parsley, Fennel, and also to Sweet Cicely, which is also unwholesome.

Fool's Parsley and Fennel are two other members of this umbelliferic family which contain poison, and indeed there are so many similar plants that perhaps only the student of botany would be able to recognise readily one from the other at first glance. Fennel is yellow and has a sickly smell reminiscent of Liquorice, and for this reason may be tempting or otherwise to children, according to whether their acquaintance with this substance has been through the unpleasant gritty powder of the sick-room or the familiar hard sticks of black paste of the sweet-shops.

Beware of the Woody Nightshade.

Commonly speaking, except in the case of small children, who may be tempted to eat anything once, the danger from poisonous wild flowers is not very great, the real snare being the Scarlet, Black and Purple Berries, so like their edible relatives and yet so deadly in their effect. One such is the Woody, or the Deadly Nightshade. The handsome purple-black berry of this plant is highly poisonous, and the fact that the flower and fruit are both rather handsome and somewhat prolific, seems to make it the more alluring.

Deadly Nightshade, or Belladonna, is the favourite plant of the devil, and he spends all his spare time in tending it. The old belief has it that he can only be diverted from his attentions on one night of the year, Walpurgis, when he is preparing for the Witches' Sabbath a pagan festival still remembered on the

POISONOUS HEMLOCKS.
On the left is the Lesser Hemlock or Fool's Parsley which, though similar to the edible parsley, is poisonous. In the middle is the Hemlock Water-Dropwort, another poisonous kind, and on the right Water-Hemlock or Cowbane.

Photos : *H. Bastin and M. H. Crawford.*]   THE POISONOUS NIGHTSHADES.   [*Mondiale.*

Although the purple-black berries of the Woody Nightshade look appetising they are highly poisonous, and children ought to be warned against touching them.   The same applies to the Deadly Nightshade (right).

Continent, but nowadays forgotten in Great Britain. On this night, if a farmer will let loose a Black Hen, the Devil will endeavour to catch it, and while so engaged the farmer will have the opportunity to dash out and pluck the plant which he can then apply to its proper purpose. This purpose is to rub his horse down with it, so that it will gain in strength. The name Belladonna comes also from an old superstition whereby at certain times the plant takes on the form of an enchantress of such exceeding beauty that it is dangerous to look upon her. Earlier ideas, too, connected the plant with the Apples of Sodom.

The active poisonous principle of Deadly Nightshade is Atropine, of Woody Nightshade or Bittersweet, Solanine, which produces giddiness and sickness. The berries especially are very harmful.

Equally handsome and quite as potent is the Bryony whose flowing tendrils and scarlet berries are often much admired, as well as the cascade of yellow flowers which precede the fruit. It is familiar all over the country, and has even been called " Sweet Bryony." The root of Black Bryony (a small green flower in which the sexes are distinct on different plants) contains starch, and is also a purgative. It is used in popular medicine when reduced to pulp for application to bruises, and this use it is which has caused it to be known in parts of France as " Herbe aux femmes battues," or the " Plant of the beaten women." There is no harm in the stem and leaves, but the fruit is deadly.

A Flower that is full of Poison.

It is surprising to learn, too, that the Foxglove, which is one of the most graceful and popular of early summer wild flowers, is of a poisonous character, though its poison is very valuable used as a medicine in certain complaints and has a definite effect on the heart's action. Two great poets at least, Wordsworth and Tennyson, were moved to immortalise the Foxglove, and one doubts not that they were probably blind to the deadly quality of its leaves. But if one must unmask the cruel nature of much-loved plants, it is comforting to reflect that there are others as charming, which are entirely innocuous and often beneficial. The Gillyflowers, the most typically English of all wild plants, besides including the Wallflower and Rocket, count among their number the Mustard and Clove.

It is very rare nowadays to come across a family of real gipsies, and even among those who can still claim a strain of Romany blood one hardly expects to find poisonous broths being concocted over camp-fires, in the legendary manner. Nevertheless people who live close to Nature undoubtedly obtain a rare insight into the virtues or otherwise of plants, which is denied to the casual observer. It is not unusual on the Hopfields of to-day still to find gipsy folk who brew camomile tea and make use of herbs in various ways for medicinal purposes. Undoubtedly there is much commonsense wrapped around the homely remedies adopted by rural people, but when the element of magic is introduced it is really an ignorant attempt to relate cause and effect and has no place in modern medicine.

How Gipsies dyed their Skin.

Legend has it that ancient gipsies used the juice of the Wolf's foot Plant to dye themselves a blackish hue, and it is for this reason that it is known as Gipsy Wort. The Wolfsbane, too, was so-called because meat saturated with the juice of this plant was supposed to be a poison for Wolves. Many decades have passed since Wolves were hunted on these shores, but the Wolfsbane is still to be found.

Plants do not appear to have any system of danger signals with which to warn humanity that they are poisonous, and animals possess a keen instinct which protects them. One rarely, if ever, hears of an animal being poisoned in this way, although it is customary to avoid putting cows to graze in a field planted with Yew Trees, because of their poisonous nature. This may be due to the fact that the keener instincts of this creature have become dulled with long usage to domestic purposes and the subjection to the will of man. It is reasonable to suppose that the Cow takes it for granted that she may eat anything within reach in a field, since her master, man, has put her there for the purpose of feeding. Be that as it may, it is certain that Rabbits and other small creatures distinguish carefully between the various herbs they devour, almost too carefully, some gardeners would say. It is also a curious fact that animals can with impunity eat plants that would be fatal to human beings. The Privet, for example, is the daily diet of certain Caterpillars, but it is highly poisonous to the human race, as also the Hemlock. Henbane, another wayside danger, older country-folk

know, is used by the witches for their stews, and the dead in Hades are garlanded with the plant as they stroll hopelessly along the banks of the Styx.

Farmers, if questioned on the subject of poisonous plants, might feasibly exclaim that their pest lay in other directions, namely Thistles and prolific weeds. It was Falstaff who was moved to lament the fact that the more Camomile was trodden on the faster it grew, whereas the Violet, the oftener it was touched, the sooner it withered and decayed. And one cannot help mourning the fact that the poisonous tribe of Hemlocks thrive in spite of the onslaught of scythe, and even fire, while the beautiful wild Daffodils and Primroses seem to disappear with the passing years, owing to the ruthless uprooting of plundering hands. One is almost tempted to wish that they were associated with some deadly poison so that they might bloom for ever in increasing abundance.

It comes as rather a shock to realise that the lovely Christmas Rose is a poisonous plant, and one is equally reluctant to admit that the Wake Robin or Cuckoo-pint contains an irritant poison. This regal plant with its purple rod and sea-green sheath, has a beautiful spotted leaf of a spear-head shape, and even more lovely is the cluster of scarlet berries on a thick green stem which comprises the fruit. Children often call this Lords and Ladies, and Snake's food, and are sorely tempted to taste it, when it is likely to cause severe cramps and convulsions and sometimes death. The Monk's Hood is another common wild flower which everybody has seen at some time or another in the hedges, with its strangely-shaped flower heads from which the name is derived. And lastly in this list is the Thorn Apple, rather less well-known but with a very pretty flower somewhat like that of the Convolvulus, and a spiny fruit, shaped in similar manner to that of the Beech.

When is a Mushroom a Toadstool?

It is a curious fact that, while experience has taught man to beware of most wild Berries for fear of poison, there is one branch of plant life in which caution is frequently disregarded. This is the genus of flowerless plants known as Fungi, comprising among others the Toadstool and Mushroom. The latter is such a delicacy that the gourmand in his eager search will often grab a handful of Toadstool, rather than be disappointed in his search. The

Toadstools are highly poisonous, and there have been cases of wholesale poisoning from this source. The only safe way to gather Mushrooms is to rise with the Lark and scan the dew-covered fields where crops of these ephemeral plants will be found, and it is a guide to remember that they invariably have a black under-surface and peel much more easily than Toadstools, while their composition is somewhat drier. The realm of Toadstools is very varied, and they are found in many places, particularly at the foot of trees and in damp woods. They are often very attractive in colouring, and for this reason are almost irresistible to children.

Beware of dangerous Plants.

In considering the poisonous values of plants it should be remembered that poison is a relative term. The quantity of poison in a plant may be so weak that eating it does not necessarily mean that grave harm must result. Generally speaking, if the idea of deadliness is conveyed by the term poison, then we must consider it as being in the concentrated form prepared by chemists. While a few plants will cause illness if a small quantity is swallowed, it takes an excess of the Common Sorrel, for instance, which children are inclined to eat because of its pleasant sharp taste, to have ill effect. This harmless salad plant, however, contains Binoxalate of Potash, which will be recognised as the very dangerous " Salts of Lemon."

Many of the vegetable poisons which are dangerous when taken in quantities are nevertheless most valuable when employed in medicines. Some plants which provide useful products, but which eaten are very unwholesome to human beings, have unfortunately a resemblance to perfectly safe garden plants. Thus, Garden Aconite, which no one can

H. Bastin.]   *[Mondiale.*

MONKSHOOD, OR WOLFSBANE.
People have died from eating this root, which grows in moist, shady ground, in mistake for horse-radish.

mistake when in flower, has a root resembling Horse-radish, and if grown in a small garden where the latter is also cultivated, may be dug up in mistake and eaten with evil results.

Then, too, every-day flowers which we never imagine contain any poisonous substance, very often are dangerous. All members of the Buttercup family, with the exception of Water Crowsfoot, contain a poisonous acrid and narcotic principle, though in varying degrees of activity. The group includes Buttercups, Traveller's Joy, Marsh Marigold, Hellebores, Wood Anemones, Winter Aconite, Larkspur and Aconite. The chief danger is in the roots, but it is very unwise to put in the mouth the petals of Buttercups, and especially of Aconite. The latter is a deadly poison. The people of old know its value in this direction quite well, and in classic times it was fabled as an invention of Hecate from the foam of Cerberus. On the island of Ceos, Aconite poison was used to dispose of persons unwanted and useless to the state. Old men were thus got rid of.

In North India wells were poisoned by Aconite in warfare, and it was also used to poison spearheads and darts, and for destroying Tigers. In Tibet and China its uses are well known.

Poppy seeds are eaten in large quantities on the Continent in pastry and sprinkled on bread rolls. They contain faint signs of Opium, and the milky juice which exudes from Poppies is, in fact, when it coagulates, the crude Opium. The real Opium Poppies, however, are cultivated, and are of a different appearance from the wild plant in that they are larger as a rule, and have smooth stems and foliage.

Laburnum, that very attractive tree, contains a violent purgative principle in the seeds, while Smallage or Wild Celery is dangerous, though when cultivated does not develop its deleterious qualities. The milky juice of the innocent-looking Convolvulus flower contains a cathartic principle, Mistletoe is decidedly unwholesome, and Spurge Laurel Bark, if applied to the skin, may cause a nasty eruption, and if eaten by children can cause death. Recently the medical press gave warning against the handling of Ground Ivy, for it will bring about an unpleasant rash on delicate skins.

One should go out in the autumn to realise the wonders of the hedgerows, when the bright berries are bravely displayed, and the trees have on their loveliest colours. While not all hedge and tree Berries are dangerous, children should be warned against sampling any kind. The Mountain Ash, to take one, will not be classed amongst the dangerous plants, for its gay berries are made into jelly, yet cases have been known of illness subsequent to eating the Berries from the tree, though really the Mountain Ash belongs to the same family as the Apple. It is also frequently called the Rowan, and sometimes Witch-wood, from the superstition of early times that a branch or piece of this tree was efficacious as an amulet against evil spirits.

These Berried plants are invaluable sources of food supplies for birds, which seem by instinct to avoid anything dangerous; perhaps the smell warns them. They will not touch the dark purple Berries of the Laurel, though, unlike the Holly, they are not protected by prickly leaves. The leaves of the Laurel are poisonous, but the Berries more so, as are also the Berries of the Ivy.

Caution with regard to plant eating has led to many quite harmless and even savour plants being overlooked. The Dandelion, for example, which plays an important part in Continental salads, is rarely, if ever, seen on an English table, and the nasturtium leaf which has a keen flavour, is popular only among the young. Sunflower seeds, too, which are greatly appreciated in Russia, do not tempt us here.

When one reflects on the reason for the delicate colouring and handsome markings of many plants, it is obvious that their purpose is to serve as honey guides for Bees and other insects, that they are in fact a biological necessity, but probably no one could have summed up the position with regard to poisonous plants more beautifully than has Keats in *Isabella* :

" Even Bees, the little almsmen of spring
    bowers,
  Know there is richest juice in poison-
    flowers."

Photo : Harold Bastin. THE DEADLY ACONITE. *[Mondiale*

The petals of the Aconite contain a deadly poison which, according to legend, was formerly used to get rid of unwanted or useless persons. In India, wells were poisoned by Aconite, and it was also used to poison arrows

[*Robert McLeod.*

Stitchwort is a plant that should be included in all collections of wild flowers. Found growing in hedges and thickets, it is easily recognisable by its long, narrow leaves which taper to a point, and its conspicuous white flowers.

COLLECTING WILD FLOWERS

By HAROLD BASTIN

FOR those in search of an absorbing and healthful hobby collecting wild flowers presents a pleasing appeal. Few, however, know how to carry it out successfully and will welcome the advice of a specialist who tells in this chapter the best methods of collecting and preserving specimens. His hints on the proper outfit are of great value and his description of this delightful hobby will make the aspiring botanist all the more eager to adopt it.

AN important piece of advice that should be given to all collectors of wild plants is to avoid the method of ruthless picking —or, still worse, the uprooting of rare and beautiful specimens.

Already the depredations, due to the activities of the building fraternity, coupled with a widespread tendency to improve communications in our rural areas by multiplying roads and by-passes, are rendering the foothold of our choicer wild flowers increasingly insecure. Indeed, some have already given up the struggle, and are no longer to be found in their ancient haunts. Others will soon be gone, if concerted action is not taken.

Existing laws have proved quite inadequate to cope with a situation which is fast becoming desperate, in the opinion of many competent judges. Broadcast appeals, addressed to that considerable section of the public which hikes, motors and picnics on every possible occasion, undoubtedly do some good. But more radical measures are urgently needed.

Probably a carefully planned educational campaign directed against wanton destructiveness by young people would in the long run accomplish far more than we can hope to achieve through legislation, or by suasion. Nine children out of ten begin life with an innate aptitude for the pursuit of natural history, which frequently languishes and dies from sheer lack of encouragement. They should be taught to *respect* wild flowers, not merely as objects worthy of close scientific and æsthetic study, but also as national treasures whose safeguarding is a duty akin to patriotism.

If this contention is sound, then the instinct to collect wild flowers should certainly not be thwarted, but turned to good account as a means of stimulating a sense of pride and proprietorship in the English countryside and its glories. Those who are sufficiently interested in flowers to wish to preserve them from decay, and to learn their names and natures, are hardly likely to stop short here. Sooner or later they will come to regard wild flowers as objects for their special protection, and seek to preserve their habitats from desecration.

The amateur field botanist, bent upon securing specimens, should take with him a fairly large box with a close-fitting lid, preferably made of metal, so that the plants may be kept cool after gathering. Convenient collecting tins, complete with carrying straps, may be obtained from dealers in natural history apparatus. A sharp penknife, a pair of scissors, a magnifying-glass, and a notebook with pencil, if not absolutely indispensable, will all come in very useful. A small trowel will also be needed if the roots of the plants are to be examined.

Some authorities state that a sample of the root should always be preserved, together with the stem, leaves, flower and fruit. But if this is done, the greatest care should be exercised to disturb the growing plants as little as possible, and always to return to the soil all roots that are not actually needed. Then, when cutting sprays for pressing, do this with forethought and precision, so that needless waste of material may be avoided.

Take a typical stem with some leaves, flower-buds and at least one expanded bloom attached to it ; and if possible a sample or two of the fruits. In many instances, however, the

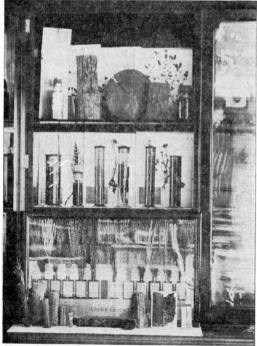

Photo : Harold Bastin]   *[Mondiale.*
A COLLECTOR'S HERBARIUM.
The collector must take care to keep his specimens in a suitable place, such as in the herbarium shown above, if he wants to preserve them in good condition.

latter will have to be gathered separately, after a lapse of several weeks ; and it is well to jot down a reminder in one's notebook to this effect.

Whether a piece of the root is taken or not, the first gathering should include two or three specimens of the root-leaves—*i.e.*, those originating low down at the base of the stem, which are often quite different in shape from those born higher up ; unless searched for these are apt to be overlooked, being often hidden among the grass and herbage. With these considerations in mind, it should prove a simple matter to snip off what is required without appreciably marring the appearance of the plant from which the specimens are secured.

How to collect without spoiling.

Of course, in the case of a small species, it may be necessary to take a whole plant. When this is so, use special precautions not to disturb its neighbours ; then no great harm will be done. No botanist worthy of the name was ever guilty of exterminating a rare plant. The menace consists in the wholesale picking and uprooting of wild flowers by irresponsible persons, who as often as not quickly throw down their spoils to wither by the wayside.

Plants gathered for preservation should be placed at once in the collecting tin, and from this transferred to a vessel of water as soon as possible. The fresher they are when taken in hand, the better specimens will they make. For this reason all unnecessary delays should be avoided.

For pressing, use botanical drying paper, or ordinary blotting paper, whichever is the more convenient, and have in readiness a quantity of sheets, cut to a suitable size— say one-quarter or one-half inch less each way than the boards of your press. The latter should consist of a couple of stout, flat boards, with carefully smoothed surfaces and slightly bevelled edges, and a pair of straps to hold them together. Dealers in the apparatus needed for botanical study supply these presses, in various sizes, from 3s. 6d. upwards. In addition to the blotting paper for drying, at least six times as much newspaper, cut into sheets of a like size, will be needed.

The method of pressing plants usually adopted may be briefly described as follows. On the lower board of the press spread several sheets of newspaper, and on this one sheet of blotting paper. Take your specimen plant, wipe off any excess of moisture from its stem, and spread it out gently upon the blotting paper, arranging the leaves, etc., to the best advantage. Usually it is wise to prevent the petals of flowers from lying in actual contact with one another by inserting snippets of blotting paper between them, where they overlap. They dry much better, and retain more of their natural colour, when treated in this manner.

FLOWERS of the Daisy sort, with bulky discs at their centres, call for special precautions. A good way is to cut circular pieces of blotting paper with holes in the middle to fit over the discs, and when these are in place to cover them with similar circles of flannel or cotton-wool. All this may sound rather tedious ; but the extra expenditure of time and patience will be found, in practice, to be well repaid by results, which will be infinitely better than those obtainable by slapdash methods.

When the specimen plant has been laid out satisfactorily, cover it with a sheet of blotting paper, with several layers of newspaper on top. This process is repeated until all the specimens that you have gathered have been disposed of, when the top board of the press is put into place and strapped down—not too tightly to begin with. After an interval of from twelve to twenty-four hours, unstrap the press, and replace the blotting paper (which will now be damp and stained in patches) by fresh sheets.

To obtain the best results, it will be necessary to do this on several successive occasions, at intervals, until the specimens are thoroughly flattened and perfectly dry. Experience must be your guide ; but remember that quick drying is the secret of successful colour preservation, and that this is attained by constant changes of paper. Each time the press is re-arranged, increase the pressure by tightening the straps, and eventually by placing weights —e.g., heavy books or flat-irons—on the top of it. Damp blotting paper, if not too badly soiled, should not be discarded, but set aside and dried for use upon some future occasion.

How to mount Specimens.

After pressing, each specimen is mounted separately on a sheet of stout paper, which may be either white or tinted, according to taste. Usually it can be fixed in place satisfactorily by means of dabs of adhesive applied here and there with a camel's hair brush to the underside of the stem and leaves. Exceptionally heavy specimens may occasionally call for the additional support of gummed straps ; but these should be used as seldom as possible, because of their unsightliness.

Photo : Harold Bastin]   *[Mondiale.*
HOW TO PRESERVE SPECIMENS.
Here is part of a herbarium, showing pressed plants, dried grasses and other specimens. The amateur collector would do very well to copy this method.

The names—English and scientific—of the plant should be neatly written at the bottom of the sheet, as well as any particulars relating to locality, time of gathering, etc., that you may wish to add—although, perhaps, these are best recorded separately in a notebook. Store your specimens carefully, preferably in dust-proof boxes or the drawers of a cabinet.

This is the time-honoured way of preserving wild plants, and when the formation of an extensive collection is contemplated it has much to recommend it. When, however, only an occasional choice specimen is to be added to one's store, the following method is well worth trying. Take your plant—or the part of it which you wish to dry—in fresh condition and lay it on a thin layer of perfectly clean sand in a wooden box or deep earthenware dish. Then fill in sand very carefully, a little at a time, so that the leaves and petals are not forced out of their natural positions.

When the specimen has been completely covered with sand, set the vessel containing it aside in a place where it will not be disturbed, and leave it for about a fortnight—longer, in the case of succulent species with much moisture in their tissues. Experience will soon

Photo: Harold Bastin]
THE WILD CLEMATIS.
[Mondiale.

This plant is worth seeking out to include in a collection. The species known as " the traveller's joy " or " old man's beard " is common in many hedgerows where it curls and creeps its way over any obstruction.

Photo: Harold Bastin] **WHITE BRYONY.** *[Mondiale.*

The somewhat bell-shaped flowers of the White Bryony are well worth preserving. They grow in groups, found chiefly in the South of England, blooming from May onwards. The flowers are of a greenish-white shade.

AT THE EDGE OF THE WOOD. [Will F. Taylor

A spot like this is the collector's Paradise. Here he may find rare specimens lurking away by the side of more common plants, and when his search is successful who can say that his hobby does not yield joy?

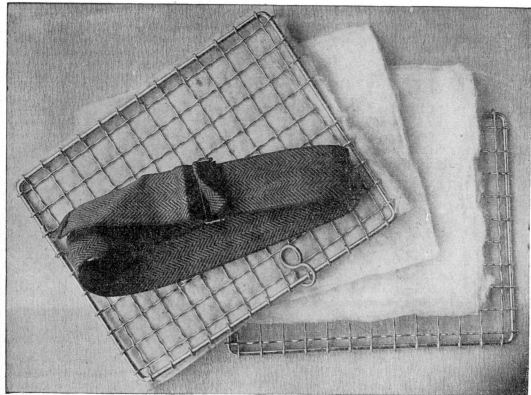

Photo : Harold Bastin] A USEFUL APPARATUS. [Mondiale.

Here is the apparatus, which is described elsewhere in this chapter, for drying specimen plants between sheets of cotton wool. By carefully following out the instructions given it is possible to preserve perfect specimens.

teach you to estimate correctly the length of time necessary in a given instance. Drying may be expedited by placing the box or pan in what cooks call a " cool oven," with the door ajar ; but probably the best results are achieved by the exercise of patience. Lastly, when you are fairly certain that desiccation is complete, pour off the sand—very gingerly, since your specimen will now be brittle and easily broken by rough usage.

ANOTHER method of plant preservation, intermediate between the old-fashioned botanical press and sand-drying, is the following. The freshly gathered sprays are placed between layers of cotton wool, and lightly bound together with a book-strap between covers of perforated zinc or wire gauze. The whole contraption—which can be purchased readymade, if desired—should then be hung up by a hook in some cool, airy place, and left for several weeks to dry. The final results, if not quite as satisfactory as those obtainable by the careful use of sand, are at all events more realistic than the output of the press. The latter are inevitably " as flat as a pancake " ;

whereas these " plant mummies," are something more than mere pictures dimly reminiscent of what they were in life.

The storage of such specimens, however, presents special difficulties, since the card upon which each is mounted must be accommodated with a shallow box or drawer, all to itself ; and this usually means that more space is demanded than the ordinary private collector can give. But for school museums, where a series of exhibits can be arranged behind the protection of glass, these plant mummies are greatly preferable to pressed specimens. Such collections might also include with advantage examples of the bees and other insects commonly found in association with the particular plants which are shown.

In the matter of fruits, it must be admitted that few—if any—of the succulent kinds can be preserved successfully, except in jars of liquid ; and even then their colours usually change or fade away with disconcerting rapidity. Moulds of plaster of Paris are not very difficult to make ; and from these models of the fruits can be cast—either in wax or plaster composition, and coloured in imitation of the real thing. There is scope here for ingenuity and craftsmanship.

Dry fruits, on the other hand, give little trouble, although care should be taken to gather them before they are quite ripe ; otherwise many of the kinds will split up and fall to pieces after they have been added to the collection. Small specimens, and seeds, are conveniently stored in boxes—or, better still, in glass tubes with corks or stoppers ; larger ones should be mounted on card, side by side with the plants which produced them.

Seeds, in themselves, form a fascinating branch of botanical study. If the reader doubts this assertion, let him gather a few samples from wayside plants during a late summer or autumn ramble, and examine them at leisure with the aid of a lens magnifying some eight or ten diameters. He will probably be amazed at the varied beauty displayed by these trifles, most of which are too small to attract attention. Every plant produces a seed which is no less characteristic in appearance than its flower. Naturally, in the case of nearly related species, the seeds are often very similar ; but even in these instances the expert can usually distinguish them at a glance.

A detailed knowledge of wild seeds is rarely possessed by the ordinary botanist, but it is very necessary to the horticulturist—or at least to those who advise him—as a safeguard against wastage and disappointment. If, when he sows clover, he sows also a high percentage of weed seeds, his crop will be seriously depleted. So that when the farmer buys his seed, he asks for a guarantee of purity, behind which stands the expert who knows one seed from another just as a shepherd knows the individual sheep of his flock.

The mention of seeds suggests gardening, which—after all—offers one of the best opportunities for " collecting " and studying wild flowers, many of which are well worth growing for their own sakes, while others are absorbingly interesting subjects in cultivation. Those who have only a small plot of soil at their disposal cannot hope to emulate the Herbaceous Ground at Kew, which Richard Jefferies described as " a living dictionary of English wild flowers . . . heedlessly passed and perhaps never heard of by the thousands who go to see the Palm Houses." But we may all raise from seed a few of our special favourites, and in this way add substantially to our knowledge of their life-histories and habits.

Photo : Harold Bastin]   THE MUSK MALLOW.   *[Mondiale.*

This is a most interesting specimen to add to a collection. The rosy red flowers when bruised emit a musky odour, from which the plant derives its name. It can be found growing plentifully on dry banks or in fields.

[*G. P. Abraham.*

In olden days few kitchens were without a branch of rowan suspended from the ceiling to safeguard the home from lightning and fire. The tree is said to have been the wood of which the Cross of Calvary was made.

WILD FLOWER FOLKLORE

By H. M. HEWSON

THROUGHOUT the centuries of civilisation flowers and plants have figured in folklore, superstition and even religious beliefs. The significance of the lotus of Egypt and Christ's allusions to the wild anemones as the " lilies of the field " —these are but two of the many examples of flowers being given a symbolism connected with life and conduct. In the chapter that follows the author traces some of the more intimate superstitions, legends and beliefs respecting flowers and plants.

THROUGHOUT Europe one finds legends and stories about the Magic Primrose, key flower of springtime, this pale yellow Butter-rose, as it is called in Devonshire. Its oldest name is Primerole, meaning the first flower of spring ; the meaning is the same in the Italian *fiore de prima vera*. The prettiest of all the legends is concerned with the story of Persephone on her return to the upper world. As she follows the dark path from Pluto's gloomy regions, coming up gradually into earth's sunlight, hosts of Primroses spring up in her footsteps, and when at last she greets her waiting mother a trail of gold lies behind her.

The first Primrose one sees in spring is a magic flower. It is a key to happiness. If you carry it in your hand you may be lucky enough to come to a castle with iron-studded door.

Touch the door with the Primrose, and it will fly open. Enter, and you will see a great pile of Primroses. Under the flowers lies a treasure. You may take the treasure, but be careful to replace the flowers. Fail to observe this precaution, and the treasure will be lost before you can get out of the castle. Like all ancient legends, this one is full of meaning and symbolism.

By the way, there is another very ancient story about Persephone and a Pomegranate If she had eaten nothing during her sojourn with Pluto she would have been allowed at once to return to her mother. But she had unfortunately eaten a Pomegranate, so Jupiter decreed that she must spend six months in the Elysian Fields each year ; the other six she may spend on Earth, and her return is celebrated by the appearance of the Primroses.

Numbers of flowers are known as Cuckoo Flowers. It shows how much we love those two ringing notes, unlike the notes of any other bird. The real Cuckoo Flower is the Meadow Bittercress, often called Milkmaids or Lady's Smocks. Ragged-robins are called Cuckoo Gilly flowers, and their relatives, the Red Campions, are known in Devonshire—that county of grotesque plant names—as geuky flowers; this queer word is easy to understand when one remembers that gewk and gog are local names for the cuckoo.

The Wild Arum of the hedge banks is the Cuckoo-pint, and the Wood-sorrel is Cuckoo's-bread. Before he begins to sing the bird takes a mouthful of the leaves of Wood-sorrel.

Plant-lore in France also contains stories about the Cuckoo and this woodland plant, where it is called Pain de Coucou. The small field Woodrush is Cuckoo-grass. Shakespeare's " cuckoo buds of yellow hue " may be Buttercups, but no one seems quite sure about this.

There is a very old rhyme about a Cuckoo in a cherry tree, and this rhyme is believed to belong to a still older legend about the three meals of Cherries which a Cuckoo takes before he stops singing and prepares to fly away.

THE MAGIC PRIMROSE.
Legend tells how, by touching an iron-studded door with the first Primrose of spring, treasure can be found.

In some places in Berwickshire a curious custom used to exist. Oats sown after the first of April were called Gowk's-oats or Cuckoo's-oats; such a sowing was made necessary sometimes by bad weather in March, much to the annoyance of the farmers, for

" Cuckoo oats and Woodcock hay
    Make a farmer run away."

The opening buds of the Hawthorn are sometimes called bread-and-cheese, and in Sussex the Whitethorn is known amongst country folk as the Cuckoo's bread-and-cheese tree.

" When the Cuckoo comes to the bare
    Thorn,
    Sell your cow and buy your corn."

Bird-life and plant-life are closely interwoven. Stories about the Nightingale and the Rose are legion. In an Eastern legend the birds charge the Nightingale with disturbing their rest by his plaintive singing; the Nightingale appears before Solomon and pleads that he is distracted by his love for the Rose, and Solomon, in pity, acquits him—though such acquittal, one thinks, would hardly satisfy the other birds. All sorts of versions of this story appear in the plant-lore of other nations; very curious is the one which tells of the Nightingale sleeping on a Rose thorn, the thorn pressing into its breast so that it may keep awake.

Our own poet Young refers to this legend in his *Night Thoughts*—

" Grief's sharpest thorn hard-pressing on
    my breast,
    I share with wakeful melody to cheer
    The sullen gloom, sweet Philomel ! like
    thee,
    And call the stars to listen.

Then, also, in Thompson's poem, *Hymn to May*, we read—

" The lowly nightingale,
    A thorn her pillow, trills her doleful tale."

Still better known are the lines from Shakespeare—

" Everything did banish moan,
    Save the nightingale alone ;
    She, poor bird, as all forlorn,
    Leaned her breast up till a thorn.
    And then sung the doleful ditty,
    That to hear it was great pity."

The Wild Peony has the power, according to old legends, to cure epilepsy. The root, fresh gathered, washed clean, and broken into small pieces, is the most beneficial part of the plant. But legend says there is danger in the remedy ; should a Woodpecker be in sight at the moment when the patient is carrying out the cure and eating the root, a worse fate is in store for the afflicted one, for it is told he will surely be stricken with blindness.

The Plant that saved a bird's life.

Many old legends persist in the names country folk have given to certain wild flowers. Vervain is called Pigeon's-grass, because pigeons and doves use it to clear their sight, and Eyebright (Euphrasia) is useful in the same way to Linnets. Galega, or Goat's-rue, is probably the plant referred to in a very old story about a peasant who watched two birds fighting. When one was exhausted it pecked at a plant which grew near and was immediately revived. The peasant stole the plant from the birds and hid it. The next time one of the little fighters needed a restorative it could not find the plant, and, in desperation, it cried aloud and died. This is an old tradition, and one also finds it in the form of a story of a fight between a Lizard and a Snake.

When Eve was banished from Paradise the snow was falling. It was a sight she had never seen or imagined, and the desolation of the earth alarmed her. She noticed that the snow was covering all her flowers, burying them out of sight, and she began to weep bitterly. To lose her beloved flowers was the worst punishment that could come to her. Her grief was so great that an angel came to comfort her. In his pity he caught a snowflake in his hand, and, to her amazement, she saw it change to the flower we call Snowdrop.

He gave the flower to Eve and she smiled through her tears. Then she saw that the flowers were springing up all round the feet of the angel. And that is how, according to legend, Snowdrops came to earth. In spite of its beauty, however, the Snowdrop is one of the " unlucky " flowers, and the first Snowdrop of spring must never be carried into a house.

Legends about pixies and flowers are numerous. Perhaps the Stitchwort is the favourite of the Little People. We may admire and love these pretty blossoms, which are amongst the prettiest of our spring flowers, but to pick them is to beg for trouble and to run the risk of being kidnapped and " pixy-led."

THE LOVE-SICK NIGHTINGALE.

The Nightingale, according to an ancient Eastern legend, was so distracted by his passion for the Rose that he spent all his nights in singing plaintively to her.

Wherever one goes one seems to find a fresh name for the flowers. Starwort is common and exactly describes the appearance of the starry blossoms in a Blackthorn hedge. Other names are Shirt-buttons, Adder's-meat, All-bone ; this last word may be turned into bony-stem to explain the meaning.

THE name Adder's-meat is more difficult to understand. It takes us right at once into the middle of the very curious subject of plant names which refer to birds, animals and reptiles. Two possible explanations may be given. One is that Stitchwort and Adders frequent similar places and appear in spring about the same time, and that Adders, according to ancient tradition, eat Stitchwort as either food or medicine (as cuckoos eat Wood-sorrel or Cuckoo's-meat). The other possible explanation is that at some time Stitchwort was considered a poisonous plant, and that the word Adder comes from the Anglo-Saxon *attor*, which means poison.

The red berries of the Wild Arum, or Lords-and-ladies, are also called Adder's-meat or Adder-berries, meaning simply poison berries.

In various districts one finds variations of a story about a girl who trod on a Stitchwort. This happened just after sunset, a magic hour,

EVE'S COMFORTERS.

[*Charles Reid.*

The first Snowdrop of springtime is thought to be unlucky and must never be taken into a house. Legend tells that it was a Snowdrop, converted from a snowflake, that comforted Eve when she was banished from Paradise.

A PRIMROSE DELL.　　　　　　　　　[*Will F. Taylor.*

When Persephone, returned from her captivity in the gloomy regions where Pluto reigned, hastened into the sunlight to greet her mother, a multitude of Primroses sprang up under her feet—so says the ancient tale !

and the fairies sent a horse which carried the girl away and she went riding till daybreak.

Elder flowers also belong to the Little People. But the whole of the Elder tree is full of magic, and there are many legends, all slightly different, about what happens when one stands under an Elder tree at midnight. One legend, widely spread, declares you will see the king of fairyland go by, followed by all his retinue. In Denmark this king goes by the name of Toly. There is a saying that he who sleeps under an Elder tree will never awake, and one comes across stories of fearful accidents to folk who have been careless.

The Elf-woman who lives in a tree.

Stories of this sort no doubt arise from the fact that both blossoms and leaves are slightly narcotic. In many places it is considered very unwise to have furniture made of Elder wood. In England superstition has always gathered around this tree, and all sorts of dreadful things happen to folk who make use of it. In some parts of England, as well as in Denmark, one hears about an elf-woman, called the Elder-mother, who lives in the tree and who objects to the plucking of the flowers.

Legend says that elves bury their children under these trees, and also that they often lie down in the shadow cast by the branches. On the other hand, one comes across stories of the beneficent action of the Elder. Sufferers from rheumatism may carry about with them a small cross made from a twig which has a joint midway and which forms a kind of cross ; a rightly-shaped cross will bring about a cure. A further condition is that the tree itself must have been grown in a churchyard. Such trees used to be found in Gloucestershire, where the country folk had a deep faith in this tradition.

Traditions and legends of lightning in connection with all natural objects are common in England and everywhere else, and plants come in for a big share. We say " Avoid an ash, it courts the flash," but Bay, Birch, Whitethorn and Hazel are endowed with protective qualities. During thunderstorms twigs of Hazel are sometimes placed in the window to protect the house.

In the time of Pliny, the old historian, Holly used to be planted near houses to keep off the evil influence of lightning. Nowadays one sees Houseleek and Stonecrop on cottage roofs for the same purpose. In Wales one meets

Photo : Harold Bastin] THE LITTLE PEOPLE'S FLOWER. *[Mondiale.*
Elder flowers are said to belong to the Little People. There is an old belief that those who sleep under it will never awake. The superstitious also believed that it was tempting fate to have furniture made of this wood.

Photo: Harold Bastin]   THE ANCIENT OAK.   *[Mondiale.*

The Oak, which is mentioned a great deal in folklore, is sacred to Thor, the god of Thunder. In bygone days it was planted on the boundaries of estates, or in the centre of a village, where it was thought to ward off evil.

legends dealing with the Stonecrop as a protection against disease generally. The "fairy-rings" caused by fungi were once believed to have been caused by lightning, and many of the old naturalists spread this belief.

MISTLETOE is the embodiment of lightning. Note its forked branches. The Swiss name is *Donnerbesen* (Thunder Broom), and country folk assert that it protects the homestead from lightning and also from fire. The same story lives in Sweden, where a piece of Mistletoe is often seen hung up in a farmhouse, just as a branch of the Rowan tree is suspended in a Scottish kitchen for the same purpose.

The Hawthorn also has its legendary roots in lightning, and in Europe has, from time immemorial, been considered a sacred tree. But all sacred plants and trees must be treated carefully and reverently; evil may come to him who handles them rudely. Therefore there are many traditions and stories about the luck or ill-luck which these trees may bring. Many people will not allow Hawthorn blossoms in a house, and from old and stunted Hawthorns, known to be trysting-places of the

fairies, it is still more unlucky to gather a leaf even and bring it into a dwelling house.

Hazel is another tree which is sacred to Thor, the god of thunder. In many legends it is mentioned in connection with lightning and fire and as a promoter of fruitfulness; hence the numerous accounts of its use in divinations relating to love and marriage. In ancient Scandinavian writings authority is symbolised by a staff of Hazel. In the hands of Mercury the Hazel rod is the symbol of peace and well-being. Tradition says that St. Patrick held a rod of Hazel in his hand when he charmed all the reptiles out of Ireland. It is by means of a branch of Hazel that one may discover subterranean water and hidden treasure, and such a branch may also be used as a lightning conductor.

The Oak is also of lightning origin, and in English folklore one sees how great is the veneration in which this tree has always been held. Oaks used to be planted on the boundaries of estates. In many parishes there are still "gospel oaks," and the name survives in a well-known London district. Peace and comfort and security were ensured when an

93

Oak, Thor's tree, was planted in the midst of a collection of dwellings.

Tales of invisibility conferred by certain plants crop up in all countries. Traditions about Fern seed are the most widely spread. They probably originated in the belief that Ferns had no seed, or that the seed was so small as to be invisible. Plenty of reason here for the wealth of legend which has grown up around Fern seed !

In Celtic countries the whole plant was formerly held sacred ; it was full of all sorts of powers ; but those attached to the seed were the most marvellous. To carry Fern seed about one's person was to possess the secret of making oneself invisible. When the charm failed one might suppose that the proper ceremonies had not been observed.

These ceremonies are difficult enough to carry out. The seeker after Fern seed must go searching for it at midnight on St. John's Eve ; he must be barefoot, clad in a single garment, and he must be in a mystical frame of mind, untroubled by worldly matters.

He must watch for the seed and catch it as it falls ; this is no easy matter, as it ripens and falls within the space of one minute.

Besides, there is the Devil to circumvent ; he also wants the seed for his own purposes, and he guards it against human beings. If a magic circle be drawn around the Fern and the searcher the Devil cannot cross the line, but he will do everything in his power to prevent its falling into other hands. He will stand at the edge of the circle and call out in the voice of some one well known and loved. " The call came suddenly ; he turned quickly to reply ; but he found he could not move his head round again ; it was fixed." In this legend the Devil could not touch the seed but the man lost it also. We are left to wonder

THE PIXIES' FRIEND. [W. F. Taylor.
If we rob Stitchwort of its blossom, legend warns us that we run the risk of being kidnapped by angry pixies.

whether he may not have been stricken with paralysis.

According to Russian legend the mystical, religious state of mind is absolutely necessary when searching for the magic seed ; one should also take a white napkin, a glass of water, a Testament and a cross. There is a legend of how a man once got the seed unwittingly. He had gone to look for a lost horse and the time happened to be Midsummer Night. The Fern seed was ripening as he brushed past a plant and some of it fell in his shoe. He thought it was sand, but he did not stop to shake it out. Presently he went home.

"No sign of the horse !" he said.

His wife looked up, startled, staring around, and he realised that she could not see him. It was only when he took off his shoes and the seed fell out that he became visible. The legend, unfortunately, does not tell us what use he made of the magic seed.

The strangest tradition about the obtaining of Fern seed is the following : "At the summer solstice, if you shoot at the sun when it has attained its midday height, three drops of blood will fall ; they must be gathered up and preserved, for that is the Fern seed."

The Fern root is also credited with magic powers and may be made into love philtres. This was a very widespread belief, as this verse from an old song shows :—

" 'Twas the maiden's matchless beauty
    That drew my heart a-nigh,
  Not the fern-root potion,
    But the glance of her bright eye."

An old story is told in Cornwall—that home of legends about the Little Folk—that a girl who was seeking work sat down to rest by the way, and idly began to break the fronds of Ferns growing around her. A man appeared

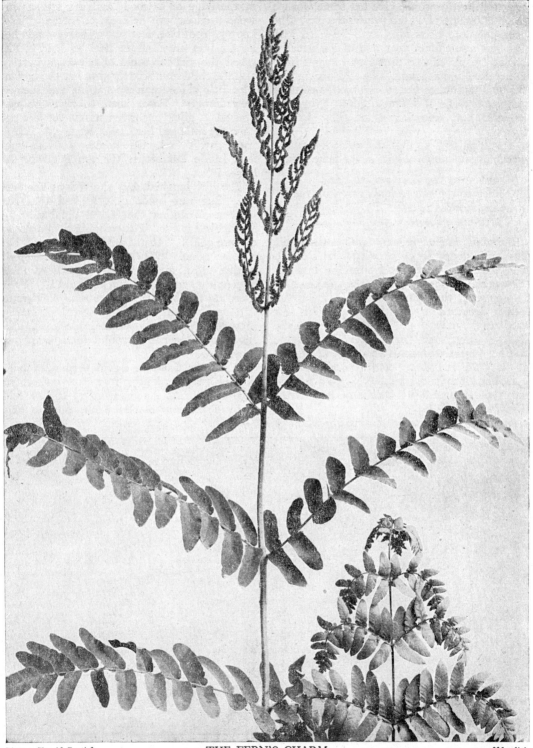

Photo: Harold Bastin] THE FERN'S CHARM. [Mondiale.
Fern was formerly considered a sacred plant, and it was believed that to carry seed was to make oneself invisible.
It is, however, very difficult to find this seed, as the Devil is said to guard it for his own dark purposes.

and told her he would give her some work if she would serve him for a year and a day. She promised, and he made her kiss a Fern leaf. She was away for a year and a day exactly, but at the end of that time found herself back in her own bed at home. She told her mother the man had taken her to fairyland, a country lying under one of the mountains. Every one believed her, and her story grew into a legend.

Tradition tells us that the quiet recesses of woods are favourite haunts of the fairy folk.

"Would you the fairy regions see?
  Hence to the greenwoods run with me;
  From mortals safe the livelong night,
  There countless feats the Fays delight."

Flowers growing in such woods share the lives and adventures of the fairy folk. There is a very old legend about Daphne, a maid of the woods. To escape danger she was changed into a shrub, the Spurge Laurel, with nectar-laden, fragrant green blossoms. In our gardens we have the Daphne Mezereon, the Spurge Olive, another plant of the same family. Copses and small woods are the homes of the Wild Strawberry and also of the Moss Folk, beneficent small people clothed in golden green moss, found in Germany and Scandinavia.

A small girl was once gathering Strawberries at the edge of a wood, and she saw a tiny woman sitting on the roots of a tree. "Her knotty, root-like feet were bare, and her height was an ell from heel to hair." She asked the girl for some of her Strawberries, and the child immediately gave her the basket. The little old woman ate several, and seemed very hungry. From head to foot she was dressed in glittering green moss. At last she gave the little girl her basket, saying, "Thank you, my dear! Go home, and do not look inside the basket till you get into the house!"

The girl laughed, but she did as she was bid. She ran home quickly and told her mother. Together they lifted the basket-lid and looked inside. They saw six Strawberries of pure gold! "It was a Moss-woman!" her mother cried. "Their clothes are made of golden moss, and, with the touch of their fingers, they can turn things to gold!" Then there are the Wood Anemones, the Wind-roses of Germany and the Star-flowers of Italy; they are typically woodland blossoms, and stories and legends surround them wherever they grow.

In former times in Egypt they were considered magic plants; it was a custom to gather the first Anemone of spring, to fold it in a piece of scarlet cloth, and to say, "I gather thee as a remedy against disease."

Photo, Harold Bastin] THE HOLLY IN BLOOM. *[Mondiale.*
The Holly, associated with many legends chiefly connected with Christmas festivities, begins to flower in May and continues to produce blossoms until August, after which the berries appear. Above it is seen in full bloom.

Three common inhabitants of our hedgerows, meadows and moistlands. Reading from left to right (1) The Glaucous Heath Sedge or Gilliflower Sedge ; (2) Couch Grass ; (3) The Lesser River Sedge, found in ditches.

GRASSES AND REEDS

By MARIAN H. CRAWFORD

TO many people grass is simply grass. To the true Nature lover the variety of grasses and reeds in the countryside forms the subject for wonder and delight. In this chapter the varieties of grasses and reeds are enumerated and their individual characteristics explained. The methods of propagation are given and the places where they best flourish are indicated.

IN the bleak days of January you may find, if you know where to look, three plants in bloom—the Sweet Violet, the Lesser Celandine, and the Annual Meadow-grass. This grass is a tiny plant, not more than a few inches high even in summer, but it flowers all the year round and its seeds will germinate anywhere.

Making a collection of the " meadow " or Poa grasses is a very interesting introduction to further study of British and foreign species. In watery places grows the Reed Meadow-grass, with stout, six-feet long stems among which water-fowl hide, and the Floating Meadow-grass, with graceful panicles and rich green floating leaves. Another name for this last is Manna-croup ; this is the name we give to the long, yellow seeds sometimes used in soup and porridge. Fish and birds also feed on these seeds.

Following the marshy places towards the coast, where the water becomes brackish, the Sea Meadow-grass appears, and on sandy sea-shores, between Norfolk and Kent, occurs one of the most interesting of all seaside plants, the Bulbous Meadow-grass. This is a small tuft of a plant a few inches high, remarkable for bulbs which are developed from swollen leaf bases. When these bulbs get detached during the summer days a high wind will send them flying along the sands ; in wet, autumn weather they take root, and the following spring send up welcome tufts of green foliage.

Growing on rocks on Scottish mountains is the Wavy Meadow-grass, found as high as 3600 feet. The Alpine Meadow-grass grows on still loftier mountains ; in the Highlands shepherds call it the broad-leaved hill-grass and value it greatly as nutritious food for sheep.

A point to be noted about this grass is that it is frequently viviparous ; the spike-lets are converted into leafy bulbs. Unfortunately, snails as well as sheep appreciate

97

this grass ; they eat the spikelets and so prevent seed formation.

We have one poisonous grass, not very common, found in cornfields. This is the Darnel. It is probably the Tares of the Bible. Other names are Reeling or Giddy Rye-grass—aptly descriptive. It is poisonous to man and to some animals, particularly rabbits, but birds do not appear to be affected by it—with the possible exception of domestic poultry. A variety of Field Brome has decidedly narcotic properties. When the seed has been made into flour the results have been described as " awkward " only, not actually poisonous.

By midsummer most grasses are in flower.

"Barnaby bright, Barnaby bright,
    The longest day and the shortest night,"

when Buttercups, Clovers and waving grasses fill the fields.

For examining the inflorescence of a grass one needs a magnifying glass of some sort. The flower spikelets are arranged as racemes, panicles or spikes, and it is chiefly the anthers which provide the colour. These may be red, creamy, yellow or purple; long or short; broad or narrow. They swing on slender filaments and in form and colour are remarkably graceful and lovely.

The pointed spike of the Meadow Foxtail is silvery grey, and the long, rosy anthers shiver in the slightest breeze. The Vernal grass well deserves its name ; its anthers are deeply yellow, though when growing in woods they are said to be purple. From the very large spikelets of the False Oat hang beautiful purple anthers. The three stamens of the floret of the Nit grass have purple anthers, and the spike is pale green and silvery.

There is a tiny grass known as Mibora or

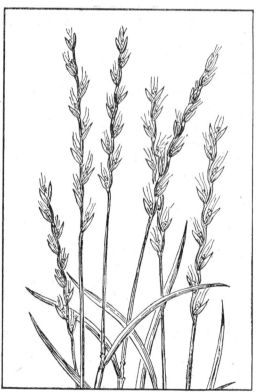

A POISONOUS GRASS.
The Darnel found in cornfields is our British poisonous grass. It is also known as Reeling or Giddy Rye-grass.

Knappia, about a couple of inches high, which usually has its flowering season over by midsummer ; it bears its curiously shaped anthers on very long filaments ; usually anthers are of an oblong shape, more or less, and forked at one or both ends, but these anthers are broader at the base than at the apex.

Sometimes extremes of length occur. In the Rough Cat's-tail and the Seaside Cat's-tail the anthers are very short. In the Floating Meadow-grass or Manna grass they are five times as long as broad ; this grass is easily recognisable and is found in ponds and slow running streams. In the Sea Meadow-grass the anthers are six times as long as broad.

How to start your Collection.

Let us suppose you set out, on a midsummer day, to begin a collection of grasses. It is only the first step which brings any difficulties—after that it is easy going. There are grasses everywhere ; on sand and on clay ; inland and around the coast ; in bogs, in streams, and on mountain tops. The collector's enthusiasm will grip you, and the joy of finding a new species, the delight of putting it into your book, will hold you in happy absorption.

That reminds me—you must, of course, take with you a collecting book. This may be quite a simple affair ; newspaper will do for the leaves, which should be made double, placed in cardboard backs. A strap or elastic ring may hold the whole together. A pencil and a trowel (small enough to be slipped into the pocket) are necessary also.

Meadows provide the best hunting-grounds for the beginner, though the first specimens will probably be gathered in the garden. The tiny tufts of green on a newly - made gravel

THREE MEADOW GRASSES.

The Quaking Grass (left) is a beautiful type, with its swaying heads of seed clusters. Timothy Grass (centre) forms silken, fur-like heads, while the Wild Oats (right) bears semblance to the cultivated types that descended from it.

path are almost certainly the Annual Meadow-grass. The rockery may give you a specimen of Couch grass; in such a situation nothing could be more unwelcome; its spreading roots extend in all directions. It has its uses, however; it is a valuable medicine for cats and dogs; they know all about it and will eat it, when they need it, of their own freewill.

The Rough and the Smooth Meadow-grasses are also unwelcome garden visitors. On waste ground will be found many handsome grasses, especially the Barren Brome, with nodding green spikelets and very long awns, and the lovely Wild Oat, an escape from cornfields. Other grasses of waste places are the Lesser Quake grass, the Cock's-foot, Rat's-tail Fescue, Wall Barley, Canary Grass, Rough Cat's-tail, and the Upright Brome.

It is in meadows that one comes to a great richness of variety. Here we have the Slender and the Meadow Foxtail, the pink Meadow Soft-grass, the False Oat, the Yellow Oat, the familiar Quake grass, Sheep's Fescue, Rye Grass, the Bristle Grasses, and some of the Hair Grasses. The Tufted Hair Grass is common · it likes a rather moist clayey spot.

Another popular name is Tussock Grass. You perhaps have seen the moving islands of Tussock Grass in certain lakes? There is one of these islands on a lake in Wales, the haunt of a fairy who had been permitted to marry a young farmer of the district. In her mortal life she was forbidden to touch iron, and a day came when this condition was broken and when the fairies carried her off. As long as he lived she came to this grassy island to talk to him; nearer she was forbidden to venture.

Great variety of species you will also find in damp, shady places. Shady woods please the bright green Bearded Wheat Grass, the Slender False Brome, which keeps green through the winter. The Melic Grasses are lovers of woodland shade; we have the attractively coloured Mountain Melic in the west of England and the more generally distributed Wood Melic, equally pretty. The tall, pale greenish purple Spreading Millet, the Wood Meadow-grass, graceful and slender, and Tall Brome, with its bright green leaves, like the same shady places.

Swampy places, ditches and pools are the homes of the Marsh Foxtail, and the Cut

H. Bastin.]
BURR-REED AND KNOT-GRASS.
[Mondiale.

The Branched Burr-Reed (left) bears pretty spikes of tiny flowers. Knot-grass (right) is really not grass at all, but a wild flowering plant. Its flowers are small and pink in colour, the plant flowering from May to September.

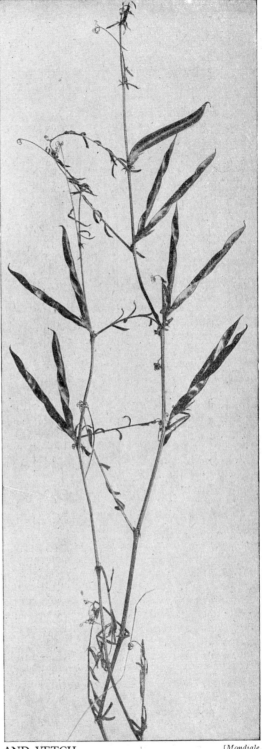

H. *Bastin*.]   WATER PEPPER AND VETCH.   [*Mondiale*.

The Persicaria, or Water Pepper (left) has pink flowers in long spikes. It flowers in moist places. The Vetch has several varieties, each having tendrils, yielding seeds in long pods. The picture (right) shows empty seed shells.

Grass, once rare, now spreading among slow-running streams in southern counties. The tall and well-known Reed, with its brown and silky panicles, growing from six to twelve feet high, likes a muddy habitat with a few inches of water over its roots. The Wood Smallreed and the Purple Smallreed are two tall, perennial grasses well worth looking for in marshy woods and similar places; neither is generally common, though abundant in certain districts. Still rarer is the Narrow Smallreed, and the slender Meagre Smallreed is found, I believe, only in the north of Scotland.

Another very interesting aquatic grass is the Catabrose or Water Whorl, the tall stems carrying green and purple panicles of pyramidal shape. It is rather scarce though widely distributed. The stems taste sweet, like liquorice, and is eaten by both cattle and water birds. Manna grass (already mentioned) is often found partly floating in slow-running water; the green spikelets are erect, with greenish tips.

Heaths, hilly pastures and sandy fields produce totally different sorts of grasses. There is the Silky Bent or Silky Agrostis, a tall, slender, lovely grass, with flat, ribbed, narrow leaves, growing in sandy fields near the coast. In the same neighbourhood may be seen four of the Hair Grasses—the Wavy, the Grey, the Early and the Silvery, none more than twelve inches high.

Amongst the most interesting of these sand-loving grasses is the Reed Grass or Reed Diagraphis Grass; a sandy place beside water is its favourite habitat; the familiar Ribbon-grass of the garden is a variety of this species. The little Squirrel-tail and the rather taller and very ornamental Hare's-tail are seaside grasses. One of the Finger Grasses (*Panicum glabrum*) grows in sandy places in Southern

[*Mondiale.*

THE PLUMES OF THE COTTON SEDGE.
Cotton Sedge, with white, shimmering heads, grows in boggy ground. The hairs lengthen as the fruit develops.

England; like many others, it is a native of warm countries. On sandy shores grows the Darnel Poa, a tufted little annual from the Mediterranean and Western Europe.

Salt marshes have a few typical grasses, such as the Perennial Beard-grass and the Cord-grass. The Cord-grass is one of the useful species; it grows on the east and south coasts, and in some places is cut and used for thatching. The leaves are about half an inch broad, rigid, erect and flat. Some species are very useful as sand-binders. For this purpose the Lyme-grass is well known; fortunately, it is fairly common on most sandy seashores, where the rigid stems and leaves catch and hold the sand, making it into a barrier which successfully defies the advance of the sea.

An interesting feature of this grass, which has been called the sugar-cane of Britain, is that it contains a large quantity of saccharine matter. One of the varieties of the common Couch Grass is also a good sand-binder. So is the rare Dog's-tooth Grass, found on sandy shores in the southern counties, with its long, tough runners. But the most valuable species is the Marram or Murran, a perennial, with roots which creep deeply in the sand, spreading in all directions.

Reed Grass is of great use in transforming marshland into fertile fields; it is sown on the marshland and requires about four years to do its work. The Finger Grass grows in fields in the south, but it is really a native of warmer climates; as Crab-grass it is used in some parts of the United States as a good fodder plant, and in Bohemia the grain is cooked as porridge, but we cannot make much use of it in England.

The popular names of the grasses are sometimes very curious, containing references to

H. Bastin.] THE WEEDS IN THE WHEAT. [Mondiale.

The above photograph shows the weeds growing in a field of wheat. Weeds take moisture and food from the ground and help to weaken the cereal crop. Poppies are here in evidence. They are not welcomed by the farmer !

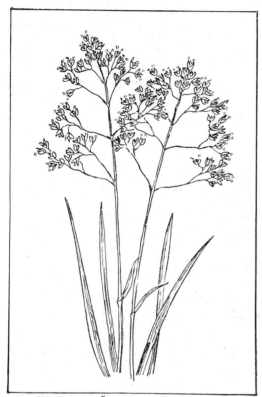

HIEROCHLŎE, OR HOLY GRASS.

This grass, which derives its name from the Greek, is rare in Britain and found wild only in Scotland.

Fowl-grass, Mouse-barley, Rabbit-grass ; and we have a Witch Grass, a Painted Lady, Bride's Laces, Gardener's Garters Finger Grass, Lady's Hair, as well as Grey, Tufted and Wavy Hair, and Timothy Grass called after the American cultivator, Timothy Hanson.

Many rough, marshy grasses in Norfolk are called Hassock ; hence the word " hassocks " for church foot-supports ; but the real hassock is not the sedge with which these are filled, but the *Aira exspitosa*, other popular names for which are Tussock, Tufted Aira and Tufted Bent.

The common Quaking Grass can boast many names. I have collected the following :

Cow-quakes, Totter-grass, Rattle-grass, Quake or Quaking-grass, Maiden's Hair, Lady's Hair, Wagwant, Trembling Jockeys.

A goodly list ! The last name comes from Yorkshire. In that country they say that mice run away from quaking grass, and a Yorkshire proverb declares—

" Keep a trimmling jock in the house
An' ye'll never see the tail of a mouse ! "

the folklore of the district in which they are found. The Holy Grass, or Hierochlŏe, is found in Northern Europe, Asia and America ; like the Sweet Vernal Grass, it is fragrant, and both in England and Germany has been used to strew in churches and before church doors. It is very rare in Britain, growing in a wild state only in Scotland.

Many of the names have got twisted and have lost their original meaning. Lyme Grass takes its name from Elyma, the Greek town where this grass is common, and the word Panic (Cockspur Panic, Loose Panic, Green Panic) comes from the Latin *panis*, bread, because the seeds used to be ground into flour and made into bread. It was inevitable that many grasses, on account of their suggestive shape, should have been dubbed " tails " ; we have several Cat's-tails, one Mousetail, four Foxtails, one Hare's-tail, two Squirrel-tails, three Dog's-tails (one of which is crested !), one Rat's-tail. Other grasses named after animals and birds are the Cock's-foot, the Cockspur, Cow-quakes (a disease of cattle), Deer's-foot, Dog's-tooth, Dog's-wheat, Sheep's Fescue,

CANARY GRASS.

This grass with its large heads grows on waste lands and is common. It is generally used for bird food.

The farmer sees Nature in all her moods. He has to wrestle with her, woo her, cajole and assist her that he may bring to a successful consummation his dealings with her. Preparing the ground is one of his annual duties.

THE FARMER AS NATURE LOVER

By DOREEN WALLACE

THE farmer is Nature's husband, not her lover. Ecstasies at her beauty are not his. He has lived with beauty all his life ; and familiarity has bred, not perhaps contempt, but a quite unemotional acceptance of Nature's most striking efforts at adornment. A flaming sunset moves him to think of the morrow, a lowering, flushed dawn makes him hastily rearrange in his head the work he had planned for the day. Spring in her lacy green, frilled with white fool's-parsley, irritates him, as often as not, because she will not weep, or else she weeps too much. With Summer he quarrels constantly ; her splendour of blue-black cloud in sunshine, against which the heavy-clad trees gleam out as though cut in metal, means thunder to spoil the haysel, thunder to lay flat the tall, unripe corn, or thunder to delay harvest. With Autumn he is usually on better terms, for a really wet autumn, which would hold up the ploughing and make the harvesting of sugar-beet laborious and expensive, is happily un-common. But perhaps it is in winter that he is most nearly at peace with Nature. There is a brief lull in his eternal battle against Time.

There is the ploughing after root-crops to be done, for the reception of the spring sowings, but there is time in addition for the tidying-up so dear to the good farmer's heart—the " flashing " of ditches, the trimming and laying of fences, the mending of gates. Smoke of bonfires dims the day, between the mists of the morning and evening frost.

Yet a capricious woman is Nature, even in her winter drowsiness. Frost being needed to kill the wireworm and other pests in the soil, frost is denied until too late—until the spring sowings are due. Rain being required, in moderation, to germinate seeds, rain is with-held, or else rain descends so persistently that the young green blades rot and turn yellow.

How can a man love such a mistress ? She is too like a wife.

No, the farmer, inured to Nature's contrari-ness, seems far less of a Nature-lover than those townsfolk who take country holidays in order to rhapsodise over rather obvious scenic effects. These people have in them the germ that, developed in favourable conditions, afflicts the nature-poet with the desire to paint in rhyme the prettiness of the world's face.

They are concerned with appearance only, having no knowledge of the labour that goes to make a cornfield, the anxiety and long watching that has brought about a sheepfold full of sprightly lambs ; yet they claim to be lovers of Nature. Theirs is the lust of the eye alone.

And there is a second school of thought which interprets love of Nature as a patient familiarity with the life and habits of the Painted Lady or the Drumming Woodpecker. These are the people with yearnings but no poetry, and affiliated with them are those amateur gardeners who know the Latin names of flowers and the difference between compost and common earth and very little besides.

The Farmer does not rhapsodise.

All of these, the lyrical and the painstaking, would deny to the farmer any love of Nature at all. Touring his fields, he will pass by the edge of a copse in which a mist of bluebells is canopied by the pale-gold tapestry of young oak-leaves, and will say no word, save to anathematise the rabbits that come out of the copse to browse on his springing barley. Nor does he know much of the habits of birds, except of rooks and pigeons which are pests, and of pheasants and partridges which are game. It is doubtful if his watchful senses are ever drenched in showering lark-song. Lepidoptera he entirely ignores ; and the insects which interest him are chiefly the unattractive ones—parasites mostly, liver-flukes and gadflies and the less mentionable worms. As for gardening, the farmer usually leaves this to the careful supervision of his wife.

He knows the truth about Nature.

A poor candidate for honours as a Nature-lover. Yet surely Nature has more than one dimension : she is not all surface, like the lid of a chocolate-box ; or like a movie-star, to be adored only on the screen. Perhaps it is the generality of Nature-fans who are wrong about the character of their goddess, while the farmer, who is married to her, knows the truth. . . . Knows the truth, and still does not divorce her. Knows her caprice, her obstinacy, and yet her fundamental generosity ; knows that her superficial beauty means little, her irritating mannerisms more, and her deep willingness to serve means most of all. After a run of bad seasons, the farmer will curse the land that bore him, but nothing short of bankruptcy will drive him off it. In towns he is homeless ; he cannot be happy for long away from the gently-swelling breasts of his own fields. Is not this love of a sort ? It resembles the love of a long-married couple, who have ceased to expect good looks and pretty speeches of each other, who often quarrel and wound one another, yet who have between them a bond of shared experiences. Humanity supplies examples by the thousand, of couples who, though not conspicuously happy together, would be lost and miserable apart. Of such are the farmer and his farm.

And as a man is filled with content at sight of his wife among her children, so is the farmer deeply and inarticulately satisfied in contemplation of Nature's providence and fecundity. He feels that he has his part in it. Though Nature is independent of him—parthenogenetic, as it were—in her reproductiveness, under his guidance she raises a far bigger and better family of crops and creatures than ever she could if left to herself. The farmer who loves her sees that she is aided by every means within his power, by thorough cultivation of the land and suppression of weeds, by careful breeding and housing of stock, by the elimination of hedgerow trees and the encouragement of trees where they are needed for shelter, by field-drainage and the trimming of hedges and ditches, and by vermin-killing.

Efficiency tempers his Nature-love.

Much of his activity is not consonant with Nature-love as understood by the poets. He is the enemy of the straggling, rose-starred fence and the dyke brimming with purple willow-herb ; picturesque mossy thatch on his buildings does not delight him ; he is prone, in his present poverty, to keep out the wind and weather with corrugated iron, which is not only cheap but also efficient. Efficiency, in fact, is his goal. Without it, he has no hope of remaining on the land he loves, any more than the inefficient clerk can hope to keep his suburban home together.

For love—chiefly—the city worker passes his drab day in an office, and fights for his place in crowded trains morning and evening ; superficially, there is not much poetry about his existence . . . until one perceives that he is animated by love. Similarly one must not deny poetry to the farmer when one sees him ruthlessly reducing his fields to an unpictorial uniformity and patching his buildings with that hideosity, corrugated iron : it is done through the influence of love.

TIT-BITS FROM THE SHEPHERD. [G. P. Abraham.

High on the Lakeland fells the shepherd, if he is to have a friend at all, must make friends with his sheep. This happy scene shows his charges exhibiting cupboard love, as the dainties are doled out to them

Sunday is the farmer's day for indulging his passion. You will see him visiting the yards where his stock is kept. He carries a stick, with which to prod drowsy bullocks and sleeping pigs into activity. Having stirred them up, he leans long on the yard-gate and watches them, with a perspicacity which you would not suspect from the look of him. He is estimating their weight, calculating their increase since last week, balancing it against the food they have eaten, speculating as to whether a slight addition of fish-meal in the diet might not be an improvement, noting a sign of sluggishness in this one, a staring coat in that one, and taking great pleasure in the well-kept appearance of the whole.

Then he goes down to the lambing-fold, where he finds his shepherd, who is on duty night and day, and the two of them lean on their hurdles and say very little, while the lambs, in irresponsible good spirits, give a sudden display of bucking and skipping, and as suddenly decide that the two immobile humans are not worth such energetic efforts, and wander off to their mothers.

"Average a lamb and three-quarter, do nawthen come along to spiel that," observes the shepherd, and both men know that this good average is a triumph of breeding and midwifery, but make no comment.

POSSIBLY the farmer, on his Sunday tour, is visited with sorrow at thought of the inevitable death that awaits the numerous progeny of Nature and himself. If so, he says nothing about it. Probably he is comforted by the reflection that there are plenty more where these came from. His relations with Nature are indeed very like those of the average man with his wife ; the woman is more to him than the children ; the woman provides homeliness and repose—anchorage, a place in life, and scions to carry on his name. And Nature is a better-than-human wife, for she is constant in her duty and obedient to her master as long as he treats her well. She cannot disappoint him of children, or fly off with a new lover. She is his.

To make sure that he has done all he can for her, he extends his Sunday tour to his fields. He roots with his toe in the soil to test the tilth ; it crumbles sweetly to his touch, and

HARVESTING THE ROOT CROP.   [*Chas. Reid.*

Root Crops are of immense value to the farmer. Though he may welcome fine weather and sunshine for his corn, he needs moisture to swell his turnips. Here is a good crop, lifted and trimmed, being carted off for safe storage.

PITTING POTATOES.   [*Chas. Reid.*

The potatoes have been dug up and armies of women and girls have gathered them from their earthy bed. Now comes the task of storing the useful tubers in covered pits until they are needed for sale or home consumption.

BRINGING IN THE HAY. [*Donald McLeish.*

Hay-making begins the farmer's work of taking produce from his fields. It is the prelude to his harvesting. Here, on the banks of Loch Lomond, the farmer who loves Nature may find find that " every prospect pleases."

THE VALE OF PLENTY. [*Donald McLeish.*

Under the shadow of Ben Venue, in the beautiful Trossachs, with Loch Achray at its foot, half hidden from view by the trees, the farmer's men perform the last rites before the harvest is gathered for the threshing machine.

he is glad. But in the next field the ploughing was done under unfavourable conditions perhaps—the furrows are ridged up in great slabs as hard as iron. He scans the sky for rain, and sighs, and makes a mental note about heavy harrows, and wishes he could have afforded extra labour to have the job done before the dry weather set in. Nature is always asking for money, drat her ! Then he passes on to a field where the young corn looks limp and yellow, and stooping, he pulls up blade after blade, rootless, bitten off just below the ground. Wireworm !—one of his love's unpleasantest habits. He has tried, by untiring cultivation, to cure her of it, but wireworm, along with rooks, pigeons and spear-grass, seem rooted in her soul. She says the rooks are there to eat the wireworm (even as a human wife says she takes aspirin to cure the headache brought on by over-smoking), but the cure is as bad as the disease, for those blades of corn which the insect has not nibbled the bird has dug up—the deep nibbles of beaks can be traced along the rows.

Nature over-opulent, giving birth to evil as well as good, how little your poets know of you ! Nature dealing wholesale death, how little they would love you if they knew ! But your farmer loves you, cherishes you, disciplines you. Soft words and pretty speeches are all very well in public, and an attractive woman like you may well expect them, but in the privacy of home, shared by the companion of years, you get a sincerer if less wordy tribute. This silent man with the sharp eyes and the hard mouth, who knows all your idiosyncracies, weaknesses and extravagances, will stand by you till he dies. He is no fair-weather lover : his is no summer-holiday flirtation. He is your husband, for better or worse ; and a man does not enter upon such a long and uncompromising contract, nor abide by it without the smallest attempt at evasion, unless love truly abides in his heart.

THE REWARD OF HIS TOIL.   [*Charles Reid.*

The ground prepared and the seed sown, the farmer is completely at the mercy of Nature through the spring and summer days. If Nature is kind the harvest is ample reward for the hard work done and the skill expended.

[G. P. Abraham.

These Pines, wandering to the edge of the lake, are relics of the days when Pine Forests were abundant in Britain. These trees, which are sometimes incorrectly called the Scotch Fir, may grow to a hundred feet high.

TREE LORE

By RICHARD ST. BARBE BAKER

TREES, which have been called the Oldest Living Things on the earth are one of Nature's masterpieces. Apart from their ornamental value, they serve humanity in many ways, providing medicine, clothing, and furniture. Almost like humans, they have heart-beats and blood in the form of sap. Their interesting life-story is here unfolded.

TREES are general favourites, and we are all tree-lovers at heart, if we only stop to think, for a tree is the grandest and most beautiful of all things on earth. It is little wonder that they held an important place in the life and imagination of the early races of men, and formed a basis for their mythology.

One of the very earliest cults was that of tree worship. Woods and forests were the earliest sanctuaries of many races. Grimm tells us that although individual gods may have dwelt in caves, rivers, or on hill tops, the festal, universal religion of the people had its abode in the woods.

Georgina Mase in her *Book of the Tree*, points out that we get some idea of the reverence in which these sanctuaries were held from the severity with which old German Law treated any one who dared even to peel bark from one of their trees. Evidently such trees and groves were believed to be under more than human protection, for nearly every country has its legends of the mysterious punishment which follows the violation of holy groves. Here is a story that comes from Ireland which illustrates this point :

" During a severe winter a farmer decided to cut some branches for firewood from an Alder that overshadowed an ancient holy well. While he was doing so he chanced to look towards his cottage and saw that it was in flames. Hurrying home, he was surprised to find no trace of fire, so he returned to his work on the Alder. Again he saw flames rising high over his house, and again he ran to put out the fire, only to find that all was well. A third time he returned to the tree to procure his wood. He lopped off as much as he needed and carried his bundle home, when, to his dismay, he found that his cottage had been burnt completely to the ground."

III

The Oak was held sacred by the Greeks and Romans as well as by the ancient Britons, who consecrated its shade with the solemn ceremonies of the Druids, who get their name from the old Celtic word Drew, an oak. The Greeks called the tree Drys, hence Dryads, the little folk who peopled the woods. The well-known chorus of "Hey, derry down," according to Professor Burnet, was a druidic chant, signifying literally, "In a circle the Oak move around."

Worshipping under the Oak.

With the coming of Christianity the early preachers proclaimed their message from under the Oaks which often marked the boundary between parishes, and which afterwards were known in many parts of the country as Gospel Oaks. Many stories are told of these, as also of the Royal Oaks. Evelyn, who wrote his *Sylva* in the reign of Charles II., thus dedicated the fourth edition : "To you then, Royal Sir, does this Fourth Edition continue its humble addresses . . . as having once had your temple, and court too, under that sacred Oak which you consecrated with your presence, and we celebrate, with just acknowledgment to God, for your preservation."

We are told that this tree, called The Royal Oak, formerly stood at Boscobel, in Shropshire, but was destroyed soon after it attained its notoriety by the ill-judged curiosity of the Royalists. Apparently it came to grief at the hands of thousands of souvenir-hunters, for the people never stopped hacking the boughs and bark until they had killed the tree. However, several saplings were raised in different parts of the country from its acorns, one of which grew near St. James's Palace, where Marlborough House now stands, and there was another in the Botanic Gardens at Chelsea, but both these have long since disappeared.

Famous Men and the Oak.

Evelyn says of the Oak : "To enumerate now the incomparable uses of this wood were needless : but so precious was the esteem of it, that, of old, there was an express law among the twelve tables concerning the very gathering of the acorns, though they should be found fallen into another man's ground." He refers to the many uses of its wood, including houses and ships, cities and navies, and, after an extensive list, he ends by saying : "The very bark is of price with the tanner and dyer, to whom the very sawdust is of use, as are the ashes and lee to cure the roapishness of wine.

The Ground-oak, while young, is used for poles, cudgels, and walking-staffs."

Shakespeare knew the qualities of the Oak, when he wrote :

"Thou rather with thy sharp and sulph'rous bolt
Split'st the *unwedgeable* and *gnarled* oak,
Than the soft myrtle . . ."

Gilpin says : "Many kinds of wood are harder, as box and ebony ; many kinds are tougher, as yew and ash ; but it is supposed that no species of wood, at least no species of timber, is possessed of both these qualities together in so great a degree as British oak."

Virgil noted its chief characteristics in this order : firmness, stoutness of limbs, the twisting branches, expansive spread and longevity.

The Symbol of our Race.

It is only natural that we should like to regard the Oak tree as symbolic of our race. The associations which immediately come to our mind are those of power and independence. Oliver Wendell Holmes once wrote :

"There is a mother-idea in each particular kind of tree, which, if well-marked, is probably embodied in the poetry of every language. Take the Oak, for instance, and we find it always standing as a type of strength and endurance. I wonder if you ever thought of the single mark of supremacy which distinguishes this tree from all our other forest trees ? All the rest of them shirk the work of resisting gravity ; the Oak alone defies it. It chooses the horizontal direction for its limbs, so that their whole weight may tell, and then stretches them out fifty or sixty feet, so that the strain may be mighty enough to be worth resisting. You will find that, in passing from the extreme downward droop of the branches of the Weeping Willow, to the extreme upward inclination of those of the Poplar, they sweep nearly half a circle. At ninety degrees the Oak stops short ; to slant upward another degree would mark infirmity of purpose ; to bend downwards, weakness of organisation."

Every tree has its individual character, and every group its harmony. Who cannot thrill at the sight of an ancient sire whose boughs in Shakespeare's language are

"mossed with age,
And high top bald with dry antiquity."

Photo: St. Barbe Baker] THE LARGEST CEDAR-TREE IN ENGLAND. [Mondiale.

In prehistoric days Cedars had a wide distribution north of the Equator, but in later times they migrated to the hilltops, adapting certain features to suit their climatic conditions. This Cedar is growing in Cobham, Surrey.

It may even be hollow, like the famous Winfarthing Oak in Norfolk, but still, year by year it has the courage to force out fresh leaves from its gnarled and knotty stem and take on, as it were, another lease of life. It is often said that an Oak takes a hundred years to grow to its full stature, and remains static for another hundred, and takes another hundred years to die, but from my own experience, I believe all these three periods are underestimated. On the continent of Europe I know a forest where the Oaks are grown for three hundred and twenty years, when they give the highest possible returns, and in England there are still a few old Oaks said to be at least nine hundred years.

The English Oak ranges from the Urals and the Caucasus, from Mount Torus and Mount Atlas, almost to the Arctic Circle, growing at an altitude of well over twelve hundred feet in some parts—chiefly in the Highlands of Scotland. No one denies that the Oak is one of our fellow-countrymen, but if any one were bold enough to do so, we could easily refute him, not only by pointing to the ancient living trees, but by noticing the trunks of trees preserved in peat bogs which have been prostrated in the soil for hundreds of years.

England, although once well-wooded, could not boast of having many species, twenty-eight in all, including besides the Oak, at least one variety of the following : Poplar, Birch, Lime, Maple, Sycamore, Holly, Hawthorn, Cherry, Mountain and Common Ash, Elm, Beech, Hornbeam, Yew, Alder, many kinds of Willows, chief of which are the White, Bedford, and Cracking Willow. The Scots Pine is the only indigenous conifer to Great Britain. From this we see that of the many trees at present cultivated in British woods and plantations, only a small proportion are real, spontaneous growths of the country, but far the greater number have been introduced from time to time.

TO-DAY there are over three hundred different kinds of trees growing in our woods which attain to timber size. But it is safe to regard as native trees all those which propagate themselves freely from seed, without our agency, and which are known to have existed in our country beyond the earliest records. Many of these introduced are now regarded as our own, such as the Spanish Chestnut, which is generally regarded as having been introduced by the Romans for the express purpose of feeding their armies.

Photo : St. Barbe Baker.]　　　ANCIENT ELM TREES.　　　[*Mondiale.*

This picture shows how, in bygone times, hollowed-out elm trees were joined to form water-pipes. They were discovered by workmen who found that, in spite of their long internment, the bark was still in good preservation.

B.W.N.   E

QUEEN ANNE'S LIMES
On a hot day it is pleasant to seek the cooling shelter afforded by shady lime-trees. This avenue,
planted by Queen Anne in memory of her children, can be seen at Ashbridge Park, Berks.

THE TWELVE APOSTLES. [*Frith*

These fine poplars by the Severn have become known as the Twelve Apostles. It will be noted that one of the twelve stands apart (on the left of the picture). Possibly this is Judas, outlawed by his more loyal brethren.

Although most of us, if not all, are tree-lovers, few really thoroughly understand them. We have been accustomed just to take them for granted, not even considering how they grow.

Picture a tree, then, as it stands : the obvious portions are the stem and the branches, and out of sight is the root system which provides support and food. When a tree grows, the root fibres absorb moisture and food in solution. This rises in the stem to the leaves, which provide the laboratories of the tree. Under the influence of sunlight carbon dioxide is assimilated from the air and is transformed into sugar-compounds forming the xylen or heart of the tree.

The construction of wood is extremely complicated, each cell serving its own function; some are thick-walled and act as supports to the trunk and enable it to withstand the stresses and strains to which it is continually exposed. Other cells may be thin-walled and act as conveyers of water from the roots to the leaves. Such cells are always found in the outer-portion of the trunk.

The growing layer is called the cambium, and the famous Indian botanist, Sir Jagadis Bose, with the help of his Electric Probe, has been able to show that there are definite heart-beats in this region. So long as life continues, these heart-beats are audible, but at the moment of death, they cease, as in a human.

In the spring the cambium or growing layer becomes intensely active and by the division of cells the tree increases in girth, the actual growth being known as an annual ring ; from these, as a general rule, the age of a tree may be estimated. This does not apply to many tropical trees where growth is continuous throughout the year, and it is not always safe to estimate the age of an Oak by this method. The reason for this is that some-times an Oak is completely defoliated during the summer, and in consequence the cambium is given a rest before a fresh crop of leaves appear ; thus a biennial ring is formed. When a tree is felled you may count the annual rings outwards from the heart of the tree towards the bark.

A tree provides its own food. When its roots dig into the earth, they tap valuable minerals, and the leaves, when they have served their function, fall to the earth and form a humous or leaf-mould, which provides the best kind of food for the growing tree. For this reason leaves should be left lying on the ground, otherwise it is robbing the tree of its food.

Trees grown singly in the open tend to form strong side-branches, and when grown in forest formation they are continually being drawn up in their search for light, while the side-branches are gradually suppressed by the crowding that takes place as they develop.

How Forests are Thinned.

The art of controlling the crowding which is necessary to produce clean timber is one of the most important operations in forestry. Constant thinnings are necessary, and great care is required to prevent opening up the forest too much. Yet at the same time not more than two-thirds of the lower branches should be suppressed, otherwise girth growth may be checked and the trees become spindly. Only long experience will enable this operation to be carried out with assured success.

When a tree is pruned and a clean surface is left, a callous will quickly form to heal the wound. Dead branches should always be removed, otherwise they become imbedded in the heart of a tree by its natural growth and present a weakness in the timber produced. A dead branch forms a knot, and makes the timber defective. They also tend to cause the stems of trees to taper and retard the growth by obstructing the sap. A tree tolerably free from knots is likely to give the greatest height and thickness and will certainly be of greater value when the time comes for it to be felled.

In the forest, with proper thinning and pruning, Nature does the rest by way of producing clean timber, and the treatment of wounds would not be considered, but in dealing with park or garden trees very often it is necessary to dispense with growing branches, either to assist the tree in its formation to obtain the required length of clean trunk, or possibly to lessen the leaf surface, to reduce the demand made on the root system.

When it is necessary to remove large branches, a saw-cut should be made on the under-surface, close to the stem of the tree, and should be continued upwards until the saw is pinched by the weight of the branch. A second cut is then made on the upper side to meet the undercut. A sharp chisel will be found useful to make a clean surface which should then be treated with Stockholm tar, as a dressing.

In an old tree it may be found necessary to treat a deep wound in the trunk, and cement is often advocated as a filler. My own feeling is that little good can come of filling a hollow tree with a foreign material of this nature. For one thing it is rigid, while the tree is flexible ; it is liable to expansion and contraction in changes of temperature, and unless great care is taken in preparation of the wound surface, it is liable to fungal attack. This is all the more dangerous to the tree, as it may go on for some time unobserved under cover of the cement. Surely it is far better to clean and irrigate carefully the hollow portion so that water does not stand in the trunk, and treat the surface with a natural protective agent such as Stockholm tar distilled from trees

" I am often asked the question : " Which is the tallest tree on earth ? " Many claims have been made for different species, some saying that the Eucalyptus tree of Australia is the tallest, others that the Coast Redwood of California predominates in height. Until my recent world tour, I should not have dared to express an opinion, but now, having visited the grandest forests of the world, I am of the opinion that the tallest tree is a Sequoia sempervirens, which is growing on the Bull Creek Flats in Northern California. This tree is said to be 364 feet in height, but I measured it with my hypsometer and each time found it to be 354 feet. Even at that height I have seen no tree to equal it.

The tallest Eucalyptus tree that I measured was 325 feet, though I am told there are taller ones. However, I am only speaking from my own experience, and I should be delighted to hear from any reader who has found one to surpass this. That Coast Redwood, I should mention, was 54 feet in girth, and in bulk did not compare with a giant Sequoia, known as General Sherman, that I saw in the Sequoia National Park. True, it was only just over 273 feet in height, but its base circumference was 102 feet. Its greatest base diameter was 37 feet. Its mean base diameter 32 feet, and 8 feet above the ground, 27 feet. The height of its largest branch was 130 feet from the ground and the diameter of this branch was over 7 feet. The total weight of the tree is estimated at over 5000 tons. It would take at least thirty large railway trucks to remove the timber, and there is enough wood in it to build a couple of hundred houses. Just think of it ! And that great leviathan of the forest sprang from a tiny seed, half the size of the head of a match. It is as if the Almighty Himself was showing us what He could do with a tree growth.

Photo: *St. Barbe Baker.*]   **THE PRAYER.**   [*Mondiale.*

A tree is more to the Indians than mere wood. It has a spirit behind it, knows the secrets of the ages, and can whisper counsel to those seeking aid. A striking example of this forest worship is shown in this picture.

Photo: *St. Barbe Baker.*]   **A HIGHLAND FOREST.**   *[Mondiale.*

This large forest at Glenstriven shows how high a standard the art of forestry has reached in Scotland. Many of the Scottish lairds depend very considerably on their woods to tide them over lean years on the land.

BY THE RIVER SIDE.   [Charles Reid.

The River Tweed, near Abbotsford, the home of Sir Walter Scott, is bordered with Larch trees. Larches
are greatly valued for their wood and for the turpentine they yield. The bark is used in tanning.

Next to the Redwoods and the Eucalyptus come the giant Kauris of New Zealand. I visited the virgin forest where they grow in North Auckland. At one time they covered a large proportion of the North Island, but there I found them making their last stand, for man has a bad record as a forest-destroyer in New Zealand ; cutting and burning, greedily and recklessly, he has sacrificed those grand trees for tillage and pasturage. The old Maoris were friends of the forest, and whenever they wanted to cut down a tree they used to ask its permission first, and then cover up the stump with foliage so as to protect the inlying spirit. Throughout the greater part of the island, the Children of Tane, the Lord of the Forest, have disappeared.

Thus deserts have been formed the world over, and the process still goes on. We must stop this mad ruin, or we shall be confronted with a timber famine ; and our beautiful world will become a waste.

It is a fact that trees are always giving out more than they take. They are healthful, exhilarating, especially the wild ones. In this much-vaunted civilisation in which we now live, Man is too often inclined to think that the Infinite made the world in the rough and left it altogether for him to improve. Are we really doing this in destroying the natural forests, as well as the birds that go with them ?

The late Professor Sir J. Arthur Thomson, that great naturalist, in his Foreword to my book, *The Brotherhood of the Trees* wrote : " For it is not merely that the world is bettered by saving, replacing and multiplying trees, it is that an aim of this kind becomes an impulse towards developing a mood and an outlook which will increasingly feel it to be natural to think for the future, for other people, for generations yet unborn. Planting a tree is a symbol of a looking-forward kind of action— looking forward, yet not too distantly."

Trees hold the rains as they fall, and condense the fogs precipitating their moisture. When the trees are gone, rainwater rushes down the hollows and valleys, cutting deep watercourses which carry off the water before it can saturate the ground. The mists, no longer held in the foliage, drift away without depositing moisture. The rushing stream carries in its flood the soil and fertile humus. The springs are not fed, because rain has not had time to percolate down to their level. Streams and rills become torrents during the wet season and barren ravines in the dry.

STURDY RELICS. [*F. Frith & Co. Ltd.*
Historical Yews, as spoken of in the Doomsday Book, are seen above. They are estimated to be over a thousand years old. The durability of the timber is remarkable, and it is said that a post of yew will outlast a post of iron.

[G. P. Abraham.

The Scotch Fir is a noble tree dominating the landscape wherever it rears its stately head. Its fir cones, the shells of its seeds, are eagerly gathered by children, for from them curious animals and birds can be fashioned.

HOW TO RECOGNISE TREES

By FORSTER ROBSON

IT is at times exasperating to be asked by a friend or travelling companion to name some tree seen on the way. This chapter offers some useful clues to the identification of our principal British trees. By bark, leaf, fruit and general shape can trees be recognised. To assist and to supplement generally our author's detailed instructions a veritable portrait gallery of trees and their leaves has been included in this chapter.

" Willows whiten, aspens quiver,
Little breezes dusk and shiver."

THE poet Tennyson in this couplet gives the salient characteristic of both trees. When the gentle summer breeze frolics amongst their leaves, it wantonly lifts those of the Willow showing their white and silvery undersides, and the slender delicate stalks of the Aspen leaves respond to its lightest airs, causing the leaves to quiver and rustle, the rustle of my lady's silken skirts as she passes by.

It is not possible in this chapter to give sufficient data to enable one to recognise all our British trees, but it is hoped that the few facts given may engender a desire for more and lead to the study of one of the most beautiful and useful features of the landscape. Implanted in most of us is a liking for trees, and in some, a deep love for them. Shakespeare says there are " Tongues in trees." An ancient tree tells many stories to those whose spirit is attuned, and when we gaze upon its rugged strength and think of the evil it has overcome to attain that strength, the tales of joy and sorrow it has listened to in its shade, our own petty troubles become less poignant and we stretch ourselves at its foot in peace.

There are two great classes of trees. The deciduous and non-deciduous, those which shed their leaves in the winter and those which retain them ; the latter are usually termed evergreens. The Conifers or Pines in Britain, with one exception, the Larch, retain their leaves through the winter. The Larch sheds its leaves and is remarkable for the delicate pale green of the new leaves in the spring and their golden colour in the autumn.

In winter the yellowish brown cones stud the slender drooping branches. The general form of the conifers is that of a cone with a straight tapering stem, the Noah's Ark trees of our childhood days. Other examples of the evergreens are the Holly, its spiny leaves and red berries familiar to all at Christmas time, the Holm Oak or Ilex, the Box, used for the edging of garden walks but which grows, when allowed to, twelve or fifteen feet high, and the Bay Laurel.

In studying trees it is well to remember that they are in many respects like human beings. In youth they are straight and slender, in middle age sturdy, showing vigorous growth, in old age gnarled and roughened, with twisted or broken limbs, telling of their struggle for existence against inimical surroundings and winter storms.

With these last thoughts in mind the trees may be recognised in winter by the character of the stem or trunk and the ramifications of the branches. Some have smooth stems like those of the Beech, Hornbeam, White Birch, Sycamore and London Plane. Both the Sycamore and the London Plane shed their bark when it is fouled, the Sycamore not to the same extent as the London Plane, on the stems of which light, yellowish grey patches alternate with sooty black ones ; the bark having been shed on the light patches, the tree is thus cleansed from the soot and grime of the city.

How to identify Tree trunks.

Trees with rough stems or trunks are more difficult to recognise when the leaves are absent, and stems of young trees do not show so rough, but grow more channelled and fissured as they grow older. The trunk of the Elm is dark greyish brown in colour ; in old Elms very rough, long fissures run up the trunk and are joined by lateral cracks at irregular intervals. The stem of the Oak is of a light grey in colour and is often covered with a grey green lichen patched with bright yellow, making the trunk a beautiful colour harmony. Near towns the colour of the tree trunks is generally blackened and dirty. When the colour of the trunk is described, it is the colour of the trunk in a clear, pure atmosphere. The colour of the trunks of the trees in Kew Gardens is spoiled by the sooty atmosphere of London and is no true guide to their real colour.

The ramification of branches is a study in itself. In trees with slender branches and twigs, their outline melts into the winter sky ; an example of such is the White Birch. The forms of trees with stout branches and twigs are sharply etched against the sky like those of the Oak ; the branches of an old Oak make one think of a mass of writhing serpents, and it is by their twisted and contorted forms you may recognise the tree. The Elm, as a rule, throws out one or two large, horizontal branches, and then the trunk divides into two large limbs each throwing off a number of smaller branches and twigs forming a rounded top. The Elm is a tree of the hedgerows and fields, and is not often found in woods ; very often the farmer lops the lower branches, to let the light through on to his field, leaving the trunk bare and the tree then resembles a gigantic umbrella. The Sweet Chestnut is another thick branched tree easily recognised by the twisted and rugged character of its trunk. The bark is fissured, the fissures curving round the trunk as if two mighty hands had seized it and twisted it like a length of rope.

Study also the Leaf-scars of Trees.

Another means by which we can recognise trees, is by the leaf scar. When a leaf drops off the twig in autumn it leaves a scar where the stalk joined the twig. These scars vary on different trees. Suppose you suspect the tree under observation to be a Walnut, the time being winter and you are not sufficiently acquainted with the ramification of the branches to be sure. Look on the twig for the leaf scars left by the fallen leaves of the last year. On the Walnut the scar is triangular in form, the two sides at the apex being slightly concave ; the base which is the longest side of the triangle is doubly curved, and in each angle of the triangle are a group of small black dots. Should the scar conform to this description the identification is complete.

Noting the character of Buds and Twigs.

In winter and spring the disposition and arrangement, colour, size and character of the surface of the buds on the twig is another aid to the identification of the tree. The buds of the Oak are placed alternately, the twig terminating in a cluster of buds, those of the Hawthorn in the same way but terminating in a thorn. The Sycamore, Elder and Ash are examples of buds placed opposite one another.

The colour of the buds may be brown, green, grey, red or black. Many of the trees have

H. Bastin.]   **HORNBEAM.**   *[Mondiale.*

The corded appearance of the hornbeam trunk is
characteristic of this tree, so useful for hedging.

H. Bastin.]   **DOUGLAS FIR.**   *[Mondiale.*

Cracked and deeply scarred is the bark of the fir. As
trees grow older the fissures show up more clearly.

H. Bastin.]   **BEECH.**   *[Mondiale.*

The smooth trunk of the beech shows up clearly in comparison with the cracked and seamed barks of other trees.

H. Bastin.   **OAK AND IVY.**   *[Mondiale.*

The ivy has here fastened itself round the oak and
fattened on the nourishment provided by its host.

green or brown buds. The Alder Buckthorn has small grey buds set alternately. The Lime has crimson red buds placed alternately and a fairly long distance apart. The buds of the Ash are opposite one another and are large and black. The Rowan or Mountain Ash has black downy buds, and this is one characteristic which serves to distinguish it from the True Service Tree of which the buds are green and smooth. The two trees are very much alike and often mistaken for one another.

The Horse Chestnut with its large buds, and Black Poplar are examples of trees with sticky buds ; these are covered with a kind of varnish to protect the bud in cold weather ; this varnish melts as the season advances, and becomes sticky.

The Wayfaring Tree is a good example of Mother Nature's care for the young buds. The buds are naked ; most buds have a scaly covering, erect, with two leaves folded so as to protect each other ; but they are covered with a thick coat of hairs, so thick that they form a grey, felt-like covering to protect the bud from winter frosts. The tree derives its name from its dusty appearance due to the hairy covering of the leaves on their upper surface ; underneath is white and woolly.

Hiking has become a popular pastime with the modern youth ; their hiking takes them through the fields, woods and lanes, and what could be more interesting than to combine with it a study of the trees ? Everyone loves flowers, but not many associate flowers with trees, yet every tree has its flower and fruit ; in many cases, however, the flower is inconspicuous, and wants looking for. Man is by nature a hunter, and what gives greater pleasure than the running to earth of the quarry—even if it be only a modest blossom?

How " Lamb's Tails " Grow.

Most woodland trees bear their flowers in catkins, called " Lamb's tails " by the country children, and these catkins appear before the leaves. The catkin consists of a central stalk, covered throughout its entire length with little florets, each on its own tiny stalk. The result of this arrangement is a pointed, cylindrical tassel which hangs from the twig. These in some cases are so numerous that at a distance they colour the whole tree. I have seen an Alder in spring a mass of golden brown, the catkins being so numerous that they almost hid the branches.

Sometimes the male catkins and the female

H. Bastin.] THE FRUIT OF THE ALDER. [*Mondiale.*

The flowers of the Alder appear in the form of catkins, long slender clusters of tiny flowers closely packed together : its fruit in the form of cones, from which the seeds fall as the scales open in their due time.

H. Bastin.]　　　　　　　　　　THE HAZEL COPPICE.　　　　　　　　　　[Mondiale.

The above photograph shows the hazel coppice in winter. The spring clothes the trees with catkins and flowers, while autumn brings nutting time, when young and old search for the tasty, oily nuts which are the tree's fruit.

grow on individual trees, and you have a male and female tree, fertilisation being effected by the wind or insects. On the Silver Birch the male and female catkins are on the same tree, the female catkin smaller and at first erect.

THE Hazel, the tree of the hedges and dear in autumn to the children for its nuts, has a distinctive female flower. The male catkins when ripe are two inches long and golden in colour, and hang from the twig. Somewhere on the upper side of the lower twigs, very retiring, will be found the female flower, a little bud-like thing out of the top of which project a number of bright crimson filaments. Any movement of the tree caused by wind or otherwise, causes the golden pollen of the male catkin to be precipitated on to the female, and Nature in that way makes sure of the nuts. An almost similar arrangement occurs in the Alder, but the female flower is small, dark crimson in colour and stalked.

The Ash flowers are borne in dense, dark purple clusters on the twig a month before the leaves. Sometimes both male and female are found on the same tree, at other times one will bear male flowers and another female.

About the end of March or early in April, according to the season, the Elms in strong sunlight have a purplish crimson tint; this is caused by the numerous clusters of purplish crimson flowers which stud the twigs.

The Sallow belongs to the same family as the Willows and is the earliest of the willows to flower; its gold and silver catkins, pear-like in form, are known to most children as Palm and are strongly in evidence on Palm Sunday. The golden catkins are the male flowers, and the silver the female; they grow on individual trees and here again the wind is made to serve Nature in her work.

Leaf-study aids Identification.

Enough has been said to show that the flower is an important factor in recognising a tree. All trees can be named by their florescence, and the study of it is an interesting and absorbing pastime for the leisure hours.

In summer the wanderer through the leafy glades of forest and wood has an easier task in recognising the trees. The leaf then becomes the guide. Leaves, as is well known, have various forms, and often different trees have the same form of leaf, but Nature pro-

125

vides a means of distinguishing one from the other by the character of the margin of the leaf.

In describing a leaf we have sometimes to use the terms Base and Apex. The Base is the part nearest the stalk. The Apex is the part farthest away from the stalk.

The margin or edge of the leaf may be : *Entire*—the term is used by botanists when the margin is smooth ; *Serrate*—that is, with teeth like a saw, the points of the teeth point towards the apex of the leaf ; *Doubly Serrate*—Smaller teeth occurring between larger ones ; *Dentate* —simply toothed, the teeth pointing outwards.

In examining the leaves of a tree be careful to select for observation a well-grown, mature leaf, not a specimen which has been warped or dwarfed in its struggle for light or against the attacks of insects. Leaves vary to a great extent on the same tree, and the shapes given are the simple forms to which the large majority of the leaves approximate.

Examining the shapes of Leaves.

Lobed leaves are those where the edges are deeply cut so that the leaf has several projections. The projections may be symmetrical or irregular. Examples of a symmetrically-lobed leaf are the Sycamore, Field Maple, and Hawthorn. The Sycamore is distinguished from the Field Maple by its margin, which is doubly serrate and the lobes pointed ; that of the Field Maple is simply serrate, occasionally entire, and the lobes are rounded at the points. The leaves on both trees have five lobes. Examples of an irregularly-lobed leaf are the Oak and the Turkey Oak. The Oak has rounded irregular lobes, the Turkey Oak has pointed lobes.

In *Heart-shaped leaves* the base of the leaf is indented and the leaf itself more or less heart-shaped in appearance. There are only three British trees with heart-shaped leaves, these are : the Lime, Lilac and Mulberry.

Knowing Trees by their Leaves.

The Gean and Wych Elm, Mountain Elm, or Witch Hazel—all three names are applied to the latter—have *leaves broadest near the apex*.

The Poplars have leaves *broadest at the base*. The Black Poplar has a large, triangular leaf with a serrated margin. The White Poplar, Grey Poplar, and Aspen—the Aspen is a Poplar—leaf margins are irregularly cut. The leaf of the White Birch, which is in this category, is small and the margin doubly serrated.

The distinguishing mark of the tree is its white, graceful stem. It is often termed the Silver Birch or Lady Birch.

The Beech, Wild Pear, Hazel, and Wayfaring Tree have broad oval leaves. The Beech leaf margin is entire, the Wild Pear serrate, the Hazel doubly serrate and the Wayfaring Tree dentate.

The Alder Buckthorn, Purging Buckthorn and Hornbeam have oval leaves. The leaves of the first two are small and very much alike, but the margins are different, the first entire, the second serrated.

Two examples of oblong leaves are the Rowan and the Holm Oak. The Rowan leaflets have serrated edges. The leaf of the Holm Oak is entire.

All the Willows have leaves much the shape of a lance head ; the Ash, Osier and Bay Laurel are other examples. The margin of the leaf of the White Willow is finely serrated, that of the Osier which belongs to the same order, is entire.

Of the trees with awl-shaped leaves there are only two, namely, the Tamarisk and the Juniper. In the Tamarisk the leaves are very minute and packed closely round the shoot, giving it a scaly appearance. The Juniper is easily recognised by the arrangement of its leaves, which have sharp points and are arranged on the twig in groups of three.

Yew, Pine and Cypress Leaves.

The Yew and the Irish Yew both have leaves narrow with parallel sides. In the Yew the leaves are placed opposite one another on the twig, in the Irish Yew they are arranged all round it.

The Pines have all needle-shaped leaves. The different varieties are distinguished by the arrangement of the needles. The Scots Pine, the Austrian Pine and the Stone Pine bear their needles in groups of two. The Scots Pine branches in the upper portion of the tree, are a brilliant orange in sunshine, the stem and branches of the Austrian Pine or Black Pine are a dark brown, nearly black, all the way up.

The Bhotan Pine has its needles in groups of five which droop round the twig. The Larch, Cedar of Lebanon and the Deodar or Indian Cedar, grow their needles in tufts. The Spruce Fir, Douglas Fir, and Silver Fir grow their needles singly.

The Lawson's Cypress and the Common Cypress have minute, scale-like needles which completely overlap and hide the twig itself.

BIRCH.

WEEPING ASPEN.

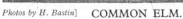

Photos by H. Bastin]   COMMON ELM.   WYCH ELM.   *(Mondial.*

This page and the two following pages show the form and character of twelve British trees. They will enable the reader the more readily to recognise trees from a distance by comparing the differences of branch and leaf form.

SILVER FIR.   LARCH.

Photos by H. Bastin]   ALDER.   BLACK SPRUCE.   [Mondiale.

The Silver Fir, really the true fir, is a tall, graceful tree.   The Larch often reaches a height of 100 feet, and sheds its needle-like leaves in winter.   The Alder is a smaller tree, delighting in a moist situation.   The Spruce was introduced from the Continent hundreds of years ago.   Black spruce wood is used abroad for making paper pulp.

MARSH CYPRESS.

LOMBARDY POPLAR.

Photos by H. Bastin.] HORNBEAM.

SYCAMORE.   [*Mondiale.*

Tall and lightly clad is the Marsh Cypress. The Poplars lift up their branches and so mass their foliage as to provide landmarks in the countryside. The Hornbeam clothes itself with a wealth of leaves and presents a rounder appearance, while the Sycamore with its profusion of five-pointed leaves is majestic and beautiful in appearance.

Holly.
Privet.   Holm Oak.   Barberry.
Cherry Laurel.   Ivy.
                                     Box.

Ash
(3 on left).

Walnut
(2 on right.)

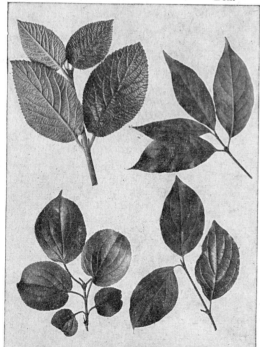

Photos by H. Bastin]

(Mondiale.

Wayfaring Tree.   Spindle.   Laburnum.   Wild Pear.
Buckthorn.   Dogwood.   Box.   Turkey Oak.   Holly.

HOW TO RECOGNISE TREES BY THEIR LEAVES. L

Spruce Fir.   Pine.   Norway Maple.   Box Elder.
     Douglas Fir.   Scots Pine.   Sycamore.   Field Maple.
         Lawson Cypress.

Photo: Harold Bastin]   *[Mondiale.*
   Oak.   Holm Oak.   Sweet Chestnut.
       Plane.   Horse Chestnut.

HOW TO RECOGNISE TREES BY THEIR LEAVES. II.

Aspen.   White Poplar.   Sallow.   Crack Willow.
Black Poplar.   Lime.

Photo: Harold Bastin]   [*Mondiale.*

Guelder Rose.   Common Elm.   Hornbeam.
Hazel.   White Beam.   Wych Elm.

HOW TO RECOGNISE TREES BY THEIR LEAVES. III.

The Hedgerow in spring is a delight to the eye of the Nature lover. Nature sends forth the new green, with promise of brighter things as buds burst into flower. Here the bees suck their honey and insects hum all day long.

THE HEDGEROW: ITS GLORY

By FORSTER ROBSON

WALKING in the country, the first thing to catch the eye of the wayfarer is the diversity of wild life in the hedgerow. The background of trees and shrubs, with tender green leaf buds, blossom, or colourful fruits, according to season, then the flowers and the stately grasses, these all blend into a picture that is as refreshing as it is satisfying.

WHEN man first began to till the earth with his primitive spade the amount of ground he could prepare for cultivation would be limited and small, and the growing crop could be easily protected from the incursions of unwanted visitors by the women and children of the tribe. The advent of the wooden plough enabled the husbandman to prepare much larger pieces of land, more or less rectangular in form, and as the perimeter of these pieces increased so did the danger of irruption by the domestic, wild cattle, and other animals. Some other form of protection became necessary.

What more reasonable to suppose that the primitive farmer spared the smaller trees and bushes that bordered his acreage and filled in the gaps between by branches cut from the bushes available, particularly those that were thorny ; these would in many cases root and the growth would eventually fill the spaces,

and, with a little attention, a barrier would be erected to prevent the depredations of the larger animals.

Such procedure we can imagine was the genesis of the English hedgerow, a feature of the landscape almost peculiar to England alone. Foreign visitors are delighted with them, their colour, the abundance of blossom in summer, the flowers that nestle under their protection in spring and summer, and their wealth of richly-coloured leaves and berries in the autumn, rich harvest for the feathered denizens of the little homes hidden away in the depths of the interlacing branches and twigs.

The good farmer endeavours to keep his hedges trim and neat. In some ways they are a nuisance to him, they harbour weeds and their seeds are scattered over the fields. Impenetrability is the farmer's ideal, a strong protection against all marauders, but often through lack of time and labour the hedgerow becomes straggly and wild. The trim, impenetrable hedge is not without its beauty, but it is the straggling ones that are the most beautiful and pleasing to the eye ; it is when walking along by their side that we come across the unexpected, always a thrilling sensation.

In the trim hedge that which would cause the unexpected has been ruthlessly cut away by the hedger, whose billhook spares nothing that is not likely to be useful in building up a thick, strong hedge. Follow the hedger in his labours, it is interesting to watch him, and incidentally by judicious and tactful questioning, you may become the richer by some quaint scraps of knowledge gleaned from his store of years, and also one or two good Ash or Hazel walking sticks with natural handles.

HAZEL CATKINS. [*Mondiale.*

The Hazel puts forth its catkins, known popularly as "lamb's tails." These give the tree a dainty appearance.

In winter the hedges look dark and dreary under the grey, lowering sky, but once let the sun break through the mantle of cloud, the dreariness vanishes ; the top of the hedge is a pale purplish grey in tone and the sides red, brown and purple, broken by the rich brown of an upthrusting clump of dead bracken, the ochre colour of the tall dead grasses at its foot, here and there the dark green and brown of the dead leaves of the Blackberry, the leaves of which, in the southern counties, hang on until pushed off by the new growth, and the shining, dark green leaves of the Holly, which is waging a grim fight through the years against the onslaughts of the hedges.

Winter's grip gradually relaxes, the sap begins to rise in February, and the branches and twigs take on brighter tones of colour ; in March the buds begin to burgeon, and towards the end of the month they vie with each other in donning their new dresses to give a gladsome welcome to Spring. The hedge is now tinged in places with a delicate green. The dainty, creamy little flower buds of the Blackthorn, set like jewels on its twigs, and the larger, crimson, brown ones of the Whitethorn add to the charming variety of colour.

Blackthorn: herald of the Spring.

Under the hedge and on its banks are the early growths of the plants that love the hedge-rows, thrusting their vivid green young leaves between the brown and red dead ones of the year that has passed, making an embroidered carpet of green, red, and brown.

When the north-east winds blow at the end of March or beginning of April, there is a spell of cold weather, known by the country people as the Blackthorn winter and it is at this time that Blackthorn puts forth its blossom before the leaves and then the hedge in parts looks powdered with snow. The flower of the Blackthorn is pure white with central threads (*stamens*) tipped with gold and about half an inch across, but so prodigal is the bush of its blossom that the flowers almost hide the dark purple twigs and delight the eye with their purity and beauty.

The yellowish bronze of the Hazel catkins turns to gold ; they hang like bunches of golden tassels from the twigs and in the lightest airs scatter their golden pollen abroad, fertilising the modest little female flowers patiently waiting on the upper surface of the twigs and branches below.

The hedgerow now begins to put on its

spring garment, the purple shades of winter become various delicate shades of green, the young leaves clothe the twigs and the various plants underneath, and on the banks, hiding the interlacing stems and branches of the bushes. The birds become busy repairing old nests in the dark recesses and building new ones, and there is a constant musical twittering accompaniment to the coming and going with materials for that important matter, the making of a home.

From earliest times the Hawthorn has been used for hedges, its dense mass of twigs, liberally armed with thorns, keeps cattle and other intruders at bay, and it is also one of the chief glories of the hedgerow in spring. It is called by the children the May Tree, the wealth of blossom being borne in May, also the Whitethorn, to distinguish it from the Blackthorn, the stem being a dark grey in colour, that of the Blackthorn almost black. The white clusters of fragrant blossom scent the surrounding air, and each little blossom with its pink, pollen-bearing vessels, termed by botanists *anthers*, is indeed a delight in itself.

Speedwell is called Bird's Eye.

Now the banks of the hedge challenge our attention. Here is a patch of blue, the colour as pure as that of the blue sky above, it is a patch of Germander Speedwell, one of the earliest of the spring flowers and called by the maids Bird's-eye, from the small white centre of the tiny blue blossoms. The White Bryony, with its vine-like leaves and tendrils climbs over the hedge, its white flowers, borne singly, peeping out from the leaves. The Black Bryony is to be seen also. It is a climber, but not vine-like ; its leaves are heart-shaped and shiny with a sharp point and dark green in colour ; the flowers are small, yellowish green and grow in a cluster. The White and Red Dead Nettle are ubiquitous and the common Hedge Parsley with its fern-like leaves forms beds of white bloom, each cluster of which is composed of a number of tiny flowers.

In the shade, the Dog Violet with its deep ultramarine blue petals blooms modestly, and if you are lucky you may espy its relative, the Sweet-scented Violet with its purple petals ; it is not so common as the Dog Violet. The satiny white flowers of the Stitchwort greet us as we move along, each petal of the five-petalled flower cleft deeply so that they look like ten and shine almost like stars against the green of their background.

H. *Bastin*.]   **THE WHITE CAMPION.**   [*Mondiale*.

This delicate flower is one of a family that includes the Red Bladder, Rose. Moss and Sea Campions.

Should you believe in the efficacy of herbs, there is some Black Horehound. Note the purple flowers growing in rings on the stalk ; you will also find it has a nasty smell, but a decoction made from the plant is very good for lung troubles. Close by is some Ground Ivy ; mark the kidney-shaped leaves and the little snapdragon-like flower with two crimson spots on its lower lip ; an infusion made with the leaves is a tonic ; the old name of the plant was Alehoof.

Herb Robert and the Red Campion await us farther on ; they are both red flowers but the petals of the Red Campion are deeply cloven, those of the Herb Robert are not. Herb Robert was used in olden times for stopping bleeding and healing wounds. Those little pea-like flowers in groups are those of the Bush Vetch, which goes trailing over the hedge in all directions, its little tendrils at the end of its leaf stalks clinging to whatever will give support.

Last but not least you will notice here and there the upright fronds of the new bracken with their crozier-like finial, fit pastoral staff for a fairy bishop.

JUNE, the month of roses is upon us. The May has faded but its place has been taken by the roses and the blossom of other flowering shrubs. The foliage of the various bushes and plants take on the deeper green of summer and the hedgerows are bespangled with blossom. The large, white, scentless flowers of the Trailing White Rose in groups of three or four are conspicuous, those of the Dog Rose are smaller and tinged with pink, but the prettiest and sweetest is the large pink bloom of the Sweet Briar with its delicate aromatic perfume. On the rose, that pretty gall the Bedeguar, may be found, it is called by the youngsters the Fairies' pin-cushion.

The white clustering bloom of the Guelder Rose, the waxy-looking white blossom of the Wayfaring Tree, the creamy white, flat clusters of the Elderberry flowers and the greenish cream, long-stalked clusters of the Spindle Tree add their quota to the hedgerow's glory.

Here and there are the starry clusters of the creamy white blossom of the Dogwood breaking the green, the small yellowish green flowers of the Buckthorn, either single or in clusters, and the triple thorned Barberry with its pendant spikes of golden yellow bloom, often covered with an orange-coloured dust caused by a fungus which attacks it. The farmer blames the Barberry for producing blight or rust in corn growing near it, whether that is true or not the verdict is " not proven."

The summer flowers that nestle in the shelter of the hedgerow are numerous and vary in different districts. The Great Bindweed flings its white trumpets over the hedge in profusion and the Small Bindweed trails its pink flowers underneath and on the banks, the Tufted Vetch with its numerous, drooping spikes of bluish purple-coloured flowers, aided by its branched tendrils climbs everywhere, the yellow Toadflax, sometimes called the Wild Snapdragon, stands up erect, its stem crowded with its pale yellow, orange-tipped blooms, the small St. John's Wort with its yellow clusters of flowers. The Hemlock, its flowers in white flat clusters, and the Foxglove and Nightshade side by side. Summer passes and with it the flowers, the flaunting summer colours are exchanged for those of a more sober character but none the less rich in variety.

H. Bastin.]   BARBERRY FRUITS.   [Mondiale.

The Barberry has egg-shaped leaves edged with spines. The yellow flowers gradually turn to orange, long red berries in autumn. The bush grows to a height of about six feet and is to be seen flourishing in our hedgerows.

THE GLORY OF LEAF AND TREE. [J. Dixon-Scott.

The Hedgerows that once lined our country roads have often to be sacrificed owing to the widening of thorough-
fares. Left alone, however, trees often spring up from the bushes and break the monotony of the landscape.

Stroll along the hedge in the early morning when the tang of autumn is in the air and the " Pride of the morning," as the country men call the rising mist, softens every outline. The hedge is grey, not altogether due to the mist, for if you look closely you will find it covered with tent-like structures formed of grey silken gossamer threads stretched among the leaves, each tent occupied by a small army of caterpillars busily engaged in feeding on the foliage enclosed ; they are the gregarious larvæ of the Black-veined White Butterfly, the Ermine Moth and the Geometers. When the the sun pierces the mist with his rays, the drops of moisture deposited by the mist on the silken threads become diamonds, glistening and sparkling, the hedgerow jewelled by a master hand.

One great charm of the hedgerow is its fruits. The children in September go nutting and blackberrying, gathering the harvest of green-cupped nuts and luscious blackberries. The Sloes, the blue-black plum of the Blackthorn, are gathered for the making of the cordial Sloe Gin and also for mixing with the Elderberries for making Elderberry wine, which, when served hot on a winter's night, is comforting and soothing, especially if one has been so unlucky as to catch a cold ; both the Elderberries and the Sloes ripen late ; the Elderberries are loved by the starlings and they will soon strip a tree of its fruit.

The Hawsor Haigs, the small red berries of the Hawthorn, in Anglo-Saxon *Hagthorn*, which means hedge-thorn, are sometimes so profuse that in sunlight the bush appears a mass of scarlet ; the Hips, the fruit of the Dog Rose, are not so plentiful, both fruits are fleshy inside and afford the birds in some measure food for the winter.

The fruit of the Guelder Rose is a rich crimson-coloured berry ; the fruit of the Wayfaring Tree resembles it at first, but gradually turns to a purple black as it ripens.

Beware of the blackberries of the Buckthorn, their effect on the internal organs of the human body are not pleasant ; the berries in olden times were used as a purgative, hence it is sometimes called the Purging Buckthorn, to distinguish it from the Alder Buckthorn, whose berries are also black and the same size, about half an inch in diameter. You can distinguish by the leaves : the margin of the Purging Buckthorn leaf is serrated, that of the Alder Buckthorn is smooth and not broken.

The fruit of the Spindle Tree differs in shape from the other fruits, its beautiful coral pink berry is, in section, heart-shaped, with four deep groves dividing the berry into four lobes, each of which contains a seed.

As autumn wanes, nowhere in the landscape do you find richer colours than those of the hedgerow, they run through the whole gamut of an artist's palette and range from the bright lemon yellow of the Field Maple leaves to the dark purple of the shadows at its foot.

This riot of colour, broken by the rich dark green of the Holly and probably the dark grey bole of an Elm, makes of the hedgerow a feast of colour for the eye, a marvel of Mother Nature's handiwork and a glorious adjunct to the beauties of the English countryside.

H. Bastin.]   **FRUIT OF THE HOLLY.**   [*Mondiale.*

That hardy evergreen, the Holly, grows its brightly-coloured fruit in the form of clusters of red berries. These are in great demand at Christmas time for the purpose of house decoration. The Holly is a typically British tree.

The graceful flight of birds as, silhouetted against the sky, they wing their way to the open sea, is a sight that remains long in our memory. The perfect formation of their flight fills us with admiration of their skill.

A MEMORY OF BIRDS

By E. ARNOT ROBERTSON

IT seems strange, at first thought, that the most hauntingly melancholy sounds that earth knows, as well as the happiest, should come from the throats of birds : they are such small creatures to range over so grand a scale of emotions. But then they consist of practically nothing but emotion—emotion constantly in an extravagant state of expression— and although thought needs actual physical space in which to develop, so that only the comparatively big-headed animals have reflective brains, the wildest emotion apparently does not : it may be compressed into the tiny, delightful compass of a humming bird, and yet remain as hot and fierce and tender as anything that most of us are ever likely to feel, if more ephemeral.

Take almost all the strongest emotions that man has, but only a bare half-dozen of his teeming thoughts, and wrap them exquisitely in feathers, and make them audible, and blow magic into them in such a way that voice and shape and movement have power to go straight to man's heart, not through his mind but through his senses ; and you have a bird.

One of the secrets of mankind's almost universal fondness for birds lies, I believe, in this high emotional quality of theirs. All our legends and tales of human heroes are devoted to the praise of those who let themselves go in love, in war, in adventure. Most of us are— perhaps fortunately—unable to do this, through pride or prudence or self-consciousness. But birds do little else : and there may be more than a touch of envy in the usual human being's slightly patronising attitude of approval towards these enchantingly temperamental creatures.

One of my earliest literary disgusts was over a book of the *Our Feathered Friends* type, sentimentally humanising, *Mr. and Mrs. Robin*, given me by a relative who felt that one could not get in touch too early with Nature, in a carefully pre-digested form. It might easily have quenched for ever the beginnings of my interest in birds, and in fact very nearly did, but that I had a comforting suspicion that if families of Robins really chatted together as it alleged, at least their conversation could not be of such a calmly improving kind, so like my own parents' in their more pompous moments, and delicately devoid of any reference to the shredding of insects for food or the killing of the old birds by the young.

The secret of the Birds' cries.

It was not for some years after this that birds became suddenly important to me, and then they flew into my imagination on a white cold night when I had gone out after mullet with an east coast fisherman, and we had drawn blank several times with the net and were rowing back up the moon-silvered creek towards the village, where lights were going out one by one because of the lateness of the hour ; nothing living besides ourselves seemed stirring in the desolation of the Essex marshes. I think it was excitement at being up at night, or possibly disappointment over the fish—a sense of expectancy unfulfilled—which quickened my sensibilities for the moment, giving significance to an ordinary occurrence, for when the whir of wings passed close to me, and I could not see the creature that cried out heartrendingly in the half darkness, all at once it seemed to carry with it in its flight, away into the night, the sum of the age-old, unavailing sorrows of the world, too great a cargo for this frail craft of wings and spirit to bear. I could not have moved or spoken without a great effort, and the boat which I had been rowing floated idly on the shining surface of the creek, the green fire of phosphorescence waking and fading where the oars dripped into the water. And then in a few seconds the whole air was alive and plaintive with the cries of the birds—Curlew and Widgeon and some other species of the wilder sea-fowl, driven into the shelter of the marshes by the hardness of the weather off shore.

The whirring wings of the Sea-fowl.

They were everywhere about us, spreading a taut, thin network of crying over the edges of the sea as they called to one another across the saltings—the most moving, lost-soul wailing that I have ever heard. But, try as I would, I could not see them, neither against the marshes, which seemed blacker than the night warranted, nor against the brilliance of the sky : it is almost always impossible to see birds on the wing when the moon is very bright : on duller nights they are sometimes more visible.

A line of stars would blink, one after another, as I stared fixedly upwards, longing, I did not know why, to make out the shapes of these agonised spirits as a kind of reassurance to myself that they were real : but nothing solid appeared between me and the milkiness of the sky. Only on the water could I see their moon-shadows, straggling company after company passing over, all heading in one direction under some vague, contagious impulse of the hour.

When they had gone, sea and marsh and sky seemed weary from the strain of their crying ; more lonely than before ; touched with new mystery : but we could breathe again. It felt, too, as though this little part of earth had been swept of sorrow. And I knew, dimly, that I had found something that would matter long after I had ceased to care that we had not been successful in our fishing.

The dead Curlew.

I asked the fisherman what birds they were ; so that when, a few days afterwards, he mentioned casually that there was a dead Curlew lying in one of the salt pans on the marshes, I went there immediately with the excitement of a child who thinks that it is coming to the heart of a secret. I believed that in the dead bird, if I could handle it, examine it at leisure and not with the hurried, far-off glimpses which were all I could get of living Curlew by day, I should find out what it was that had moved me on the night in which loveliness and wild pain and the strange half-fear that goes with the apprehension of beauty first took on a living form for me.

But the dead bird was only a bedraggled carcass when I found it, and its eyes looked trivial, as all birds' do when one is too close to them. There could be no wild secrets here, nothing to stir the heart almost unbearably : something more than life had gone out of the bird's body when it died.

Birds, I knew from then on, are more alien to us than any animal ; unalterably so, for their spirit is for ever elusive. It is not only when they are dead that this strange, marvellous quality of theirs escapes us : caged or tamed they are no longer the same creatures ; any more than those happiest of all miracles, the living flowers that we know as Butterflies, are the same when pinned in an entomologist's collection. Only the shape and the colour

LEFT OUT! [Robert McLeod.

Young Thrushes, as we are told in this chapter, are not always well cared for by their feathered parents. The author states an instance when two fledgelings had fallen from the nest and older Thrushes refused to aid them.

141

remain ; the essence, the exciting appeal to the imagination is lost when they, who live in an enchanted self-sufficient world alongside ours but not in it, are dragged into our world, living or dead.

Two other memories of birds stand out particularly clearly in my mind ; one is of two very young Thrushes that fell out of their nest on to a tangle of twigs a foot or so below, owing to the collapse of one side of the mud-lined nest after exceptionally heavy rain. A third was killed by the fall, leaving only one survivor in the nest. Though the pair on the twigs were in full view of the nest the older birds could not be induced to feed them. Their response to the gaping beaks and increasing need of the youngsters was to work harder and harder to procure food ; never have I seen birds hunt more assiduously ; but once the food was in their beaks instinct was too strong for them ; they gave it all to the one in the nest.

For once that almost insatiable creature, a growing bird, had more than enough to eat. Looking bloated and peevish, it sat with its eyes closed and its beak languidly open, while its parents, as they continued to stuff it, gazed down with bright, troubled eyes at their other offspring, and then, spurred on by those demanding beaks, flew off again in agitation for further supplies. But the problem was too much for them : the end was tragedy.

Tragedy, too, must have ended the struggle of a maimed Sea-gull that day after day bluffed for its living on the Embankment in London, getting its share of scraps by ferociously threatening any other Gull that came near. It could not possibly have fought had its challenge been accepted. In some mishap it had lost one claw (many Sea-gulls do ; I do not know how) and so many of the long outer feathers of one wing, on which balance depends, that it could scarcely fly at all. A hopeless, gallant, heart-stirring pretence.

But more moving than any recollection of individual birds remain with me always the echoes of those thin, high voices of impersonal, inhuman despair, wailing through a marshland night throbbing with the pulse of unseen wings.

[*F. Frith & Co.*

Sea-fowl, congregating round the harbour in the hope of finding some tit-bit left in the fishing-boats, bring with them the mystery of the sea and a breath of the far-off lands which they visit in their distant flights.

The fierce Golden Eagle prefers to make his home where he can be lord of all he surveys.
He is happiest on the perilous ledge of a mountainous crag where no one can intrude on his privacy.

SOLITARY BIRDS

By ARTHUR BROOK

MANY birds, chiefly birds of prey, prefer the solitude of impenetrable cliffs to the more sociable of feathered communities. In this chapter these birds are dealt with by an actual observer of their home life and habits. In the next chapter they are described by another naturalist, and the reader may compare the records and secure a complete picture.

GENERALLY speaking, the solitary living birds of Great Britain are on the large side, and many of them are flesh eaters, strong, powerful creatures, magnificent on the wing. Their habits tend to keep them away from the haunts of men where they can be more generally observed, and so to study them the enthusiast must seek the wilds of Scotland and Wales and the hills of the Lake District. Thus the finest fellow of his kind, the Golden Eagle, no longer nests south of the Scottish Highlands—a fitting home for this splendid bird. Upwards of two hundred years ago it nested in Wales and Derbyshire, and for about one hundred years longer in the Cheviots and the Lake District—it is said no longer to nest in Ireland.

The romantic stories told of the Golden Eagle being a fierce bird, carrying off babies, a bird whose very name whispered terror, can be looked upon as fairy tales. In reality the Golden Eagle is timid and cowardly. It is certainly a magnificent and very powerful bird to look upon, especially when battling with the elements high above some Scottish deer forest, but who has ever known one attack a visitor to its nest, whether for the sake of study or for robbery?

In 1925 I spent several weeks studying and photographing a pair of Golden Eagles at their eyrie far up in the Scottish Highlands. What a truly fascinating experience it was to be hidden within a few feet from the King of Birds, and watch him and his royal spouse, brooding and tending their young, from the time the latter were small downy chicks until the day, eleven weeks later, when they both took to the air and disappeared from my ken! Let us hope they still live—and have tended young of their own.

How gentle the Golden Eagle is for so huge a bird—that is, when attending its young!

Only the titbits of flesh are given them to eat, and neither storm nor sun is allowed to cause the young any discomfort. On the first day of my observation in the " hide " I stayed seven hours, and the hen Eagle left the nest but once during that time. She was away only for seven minutes, probably to stretch herself. As the young get older they are left to themselves for longer periods, and when they are about a fortnight old the hen Eagle rarely broods them during a fine day.

The Golden Eagle is not a welcome tenant on a grouse moor, nor can it be wondered at, for the amount of grouse a pair of Golden Eagles bring to the eyrie is considerable. I once looked into a nest containing the remains of nine grouse and several mountain hares. But in a deer forest the Golden Eagle is often tolerated, in fact welcomed, for the deer stalker frequently has the chance of a good shot ruined by a startled grouse or mountain hare.

The Golden Eagle's nest, though not infrequently built upon a tree, is usually on some steep, hillside crag. A rope is not necessary to reach the greater majority of nests ; some are almost on the ground, in ridiculously easy situations—the very isolated spots, no doubt, accounting for this. Two eggs generally are laid, three is not unknown, but this number is of extremely rare occurrence. They remind one of huge Buzzard's eggs. Not often will a Golden Eagle lay again in the same year should her eggs be taken.

The Bird that is a coward.

The Common Buzzard, like an Eagle in miniature, is a bird of prey which has increased of late years. A quarter of a century back it was comparatively rare in most parts of Great Britain, with the possible exception of certain districts in Wales, where nowadays it is really common. The nest is built on rocks, in trees, and occasionally even on the ground. I have seen one in heather, after the manner of a Merlin, and again in a patch of bushes, on a Welsh hillside, in a spot one would expect to find a Curlew. On the inland crags it is rare to find a Buzzard's nest—which cannot be approached without the aid of a rope. With sea cliffs the reverse is the case.

Of late years the Buzzard, in Central Wales in particular, lays bigger clutches of eggs than formerly. In the early part of the present

Photo : Arthur Brook.] DINNER IS SERVED. [Mondiale.

The Buzzard, another solitary bird of prey, builds its nest in an isolated spot and there feeds its young on the spoil of a foraging expedition. Its desire for solitude is partly due to cowardice, for the Buzzard is not a bold bird.

Photo : D. N. Dalton]   THE MONARCH.   [Mondiale.

The Peregrine does not tolerate interference from anybody and, with his vicious-looking beak, is well able to rout intruders. He makes hilly districts and sea cliffs his haunts, sometimes taking possession of other bird's nests.

century two eggs was the rule, three was uncommon, four almost unknown. To-day, three is quite a common number, and four by no means rare. The Buzzard is a coward at heart, and other birds delight in " taking it out of him." The Peregrine, Raven, Carrion Crow, Merlin, and Kestrel all send him hot foot from the vicinity of their nest haunts.

How a small bird terrifies the Buzzard.

It is a ludicrous sight to see a tiny Merlin swoop down on a bird many times its own size, and strange to hear the larger bird cry out as though in terror. By a rare chance, however, you will find a pair of Buzzards display a certain amount of courage by swooping down on a human intruder at their nest containing small chicks.

Because the Buzzard is a big bird with a hooked beak many accusations are levelled at it. It does comparatively little harm, however, feeding on carrion, rats, moles, frogs, beetles, earth worms, young rabbits, and wounded or weakly birds up to the size of a grouse. The female Buzzard is larger than the male, being about two inches longer. It is a fine sight to watch a pair of Buzzards in an aerial display,

rising, soaring, diving and illustrating complete mastery of the air.

In the Buzzard's mountain home you may be fortunate enough to chance upon Peregrine, Merlin, Kestrel and Ring Ouzel. The handsome Peregrine is monarch of all he surveys. One Welsh cliff which I have in mind was for many years the abode of countless Jackdaws. One spring a pair of Peregrines took up residence there. I visited the spot during the April of that year, and not a Jackdaw was to be seen. The Peregrines had taken possession of a Raven's nest, torn out the wool lining, and laid four handsome eggs in it. The eggs were not allowed to hatch, however, as the lessee of the adjacent grouse moor would not tolerate a " hooked beak " about the place. So the Peregrines had to go—and the Jackdaws returned. The mischief done by that colony of Jackdaws doubtless exceeded that done by the Peregrines many times over.

In a patch of heather just over a certain hill is the home of a little Merlin. This bird lays its eggs about a month later than the Peregrine. Usually the eggs are laid in heather, but sometimes the old nest of Crow or Magpie is made use of. Merlins become attached to their chosen nesting site, and will return year by year to the same patch of heather. I have seen the eggs laid within a foot of the spot used successfully the previous year. The Merlin is a close sitter, often remaining on the eggs until almost trodden on. Once the nest has been found, however, I have observed that the bird is prone to leave more quickly on the next visit.

In 1913 I watched a cock Merlin alight in a small patch of heather, and heard him feeding the hen. Although I searched, every inch as I thought, I failed to flush the hen. When I was at a certain spot the cock Merlin was very excited and swooped down at my head, almost touching it. Eventually I gave up the hunt and repaired to a keeper's cottage. Later the keeper, his son and I paid another visit to the heather patch. I went to the spot I had marked as being the likely one, and shouted to the keeper, " Somewhere here, I think it is." As I spoke, up got the hen Merlin literally at my feet, in fact my one foot was barely three inches from the eggs. The " killing places " of the Merlin advertise the fact of the nest's proximity.

The Kestrel, or " Wind-hover," is often neighbour to the Merlin, nesting on a crag or tree overlooking the Merlin's abode. The former bird also frequents cultivated land, woodlands and the sea coast. It is a past master in the art of hovering, no other Hawk can do it quite so well. Frequently it hovers above the Pheasant's rearing-field, but the attraction there is the mice, not the chicks. It will certainly take Pheasant chicks occasionally, should no other food be available to appease the voracious hunger of the four or five lusty youngsters in her family.

Queer sites for Nest-building.

The Kestrel builds no nest, merely laying its eggs in a hollow scratched on some ledge, also in old ruins, farm buildings, church towers, hollow trees, and old and deserted nests of Raven, Crow, Magpie, Buzzard and other birds. The eggs, laid at the end of April or early in May, are from four to six in number. In contrast to most of the birds of prey, very little difference in size occurs between the male and female of this species.

The Kestrel may have as a near neighbour the Ring Ouzel, a solitary bird in its domestic abode, but as autumn approaches it is often observed in small flocks feeding on the fruit of the mountain ash. In the Ring Ouzel's haunt you will often find a nest of the Raven, largest and most intelligent of the Crow tribe. The Raven has increased of late years. Thirty years ago if you wished to see this bird in its home, some of the wildest parts of the country would require to be visited—the rugged sea cliffs or sequestered inland crags.

Ravens that nested in a Quarry.

In those days very few Ravens nested on trees ; to-day, however, many tree nests are in existence, and the bird has extended its range—even to the cultivated areas. Many people look upon the Raven as a rare and extremely shy bird. Wary it undoubtedly is, but there is a nest in Central Wales built in a quarry which is in daily use, bordering on a main road. Blasting takes place regularly not twenty yards from the Raven's nest, but does not appear to disturb it in the least.

It is a typical early bird too, and often lays eggs in February. Snow may be deep on the hills when the eggs are laid, or even hatching. The food supply rather than the weather, regulates the Raven's nesting period. When the weather is hard more food is usually to be had, in the shape of mutton ; consequently nesting is earlier and the clutches of eggs larger. Four or five eggs is the average, but six is not uncommon, and I have seen even seven on several occasions.

This is one of the few kinds of birds which pair for life, and they are very jealous of their nesting sites. Rarely will you find Ravens nesting within a quarter of a mile of each other—generally a much greater distance will separate two pairs. If taken young and brought up, the Ravens make amusing and entertaining pets. Some talk quite well. It is, however, surprising that many people still think the tongue should be split with a sixpence to create ability to talk. But such nonsensical ideas will persist. Pet Ravens enjoy a bath, and during winter will even break the ice to get at water ; they also love to roll in the snow. Like careful managers they have the habit of hiding any food they cannot eat at once, often tucking it in some hole or corner, and covering it with any bit of paper, stick or rag that is handy. This habit of hiding food must be an inborn instinct to provide against a " rainy day " in the wild state.

Another solitary species commonly found nesting in the vicinity of the Raven's abode, for the Raven loves to nest near a mountain

Photo: O. G. Pike.]   A RARE BIRD.   *[Mondiale.*

One of the rarest of mountain birds is the Kite, which is now a very solitary bird. It is pestered so much by enemies such as the Carrion Crow that harries its nest, that there is danger of it being exterminated altogether.

stream, is the cheery, rotund, white-breasted Dipper. Wandering near a mountain stream on a cold winter's day one may often hear the sweet, wren-like song of the Dipper, to the accompaniment of the tumbling waters.

The Bird that " says it with Music."

In the courting season the cock sings whilst running, and sometimes when flying after his mate, as they dash up or down stream, taking the hairpin bends in great style. The nest is a large, oval structure of moss, grass and leaves. In a damp situation, as on the side of a waterfall, where the spray drenches the nest, green moss is used, but on dry, grey rocks, the bank sides of a stream, under bridges, on a branch overhanging water, and in like situations, dry moss is generally used. The pure white eggs, four to six in number, are laid in March or April.

This year I saw five eggs on March 10th, which is an early date, although eggs have been found in February. Two or three broods are reared in the season, often in the same nest, a new lining of oak, beech, or other leaves being added after each brood has matured and flown.

The most characteristic habit of the Dipper is its remarkable action when standing on a rock in mid-stream. Every five or six seconds it bobs its plump little body; the legs appear to be bent at the knee-joint, the body is lowered an inch or more, then the bird bobs up again; it is this strange habit that has given the bird its name, for it spends the whole of its existence in dipping.

Birds that are expert Divers.

It dives well, and swims under water, using the wings to propel itself. Young Dippers are expert swimmers from the moment they leave the nest.

Great care should be exercised when examining a Dipper's nest containing fledged youngsters, as the least disturbance will cause them to leave the nest, dive into the water below, and swim on or beneath the surface. They will travel some distance before climbing on to a stone or rock, where they " bob " in the approved Dipper style.

The Kingfisher is another bird of the waterside, but not of the rapid, tumbling mountain streams so beloved of the Dipper. It prefers the sluggish stream, canal, pond, or lakeside. The legends and superstitions connected with this brilliantly-feathered bird are numberless.

Another jolly little bird of the streams and rivers is the Sandpiper. This bird arrives in its breeding haunts during April. The lonely angler fishing the mountain streams, often disturbs the bird from its nest containing four eggs.

The Carrion Crow, solitary in its nesting habits, and for the greater part of the year, although they roost together in winter, is hated more than any other bird. The sable villain is the sworn enemy of farmer, gamekeeper, and bird-lover alike—and also of the furred and feathered denizens of the wild.

The Bird that acted as Scavenger.

At one time the Kite was so common that it swarmed the streets of London, and did useful service as a scavenger. In those far-off days it is probable that the Kite was a gregarious bird; nowadays it is an extremely solitary bird. It is a far cry from London to the Kite's last British nesting site—Central Wales. Even here, despite the laudable attempts at protection, it is still harried—by the egg collector and also by the Carrion Crow. The protectors of the Kite should pay more attention to the Carrion Crow than they do, for this rascal does more harm than the human one by taking the eggs and the young birds up to about ten days old.

Upon several occasions I have watched Carrion Crows, any number from two up to ten, escort a Kite back to the nest. In one instance a Carrion Crow lit on the nest, and began pecking at the Kite's breast to make her rise in order to get at the young ones beneath. In Wales, the Kite nests in a tree—nearly always an oak. It builds its own nest, though not infrequently a Buzzard's or Carrion Crow's old home is used as foundation. The nest itself is a heap of rubbish, lumps of turf, tufts of hair, grass and its roots; the lining is of sheep's wool, augmented with paper, rags, string, bits of rope, and anything else which takes the Kite's fancy. The nest is flat, and the sitting bird is very conspicuous.

If disturbed the Kite will usually return to the nest in a very short time. In fact, I have watched one return before a friend of mine had gone fifty yards from the nesting tree. At the present moment the fate of the Kite in the British Isles is in the balance.

If no better success attends the efforts of protection in future, then one of the delights of the air—for the Kite is a magnificent bird on the wing—will disappear from our countryside.

Here is the Golden Eagle flying to its mountain home with a store of heather for its nest. It prefers a lofty fortress from whence it can look down upon the surrounding country in search of its prey.

BIRDS OF THE MOUNTAINSIDE

By OLIVER G. PIKE, F.Z.S., F.R.P.S.

MANY of the feathered kings of the wild mountainside are as grim as their surroundings, descending to the plains only to swoop down on their ill-fated prey and bear it off to their unapproachable eyrie. They are silent birds, as far as singing goes, but utter queer wild cries that strike terror into the hearts of the smaller creatures. We are taken into their lofty hillside fortresses by the author of the following chapter.

ON the bleak mountains of Scotland and Wales we find a class of birds very different from those of the lowlands. Many of these are birds of prey, for other kinds of food are absent on the bare moors and slopes. These birds have no song ; their wild cries are well in keeping with the lonely tracts in which they live. Some may have to go for days without food, but when they do have good hunting they gorge themselves until flight is not too easy.

The lordly White-tailed Eagle is now extinct in these islands ; until recent years a pair nested in a giant crag in the Shetland Isles, but the Golden Eagle is fairly well distributed in some of the wilder parts of Scotland. This large bird preys on all creatures found on the mountain side ; lambs, fawns, grouse, mountain hares and rabbits form the chief food ; it is surprising what power these birds have, especially in lifting heavy objects.

On one occasion I was sitting against a rock immediately under a Golden Eagle's nest ; while waiting, I saw the Eagle returning with a large hare in its talons, as it came across the great valley it flew without the slightest effort, but when a few hundred yards from its eyrie it saw me, it dropped the food and quickly disappeared. Another day I was in a hide only thirty feet from the nest, and within half an hour from entering my shelter, both Eagles returned, one with a hare and the other with a grouse.

On the Welsh mountains the Buzzard takes the place of the Eagle ; in certain parts this fine bird of prey is fairly common, but you seldom find more than one pair in a large tract of moorland. Their territory may extend for three miles, then another pair is in evidence ; but we often find Ravens and Buzzards nesting within a few hundred yards of each other. The males, however, seem to wage a continuous warfare ; day after day when I have visited the districts, I have seen the two male birds circling around high up over the nest, one repeatedly striking at the other ; sometimes the females leave their nests and join in.

IN a Welsh wood I saw a pair of Kites and two Carrion Crows having a great fight ; it was a magnificent exhibition of aerial manœuvring ; as the graceful Kites with their long wings and forked tails glided backwards and forwards, the angry Crows rose above them, then darted down, attempting to strike in passing ; but the Kites, with better powers of flight simply moved to one side or the other, and the Crows, becoming more furious with each baffled attempt, at last gave up. The female Kite then glided down gracefully to her nest, while her mate took up a stand not far away where he could warn her of approaching danger.

In one Welsh dingle, a pair of Kestrels attempted to rear their young, but the Ravens which already had young in their nest, very much resented the appearance of the smaller birds. We saw many fights in the air high up above the glen. One spring morning the two male birds fought furiously, and it was a delight to watch the ease with which the Kestrel avoided the mad rushes of the Raven. The latter would rise fifty feet above the Hawk, then with wings brought to his side he came downwards like a great feathered dart.

The Kestrel, with just a flick of his wings, or a movement of his tail, slipped aside and made rings round the furious Raven as he returned to the attack. What finally happened was not easy to see, but the Kestrel evidently misjudged one of the Raven's attacks, and a moment later we saw the dead Kestrel tumbling over and over as it fell to the valley far below.

But even the powerful Raven has his enemies. At one nest the male was on guard during the night, but that cunning wild mammal the Polecat, stalked him in the darkness and succeeded in killing him. The hen continued to sit upon her eggs, and within twenty-four hours another male raven appeared ; the birds mated up, and the newcomer assisted in rearing the young birds when they arrived.

How Birds send Wireless Messages.

This "wireless" of the wilds is a wonderful thing ; I have known several instances of birds losing their mates, and yet without leaving the district another has turned up in a very short time. Some years ago a pair of White-tailed Eagles became parted, the male was trapped and shot, and although there was not another Eagle of that species within three or four hundred miles, another male arrived within a week !

All entomologists know that if the female of a rare Moth is captured and confined in a box, and if this is placed in a room with an open window, males will presently arrive, even if they have never been actually seen in that district.

The Buzzard builds rather a massive eyrie, that is, if it has been used on several occasions. As a rule a pair of Buzzards will build two nests in their territory, using them in alternate seasons. The eggs of this fine bird vary greatly. Some are very magnificent, while others are almost bare of markings.

Those birds which nest on the coasts of Devon and Cornwall where they are fairly common, find that there is plenty of food, and they will sometimes succeed in rearing four young, but on the bare Welsh hills where it is not always easy to find food, only one youngster is brought up. Three or four eggs are laid, and the birds leave their shells, but all except one disappear a few weeks later.

Photo : Arthnr Brook.] [Mondiale.

KESTREL AT NEST.
The Kestrel nests on lonely ledges, and is the farmer's friend, for whom it keeps down many small pests.

THE SMALLEST BRITISH FALCON.
The Merlin, which breeds on hill and moorland, is a very bold hunter, daring many dangers so that its young may be well fed. Although only about the size of a Blackbird it is very swift, and a deadly enemy of smaller birds.

Photo: Arthur Brook.] THE MEADOW-PIPIT'S FOSTER-CHILD. [Mondiale.
The Meadow-Pipit is one of the commonest birds seen among the hills. It gives shelter to another neighbour, the Cuckoo, and is seen here with its charge, which has grown many times larger than the foster-mother.

After the Buzzard has laid her first egg she commences to sit, two days later the second egg arrives, and another two days may elapse before the third is deposited. The result is that one youngster comes out of its egg six days or so before the last; this baby grows fairly quickly, and is, of course, much stronger than the small, weaker, nest companion.

WHEN the parents are absent from the nest for long periods searching for food, the youngsters in the eyrie become very impatient, and what often happens is that the first arrival pounces upon his weaker brothers and sisters,

haunts, where he picks up his game, are usually a good distance from the nest itself, although within a couple of miles. When he has captured a bird, the first thing is to kill it, then he removes the feathers; this is usually performed on a favourite mound. When he has plucked his prey he flies off to the nest, and when within about a hundred yards he calls his mate to him, and passes the food to her. She quickly returns to her family, and standing before them gives a small portion to each, eating the hard parts, such as the bones and skull herself. When the

Photo: Arthur Brook.] THE CROW'S FEAST [Mondiale.

The Carrion Crow, which is seen above at work on a dead sheep, is very fond of mutton, and scours the hills in eager search of any carcass. Its stout beak provides it with an excellent knife and fork.

kills and afterwards devours them! This remarkable incident, which takes place also in the nest of the Golden Eagle, has been filmed on several occasions.

One of the pluckiest birds of prey found on the large, open, mountain moors is the Merlin. This dashing little falcon is a great hunter, and there is little hope for a bird when once it gives chase. The nest is made on the ground among the coarse heather. Although the Merlin is persecuted by gamekeepers, I have known several instances of Grouse having brought up their young successfully within a few yards of a Merlin's nest.

The male does most of the hunting, and his

young are three weeks old, she will often throw the food to them, and allow them to pull it to pieces themselves.

In a lifetime spent in birdland, I have often come across instances which showed that birds are able to reason to a certain extent. One concerned a Merlin which was captured in a noose. One foot appeared to be fixed firmly in the stout, knotted piece of string, and for a time the bird struggled violently, but finding that this did not help, she sat down and carefully examined the knot; she looked at it for several minutes, turning her head from side to side, and at last carefully pulled at it with her beak; she found that by persevering she was able to loosen the knot, and eventually opened it to such an extent that she was able to step out a free bird.

The most musical sound to be heard on the mountains is the spring call of the Curlew. This large bird spends the winter months on the sea-shore, but in the very early spring it goes to the large, open spaces on the hillsides for nesting purposes. Although the eggs are large, they are not easy to find, for the bird seems exceedingly clever in selecting a spot for her nest which is difficult to come upon.

The foolish Bird that is really clever.

In the company of the Curlew we find other moor birds, all exceedingly wild : Golden Plovers, Redshanks, Snipe and Greenshanks, while on some of the lonely table-like tops of some of the most desolate mountains we come across that delightful little bird, the Dotterel. It prefers mountains over 3000 feet in height ; some say that it derived its name from dotard, because it is a foolish bird. It certainly shows no fear of man, for we can approach to within a few feet without its attempting to move, but when it has young it will attempt to attract an intruder from the nest by feigning a broken wing, and dragging itself along the ground, it

will lead him away for a distance of a hundred yards or more before taking to its wings.

The commonest bird to be found on the moorlands and mountain sides is undoubtedly the Meadow Pipit. Some think this bird is the commonest in the country in the summer months, but I give this distinction to the Willow Warbler. As we wander over the moors we flush Pipits every few hundred yards, but although the Merlin and other birds of prey take a large number of these birds, they continue to thrive and increase. The Meadow Pipit is undoubtedly the favourite fosterer of the Cuckoo, that strange bird around which so many fables have been woven. The Cuckoo also is a frequenter of many of these lonely, mountain moors.

To those who love the open spaces, the birds of the mountain have a wonderful fascination ; we have to travel long distances to observe them, and if we wish to see and study their habits we have to tramp over the roughest country. I have sometimes walked and climbed thirty miles in a day, and during the whole of that time have come across very few birds, but those which have been observed, and occasionally photographed, have more than recompensed me for my arduous labours.

A GATHERING OF WARBLERS.   [Charles Reid.

In the summer Willow Warblers are found in great numbers all over the countryside. Occasionally they winter here, but usually are birds of passage. Allied to the chiff-chaff family, they are sometimes called Willow-Wrens.

[Charles Reid.

The Woodcock often leads the sportsman a dance with its queer, dodging flight. Its plumage also is so harmonious with the background of trees among which it lives that it is often very difficult to distinguish.

GAME BIRDS

By IAN THOMSON

MOST birds are useful to us in some ways, but game birds are doubly welcome, both to the sportsman and the housewife. Nature has provided each with a sporting chance of evading its enemies—the Woodcock with its peculiar dodging flight, and the Grouse with its colouring that matches its lonely moorland home. The Partridge, too, another mark for the sportsman, harmonises with the stubble on which it crouches, so that there is no unfair conflict.

OUR game birds can be roughly divided into those of the hill and moorland, those of low-lying country and woodland, and those species which are border-line types, being sometimes found in both areas. I will speak first about those which frequent the low-lying.

Probably the Pheasant is the best known of any game bird, as its wonderful and varied plumage, with its typical long tail, when once seen are not at all likely to be forgotten. The Pheasant is not natural to the British Isles, but it has been so long established that we look upon it as one of our own birds. Much water has flown under the bridges since this attractive and useful bird first came to us, and it is not recorded when it was first introduced. It is thought that the Romans may have been the prime instigators of this introduction, but as there are several types or varieties of the bird, it may have been, and

probably was, traded here by different races who visited our islands, and at different times. Certainly the Chinese bird is recorded as being brought here some two hundred years ago, and owing to the crossing of this and the original bird from the district around the Black Sea, pure birds are non-existent.

As a table bird the Pheasant takes a great deal of beating ; probably for its size it has more flesh than any other bird which is eaten. The Pheasant cannot really be called a wild bird ! Semi-domesticated would be more akin to the truth in describing it. This is due to the care bestowed upon it by those who preserve the game on their land. These birds, on any estates where a lot of shooting takes place, are usually reared artificially.

There are several methods employed. Probably the most usual is the hatching of the eggs by hens which, after the chicks emerge, are placed in coops in what are known as the rearing fields. Some keepers employ different methods. On one estate as soon as the eggs begin to chip (that is, when the chick inside starts to crack its shell a little before it makes its way into the world) they are put into incubators and hatched out there and dried off in boxes before a fire for twenty-four hours before being put back with the hens.

This is a splendid method, as the tiny chicks by then are strong on their little legs and not so likely to be crushed by the heavy old barn-door foster parents. The chicks are fed and watered regularly on the rearing-field, and, apart from the food given them, find any amount of other food in the grass, such as seeds of many kinds and insects and grubs.

How the Pheasant is hoodwinked.

Most rearing is done after this method. The hen Pheasant is supported like a poor parent, but this has been rather disproved by a system known as the Euston system. This is varied slightly, but the main idea is the removal and chipping of the eggs under hens, pot eggs having been substituted under the Pheasant. The eggs are returned to the Pheasant when due to hatch. All eggs which are put into a nest being reckoned to produce a chick at about the same time. This is done because the hen Pheasant is known sometimes to leave a nest of eggs when only four or five chicks are hatched, the others drying in the shell. If they all emerge from the shell about the same time then she will have a good brood with her when she moves away with them as soon as they are strong enough to follow her.

In this country the Pheasant is polygamous, each cock as a rule having several hens. He, therefore, has nothing to do with the bringing up of his family. In the natural state these birds may be monogamous. The Pheasant is a woodland species roosting in trees at night, but nesting on the ground and feeding there, whereas the Partridge is a bird of the culti-vated farm land. This jolly little brown bird is probably almost as well known as the Pheasant, because of its protection by sports-men and by those who consider the bird as a very great delicacy for the table.

The Partridge is a good parent ; both birds rear the family and are extremely brave in the way they will attack any enemy that may threaten their tiny charges. During February the old birds begin to pair up again, and most amusing fights occur, the old birds running after each other and apparently going to harm each other quite seriously, but nothing much comes of it. The Partridge, without doubt, would be a comparatively rare bird if it were not for the protection it is afforded by owners of estates, who keep down vermin such as Stoats, Weasels, Rats, etc., which would prey on the eggs and young birds.

Being of a brown colour the Partridge seems to merge to a most marked degree into its surroundings, especially in stubble and in ploughed land. We might perhaps call even the Partridge a border-line bird in some cases, as I have seen the bird when shooting Grouse at quite an altitude, and in the heather. The Red-legged, a French Partridge, is not native to this country, but was introduced as far as records go about the end of the eighteenth century. It is bigger than our bird, and is identified by its barred sides and black-edged face and throat and red legs and feet.

The Frenchman gives the sportsman an excellent shot when on the wing, but it is much more inclined to run than take to the wing. I have often seen the birds " flick " over a hedge at the end of a field of roots after walking through these, the Common Partridge having long before left on the wing.

We must not fail to mention our smallest game bird, the Quail. It visits us, though rarely in large numbers, in the summer, arriving in May and leaving us usually in October. A few stop sometimes to winter with us. This sand bird is very clever at concealing itself, its small size aiding it in this respect, scanty growth affording it quick and suitable cover. It strongly resembles its larger cousin, the Partridge, in many respects, the general colour being a sandy buff.

The Bird with a dodging flight.

Before passing to the moorland species, mention should be made of that most sporting of birds, the Woodcock. This charming bird with its large eyes and well back audits, long bill and beautifully barred buff, black and brown feathering which make it so unlike any of the other game birds, is resident in the British Isles, though by far the greatest number of the birds seen and shot are immigrants from abroad. The Woodcock, as its name implies, is a bird of the woods. Here it nests quietly, and because of its wonderfully harmonious plumage merges so perfectly into its surround-ings that it is wellnigh impossible to see it until it is flushed, when it soon vanishes amongst the trees with its quaint, dodging flight. As a

Photo : O. G. Pike] THE PARTRIDGE GUARDS HER CLUTCH. [Mondiale.
This popular game-bird takes great pains to rear its brood in safety. Its nest, placed on the heather or under a bush, is made inconspicuous when the mother has to leave it by a covering of dead leaves and grass.

COMMON PHEASANT ON NEST. [*Niall Rankin.*

The best known of our game birds is often brought up with a hen acting as their foster-mother. Keepers collect the eggs, and have them hatched under their careful supervision, later letting the birds go free.

THE GROUSE AT HOME. [*Charles Reid.*

Grouse-shooting is a popular sport on the Scottish moors, where the birds are prolific. They are valued as table-birds. The cock is very handsome, with colourful plumage and crimson crest. The hen is of a quieter appearance.

rule it will drop down again ahead and can be flushed as before.

Recently when walking through a rather thick wood, I flushed a Woodcock and it went dashing away and appeared to settle well ahead. It was flushed like this three times. The nest is placed in the dead leaves in a wood, and when the bird is sitting immovable it is practically impossible to see her. It is only the large eye which enables one eventually to make out the rest of her body. The birds sit very tight, and unless they are practically trodden on will not leave their eggs.

THERE are many stories of the Woodcock carrying away their young ones, and the different methods employed. The usually accepted method is the carrying of the chick between the thighs. If the chick slips slightly the appearance of it being carried in the feet may be seen, and at such times the old bird may place its bill almost perpendicular with its body and hold the chick by pressing against it with the mandibles.

We can now move to the hill country with its heather, bogs, small pools, and streams or burns as they call them in the north, which are replaced the higher we go by close growing grass and rocky mountain crops. As we reach the heather country we will probably before long be startled by a whirr of wings and a dark brown bird with a flight which resembles that of the Partridge. When we hear his call, " Cock, cock, cock," and in landing a threatening, " Go back, go back, go back," we have put up our first cock Grouse, or Red Grouse, to give him his correct name to distinguish him from his cousin, the Black Grouse, to be mentioned later.

I remember well photographing a Herring Gull here and noticing chicks of a few days' old being fed by what I thought was egg. After I came away from my " hide " I went over to the nest and found nine Pheasant eggs together under a dock leaf. These had been brought from the mainland to this island by the old Gulls, and from the two broods of Grouse I saw in three weeks on this moor, which to me seemed ideal for them, I have no doubt that the eggs went the same way as the Pheasant's, which were so appreciated by the young Gulls.

Grouse vary in their numbers considerably from year to year on a moor, even if it has been heavily shot over, in fact, unless the old birds are kept down the stock will suffer considerably. Too many birds may bring in

THE SNIPE. [*Niall Rankin.*

This long-beaked bird, found in marshland, is a mark for the huntsman, who considers its flesh a delicacy.

disease, and hundreds of birds may perish due to this. I remember being stationed during the War in Scotland in 1916, and having to visit a company of men under instruction on a rifle range up on the moors. Here the Grouse had not been shot for two years and the stock had increased considerably. The birds seemed to be everywhere, and I fear occasionally were bagged with a service rifle—all against King's regulations, of course. I heard later that disease set in and this splendid stock of birds was sadly depleted. I mentioned the Grouse and heather, but the bird is found in many areas almost devoid of heather. A small shoot I knew in Scotland, which was more of the Green Deer Forest type of country, held quite a number of Grouse, and in this locality there is little doubt the birds subsisted on the Blackberry and such plants which abounded there.

The cock Grouse is a handsome bird with his chestnut-red plumage barred with many black lines, and his erect, crimson crest. The hen as a rule is more spotted and shows sometimes a good deal of white.

On this shoot I went on there were rocky hills rising to the 3000-foot contour, and here I first saw the Ptarmigan or White Grouse.

The summer plumage of the Ptarmigan is mostly grey with speckled, wavy lines of black. It is the winter plumage which most of us know best, as we see White Grouse hanging in poulterers' shops. Except for the black on the tail the white plumage is outstanding ; in snow it is nearly impossible to detect the bird.

How the Black Cock does his wooing.

Probably the most striking of the Grouse family is the male of the Black Grouse, the Black Cock. What could be finer than this grand fellow with his glossy, blue-black plumage, brown wings with their white bar, and his white undertail feathers surmounted by the wonderful and well-known lyre-like tail. In the spring, the cocks assemble at certain spots and go through the most remarkable gyrations and displays, scrapping with each other and beating with their wings, little damage being done, however. The ladies, much attracted by the showing-off of their prospective mates, collect on the outskirts of the sparring ground, and eventually the successful suitors depart with their wives, polygamy being practised by these gay suitors.

The hens are quite different in plumage and are known as grey hens in spite of being more reddy buff, mottled and barred with black. Both birds have a red wattle above their eyes, but the cocks, as is general, are much more easily marked than the hens.

Mention must be made also of that very large bird, the Capercailie. It was originally natural to the pine forests of this country, but became extinct, I think, some time in the seventeen hundreds. It has been since produced from Scandinavia and is to be found in suitable localities in Scotland, though it is never common. The cock is a huge fellow, with a grey-black general plumage and a striking whitish and strong curved bill. The hen is about a third of his size and much resembles the Grey Hen. The food value of the Caper is not of much note, as it has a turpentine flavour due to its fondness for the young shoots of the pine trees.

The Snipes, are long-billed birds like the Woodcock, and are frequenters of the marshy and muddy areas of the streams. The Common Snipe is resident in the British Isles, and as spring approaches we may hear that strange drumming sound made by the birds as they fly high in the air, diving and twisting downwards. This drumming is made by the two cut tail feathers, and although some people state that it is made only when flying into the wind, I have heard the sound made by a bird as it flies in a large circle and as it turns to every point of the compass.

Photo : Arthur Brook.] THE CAPERCAILIE. [Mondiale.

This big game bird, formerly almost extinct, but now reintroduced into Scotland, provides good sport, but is not much favoured as a table bird. Its fondness for the shoots of pine trees gives its flesh an unpleasant flavour.

In flight, the white-plumaged Gannet, with its black wing feathers, presents a wonderful sight. It has an enormous wing spread, and travels great distances, without any appearance of strain, to seek the fish on which it feeds.

BRITISH SEA BIRDS

By PETER WEBSTER

WHO that loves the Sea does not love the Sea Birds also—their noisy clamour on the rocky islets and the sheer clean beauty of their flight? Gull and Gannet, Guillemot and Tern, they are a joy to watch as they mount and soar and swerve with the very rhythm and motion of the sea. They are clad in the sea's livery, too, in the grey of the waves, the stark black of the rocks, and the dazzling whiteness of the spray.

WHO that has visited a Sea Bird colony in the nesting season will ever forget the whirling, screaming clouds of birds which arise into the air to scold the visitors?

To most of us it is inconceivable that so many birds can find room and food to exist in such concentrated masses. Yet from the fact that they persist in returning year after year in ever-increasing numbers to the same site is proof that they not only do exist, but live well.

When one considers the thousands of small fishes which must be collected and consumed in the immediate vicinity of their breeding haunts for three months of the year, it is a mystery how certain species of fish are not entirely exterminated in these local patches of the sea.

In a suitable colony, such as the Farne Islands, one would see three or four species of Gulls and of Terns, also Puffins, Guillemots, Razorbills, Cormorants, Shags, and a few representatives of the Duck family. Gannets —the largest of the sea fowl—are found on a few isolated sites, but when they are found they are there in countless thousands.

It is striking to observe how the various species separate themselves into cliques, according to the nature of the ground and overlap or intermingle with another species only in exceptional cases.

The Terns (which are the smallest of the Gull family) are always the most interesting. In some sites their eggs are so numerous that it is difficult to walk amongst them without crushing them. In the case of the Sandwich (the largest), and the Lesser (the smallest), the eggs are laid on the bare sand or shingle. The wonderful variety of markings on the Sandwich Tern's egg makes them the most sought after by the collector.

The Terns are easily distinguished from the Gulls by their longish, pointed bills, short neck, and forked tail. They range in size from about that of a Pigeon to that of a Thrush. The Common and the Arctic Terns are so much alike that they have to be handled to see the distinguishing colour and markings of their beaks.

These two species appear to have progressed a stage further than the remainder of the Terns. They make a nest which in quite a number of cases is equally as good as a Gull's.

The Tern's distinguishing screech.

The Roseate Tern, which is very scarce, is usually represented by a few pairs breeding with Common Terns. Again the colour of the beak is the distinguishing feature, but in addition to those who have a finely trained ear, its screech will be found to be different from that of its confrères. The eggs of all these three species vary so much in ground colour and markings that it is impossible to identify them definitely.

The Terns feed on small fish which they catch by diving—or so-called diving, for it is more splash than dive—accomplished by closing their wings and dropping headlong into the sea often from a good height. In flight they are as graceful as the Swallow, and, as a matter of fact, are oftener referred to as " Sea Swallows " rather than Terns. All the Terns nest on the ground, and two or three eggs are laid.

Terns are a good guide to the fisherman, indicating where the shoals of fish are feeding. When the Terns hunt in flocks, screeching themselves hoarse, it is a sure indication that they have found a school of fry fleeing from a shoal of fish. Taking the Terns all round, they are very gentle and attractive ; not so with the Gulls, however.

We may start off with the huge Great Black Back Gull, which, by the way, is the real Big Bad Wolf of the Gull family. It is as big as a Goose and much more powerful, but, thank goodness, there are very rarely more than one pair of them in a sea bird colony. This big Gull will gouge out the eyes of a sheep if he finds one on its back, and would then gobble up a whole brood of young Ducks or a nest of eggs—all at a meal.

Then his smaller brother, the Lesser Black Back Gull, in common with the Herring Gull, is not much better. These two are about the size of a Duck, and are the commonest Gulls we see round our shores and harbours for nine months of the year. The mottled grey specimens which predominate in numbers at the end of the summer are not a separate species, but merely the young birds of the two foregoing Gulls. They do not assume the adult plumage until their fourth year. These two Gulls will neither work nor want, but love to prey on the smaller Gulls.

How the Gulls bully each other.

As the tide is ebbing they hang around the rocky shore waiting for the water to be shallow enough for them to dive after anything in the form of food. (Gulls cannot dive in the true sense of the word.) It is always the smallest Gull which takes the plunge first and then the fun begins—but not for the diver, whose first frantic endeavour after securing the food is to swallow it. This, however, does not save him from the persecution of the larger Gulls, who pursue him indefinitely until in desperation he is compelled to disgorge his tit-bit, which is immediately pounced upon by the bully.

Another favourite trick of these gulls, particularly the Lesser Black Back, is to watch for the Ducks being disturbed from their nests, leaving so hurriedly that they have not time to cover over their eggs. The reason why the Ducks pluck the down from their breasts when

SELF-POSSESSION. [Robert McLeod.
This baby Arctic Tern maintains his balance—and his poise—on the extreme edge of an unscalable cliff.

Photo: *Arthur Brook.*   THE GULL COMES HOME.   [*Mondiale.*

The Black-headed Gull likes to stay near the water even when nesting, and builds a peculiar home among water-plants in marshy ground or on the edge of an inland lake. Its brood usually consists of three eggs.

THE GREATER BLACK-BACKED GULL.   [Mallinson.

This bird, as big as a goose and far more fierce and powerful, is looked upon as a fearful ogre by smaller sea-birds. Its appetite is so great that it takes a whole brood of young ducklings to satisfy its needs.

sitting is not only to make a lining for their nests, but principally to form a warm, protective covering with which to hide the eggs when they leave the nest voluntarily to feed.

There is no trick too low or food too dirty for the Black Backs. They are in many colonies shot down by the keepers and watchers. The only time I have ever seen a Black Back Gull work hard for his own food was one winter's day when I heard something drop ahead of me on the shore. It proved to be one of these beauties flying up into the air with a mussel in his beak, dropping it on to a large boulder. I watched him for some time and noticed that it took three or four repetitions of the process before he swallowed the mussel and went after another.

The wise Bird that builds for safety.

The Gulls adhere religiously to the same type of nesting site. The Greater Black Back picks on some promontory away by himself where he can watch a visitor approaching and slip off to sea in plenty of time before he is recognised. These Gulls are difficult to distinguish from the lesser variety as size is deceptive when they are on the wing, but if one can get close enough, the pink legs of the Greater always distinguish him from the Lesser, which has yellow legs.

The Lesser Black Back Gulls always select the tufty grass on the top of some sea-bound rock when they can find such a site where they will be undisturbed. There they will then nest in colonies, but otherwise they are found in single pairs dotted about the cliffs. It is not, however, uncommon for them to nest inland.

The Herring Gull always selects the upper recesses and shelves of the marine island cliffs for its nesting site, but keeps well away from the Kittiwakes, who are lower down the cliffs. Most Gulls lay three eggs in a well-formed nest, and the colour and markings of one species closely resemble those of the others.

The smallest of the Common Gulls (the " Common " Gull is the rarest) is the Kittiwake —the daintiest of them all in habits and form.

I have seen a whole flock of them, composed of thousands of birds, spend hours hovering over a wounded member of their own species, which was floating on the sea, in their endeavour to assist the disabled bird.

This Gull has fixed ideas in so far as a nesting site is concerned. They are always to be found on the face of the cliffs on projecting ledges and recesses nearer the bottom than the

Photo : Arthur Brook.]   *[Mondiale.*
THE GULL'S NEST.
The Common Gull, the rarest member of the Gull family, is seen alighting on its nest. Its eggs are edible.

Herring Gull ; never on the top of the rocks. They live peacefully together, even when their nests are touching each other.

I ONCE picked out with my glasses what appeared to be a newly formed colony of Kittiwakes on an easily accessible grassy slope on one side of an island where the Kittiwakes had never nested before, and which I knew to be entirely unsuitable for them. The birds were very numerous and closely packed together. On the boat approaching closer the birds made off, when it could be seen that what had once been a grassy, sloping bank now looked more like a ploughed field. The Kittiwakes had simply been digging up the short grass by the roots for the purpose of lining their nests.

Next to the Gulls, the Guillemots predominate in the colony. These and the Razorbills are of similar form and habit, but the Razorbills, as their name implies, have a broad, razor-shaped beak as compared with the Guillemot's sharp-pointed beak.

They are all classed as divers by the fishermen. This misnomer is not far wrong, as they

Photo : *O. G. Pike.*] THE FULMAR PETREL TURNS ON HER NEST. [*Mondiale.*
Thousands of these beautiful birds are found on the cliffs of the lonely island of St. Kilda, where they used to
form the chief food supply of the natives. For winter use, their bodies were salted and packed away in boxes.

A CORMORANT COLONY.   [*Robert McLeod.*

These birds are renowned for their remarkable speed in swimming and their powers of diving deeply in search of fish.   They have voracious appetites, collecting an extra supply of food in the pouches at their throats.

are certainly expert divers. They use their wings more than their feet, when under water, and can travel submerged long distances away from the place where they dive.

Guillemots are extremely interesting, if it is only from the incredible jam at the nesting site. They are always on the flattened top of the rock and in a solid mass. So congested are they in some seasons that the birds returning from fishing land blindly into the centre of the mob and slowly shuffle their way to their own particular few square inches. This means that those on the outside edge are constantly being bumped off into the sea, which results in a more or less constant circulation. The heat of their feet is quite enough to keep the incubation of the egg going, so that no great harm is done by the everlasting jockeying for position.

The Razorbills are found in small bunches lower down on the face of the cliff. The single, sharply pointed egg of these two species is laid on the bare rock. If the bird leaves in a hurry, the egg cannot roll off the ledge owing to its shape, but simply rolls round in a small circle. The peculiar croaking call they use is distinctive from the hiss of the Guillemot.

Puffins are the next most numerous, and can run a good second to any rabbit at digging out a nesting hole. They burrow into the peaty deposits on the ledges of the rocks, or sometimes take entire possession of a peat-covered island and absolutely honeycomb the ground with their burrows.

If a visitor lands quietly on one of these islands it looks deserted, until something warns the sitting Puffin of danger. Then, as though by magic, there is a funny little parrot-like bird with gaily coloured beak at the mouth of every burrow, waiting for somebody to say "go." When off they go like a white cloud with their bright orange feet dangling.

A Colour Scheme inside an Egg.

They lay a single dirty white egg at the end of their burrow, and as there is no one in the burrow to admire any colourings or markings such as we find on the Gulls' and Terns' eggs, they put some violet blotches and markings inside the shell, no doubt for the entertainment of the little Puffin chick inside the egg. No other bird seems to have thought of this colour scheme.

A Puffin in the nesting time is a totally different bird from one in the autumn or winter. He grows especially for the mating

Photo : O. G. Pike.]   A PARTY OF PUFFINS.   *[Mondiale.*
These birds, because of their comic appearance, are sometimes called the clowns of birdland. They are found in large colonies on St. Kilda. Their nest is a dark burrow in the ground, and their brood consists of one solitary egg.

Photo : P. Webster.] ON THE EDGE OF THE CLIFF. [*Mondiale.*

Razorbills seem to delight in perching themselves in precarious positions and even deposit their eggs—without building a nest—on narrow cliff ledges. The eggs are so shaped that there is no fear of them rolling over.

season a huge, crudely-coloured, parrot-like beak, but man-like, when the family is reared and he is getting rather fed up with life, he sheds his bright beak and slips back into his real old, shabby, unattractive self : not unlike a common Guillemot.

Before leaving him, however, there is one clever little trick one must give him credit for which many another sea bird would give a lot to learn. He comes ashore with eight or nine small fishes in his beak, all held by the head or tail—but how does he open his beak to catch the last one without losing all the others ?

Why " Old Nick " keeps to himself.

Cormorants, referred to by the fishermen as " Old Nick," and their crested smaller relations, the Shags, are not found in all sea bird colonies, but where they are they are well worth seeing. Cormorants like a ledge of rock or an island all to themselves, or probably it would be nearer the truth if one admitted that they had to keep to themselves. They are so filthy in their habits that no other self-respecting bird would mix with them.

Shags prefer the dark interior of some inaccessible cave where they croak away all to themselves like a lot of old men. Both these

birds build a bulky nest of dried seaweed and lay several eggs of a greenish ground colour, thickly coated with a white, chalky substance. It is very remarkable that they never appear to have time to whitewash completely the green shell before the egg is laid ; there are nearly always a few patches left uncovered. The Gannet is another of these birds with the white-washing habit.

It is common belief amongst fishermen that a Cormorant eats several times its own weight of fish in a day. He is an expert diver and can swallow a half-pound of fish easily. I once took an exhausted Cormorant from the water with a six-inch flat fish lodged sideway in its throat. The only way it could be released was to take the bird ashore and cut the fish out with a pair of scissors.

The Cormorant's flight is very laboured and close to the water, and it takes it a long time to gain any altitude. The penalty for a visit to a Cormorant colony is at least a new suit and boots. No washing or cleaning will remove the aroma left by walking through a twelve-inch layer of droppings and decomposed fish.

The young Cormorants are not fed like other birds. As soon as the parent arrives ashore with the morning's catch, there is a mad scramble amongst the brood of four or five youngsters to see who can get his head, and very nearly his shoulders, into his father's crop to help himself. Any fish that is dropped in this process is allowed to remain round the nest, with the result that fish in varying degrees of decomposition is found in abundance round every nest in the island.

Eider-downs in their living form.

Other interesting sea fowl which associate with the Gulls and diving birds are the Ducks. The Eider Duck, famous at least in " down quilt " form, is very numerous on some islands, although entirely unknown in many districts. They are exceptionally timid, except in the nesting season, when the very reverse is the case. It is not unusual for the female to allow one to stroke her back when sitting on her eggs. What with the collectors of eggs, the collectors of down, the marauding of the Gulls, the damage by rats, it is rarely that the full clutch of five eggs is reared.

A sitting bird harmonises with the surroundings to a remarkable degree. So much so that often the first warning one has of the Duck's presence is that she has been flushed off her nest owing to being touched. This is the sole reason why visitors are not welcomed to the Eider Duck colonies. The large Gulls are ever on the watch for uncovered eggs which are then quite conspicuous. The males are hand-some birds in common with most of the Duck family ; whereas all the females might be said to conform to a standard drab pattern. Although wonderful divers, they appear to feed exclusively on the numerous varieties of shell fish, swallowing shell and all.

The Gannet is the largest of the sea fowl which nest round our shores in colonies. On sites like the Bass Rock and Ailsa Craig they come ashore in their thousands to nest and make a wonderful sight. They have an enormous wing spread and travel long distances in search of food, which they catch by dropping perpendicularly from a great height on to the unwary fish, making a tremendous splash. It is a wonderful exhibition of flight to sit on a Gannet rock and watch the endless procession of birds soaring past one, effortless and graceful in the extreme.

Their single large, chalky egg is laid in an enormous bulky nest composed of decayed seaweed, placed on the recesses and shelves of their chosen site. They are exceptionally tame when visited, and allow one to approach within a few yards of them, when they waddle to the edge of the rock and jump off. Like many other birds with long wings, they find great difficulty in rising from the ground, or even from the surface of the sea.

Then there are Petrels, Shearwaters, and other rare sea fowl to be met with on some of the remoter, unfrequented islands, but not generally in the average colony of sea birds.

GANNET ALIGHTING. [*Niall Rankin.*

Here is an exquisite study of a Gannet alighting on its nest—a casual affair of grass and seaweed. This large **sea bird,** known also as the Solan Goose, breeds on the Bass Rock in the Firth of Forth and in Ireland.

The most graceful of our water birds is welcomed on lake and river where it adds a decorative touch to the surroundings. The Swan, seen above with its fluffy brood of cygnets, looks very proud of its family.

WATER BIRDS

By IAN THOMSON

OUR lakes and inland waters are brightened by the presence of the feathered creatures that make their homes near the edge of the water and swim gracefully, as only a bird can. Of these, the swan, duck and geese family are the most conspicuous and are each dealt with in this chapter. Their interesting habits and curious water-side homes are described.

WATER has a fascination for most of us, and especially so when we think of the many happy moments we have spent watching the wild life associated with it. We may have been sailing on the tranquil waterways of the Norfolk Broads, fishing from the shores of some Highland tarn, or perhaps merely watching the cattle drinking from some picturesque pond whilst on one of those delightful holidays spent at a kindly farm.

On all these waters, if we are imbued with just a little of that power to notice things which we call observation, and have learnt to move without much noise, we can see the numerous types of bird life which the different areas and their varied waterways hold for us. Even if we are unable to visit any of these places mentioned, the parks with their lakes in our cities and towns usually have a variety of water birds swimming on their smooth surfaces.

Most of us associate the Ducks more than any other species with water. The Mallard or Common Wildduck is probably the best known to most of us ; the Drake, with his yellowish bill and lovely, glossy green head and neck with a white ring, his chestnut breast and grayish back with curled up, black, tail feather, and, we must not forget, the greenish purple wing stripe which is so noticeable. His mate with her general plumage mottled with brown and buff is much more subdued, but it is she who rears the family, and her feathering is so designed by Nature in order that she becomes practically invisible when sitting on her nest, or hiding in the reeds with her flotilla of tiny ducklings.

All the Ducks pluck the down from their under breast and line their nests with it, forming a wonderfully warm lining which helps to prevent the eggs from becoming unduly chilled if they are left for any length of time. The Drake towards the end of May starts to emulate a plumage similar to the Duck, and as his quills are usually cast at the same time, he is unable to fly until he has passed through the moult. Here again this mottled plumage assists him, in his adversity, to hide from his many enemies, until he has once more acquired his resplendent gown and the power to rise rapidly from the reed beds, where he has been so secluded.

That jolly little diving bird, the Tufted Duck, is probably the next best known to the majority of people, and it is to be seen on most of our park lakes. The Drakes with their black and white plumage and long crest and brilliant, golden yellow eyes, and their more sombre Ducks, with sooty brown plumage, are easily identified. Their diving is a joy to watch as they leap into the air before taking a " header " in search of aquatic plants and other such food. I always remember the thrill I had when photographing this bird in the south of Scotland. I was being rowed on a loch by the old keeper, and I suggested that some reedy spots on the shore might be suitable for them to nest amongst, but he assured me that they never nested there, choosing only the islands with which the loch was studded. We searched some of these without avail, and, seeing a pair of Great Crested Grebes swimming from a larger area of reeds on the shore as we approached, I tactfully asked him if he would put me ashore at that spot to see if I could find their nest. I had not moved more than fifteen yards when I flushed a Tufted Duck from her nest of eight eggs.

Snapping a Feathered Beauty.

I photographed her some days later from a hide I had gradually erected, and it was charming to watch her quietly swimming up to her nest to a platform of trodden down reeds beside it. There she sat and preened herself for some minutes before jumping on to the side of her nest and eventually settling on her eggs. The moisture in the feathers of these water birds helps to soften the hard shell as incubation reaches its completion, and so assists the ducklings to emerge successfully from their eggs.

In the winter these Ducks are shot, as are the Mallard, and provided they have been feeding on vegetable matter and not animal, they are very good to eat. The Common Teal, so called to differentiate it from its rarer cousin the Garganey Teal, is most abundant during the winter, when large numbers of it arrive here from abroad—our winters being less severe than in the countries which they leave to visit us. The Teal breeds in most areas of the British Isles, though in many it is scarce.

The Common Teal Drake is a very charming little fellow with his blackish bill, chestnut brown cheeks and nape which show off to perfection a wonderful elongated area of green behind his eye. His upper parts are delicately marked with black and white. This bird also has a bright green patch on the wing. The Duck is mottled with brown and her wing patch is not so brilliant as her handsome little mate. As in the case of the Mallard the Drake goes into the eclipse plumage during the moult, assuming again his striking dress in October.

The Bird with the shovel-like Beak.

Probably the most striking Drake in the Duck family is the Shoveller, whose lead-coloured bill and yellow eye are shown up to perfection, being set in a head and upper neck of green suddenly changing to white on the lower neck and chest. The featherings on the middle of the back are dark brown and the shoulders a pale blue. The wing coverts being white and the secondary feathers dark brown in conjunction with the almost black rump tail and primary feathers make the Shoveller Drake a magnificent sight on a frosty spring morning as he flies overhead, showing his chestnut breast and belly and reddish legs.

The Duck, as in the other species, has a mottled brown plumage, but her eye is brown. I have seen many Shoveller nests on the dry marshes of Norfolk, and each time I see these birds I admire them more and marvel at their strange, spatulated bill with which they seem to suck along the surface of the water.

The other species of Duck we may find on our waterways are not as common, although vast numbers sometimes arrive in winter, such as the Pochard and Widgeon, both of which breed sparingly at times with us.

The Grebes are another race of water birds which can be seen in suitable localities, the most common being the Great Crested Grebe and the Little Grebe, which is also known as the Dabchick. Grebes are divers and are streamlined, to use a modern expression, their long, tapered bodies being well adapted to their underwater habits. Their legs are placed far back on the body, making it wellnigh impossible for them to travel on land. Their feet, too, are strangely webbed, not right across as in the case of the Ducks, but each toe is separate with a flange-like web to each.

The male Great Crested Grebe is a most handsome bird with his crest and head dark brown, and whitish cheeks : his back and

Photo : O. G. Pike.] THE SHOVELLER DUCK. [Mondiale.

The Shoveller, a handsome duck with many-coloured plumage has, as its name suggests, a very broad beak which is useful to it at meal-times. The Drake, especially, has a very colourful appearance when on the wing.

THE WILD DUCK'S NEST. [Mondiale.

The nest of the Wild Duck is lined with down plucked from the mother-bird's breast. This provides a warm shelter for the Ducklings. The females have a loud voice, but their cry is only feebly echoed by the males

Photo: F. Frankenhauser.]   THE ELEGANT HERON.   [Mondiale.

This great bird, easily distinguished by its long neck, beak and legs, has a slow, flapping manner of flight.
Its nest is usually made in the tree-tops, though sometimes it is found in reed-beds. It is an expert fisher.

Photo : Arthur Brook.]　　　　GREAT CRESTED GREBE.　　　　[Mondiale.

Grebes are well fitted for underwater activities, being expert divers and having webbed feet.   They make floating
nests of water plants, and have their legs placed so far back on their body that they find progress difficult on land.

Photo: R. Atkinson.] THE MOORHEN'S NEST. [Mallinson.

The Moorhen, or Water-hen, jerks its head and tail in a queer manner as it swims. It wages perpetual war, as do most water-fowl, with the rats that infest the water-side and are always eager for a meal of young birds.

A BROOD OF YOUNG SHELDRAKES. [Charles Reid.

The Shelduck, with its striking contrast of plumage, has some of the characteristics of a goose and some of a duck. It is an ornamental addition to ponds, but is often found on flat coasts, sometimes nesting in an old rabbit-hole.

upper parts are dark brown and his under parts silvery white. The legs are olive green. The hen is smaller, with not quite such a large crest.

Fortunately this bird has increased in numbers since the ladies gave up the dreadful habit of wearing Grebe boas and such additions to their finery, with the result that the poor birds are not slaughtered to meet this demand. The Grebes make a floating nest of dead water plants, and it is attached or moored, shall we put it, to reeds or other herbage in the water. On the slightest sign of an enemy they rapidly hide their eggs by pulling nesting material over them and quickly dive, rising to the surface some distance away, often first showing only their head, submerging their bodies and so attracting very little attention.

As the nest is usually awkward to approach except with a boat, photography or observation is extremely difficult. I was able to take a few photographs and watch the birds at the nest some years ago by being fortunate enough to find a nest fairly close to a hard shore, but it was not until I heard of a pair of birds which refused to leave their nest even when one approached quite close to them that I was able really to study them as I had always wished.

Three of us hired a boat and went out to where the nest was situated. There was the old Grebe sitting on her nest, and as we approached I expected her to move away as I had always seen before. All that happened was that she showed her obvious dislike of an intruder on her privacy by greeting us with squawks and much puffing up of her feathers and shaking of her head.

When we got some twelve feet away, or perhaps even less, the cock bird suddenly rose from a dive beside the nest and jumped up beside his mate. She then left, and so, gently nosing the boat to the nest, I leant over to stroke the sitting cock—only to be pecked by his dagger-like bill. I offered him a long reed, which he held on to, and I gently pulled him off the nest into the water. This did not perturb him, he simply let go and jumped on to the nest again and settled down.

WE spent two most entertaining days with this pair of Great Crested Grebes and saw the many aspects of their life at the nest : for example, the change over as one bird relieved the other ; the obvious annoyance if a boat passed nearby ; and even the strange sight of the bird tucking its head into its back feathers and going to sleep within eight feet of us.

I spent a holiday in the west of Scotland one year and in a loch there with reedy sides I saw several pairs of Dabducks. What dainty little fellows they looked as they floated buoyantly on the surface, with their head and upper parts brown and their chestnut cheeks and neck ! There were several of their little floating nests, and many times I tried to stalk a nest near the bank to see if I could surprise the bird from her eggs without her covering them up. However much I succeeded in getting close to her she always managed hurriedly to cover her treasures. One day, while fishing from a boat on this loch I saw the newly-hatched chicks having their first swim. After some difficulty I managed to catch one in a landing-net and was able to examine those strange feet I have already tried to describe.

Other kinds of Grebe are on the British list such as the Slavonia Red Necked and Black Necked Grebes, but they are so rare that one can only mention them in passing.

The Water-hen or Moor-hen can be seen in most ponds and stretches of water with its

Photo : O. G. Pike.]   A RARE GREBE.   [*Mondiale.*

This Black-necked Grebe is so rare that it is seldom photographed. Here it has been caught on its nest.

quaint jerking of head and tail as it swims or moves about the banks. The name Moor-hen is really " mire " hen or marsh hen, and has nothing whatever to do with the word moor as we know it to-day. The nest is usually a bulky affair built of dry reeds, sedge and flags more or less woven together, and can be found mostly in moist situations attached to water-plants or tree roots. It is sometimes placed in a tree which is quite high above the water.

Out of the Nest and into the Water.

One pair of birds make their nest every year in a hawthorn bush overhanging a pond, and the tiny, greyish brown Ducks, with their dull green legs and beak are first toppled out of the nest into the water with apparently no harm to them whatever. Rats are a very great source of trouble to most young aquatic birds and in this case it is a much depleted brood that reaches maturity.

The Coot is found in much greater stretches of water than the Moor-hen and builds a similar type of nest though larger ; the eggs are of one colour and speckled with tiny dark spots, whereas the Moor-hen's are buffish, speckled with reddish brown and sometimes purplish underspots. The Coot is quite distinguishable from its cousin, as it has not the jerking movements and is sooty black in plumage with a most noticeable patch of pure white on the forehead. From this white mark it has often been known as the Bald Coot. In Norfolk vast numbers can be seen in the winter, having come to us from the frozen districts abroad, and organised shoots are at times arranged, the spoil being divided amongst the local villagers, who skin and stew them, much to the disgust of the village butchers.

We all know the familiar Swans of our parks and ornamental waters and the story of the Ugly Duckling. A Cygnet (the young Swan), however, is a quite attractive little bird and far from ugly. The species of Swan usually seen is the Mute, but Wild Swans, such as the Whooper or Bewick, visit our shores in the winter, but are very timid in their nature.

THE COOT'S RETREAT.
On inland waters this slaty-black bird with a white bill can be found nesting on water-plants and dry rushes. The expression " bald as a coot," has arisen from the fact that this bird has an unfeathered patch on its forehead.

Photo : Mrs. M. Livingston.]　　　　　　　　　　　　　　　　　　　　　　　　　　　[Mallinson.
Although the Blackbird does good in disposing of grubs, the destruction it causes outweighs its usefulness.
Fruit-growers find that its appetite is too keen for their liking and that it is appeased too often with their fruit.

FRIENDS AND FOES OF THE BIRD WORLD

By HAROLD BASTIN

NO matter how much we welcome the gay companionship of the birds, there are some with which we can never be friendly, and when we see the havoc they cause to garden produce we are inclined to forget the leaven of their sweet song. Others, however, are applauded for their activities, and the energetic way in which they dispose of destructive pests wins the approval of the gardener. Their case, for and against, is stated below, and the reader is left to choose which of our feathered friends are worthy of his notice.

APART from the Game Laws, no measure for the protection of wild birds in Britain existed before the year 1880. Prior to this date, gamekeepers and farmers had been in the habit of destroying at sight all kinds of birds that they suspected of being injurious, in however small a degree ; and it must be added that they rarely, if ever, gave any species the benefit of the doubt. For example, that wholly insectivorous bird, the Nightjar, which is of the utmost importance to forestry, has suffered such persistent persecution as a " Hawk " by successive generations of unintelligent gamekeepers that it is now a comparative rarity. So, too, with the Barn-owl, the Brown-owl, and the Kestrel, all of which do far more good than harm, whatever the rustic wiseacres may say to the contrary. It is true that the Kestrel occasionally works havoc among young Pheasants ; but careful

investigation has brought to light the fact that such misdemeanours are usually chargeable to the Sparrow-hawk—a species whose protection in this country cannot reasonably be advocated, not only on account of its overfondness for game and poultry, but also because it destroys a certain number of wild birds which are actually beneficial to agriculture.

There can be little doubt that the passing of the first Wild Bird Protection Act in 1880, as well as much subsequent legislation aimed at achieving the same end, although conceived with the best intentions, led to results which were largely unexpected, and to a certain extent undesirable. Too much attention was paid to the behests of inconsequent bird-lovers, too little to the interests of farmers, fruit-growers, etc. Hence, Sir Walter Gilbey had behind him the wellnigh unanimous support of expert opinion when in 1910 he wrote : " Bird protection within reasonable limits is an excellent thing, but sentimental ideas cannot be allowed to over-ride practical considerations, and those who know the extent of the injury done by birds will agree that protection has been carried too far." One obvious result of the wholesale protection of wild birds is the very large increase of certain vigorous and pushful species at the expense of others which can be ill spared.

The Starling's good and bad points.

Again, a reciprocal alternation in the habits of two or more species may take place. Thus, authorities are pretty generally agreed that our Starling population has increased enormously during the present century, this being due in part to immigration from abroad, but mainly to the protection afforded to wild birds in general. Now the food of the Starling is in normal circumstances not very dissimilar to that of the Rook and the Jackdaw. Hence, these larger birds have been forced to forage more widely. They pillage large quantities of the farmer's grain, consume much fruit, and devour the eggs not only of game birds, but of many ground-nesting species—including the Lapwing, or Plover, than which " there is no bird more beneficial to the cultivator." The moral seems to be that the good deeds of the Starling and the Rook—to say nothing of the Jackdaw—would outweigh their bad ones, if only these birds were less numerous than, in fact, they are.

During recent years much valuable work has been done in " economic ornithology "— that is to say, the study of birds in so far as they affect the interests of mankind as a whole, and especially those of the agriculturist ; so that it is now possible to draw reliable conclusions with regard to most, if not all, of our native species, and to suggest to what extent their increase—or suppression—is desirable. This work has proceeded for the most part along four lines of inquiry, viz. : (1) examination of the stomach-contents—if necessary with the aid of the microscope—in order to determine exactly what the bird has eaten ; (2) observation through field glasses of birds feeding in their natural haunts ; (3) similar observations of the food conveyed to nestlings ; and (4) examination of the droppings of birds and of the pellets of indigestible matter thrown up by many species.

Investigations falling under the last of these headings have brought to light a number of facts which cast doubt upon the assumption once commonly made, that birds which feed largely or exclusively on weed seeds must for this reason be ranked as weed destroyers, and hence as beneficial to the farmer and gardener. Beyond question, enormous quantities of weed seeds are eaten by wild birds. But it has been found that an appreciable percentage of these are ejected with unimpaired vitality, and that they subsequently germinate, perhaps after they have been carried to a considerable, distance from their place of origin. We have, therefore, good grounds for believing that seed-eating birds play an important part not only in the perpetuation of weeds, but also in their distribution from one locality to another.

Darwin was perhaps the first to discuss this question in his *Origin of Species*, and to show incidentally how even carnivorous birds are indirectly involved. " Some hawks and owls," he says, " bolt their prey whole, and, after an interval of from twelve to twenty hours, disgorge pellets which, as I know from experiments made in the Zoological Gardens, include seeds capable of germination." In another passage, he adds that birds may be responsible for the wide dissemination of seeds originally eaten by fish. " Herons and other birds, century after century, have gone on daily devouring fish ; they take flight and go to other waters, or are blown across the sea ; and we have seen that seeds retain their power of germination when rejected many hours afterwards in pellets or in the excrement."

When Birds are useful.

In so far, therefore, as the food of birds consists of weed seeds, their activities appear to be of little importance from the standpoint of the agriculturist. When, on the other hand, they habitually devour large numbers of noxious insects, the farmer and gardener benefit—often so substantially that they can well afford to overlook a relatively small amount of injury inflicted by the same birds. Indeed, only in a very few instances can a species be written down unhesitatingly as wholly beneficial, or wholly harmful. Each case has to be decided on its own merits, after all the available evidence has been sifted and weighed.

An admirable summary of what is known concerning the food and feeding habits of British wild birds was published some years ago by Mr. W. E. Collinge, to which he added,

YOUNG THRUSH.

[*R. McLeod.*

This bird does noble work as a consumer of slugs and snails and is so useful to the gardener that the damage it does to fruit is forgiven. Although fond of occasional strawberries and cherries, its regular diet consists of garden pests.

in tabulated form, the results of much first-hand observation and experiment. Of about two hundred and eighty species to which the term " British " can be applied, some are so rare, or so sparsely represented with us, that they scarcely count either as friends or foes to agriculture. Others, including the aquatic, shore and sea birds, may also be excluded from the inquiry.

THESE deductions reduce the number to about eighty-five species, fifty of which are known to feed exclusively on insects—such, for example, as the Swallow tribe, the Fly-catchers, and the Wagtails. Except in so far as these may destroy useful insects, like Lady-birds and Hover-flies — and this seems rarely to happen—all these birds play into the hands of the farmer, and should on no account be molested. There remain, however, twenty-nine species, all more or less commonly represented in most districts, as to whose status considerable suspicion existed ; and Mr. Collinge's investigations were undertaken in the hope that this uncertainty might be dispelled.

Probably the average reader is most interested in the birds which occur most frequently in suburban districts—the region where town and country merge. For the sake of convenience we may call these " garden birds," and consider briefly the effects of their presence in and about the orchard, the vegetable plot and the small-holding.

To begin with, let us see what science has to say about the ubiquitous House Sparrow, which is never absent from these localities. One of the present writer's friends, who has devoted the leisure of many years to bird-watching, always insists that " even the Sparrow " deserves respect. Up to a point, this is undoubtedly true. House Sparrows

[Charles Reid.

THE FARMER'S FRIEND.
The farmer looks on the Wagtail with great friendliness, knowing that it will remove many pests from his crops.

destroy enormous numbers of injurious insects, and rear their young largely on this diet. Mr. Collinge's investigations led him to conclude that in fruit-growing districts, and probably also in gardens, the good done by these birds far outweighs the harm of which they are capable. But in agricultural areas they consume so much grain that " the present attitude of all farmers must be one of extermination." It has also been proved against the Sparrow that it is a very active distributor of injurious weed-seeds. So that the summing-up of our authority is against its protection—with the proviso that if its numbers could be reduced, so that it were no commoner than the Robin, it might then be ranked as a friend, instead of as the dire foe which it is at present.

The pugnacious exclusiveness of the Robin apparently serves to retard its undue increase, even in the most favourable circumstances. Hence, while you can always count upon a few in every district, the population never increases beyond reasonable bounds; and as the food consists almost entirely of insects—with perhaps a little seed and kitchen refuse, especially in hard weather, it fully merits the affectionate regard in which it is commonly held.

So, too, with the Wren—that wee bird coupled by tradition with the Robin as " God Almighty's friends." It is almost exclusively insectivorous—except that when food is abnormally scarce it may succour itself with a few small seeds. Its chief diet, however—as well as that which is provided for its young —consists of green-fly, small caterpillars, and daddy-longlegs or crane-flies. Every gardener will agree that if it did nothing else besides helping to keep down the last-named pests, whose grubs are the nefarious " leather-jackets," it would deserve special laudation.

Photo: Arthur Brook.] THE SPARROW HAWK'S EYRIE. *[Mondiale.*

The Sparrow Hawk is the terror of the smaller creatures of the feathered world, and preys so much upon game-birds and poultry that it is by no means popular. It is especially fond of a meal of Pheasants.

183

"A pair of birds nesting close to my house," writes Mr. Collinge, " were carefully watched, and counts were made of the number of visits the parents paid to the nest. Between 2 and 3 p.m., thirty-eight visits were made ; between 3 and 4 p.m., thirty-six ; and between 6 and 7 p.m., twenty-nine. On all these occasions crane-flies constituted the bulk of the food." Truly a marvellous record !

A sweet Singer and a great Thief.

Blackbirds and Thrushes are always in evidence in orchards and gardens, and while the latter do much good and comparatively little harm, the former have become too numerous, in view of the large amount of vegetable food which they consume—especially fruit. Authority states that at the present time the Blackbird is one of the most destructive species with which the fruit-grower has to contend. This will seem a hard saying to those who love to listen to the Blackbird's mellow song. But facts are stubborn things, and cannot be glazed over.

The Song Thrush is a greater eater of slugs and snails, as well as of insects and worms. It often does some damage to cherries and red currants, occasionally to strawberries and raspberries ; but the aggregate of its spoliation never outweighs the benefit conferred by its good deeds. The Blackbird, on the other hand, while it destroys in their season a certain number of noxious insects, does so much damage to fruit of all kinds that it inflicts a serious loss upon growers.

The Tits, three or four species of which are often common in gardens, where they attract much attention by their gay colours and quaint antics, subsist on a far more varied diet than was formerly supposed. Insects figure in it to a large extent, but by no means exclusively. The Great Tit, for example, sometimes does considerable damage by picking fruit blossom to pieces—possibly when searching for tiny caterpillars or beetles, though some of the bud-scales may also be eaten.

A more serious charge against this bird is that of injuring pears by picking holes in them ; while it has a bad name with bee-keepers, since it is apt to prey upon the inmates of the hive. Nevertheless, it collects so many caterpillars to feed its young during the nesting season, and devours so many hibernating aphids, scale-insects, small weevils, insects' eggs and the like during the winter, that the relatively small amount of damage

A " BOUGH "-ING ACQUAINTANCE.   [Robert McLeod.

Blue Tits are often blamed for damaging the fruit harvest by pulling the blossoms to pieces and destroying them with their beaks. Actually, however, they do much good in searching among the flowers for the eggs of insects.

Photo: O. G. Pike.]   A USEFUL APPETITE.   [*Mondiale.*

The Whitethroat chooses for its meal insects that are a nuisance to the gardener and farmer and so wins general favour. This bird, which is sometimes also called the stone-chat and the white-tail, is a summer visitor.

which it does in the orchard when the trees come into blossom may well be forgiven.

The same is true of the Blue and Coal Tits, whose habits are similar. The tireless activity of these birds, especially the Blue Tits, and the apparently wanton manner in which, at times, they are seen to tear in pieces the buds and blossoms of fruit trees, has given them a bad name among those fruit-growers who have not been at the pains to discover what is actually being done. "It is not the buds or blossoms themselves that are eagerly sought for," says one authority, "but the eggs or grubs of insects with which they are so often infested. From their minute size these pests escape human observation, but the keen vision of the Tit enables it to detect them. It is scarcely necessary to add that the insects, if unmolested, would not only destroy the buds and blossoms, but would produce a countless progeny as rapacious as themselves." In short, and on balance, the Tits must be accounted the good friends of man—not his enemies.

Coal Tits are sometimes confused by the uninitiated with the Blackcap—really a very different bird, a summer visitor which arrives in these islands about the middle of April, and usually leaves in autumn to winter in North-eastern Africa and Senegambia, although a few individuals undoubtedly remain with us throughout the year, in especially sheltered districts. It is a charming bird, whose song is not greatly inferior to that of the Nightingale ; and, as Mr. Collinge's post-mortem records show, it consumes a good many insects. But unfortunately it eats and destroys so large a quantity of fruit that its presence in our orchards and gardens—except, perhaps, in very small numbers — should be vigorously discouraged by all growers.

Welcome feathered Visitors.

Of the Whitethroat, on the contrary—a bird which is sometimes seen in association with the Blackcap—the reverse is true, since its food consists so largely of injurious insects that the small amount of damage which it does to peas and soft fruit is far more than repaid. So, too, with the other summer migrants which occur more or less commonly in and about gardens—the Chiff-chaff, the Lesser Whitethroat, the Garden Warbler, the Willow Warbler and the Spotted Flycatcher : these are predominantly insectivorous, and should be accorded a welcome wherever they appear. The Spotted Flycatcher, in particular, is a delight to watch on a summer afternoon— waiting patiently at some point of vantage, then darting out suddenly to seize a passing insect on the wing, then back to its original post. Its food consists of flies, gnats and midges, including the plaguey "mosquitoes."

Among other garden birds, the Hedge Sparrow—which is one of the commonest— may be counted a good friend, since it lives, for the most part, on insects, spiders, a few worms, and a variety of small seeds. The Hawfinch is a shy bird, and not very common. If it were more so, it would probably work much havoc in plum orchards, because of its partiality for the kernels of stone-fruit, the shells of which it crushes with its powerful beak, after ripping off and discarding the succulent outer coat. Like the Jay, it has a fondness for green peas, as many gardeners, even in the neighbourhood of large towns, know to their cost.

A much commoner bird, the Greenfinch, can be a great nuisance in the kitchen garden, where it is prone to disinter freshly-sown and germinating seeds ; while in the orchard it is a great destroyer of blossoms. It seldom attacks cultivated fruit, although in the autumn and winter it pays much attention to wild berries, apparently with the object of extracting the pips or kernels which they contain.

The Butterfly Bird.

Against the Goldfinch — that butterfly among our wild birds—no charge can be brought more serious than that it assists in the distribution of weed seeds, against which must be set the fact that during the spring and summer it destroys a considerable number of insects. The Linnet likewise is a harmless bird in existing circumstances ; but there is reason to fear that it might become injurious by eating grain and the seeds of cultivated plants if its numbers were to increase beyond a certain point. The same is true of the Yellow Bunting—the bird whose song has been likened to the phrase, " A little bit of bread and no cheese," with the last syllable long-drawn-out. At present its food consists mainly of weed seeds and insects. It seldom visits the garden or the orchard, but frequents hedgerows, and is occasionally guilty of consuming a considerable quantity of grain, both in the fields and in the rick-yard.

Sad to tell, neither the Chaffinch nor the Bullfinch is accorded an unequivocal certificate by the experts. The former lives largely on seeds, but also destroys many insects, which it uses almost exclusively for feeding its young. On the other hand, this bird is convicted of much harm done to sprouting corn ; while during the summer season it is capable of considerable damage in the orchard. Concerning the Bullfinch—an especial favourite with many bird-lovers—still worse is told.

A Vegetarian Bird.

Its diet is predominantly vegetarian, consisting largely of weed seeds : only one out of 308 post-mortem examinations of adults showed that an insect had been eaten, although a considerable number of caterpillars, grubs and flies are given to the nestlings. But the damage done by the Bullfinch in fruit orchards is so great as to far outweigh any little good that it may accomplish in other directions. At the present time, expert opinion declares unhesitatingly that in this country both the Chaffinch and the Bullfinch are far too plentiful.

Among the various protective measures which have been suggested with a view to maintaining a balance of bird life favourable to the farmer and gardener, the provision of nesting boxes and nesting sites in secluded situations for the use of insectivorous species is strongly recommended. All who have gardens may do something to help forward this plan, which, in conjunction with the suppression of species known to be injurious, would undoubtedly produce a marked effect before many years had passed.

Taking the countryside as a whole : Which bird—or birds—can be accorded the highest praise, and which the deepest censure ? From this general standpoint, probably the Plover or Lapwing is our staunchest friend. Unfortunately its numbers are far fewer than they might have been if only the fact of its usefulness had been duly recognised, and practical measures for its protection adopted, long ago. As a good second to the Lapwing, we may suggest the Kestrel, which not only destroys many cockchafers or may-bugs, but is also the arch-enemy of the vole and field-mouse tribes.

On the other hand, our chief foes of the bird world are the Pigeons. Of the Wood Pigeon, Mr. Collinge says : " There are no extenuating circumstances that lead me to alter the opinion formed many years back, that no quarter should be shown to this bird, and that every means should be taken to destroy it."

[R. H. Mallinson.

The Kingfisher is a distinctive bird even in his method of home-making. No tree-top nest would ever satisfy him, but he scratches out a hole in the bank and makes his retreat there. Here he is seen at the door of his burrow.

A FEATHERED FISHERMAN

By PETER WEBSTER

THE gaily-coloured Kingfisher is one of our most handsome and interesting birds, though its young look very ugly at first, resembling Hedgehogs rather than birds. They are brought up in very " fishy " surroundings, the nest being strewn with the fish-bones left by the parent-birds after their meals. They have to learn to fend—and also to fish—for themselves for, as we learn below, they are soon driven out into the world.

THE brilliant Kingfisher is not rare. A pair will be found on almost every moderately-slow stream having high clay banks. Gaily-coloured, they are at once distinguished, the head, neck, back and wings generally being of a glossy greenish-blue colour and the breast and undersides a brick red. The consistency with which the same type of ground embodying certain features is chosen for the nesting site is nothing short of marvellous. These are a double bend in the course of a stream having high clay or sandy banks, free from overhanging roots and branches, a deep pool below, and straight or over-hanging banks, up which a rat cannot climb.

If an oval hole be found about three-quarters up the bank side, which embodies all the foregoing conditions, it may be taken for granted a Kingfisher has a home there. Should the hole smell of rotten fish and there are droppings on the roof of the burrow, then it is absolutely certain that it is a Kingfisher's hole. The only nesting hole with which it is likely to be confused is that of the Sand Martin, or perhaps a rat's hole may sometimes be mistaken for one, but the former is always a horizontal oval hole, whereas the King-fisher's hole is always a vertical oval—larger in the vertical direction than in the horizontal direction, and, further, the Kingfisher's nesting hole is the only one in which droppings will be found on the roof.

The Kingfisher tunnels out this nesting hole with its beak, its tiny little red feet which have two toes in front and two behind, being too frail for such an undertaking ; they are used for nothing more than scratching away the loosened earth. Should a stone be en-countered in the path of the tunnel, the birds simply work round it and continue operations.

The first of the little round eggs is laid on the bare earth, but by the time that the last egg of the clutch is laid the bird has cast up quite a respectable heap of undigested fish bones which form an excellent bed for the eggs. Seven eggs form the full clutch. The yolks can be seen quite clearly through the glossy white shell. Unfortunately they lose this pink tinge on being blown and become a very ordinary white. With surprising regularity year after year, with not more than a day's variation in the most backward season, the seventh egg is laid on 20th April. Two broods are sometimes reared in the season, the second clutch of eggs being laid towards the end of June. It is generally supposed that the Kingfisher sometimes occupies a ready-made hole in the bank side of a stream, but as far as the writer's experience goes this has never been found to be the case.

to be all mouth and quills, and look more like Hedgehogs than birds. Their ability to run backwards equally as well as they can run forwards tends to confirm one's first impression that they were not birds but animals. By the time that they are a month old the nesting hole has become absolutely vile. The hideous odour of decomposed fish, with the incredible accumulation of droppings throughout the whole length, and all round the burrow is enough to put into the pale of insignificance the proverbial " Augean Stables." This slimy

Photo : P. Webster.] BEGINNING LIFE ON THEIR OWN. [*Mondiale.*
There is no undue coddling in the Kingfisher family. When the youngsters are old enough to provide for themselves and have learnt the art of fishing, they are driven away from their home by their stern parents.

IT is customary for a pair of these birds to return to the same nesting site year after year if they are unmolested. A fresh hole, however, is dug each successive season, the old hole being too filthy, and too much enlarged for re-occupation, owing to the constant traffic in the later stages of rearing the young. On one occasion in Ireland no less than five nesting holes—all undoubtedly Kingfishers—were discovered by the writer in a small stretch of bank side no more than eight feet long.

The young are born quite naked, very much the same as other young birds, but at three weeks old they are positively as hideous as their parents are beautiful. They appear

green deposit is often absolutely alive with Maggots.

The food of the Kingfisher is primarily fish, but insects, Shrimps and small Shellfish are eagerly consumed in hard weather. Sticklebacks have an irresistible attraction for these birds, and when they can be found they seem to prefer them to all other small fish. When fishing the Kingfisher will sit on some protruding branch or root under an overhanging bank waiting for the small fish to pass beneath ; then it drops down like an arrow upon its prey, but apparently it makes too much splash and disturbance to be regularly successful, unless the fish is very near the surface. At times it

Photo: H. Bastin.]   HOME-HUNTING.   *[Mondiale.*

This pair of Kingfishers are probably looking for the nesting-hole they used the previous year to save them the trouble of rebuilding. The eggs are laid on heaps of undigested fish bones which make an odoriferous resting-place.

fishes quite freely in deeper water, hovering over the surface somewhat like a Tern, and will then readily take a headlong plunge out of sight. When catching a fish it takes it across the middle, and on returning to its perch turns the fish round until it is held by the tail, gives it a few sharp raps across the branch to kill it, and then swallows it head first. This habit of killing the prey is an instinct born in the bird, as has been proved by observing young Kingfishers taken from the nest at quite an early stage, and hand-reared. Although it was absolutely impossible for these youngsters ever to have seen their parents kill fish, it was their invariable custom when being fed with strips of Whiting (on which they were exclusively reared) to seize hold of one end of the strip of fish and hammer away at it as though it had been very much alive. Kingfishers are extremely solitary in their habits, and when once they have taken up their quarters on one stretch of stream they confine themselves rigidly to it. Should another Kingfisher encroach on the line of demarkation a battle royal ensues and does not end until the intruder has been beaten off. This habit of selecting a " beat " for themselves leads to their own destruction. On being disturbed the birds make off upstream, hugging one side or the other very closely until out of sight. If followed up again the bird makes another stream flight, and so on until it reaches the limit of its own beat. It then doubles back, and will go as far in the downstream direction as its beat extends. By thus following one particular track it lays itself open to destruction. By persistent stalking it is only a question of time before it is either shot, or netted under some bridge by anyone so disposed.

On the approach of hard weather Kingfishers work their way downstream until the coast is reached, where they take up their winter quarters, or at least until the frost has gone. They feed round the estuary and along the shore, picking up small animal life left by the receding tide. This kind of exposed life does not appeal to the Kingfishers, however, who make back upstream the moment their food supply is assured again. They do not migrate altogether, but a local movement invariably takes place. The young birds are driven away from their original home by the parent birds as soon as they are capable of successfully fishing for themselves.

THE KINGFISHER'S PERCH.   [Mondiale.

The Kingfisher spends a great deal of its time on a branch overhanging the stream that it has chosen for its fishing activities. It dives perpendicularly after sighting its prey, and kills it by dashing it against a stone.

Photo : O. G. Pike.]   [Mondiale.

The most amazing architects in the bird-world are the Long-tailed Tits, whose domed nest when complete looks like a ball of lichen. It is lined very thoroughly with feathers, sometimes as many as three thousand being used.

WONDERFUL BIRD HOMES

By OLIVER G. PIKE, F.Z.S., F.R.P.S.

WE can learn many lessons from the careful and painstaking manner in which the birds construct their compact little homes. They are finished workmen; we rarely see an untidy or carelessly-built nest and cannot but marvel how such small creatures, with no tools other than their beaks, can accomplish such extraordinary feats of workmanship. Many queer tree-top homes are fully described in the following chapter.

IN many foreign countries we find birds which build the most wonderful homes in which to rear their young. The Bower Birds make elaborate arbours; some of the Weaver Birds, using grasses as threads, construct nests so perfect that one would think the builders had served a long apprenticeship, and the Brush Turkeys actually manufacture an incubator with decaying leaves which performs all the duties of incubation, leaving the young to emerge later, fully fledged, and able to look after themselves when they enter the outside world.

In Great Britain we have few birds which can compete with these foreign architects, but nevertheless we have some which make very wonderful homes, and if we searched the world over I doubt if we could find any country in which so many strange sites are used for nest building.

We find that, as a general rule, the smaller the bird, the more perfect is the nest. The home of the Rook and Crow, built at the top of a tall tree, is a clever piece of work, for it will often withstand the gales of many seasons, but when compared with some of the work of the diminutive Tits, Wrens and Warblers it is very rough.

The most wonderful nest built by any British bird is that of the tiny Long-tailed Tit. The length of the bird is five-and-a-half inches, and more than half that length is taken up by the long tail. The nest is very little longer than the bird, and at first glance looks like a ball of lichen. The birds work hard on it for a fortnight or more. I have known one of these nests to contain just upon 3000 feathers, and as the latter were collected from a distance of several hundred yards, the builders must have travelled a great many miles before their home was complete; besides the feathers there was a quart pot full of other material—Moss, Lichens, Rabbits' fur and Spiders' web. The birds use a large quantity of web in building their home, and I will presently explain why.

The inside of one of these nests, when completed, would be about the size of a tennis ball, and in this small space we sometimes find a large number of eggs—I believe the record is twenty. Some birds in building their nests first build the framework, then later add the lining of feathers. Long-tailed Tits commence with the bottom, then as the walls are built upwards, they complete it as they go along, so that when the roof is reached and the last piece of lichen placed in position, the inside is quite ready to receive the eggs.

First Come, First Served.

The majority of nests contain eight or ten youngsters, and we might wonder how they all obtain an equal supply of food, for when they hear their parents approaching there is room only for two little heads at the small opening near the top of the nest. There is always a struggle to get there, and when the fortunate ones get their beaks out they remain there until they are satisfied, then they fall back, and two more push forward and so it goes on all through the day, for the parents are kept busy with such a large family to look after.

When the young are nearly full grown and about ready to leave, life inside this diminutive nest must be very crowded, and this is where the cobweb used in the construction of the nest comes to their assistance. The lichens are fastened together with this, and as the young grow, so the interior of the nest expands with them, without actually breaking open, but one nest I found with a very large family inside could not stand the strain, and it had burst completely open ; when I discovered it the youngsters were sitting contentedly on the top of their wrecked home.

I once passed one of these nests at a most interesting moment : the young were just ready to leave. The nest itself was no larger than an ordinary coconut ; near the top was a small hole, and as I watched I saw the mother emerge from this ; she saw what she supposed to be an enemy outside and gave a warning cry. Immediately the youngsters commenced to leave. They were just about the same size as their mother, and altogether nine birds came out. As they flew away in single file across the small, open space of woodland, it looked as though it was impossible for such a tiny nest to hold such a crowd ; I always look upon it as one of Nature's conjuring tricks !

All over England we find a race of Robins which have departed from their proper custom of nesting on grassy banks to build in all kinds of strange situations. It is probable that thousands of years ago a pair of Robins found shelter in an old pot left outside the camp of one of our distant ancestors. They found it a safe and successful site, and the descendants from that first nest are still carrying on.

I have found that if birds are reared in a strange place, when they grow up to build nests for themselves—and this applies chiefly to the young hen birds—they think that they must search for and build in a similar site. An instance of this occurred over thirty years ago in a North London suburb. A pair of Blue Tits built their nest inside a lamp-post ; they entered just under the glass to make their home somewhere inside the iron pillar. They reared a large family, and the youngsters succeeded in flying from their strange home. The sequel was seen later, for when five years had passed half a dozen lamp-posts were occupied by Blue Tits, showing that the descendants from the first nest thought that such a site was the one and only place in which to build. I was lecturing in that district three years ago, and a member in my audience told me that the Tits were still building their nests inside the lamp-posts.

A similar instance came under my notice in regard to Wheatears. Thirty-five years ago I found a nest of the Wheatear under an old tin. Other tins were placed in the district, and nowadays practically every one is occupied by these birds. In some parts of England, especially in the county of Hertfordshire, there is a race of Spotted Flycatchers which build their small nests inside the old nests of Blackbirds and Thrushes, instead of in the usual site, which is among the Ivy found growing on a old wall or tree.

A Home under a Pot.

In a certain garden which I knew the Great Tits built their nests under inverted flower pots, large ones, ten or twelve inches in height, and if they were able to squeeze their little bodies through the hole they went inside and built a cosy nest of moss and hair. A pair of Blue Tits made their home inside a discarded pump, going to it season after season. I noticed that when the parents fed their

Photo : W. Farnsworth.]   GREY HERON AT NEST.   *[Mallinson.*

The Heron's nest is a large structure of sticks, lined with grass and twigs, usually situated near the tree-top. This long-legged bird lays as early as the month of February and rears two broods in the same season.

Photo : O. G. Pike.] THE CHAFFINCH'S HOME. [Mondiale.
The Chaffinch is an expert builder, gathering together moss, grass, lichens, cobwebs, wool, hair, down and feathers, and making from these a beautiful nest. Here it is seen proudly surveying the result of its patient work.

young, the male Blue Tit entered the nest by the small hole at the top of the pump through which the pumping rod passed, but his mate preferred the larger hole through which the water emerged when the pump was in use.

SOME birds do not object to taking in lodgers. I have seen a Heron's nest with a Magpie's nest immediately underneath it. The latter bird makes a dome to her nest, but in this instance it had been done away with, for the floor of the Heron's home acted as a roof to hers. The great Golden Eagle is a bird feared by most other wild creatures, but in one Highland glen I saw a nest which had two lodgers. A Wren had her little domed home in the sticks immediately underneath the large eyrie, while a short distance from this a Chaffinch had made her nest. In many Rookeries close to human dwellings we often find Sparrows making their nests of hay on the under sides of the large stick structures of the Rooks. Wild Ducks will sometimes share a nest; I found one double nest containing twenty eggs in all; sometimes when I visited it one side contained eleven eggs and the other nine, then if I passed a day or so later one bird was sitting on five only, while her companion had to cover fifteen! How many ducklings they brought up between them I was not able to find out.

On the sand dunes on the seashore we sometimes find the beautiful Shelduck which makes her home in a burrow, sharing the hole with Rabbits. But the strangest wild companions I ever knew to share a home were a Shelduck and a Fox. The Fox had his lair in a big burrow in the sand, but whether he took possession after the Shelduck had laid her eggs, or before, I could not dis-

[Charles Reid.

AT HOME IN A COCONUT.

The Wren, a careful little builder, hides its home in nooks among the trees and bushes. Sometimes its young are reared in unique surroundings. Here a coconut has provided a neat and secluded home.

cover. However, both seemed quite content to carry on.

Birds of many species are pastmasters in the art of camouflage. The most cleverly-built nest that I ever saw was one made by a pair of Long-tailed Tits in a lichen-covered fruit tree. The nest was built at the base of a stout fork, and at a distance of a yard it was absolutely impossible to tell which was nest and which branch, for the builders had made the outside of their home exactly like the trunk. The Chaffinch is a clever builder. I have seen many nests which looked just like the tree in which they were built, but the birds will sometimes depart from their usual custom and cover their homes with white down which they collect from the Willow Trees. I have found two nests built in the thickest part of a hedge which had small pieces of paper dotted round the outside. Without the paper the nests would have been almost invisible, but when looked at from eye-level they appeared to be made more conspicuous. On examining them more closely, however, I found that the clever builders had actually made a most successful attempt at camouflage. Most of the enemies of the Chaffinch, such as Cats, Weasels and Stoats, would search for the nest from the ground, and I found that when looked at from their viewpoint the little pieces of paper looked exactly like the small patches of light seen through the thick leaves of the hedge.

There are many birds in this country which make no nests of any kind. Their eggs are so much like the places in which they lay them that it is exceedingly difficult to see them. The eggs of the rare Kentish Plover are laid on the bare stones of the seashore; they are the colour of the stones, and the markings on them harmonise exactly with the spots on the surrounding stones. The Norfolk Plover, a much larger bird, lays her two eggs on flint-covered moors, and they are so much like the bare ground that I have known experienced egg-collectors fail to discover them. The Ringed Plover, another shore bird, will sometimes place a small ring of tiny pebbles or shells around her four eggs, a primitive form of nest building. The Lesser Tern, which usually dispenses with any form of nest building, will occasionally do the same, but with her it is really a kind of game that causes the shells to collect around her eggs. She may find that she wants some kind of occupation during the long hours of sitting, and so she will occasionally dig a small hole with her beak, then when she finds a little shell or brightly-coloured pebble which pleases her, she holds it in the tip of her beak, throws her head right back, points her beak straight upwards and allows her prize to fall on to her back. It rolls off to find a resting-place by her side. She takes no further interest in that one, but presently searches for another, and as she does this several times each day during the period of incubation, quite a ring of little pebbles and shells accumulates around her eggs. Another Lesser Tern that I watched brought to her eggs a piece of straw sixteen inches long, and after a long struggle managed to place it in a kind of circle round them.

I found a Kentish Plover sitting hard upon two eggs—three is her usual clutch. As these were in a good position for photography, I decided to try to photograph her sitting upon them. I fixed up my camera, placed my bird-watching tent over it, went inside and waited. Half an hour later the owner returned and settled down on her eggs. After sitting for about twenty minutes, I noticed that she left them, walked about a couple of yards to the left and sat on the stones for about the same time. As she did this at fairly regular intervals throughout the day I thought it very strange, so when I had finished my photography I decided to investigate her reason for this behaviour. After a short search I found to my astonishment that this wonderful little Kentish Plover had her two eggs in one spot, and away to the left was her third, and she was actually endeavouring to hatch all three! I have never come across an incident in the bird world that looked so much like intelligence.

A LOFTY HOME.   [Charles Reid.
The Rook is not particular about the daintiness of its nest, but makes it a stronghold against gales. It perches it on tree-tops amid a colony of similar homes or sometimes chooses a convenient chimney-stack.

[Mallinson.

Had it not been for sportsmen's delight in the hunt, the Fox would have shared the same fate as the Wolf which has long been extinct in our country.   A pretty creature, its visits to the poultry-yard have made it unpopular.

ANCESTRY OF ANIMALS

By MALCOLM BURR, DSc., F.R.P.S.

IN this very interesting chapter the family-tree of the animals that run wild in our island is revealed. We are also told about creatures that used to make their homes here many centuries ago. Reindeer, we learn, flourished in Scotland in bygone days, hungry wolves roamed the country, and the Wild Boar led many kings to the chase. To all who are interested in the history of animals, the following section will prove absorbing.

WE are not very rich in mammals in the British Islands, but our list includes the smallest and the largest known kinds. Altogether we have on the list twenty-three kinds of rodents, sixteen carnivorous, three ruminants or hoofed animals, six insectivorous, and twelve kinds of Bats, and twenty members of the Whale tribe, making a total of eighty. Some of these are very scarce indeed, such as the Walrus, very occasionally taken in British waters, or confined to very small islands, like some of the Mice.

On the list we have included foreigners which have become established here, often to our great prejudice ; but we have omitted many fine creatures which have become extinct within historic times, as the Beaver, the Reindeer, the Wolf and the Bear.

Everyone knows the Rodents. They are small animals, usually slinking and nocturnal in habit. The distinctive feature is the form of the front teeth, which are like chisels. A real old Englishman is the Rabbit, for his fossil remains are found in various parts of England, but not in Ireland or Scotland, where it seems to have been introduced by man. Its cousin the Hare is nearly as well known, though perhaps more often in jugged than in wild condition. It is abundant throughout England, Wales, and the Lowlands of Scotland. In the Highlands it gives way to the Arctic or Blue Hare, which is smaller and turns white in winter. The Irish Hare is slightly different from both. They all give gamey meat and are bad-tempered pets.

The Squirrel is a beautiful little creature, once common in all British woodlands, but now much reduced by an American interloper. It makes a neat little nest called a drey. In this country there is a slight change of coat in winter, but in Siberia the same species turns grey when the frost sets in, and this is the Squirrel fur of commerce. The American Grey Squirrel has unfortunately spread over almost all this country at the expense of our native kind. Like a tiny squirrel is the Dormouse, common in southern and central England. It makes a charming but drowsy pet, as it sleeps so soundly that if aroused suddenly it dies of palpitation. Its larger cousin, the Fat Dormouse, escaped from Lord Rothschild's collection and is now established around Tring, but does not seem to do anyone any harm.

The Harvest Mouse is so tiny that it can climb and eat an ear of corn without bending the stalk, as it weighs only about one-fifth of an ounce. It is found in cornfields, in several southerly and midland counties. It weaves a nest slung on three or four corn stalks.

Country children know the Long-tailed Field Mouse or Wood Mouse, which occurs all over Great Britain. It is a little larger than the Common Mouse, with a longer tail and white hind feet. If its numbers were not kept down by Owls, Kestrels and Weasels, it would inflict serious damage on farms and gardens. It develops special local races in the Hebrides and Fair Island. In the island of St. Kilda there is a distinct species (*A. hirtensis*), and the Yellow-necked Mouse is found side by side with the common form in Herefordshire, but does not mix with it.

The Domestic Mouse is certainly an ancient Briton, as fossilised remains have been found in the Thames Valley and in some English caves, but it is not now found in the wild state. There is a distinct kind in St. Kilda.

There are no truly British Rats. The Black seems to have been introduced by ships in the fifteenth century. It spread all over the islands, but never really made good in Ireland. Early in the eighteenth century the Brown Rat appeared and, being the stronger animal,

nearly exterminated the older settler. It is believed to have invaded Europe from Mongolia in vast hordes. It crossed the Volga in 1727 and reached Paris in 1756. It spreads plague through its infected Fleas and does incalculable damage to stored food of all kinds. Modern architectural developments, with big buildings and numerous electric cables, favour the more nimble Black Rat, which is now regaining lost ground.

VOLES are not quite the same as mice. They have shorter tails and more rounded muzzles. The Short-tailed Field Vole is abundant all over England and Scotland, but does not occur in Ireland, so it must have reached this country after the separation of the Emerald Isle. It occasionally swarms, doing great damage, but is kept in check by Owls, Kestrels and Buzzards, which foolish people so often destroy.

Another interesting kind is the Orkney Vole, which is interesting chiefly on account of its origin. As its nearest relative is found only in Guernsey, and another used to occur in Kent, for its fossil remains have been found in the late Pleistocene deposits at Ightham, it appears that it reached England before we

Photo : John Markham.]   [Mondiale.

THE BANK VOLE.

This small creature is so much of a night-prowler that it is seldom seen. It does great damage to plantations.

were separated from the Continent and spread right away to the north. Competition was too strong for it in England and Scotland, but it was able to hold its own in the Orkneys, where it has developed slightly varying, but quite recognisable forms in the different islands.

A third kind is the Bank Vole, occurring all over England and most of Scotland, but seldom seen owing to its nocturnal habits. Sometimes it does much damage to young plantations. It is redder in colour and paler beneath than the Common Vole. In the island of Skomer, off the southern coast of Pembrokeshire, there is to be found a distinct form.

MERELY A MOUSE. [*Brit. Instruct. Films.*

The drowsy little Dormouse has to awake gradually from its sound winter sleep, else it will die of palpitation. It is at home in the trees and sleeps in a nest in which, with instinctive forethought, it has stored a supply of nuts.

199

Most boys in the country know the Water Vole, commonly but wrongly called the Water Rat. The true Rat swims along the surface of the water, but the Water Vole dives and swims under the water. It is a friendly little animal and does no harm to anyone. But its cousin the Musk Rat, or Musquash, is capable of doing very serious damage to embankments, bridges and so on, by undermining the foundations. It was deliberately introduced from Canada with Government encouragement to find work for the unemployed for the sake of its beautiful fur. Unfortunately, the authorities did not take zoological advice, and before many years it had escaped and started breeding, so that the Government is now spending thousands of pounds in attempts to cope with what has become in places a serious pest. It is liket he Water Vole, but twice as large.

Once upon a time Beavers had their home in Britain, but they seem to have died out in the Middle Ages. Their memory still survives, however, in place-names, as Beverley, Beverbroke, and in Welsh as Nant ffrancon.

Why the Fox is preserved.

Among our Carnivora, the most familiar is the Fox. As it is troublesome to owners of poultry, it would long since have disappeared into extinction but for the hunts, and followed its cousin the Wolf, of which the last English specimen was killed in the reign of Henry VII., though in Scotland it lingered on until later than 1680, and in Ireland later still. The Wolf was a very ancient British animal.

The Wild Cat was not long ago thought in danger of extinction, but, thanks to a more generous attitude on the part cf landowners, it is recovering lost ground. The Domestic Cat is believed to be derived from a cross between this creature and an African species.

The Weasel tribe is well represented in Britain. The Weasel itself, though the smallest, is as fierce as any. It is mercilessly killed as vermin, but does much good in keeping down the Voles. The Stoat is a good deal larger, and the tip of the tail is black. It is a determined little hunter, and very bloodthirsty and intelligent. In cold countries it turns white in winter, except the black tip of the tail, and in this state is generally called Ermine. The Irish Stoat is smaller and darker. The Polecat, once common, is now extremely rare. The country folk used to call the male, hob, and the female, jill. If a Polecat finds its way into a poultry run, it kills every living thing within reach. The Ferret is a domesticated form of the Albino.

Handsomest of all is the Pine Marten, once common, but now surviving only in a few isolated woodlands. In Russia, Latvia and other places where it is fairly common it is mercilessly trapped for its beautiful fur.

The Beast that valets the Fox.

The Badger is rather like a small Bear. It is a harmless, very intelligent animal, so hygienic in its habits that Masters of Foxhounds put Badgers into Foxes' earths to clear them of mange. Being nocturnal and shy, Badgers are seldom seen, but are by no means rare.

The Otter is also much commoner than suspected, as is shewn by the existence of several parks of Otter Hounds. The Otter usually makes its nest or holt in the bank of a stream. It is a wonderful performer in the water, and feeds entirely on fish.

Fossil remains show that these **members** of the Weasel family are all ancient **Britons**. The last of the powerful Carnivora in Britain was the Bear, which was probably exterminated before the Norman Conquest.

The Seals are Carnivora adapted to life in the sea. The Common Seal is not rare on the rocky western coasts. The Grey Seal, a more northerly kind, is fairly common on the shores of the Shetlands, Hebrides and southern Ireland. Sometimes, too, we receive visits from other kinds, as the Ringed Seal, the Harp Seal, the Bearded Seal, the Hooded Seal, or Bladder - nosed Seal, and upon occasion the Walrus pays a visit to our shores.

Monsters of the Deep.

Cetacea is the name of the order which includes the Whales and Dolphins. Some are regular inhabitants of our waters, and some occasional visitors, several familiar friends of the seaside, and several real monsters of the deep. The most familiar is the Porpoise, which often does much damage to fishermen's nets. Less familiar is the Dolphin, which sometimes swims up from more southerly waters after our Pilchards and Herrings. The extraordinary Narwhal, with its long, single-twisted ivory tusk, occasionally strays down from its Arctic home.

A school of the world-wide False Killer was stranded on the Scottish coast a few years back. The real Killer or Grampus, pied like a Magpie, is surpassed in voracity by no

Photo : Arthur Brook] RED DEER AT HOME. [*Mondiale.*

Red Deer still run wild in Scotland and in some parts of England, where they are preserved for hunting. Tame herds are also found in many parks, but they are really seen at their best in their native mountains and forests.

living creature. Risso's Grampus sometimes makes a show in British waters ; it has a world-wide range, and one specimen earned fame as the only marine creature which has enjoyed the specified protection of the law, under the name of Pelorus Jack, which used to pilot ships through Pelorus Sound, New Zealand. There are also such creatures as the Bottle-nosed Dolphin, the White-sided and White-beaked Dolphins, both stragglers from the Arctic. The Beluga, the source of the " Porpoise Hide " of commerce, is also a rare visitor to our coasts. The Pilot Whale was formerly much hunted off our northern coasts.

OF the Toothed Whales, the tremendous Sperm Whale, with the largest head of any animal, is a rare visitor. It is a wonderful sight to see him raise his huge bulk half-way out of the water and come splashing down as he ploughs through the waves. The Bottle-nosed Whale pays a call twice a year on migration. It is cruelly persecuted by whalers. There are many tales told of its nobility of character. Sowerby's Whale is rare everywhere, whilst Cuvier's Whale is recorded on the strength of a single specimen found stranded off the Shetland Islands.

Of the true Whales, half a dozen kinds are on our list. The Biscay Whale has been persecuted for its blubber and whalebone for centuries, under appalling cruelties. It produces a single baby at a birth, from ten to fourteen feet in length. The Humpback Whale is a rare visitor, and is the only true Whale which clears the waters when it leaps. It seems to be an affectionate creature, for it is often seen to pat its mate with its huge flappers in the breeding season.

Then there are the four Rorquals. The Common Rorqual is a fairly common visitor. It runs to a length of seventy feet or more, but is exceeded by Sibbald's Rorqual, the largest living animal. One stranded on the Hebrides some years ago measured over ninety feet in length. The Lesser Rorqual is only a little over thirty feet long. It is an occasional visitor from the Atlantic. Lastly, there is the Northern or Rudolphi's Rorqual, a medium-sized fellow that occasionally finds his way even into the Medway and the Thames. A small one, thirty-five feet long, was stranded at Tilbury in 1887.

The group known as the Insect-Eaters includes a few small but fierce and greedy little flesh-eaters with needle-like teeth. Every-

A SEAL COLONY   [Sport & General.

Seals are still numerous, chiefly round our rocky western coasts. They are the subject of many strange legends, and believed to have musical abilities. There is no evidence that this is true, though they are fond of music.

A HERD OF REINDEER.   [*Mondiale.*

Herds of Reindeer such as this used to be found in Scotland, even as late as the 12th century. As Reindeer Moss, on which they feed, grows freely in Scotland, it is a pity that they have not been reintroduced.

one knows the Mole, which is so foolishly persecuted, for it does more good than harm. It is a most powerful digger and seems simply to swim through soft earth. The fur can be brushed in both directions, a great advantage to an animal living in small tunnels. The hairs are hardened into spines in the familiar Hedgehog, another friend of man which consumes great quantities of noxious insects. Their near relatives the Shrews have nothing whatever to do with the Mice, though it is true they are something like them to look at. But Mice have chisel-like teeth for gnawing and are vegetable-feeders, while Shrews have needle-like teeth for catching and tearing the Worms and insects, of which they consume quantities. They are savage little fellows, so that their name has become a very word for bad temper, and, in spite of Shakespeare, it seems they are untamable. The Common Shrew, although unknown in Ireland, is an ancient British animal, for its fossil bones have been found in Norfolk. They are seldom seen alive, but seem to be easily killed, as their bodies are often found in lanes and paths, especially in the autumn.

The Pigmy Shrew is one of the tiniest of Mammals, measuring less than three inches, including the tail, and the teeth can hardly be seen without a lens. It is found throughout Great Britain and also in Ireland. The Water Shrew is the largest and darkest of the Shrews. It lives in streams and swims actively under water, where it devours water insects, fish, fry and spawn.

Ten years ago a new kind of Shrew was discovered in the Scilly Islands. It is slightly different from a common French species, and was named *Crocidura cassiterridum*, so we may call it the Shrew of the Tin Islands. It is an untamable little monster which lives on Earthworms and will not accept its dinner unless it has caught it alive and killed it itself. It may be discovered on the southern coast of Cornwall, but no fossil remains have been found in England, so it seems that it reached us from the Continent just before we were cut off from the mainland, and was able to establish itself only down in the south-west.

The Ungulates or Hoofed Animals are represented in our country by several kinds. The Red Deer still runs wild on Exmoor, where hunting has preserved it from extinction, for otherwise the farmers would certainly have shot it to death. Those once wild in Epping Forest are to-day represented by descendants from Windsor herds, which came originally from Epping. In the Highlands, of course, they are numerous. It is known as a fossil, and is an ancient British Mammal. Not so the Fallow Deer, the ornamental Deer of our parks, which was imported ages ago from the south, some think by the Romans.

FORMERLY there lived here the grandest of Mammals, the Giant Deer, often miscalled the Irish Elk, with enormous horns expanding over nine feet across. It was probably hunted by early man. The Roe Deer is still wild in Scotland, where it is a regular game animal. It survives here and there in northern England, but those in the Black-moor Vale in Dorset were turned out, like those in Windsor and Epping Forests. Its fossilised bones are not rare, so it is a truly ancient British animal, but has never occurred in Ireland; therefore it must have reached us after the separation of the Emerald Isle. The Roe lives in small parties, and mates for life. It is so active that it can leap over a six-foot wall with ease.

The Reindeer used to inhabit Scotland, and was hunted in Caithness by the jarls of the Orkneys as late as the twelfth century. It would be a good thing to reintroduce it as a food supply, since the meat is good and they do not require feeding, as they support themselves by grazing on the lichen called Reindeer Moss, which grows freely in Scotland.

The wandering herds of cattle of ancient Britain have been preserved in four parks : Lyme in Cheshire, Chartley in Staffordshire, Cadzow in Lanarkshire, and, most famous of all, Chillingham in Northumberland, each herd differing slightly from the others. Their habits are similar to that of wild animals, feeding by night, hiding their young, avoiding mankind generally, and moving very rapidly.

THE STOAT.   *[Charles Reid.*
This member of the Weasel family is sometimes called the Ermine, especially when it dons its winter coat.

Opinions are divided as to whether they are descended from the Urus, or Aurochs, mentioned by Cæsar, which lingered on in Central Europe until the Middle Ages, or from imported domestic cattle run wild. The remains of the Urus are found in conjunction with interments as late as the Bronze Age, so it was probably hunted by man, and may have been tamed, though there is no record of that. But the Celtic Shorthorn was certainly domesticated by the ancient Britons. It was the ancestor of our small dark breeds.

The Wild Boar, though still numerous just across the English Channel, has long since disappeared from Britain, where it once was abundant. Edward III. used to hunt it in Oxfordshire, perhaps near Boar's Hill, and in 1573 Squire Kitson, of Hengrove, in Suffolk, received " a bore " every Christmas from one of his tenants.

Bats are the only Mammals that can fly, and they differ in many respects from other animals. They sleep during the day in colonies in hiding places, hanging by the hind legs, and come out only at dusk to hawk insects. Although they fly at dusk, their eyes are tiny and they depend more upon the sensitive membranes of the wings and ears, and in some cases of the nose. This is seen in the two Horseshoe Bats, the Greater and the Lesser, which have membranes like leaves on their snouts. These curious creatures are not rare in the southern and south-western counties. The most common everywhere is our smallest Bat, the Pipistrelle. Our largest kind is the Noctule, which flies fast and high in our southern and midland counties. There are several stragglers from abroad, of which we may make mention of only one—the Mouse-coloured Bat — because the single specimen recorded in this country had the singular tact to be captured in the British Museum !

Here are two Badgers at the door of their queer, underground mansion which they have built with greater under-standing than most animals possess.   The twisting tunnels that lead to its home are very cleverly designed.

BROCK THE BADGER

By OLIVER G. PIKE, F.Z.S., F.R.P.S.

ABOUT a century ago the sport of Badger-baiting was very popular in Great Britain, the animals proving fierce fighters and providing great entertainment. Luckily, this " pastime " has been prohibited, and the Badger is now more or less free to live its own life.   Its skilfully-built home and its domestic matters are described in the following chapter, where the life-history of this interesting creature is also revealed.

THE numbers of towns in these islands which have the prefix brock in their names, shows that in the past Badgers were common practically everywhere. Even now this fine Mammal is not so rare as many imagine, but the fact that it is a creature of the night rather than of the day, and is therefore seldom seen, causes some observers to think that it is not found in their district. There are few counties in the southern part of England where the Badger is not found, while in parts of Devon, Cornwall and certain districts in Wales it might be called common.

The chief reason that the Badger has con-tinued to thrive in a country where every man's hand seems to be against it is the fact that it is almost omnivorous in food, eating all kinds of fruit, eggs, insects of every kind, Frogs, Mice, Snails, roots and Fungi. With such a varied fare in the countryside the

Badger never need go hungry. Also it has the most astonishing strength in its jaw with its flattened, ridged molar teeth, which aid it in crunching bones and cracking open the hardest nuts.

The home of the Badger is a deep, under-ground burrow, which the creature makes itself. It is often made on a tree-covered bank, and the quantity of earth which is seen outside shows what a clever engineer it is. The tunnels twist and turn in the most be-wildering manner, while at the end there is a larger chamber in which the bed is made. For thousands of years before man ever thought of cutting and drying grass for winter use the Badger did this. In the late summer or early autumn the Badger cleans out its living room, then collects a quantity of Bracken and Grass, places it in the sun and turns it daily until it is quite dry. It then carries it down below to make a comfortable and warm bed for the winter. I know one haunt of the Badger a few hundred yards from a stack yard. The Badgers here have enough intelligence to use the already dried straw, and at night they visit the straw stacks and purloin sufficient for their needs. The long trail of dropped straw from the yard to their burrows tells the story of their depredations.

How the Badgers play Games.

The sexes appear to keep apart, except during a short period when the young require food. They are born at any time between March and June. At birth they are blind, but within a fortnight are able to see. At a month old they are attractive babies, and at six weeks some of the most playful Puppies of the wilds. When about three months old they play the most ridiculous game. Some wild Cubs seem to have a method in their play. Young Otters will play the game of follow the leader—the parents make a very effective water chute by sliding down a sloping bank into the stream, and the young follow ; the faster they slide down the slippery bank and the louder the splash they make in the water, the more parents and young seem to enjoy the game.

Young Foxes will romp with each other like Dog Puppies, jumping over one another's backs, and using small rocks as balls. The chief game of the Badger Cubs is very different. I have often watched them at play. Two or three may be searching diligently for Worms or leather jackets, food of which they are very fond ; suddenly, without the slightest warning, the whole party will simultaneously stiffen their legs, and puff out their fur, when they look like large round balls ; having done this they bounce up and down as though made of india-rubber, turning round and round one another ; then just as suddenly the fur is lowered, and they dash at one another's throats, trying to grip the loose skin. Now they tumble over and over, break apart and commence the ridiculous dance with stiffened limbs again, and just as suddenly as they commenced this game they cease, and in a second all are searching once more for food.

The red-letter day in a Badger's life is when he finds a nest of wild Bees. It often happens that a swarm of Bees will escape from an apiary and go back to the wilds. They often choose a hole in a forest tree,

sometimes quite low down, and it is then that the Badger has the day of his life if he manages to track them down. With his powerful jaws he rips off the bark and exposes the honey to view.

I have watched one at work and was amazed at the callous manner in which the robber treated the angry Bees. They were flying around him in their hundreds, darting on to his thick fur and endeavouring to drive in their stings, they were settling on his face, but with his paws he brushed them aside and continued to devour the yellow comb with its sweet contents. With the honeycomb he devoured many Bees, but little notice did he take, and he continued to eat until satisfied. At last he was in a sticky mess, honey was trickling over his face, which was nearly covered with the furious insects, but he again brushed them off. At last, however, one or more evidently found a sensitive spot, for he jumped backwards, turned tail and disappeared.

Another interesting thing I discovered about the Badger is his method of killing his prey. Many wild animals dispatch their captures by biting them ; the Badger does not use his teeth until the animal he has caught is dead, and his method of killing is to tread them to death. I have observed them killing Frogs, Toads and Moles, and in every instance they pressed them to death with their powerful front paws, meanwhile rolling them round and round on the ground.

The Badger is really a most useful animal, and ought to be strictly protected. At present he is looked upon by country folk as a creature fit only to be hunted and killed on every possible occasion. I wonder when the people of this country will realise that the wild creatures have every bit as much right to live as they themselves, and it is certain that a Badger does far more good in his short life than many of the ignorant, so-called sportsmen who roam the countryside with a gun, killing every bird and beast they can approach.

The Badger and the Hen.

Although the Badger will devour eggs if he comes across them when hunting for food, he will not go out of his way to search for them. I have seen and filmed one robbing a Hen's nest, but it was really the fault of the bird, for instead of laying her eggs in the house and nest provided for her, she chose a bank under a thick hedge. A Badger in passing picked

Photo : O. G. Pike] COMMUNITY FEEDING. *[Mondiale.*

This Badger, which was caught young and reared on the bottle, has become a great pet, as full of playful pranks as the young puppy with which it is so friendly. They play together and even share the same dish at meal-times.

OVER THE TOP. *[Brit. Instruct. Films.*

The Badger's strong, short legs and powerful claws stand him in good stead when hurrying from some enemy. He possesses a gland that secretes a strong odour with which he lays his trail when journeying a distance from home.

up her scent and approached her, but when they met face to face the bird jumped up, spread her wings, and it was not easy to decide which was the more surprised. However, the Badger bolted, and the Hen followed, but the former thought better of it, came back on his own trail, found the eggs, and devoured two.

In some districts Badgers and Foxes appear to be rivals, while in other haunts they live together peacefully. There is an instance on record of a Vixen and a Badger having their Cubs in the same burrow. The Fox being a creature not too fond of hard work is always ready to occupy the "earth" made by the Badger. When a Fox inhabits a burrow, the strong scent at the entrance is a sure sign that he is at home. Although the Badger possesses a strong scent, he does not advertise his presence to such an extent as the former. As the Badger travels about the countryside he constantly pauses, sits down and leaves a tiny trace of his scent from his scent-gland behind him. I have on several occasions been able to locate these spots, and have found a small patch of what looks like a dull red smear on the ground. By doing this the Badger is able to travel long distances and return on the same trail when necessary.

The Badger's skin is very loose, and he is able if attacked by a Dog or other creature to turn on his adversary. I have seen two Badgers fighting, and I found that they had a clever method of dodging. If one attempted to rush the other, the latter would put his nose down, then when the attacker darted in there was only the back of the head facing him; now directly the two met, the first would continue to lower his head and turn a complete somersault, and was therefore ready to pounce on the other immediately

it recovered. It is a very rapid movement and exceedingly clever.

The Badger is the cleanest animal I know. He never soils the inside of his home or leaves refuse lying about as does the Fox. This is a great advantage, for in frosty weather he retires into his warm bed, curls up in a ball and goes into a deep sleep, which will continue for as long as the frost. He does not hibernate as completely as some other Mammals. The Dormouse sleeps for several months; the Hedgehog often does the same, but in mild or only reasonably cold weather the Badger is out and about searching for food. Sweet things are always attractive, and I suppose it is for this reason that in some burrows there have been found numbers of old tins. Where the Badgers obtained them I cannot say, but in roaming the countryside they may have entered gardens or farmyards and picked up and carried off home tins which have contained treacle or jam.

The Badger is not often heard except in the breeding season; then one may sometimes be heard calling to his mate.

The old English name of this Mammal is Brock, and it is one of the very few of Celtic origin in our language. In the Irish, Gaelic and Manx languages the name is still Brock, while in Welsh it becomes Broch. At close quarters the Badger is very conspicuous, with his bold black-and-white markings, but at a short distance these markings act as a very clever form of camouflage. On a moonlight night when the Badger issues forth from his lair he is almost invisible, and even in the sunlight when standing quietly on the edge of a wood the stripes on his face appear to harmonise in the most wonderful manner with his immediate surroundings.

[Mallinson.

BADGER AT SETT.

A picture taken by the Badger itself. As it left the hole it ignited a trapfuse—the camera being left open.

Photo : O. G. Pike.] *[Mondiale.*

The Fox pauses a moment at the door of its lair to sniff the air and learn, with its keen sense of smell, if any antagonist is on its trail. Swift and cunning in its nature, it has a notorious reputation for outwitting its pursuers.

THE RED-COATED HUNTER

By ERNEST A. GRAY, M.R.C.V.S.

PERHAPS we are too ready to condemn the wild things of the woods when their hunting leads them into trouble, forgetting that food is difficult to secure when only sharp wits and sharper claws are the means of winning it. It is difficult, for example, to judge the Fox, whose story is told below, for it has many endearing characteristics.

BEYOND the roar of the traffic at the bottom of the street, there is a countryside where my mind dwells—a wide open space in Yorkshire, where man lives fully every hour of light, entertained by the wild creatures which town tends to make us forget.

The only sounds are the plaintive crying of peewits and a distant murmuring of sheep. The moors sweep into a cup-shaped depression, and there are cottages in the hollows, a silver streak between them betrays the presence of a stream. There are few human beings—but other life abounds. Across the farther slope is a gaunt shoulder of granite humping out of the hillside. A few scattered pines shiver beneath its shadow. With a telescope focused on the base of the trees, we see amongst them the sandy pit of a rabbit warren : and there, look—what was that tawny streak that showed for a moment ? Not a rabbit, surely ! No, a fox, a mother fox who has made her home in the deserted Coney City. Our valley is known to the countryside as the Devil's Punch Bowl : and it is a famous haunt of foxes. This year, a vixen has made her home in the old rabbit warren. The rabbits have long since departed from this world : let us hope, for their sakes, to one where foxes cease from troubling and the huntsman's horn is at rest. But it may be queried, if those villagers down there know the foxes are up here, why don't they wipe them out. Foxes are expensive neighbours, killing poultry and game and so on. They do, indeed, but Brer Fox is a wily creature, he never mires his own nest. He hunts far afield and leaves the district near his own home severely alone. Therefore, our own foxes flourish in peace, until the leaves begin to redden, and the stirring tantivy once more awakes the echoes. It should also not be forgotten, apart from the sporting instinct which is in all of us, and helps to save the fox race, that foxes love rat-meat, and it remains a question whether a fox-denuded countryside may not be worse off if overrun by rats, which not only kill poultry but take the eggs also.

The fox is of the dog tribe, but has a different type of skull and has oval rather than circular pupils in his eyes. He has a narrow snout, long ears and a bushy tail. In the mountainous regions the slim Greyhound Fox is found, while the Mastiff and Cur Foxes of the lower ground are more sturdily built. The badger's lair or the rabbit's warren are alike welcome to Reynard, who adopts and adapts these "earths" to his own use and takes his mate there to rear her family.

To approach the foxes' lair demands the skill of a first-rate tracker. But he who is persevering and patient will be rewarded. The dainty red-furred vixen and her five little woolly cubs, outlined against the grey rock and the sombre tints of the pine trunks, make an idyllic picture of family life. The cubs have been brought into the world about the end of March, and there are usually three to six in a litter. For the first month the mother feeds them entirely on her milk; only when the summer is well advanced will she leave them to catch stronger meat, rats, young rabbits, and feathered game, to

A HAPPY FAMILY.   *[Charles Reid.*
The Vixen is a model mother, rearing her whelps which are blind until ten days old, in a very attentive way.

satisfy their big appetites. Vixens are devoted mothers. But mother here is now resting, and one glance shows her pride in her sturdy family. On her last trip, she brought the cubs home a pheasant: now that pheasant has disappeared into their fat little insides, and only a few feathers and a leg remain to tell the sad story of a pheasant who thought he had no more to learn. The cubs are having a fine game with the remaining leg; one tosses it up in the air, another catches it and runs away, only to be caught by his yelping brothers and sisters, and rolled over and over by a pack of excited furry rascals. Now one

of them has stolen the toy, rushed off and quickly buried it. This starts a new game, played until the cubs are tired. Fox cubs are very fond of a race, and they often have a definite running track outside their earth. There is one here in the sandpit, running from a rock round a pine stump and so home again. The pheasant's leg forgotten, and revived by their siesta, the cubs race wobbly up and down the track, until one, exasperated at being left behind, seizes the tail of the brother next ahead in his teeth, and a free fight ensues. The combatants separate, exhausted; there is a moment's pause as if to think up some new occupation, and then one scratches up that pheasant's leg again, and a new version of hunt-the-slipper begins.

But the mother is uneasy. The wind—kind friend of all wild folk—has whispered a warning. There is a strange taint on the breeze: Man! Instantly she bundles the cubs into the earth and down into the rabbit's galleries. They are gone in a flash, and the passing shepherd climbs on up the hillside, pretending he has seen nothing, but with a grim little smile about his mouth as he thinks of the ravages these fluff balls may accomplish when they grow up, and the reckoning to be paid when autumn bows out summer.

He has passed very close to the "earth" and is soon out of sight. The little red mother stirs, peers out warily, and finding the way clear, starts off on a forage to find new food for her voracious family. Now, however, the cubs have been enjoined to stay where they are, deep in the cool earth, until she returns to them. Sniffing the air outside her home, and satisfied, in another second she has slipped out into the friendly sheltering heather. She knows man's power and is not such a fool as to raid neighbouring roosts. She pads

A CAREFUL FOSTER-MOTHER

Surely no mother ever had such unusual foster-children to rear as this Spaniel that was placed in charge of two Badger cubs. She brought them up as gently and carefully as though they were her own puppies.

Photo: J. P. Taylor. **LEARNING TO TRACK.** [Mondiale.

The young Fox, though helpless for the first few weeks, soon learns, under the expert guidance of his parents, how to hunt for himself and how to outwit his enemies. He is a speedy runner, can swim, and even climb trees.

out across moors and fields for full five miles, casting round like a setter until she finds a rich scent. But always she keeps some hedge or boulder nearby for refuge in case of sudden danger. If it were dark, she would creep upwind stealthily and then pounce suddenly upon her startled victim. But when still daylight, she is compelled to adopt other tactics.

How Rabbits are lured to their death.

Foxes perhaps realise better than most the broad streak of foolishness in all animals; and where concealment is useless, they play on their victim's gullibility. Watch her antics now in front of another rabbit warren, an inhabited one this time; she approaches quietly, then commences rolling over and over, her tail between her teeth. Fascinated, the rabbits draw closer and closer, until suddenly she straightens out like a released spring—there is a sudden flurry of bolting rabbits. One fails to get away quickly enough, and the vixen trots away with a limp form hanging from her jaws. The cubs she knows are well fed, and food is plentiful; so in a suitable place she scratches a grave for her furry victim, nosing the loosened earth over it, until completely covered, and leaving it safely cached as an emergency larder. Farmers

dread vixens with cubs, for sometimes a madness will seize them, and they will kill and kill for the mere lust of slaying.

But is the fox such an injurious intruder in the neighbourhood of coverts? He certainly takes pheasants, and, unfortunately, any damage is attributed to that "dratted fox." Careful examinations of "kills," however, suggest other creatures as culprits, for instance, marauding cats; and, in any case, of all "vermin," rats are the most destructive, and the fox is the rats' natural enemy.

Certainly foxes are vermin, in that they wage red war on all small animals that man tries to keep for himself. But even man can learn some useful lessons from a fox's life; there is the fidelity of the dog fox to his mate, and the devotion and self-sacrifice of the mother. She especially has only one interest in life: to care for her cubs. Her creed, indeed, is "Sufficient unto the day is the evil thereof." The day will come soon enough when the young hounds are taken out "to be blooded" on such cubs as the huntsmen can find them. Then, indeed, the fox's family, their woolly baby coats turned to the tawny red of manhood, will need sound bodies and well trained minds. And to this end the little lady in the red coat bends all her energies.

Photo: P. J. Taylor.]   HIDE-AND-SEEK.   [Mallinson.

Fox cubs are playful little creatures, very pretty and amusing in their antics. They do not appear outside their snug lair till they are six weeks old, but after three months they start hunting and learning the dangers of the wood.

[Charles Reid.

The Hare seldom seeks shelter underground as the Rabbit does, but relies on the colouring of his coat to deceive the eyes of his pursuers, and also on the use of his powerful limbs and exceptionally keen senses.

THE RABBIT AND THE HARE

By M. V. LEBOUR

WHAT is the difference between a Rabbit and a Hare ? To many people they look alike, but their distinguishing features will be easily recognisable when this chapter, which explains their characteristics, has been read. These brave little creatures, whose daily lives are beset by many dangers, make an interesting study.

IT is well known that Rabbits and Hares belong to the large group of Rodents or gnawing animals. Let us look carefully at a common wild Rabbit and note its characteristic features. It has brownish, sandy-coloured fur, not long but very soft and thick. Its ears are long and its tail is short with a white patch underneath it. The hind legs are much longer than the front legs, and it has five toes on each front foot and four toes on each hind foot. The mouth is cleft above. (The " Hare lip " is so called because of its resemblance to that of a Hare or Rabbit.) It has long whiskers, which are very sensitive and act as feelers. The two front teeth in each jaw are long and curved with sharp, chisel-like edges, and behind the upper front teeth is another small pair. There are no canine or " eye " teeth, and there is a large gap filled with fur between the front teeth and the flat grinders or cheek teeth.

The Rabbit can run quickly in a scuttling manner, and as it runs it lifts its tail so that the white patch shows. Compare the Rabbit with the Hare. The Hare is a close relative, resembling the Rabbit in many ways, but it is a larger animal altogether with much longer ears and very much longer legs, especially the hind legs. It runs much more effectively than the Rabbit. It has no white under the tail, and its fur is a soft brown.

The Rabbit lives in burrows which it digs with its feet in the earth or sand. These are elaborately made, with many passages and nests in them, and usually at least more than one outlet—sometimes several. It thus escapes its enemies by retiring underground. The Hare lives a solitary life in the open and never burrows. It is always alert and depends on its swiftness of sight, hearing, scent and running powers to escape its enemies. Even the heart is so adjusted that the Hare is able to put on full speed in a moment. It lives in the shade in summer and in open fields in winter, getting as much sun as possible. It makes for itself a loose bed of leaves and grass,

213

known as its " form." Both Rabbit and Hare are perfectly adapted for their own particular mode of life.

The front teeth of these animals and of all Rodents are peculiar, for they are continually growing, and have what is known as " persistent pulps," instead of being closed up at a certain age as are our own. They bite on the bottom teeth, and so keep them sharpened and well adapted for gnawing ; and they can gnaw without any damage to the mouth and lips. These are specially protected, the palate having hard ridges, the tongue with a hard patch in the centre and the soft, cleft upper lip withdrawing itself as the gnawing goes on. The fur in the gap between front and cheek teeth is also a protection. If one of the front teeth should break, the whole system is put out of order.

Rabbits eat much grass, and the turf on which they feed and have grazed is said to be the finest in the world, for they devour all the stalks which the sheep would leave. They come out at dusk to feed, and retire into their burrows late at night, coming out again early in the morning before sunrise, although they are often to be seen in the daytime, scuttling into their burrows at the slightest disturbance, the white under the tail serving as a warning signal to those who are dilatory, probably the young Rabbits. Hares feed even during the darkest nights and wander about in the dark. Rabbits have a peculiar habit of drumming with their feet at the entrance of a burrow, perhaps to attract a neighbour, and have a different kind of drumming when alarmed, as a signal to the others. They often fight, using their legs for powerful blows. Hares are also capable of delivering severe blows with their legs when in conflict.

When Unity is Strength.

This keeping together and living in burrows probably accounts for the great success of the Rabbits in the battle of life ; also for the fact that they are exceedingly prolific and find their food with ease. Wherever they go they multiply. The well-known fact of how they were introduced into Australia, and have now become a pest, is an instance of this. They have been introduced into many countries, and are not even natives of Britain, but came long ago from Southern Europe.

The Hare is a true native, and has been honoured for centuries in this country. The ancient Romans kept it as a pet and did not

Photo: John H. Vickers.]   THE RABBIT'S FRONT DOOR.   *[Mallinson.*

This old Rabbit, sitting at the mouth of her burrow, has her ears alert for any sound that spells danger. Next to the sportsman's gun, her greatest dread is her enemy, the Stoat, from whose attack it is almost impossible to escape.

Photo : Farnsworth.] **YOUNG BARN OWL AND RABBIT.** [*Mallinson.*

This peculiar friendship shows that the wild creatures of the woods are not always at war with each other. The young Owl has not yet attained full plumage, and its fluffy white covering is evidently fascinating its companion.

eat it, and by the Normans it was protected as a beast of the chase. They made special parks for it where it was sheltered. If it had not been for this care the Hare would probably be very rare now, if not extinct.

The Common European Hare, which is our Common Hare, has a wide distribution. But there is another species living in Northern Scotland. This is the Scottish Mountain Hare, one of the so-called Varying Hares. This species changes its coat in winter, turning to white, with the exception of part of its back which remains grey, and the tips of its ears, which are black. In Ireland there is a third species, another of the Varying Hares, which differs from the Common Hare in its shorter and more rounded head, shorter ears and legs, and reddish-brown fur of a somewhat inferior quality.

The Irish Hare does not change its coat to white in the winter. This change of coat is caused by the coloured hairs being shed completely and new white hairs appearing in their stead. Not only is it advantageous in snowy country to have white hair so that it is inconspicuous, but, even more important, it is much warmer, as it prevents the body heat from escaping. There are some long and much coarser hairs among the fine fur which are more deeply rooted and stand out farther ; these keep the fur from matting and are a protection in the rain. There are sometimes black Rabbits to be found among the others. In several localities I know one or two are always to be seen, but they are much too conspicuous ever to be successful, although there must be quite a fair number born in order for them to survive under normal conditions.

The Crow's Cunning.

Both Hares and Rabbits have many natural enemies : Foxes, Stoats, Weasels, Cats, Hawks, Owls, Crows and Hooded Crows, not to mention men and Dogs. A Hooded Crow will pretend to be friendly with a Rabbit and then suddenly pounce upon it and kill it. Two Crows were once seen pursuing a Hare and aiming blows at it whilst the poor frightened animal was screaming, and a final blow killed it.

The Hare is very clever in evading its enemies, doubling back on its track several times. When it leaves its " form " it takes a long leap to break the scent, and on returning leaps back into it. Both Hares and Rabbits sometimes rely on keeping perfectly still to

AFTER THE STRUGGLE. [*Charles Reid.*]

The enemy feared most by the Rabbit is the ferocious little Weasel, from whose attack there is little chance of escape.
The above picture tells its own story of struggle and defeat. The victor seems exhausted after its hard fight.

Photo : Farnsworth.] THE AGE OF INNOCENCE. [*Mallinson.*

Young wild Rabbits, ignorant of the dangers awaiting them on every side, forget to be cautious when their mother
is not at hand to warn them. They are playful little creatures, very easy to tame, and make extremely docile pets.

BROWN HARE.　　[*W. S. Berridge.*]

The Hare squats nearly the whole of the day in its "form" and goes food-hunting during the night.

Noel Temple.]　　YOUNG HARE.　　[*Mallinson.*]

As soon as the Leveret is able to make provision for itself the mother Hare leaves it to its own resources.

MOUNTAIN HARE.　　[*W. S. Berridge.*]

In winter the Mountain Hare has a chance of eluding its many enemies. It is protected by its colouring, which harmonises so well with its surroundings that it is very difficult to detect, especially when it is squatting.

elude their enemies, so closely resembling their surroundings that they are seen with great difficulty. Only a practised eye can distinguish a Hare or Rabbit lying low in a field.

The Rabbit is very prolific and has several families in a year, making soft nests of grass and leaves, and tearing out its own fur for a comfortable lining. The young are born naked and helpless and quite blind, with very short ears and legs. The Hare breeds in spring and makes only a rough hollow for her young, never making a burrow. Her babies are known as Leverets, and are born with fur, the ears and legs being much longer than those of the young Rabbit. The mother, if she scents the proximity of an enemy, may carry her family right away to some safer place and there make a new home for them, where they will be entirely out of danger.

The Hare's piteous cry.

The Hare has a curious, low cry, said to sound like "bleak, bleak," and quite a different and piteous cry when hurt, like the crying of a child. The Rabbit cries only when in pain. The cry of a trapped Hare is the most miserable sound imaginable.

Both Hares and Rabbits make good pets. Sometimes a Cat will adopt baby Rabbits and bring them up as her own. Both Dogs and Cats, although usually regarded as enemies, have been known to live in a friendly way with them. I have seen the children at Plymouth sometimes bringing their pet Rabbits for a run on the grass on the Hoe, where they frisk about quite safely. The most celebrated pets of this kind are the tame Hares belonging to the poet Cowper. He kept three wild "Jack Hares," as he called them. Their names were Puss, Tiney and Bess, although they were all males. Puss would sleep on Cowper's knee, and was so grateful for being nursed when ill that he would lick the hand of his benefactor. He was carried into the garden, staying there all day and carried back at night. He would invite his master into the garden by drumming on his knee, and preferred the society of human beings to those of his own kind. Tiney was never quite property tamed, but Bess was always tame and gentle. Each had a character all his own, and each could be recognised by the expression on his face. They were fed on leaves—Sow Thistle, Dandelion and Lettuce and herbs. They ate grass only occasionally, and apparently for medicinal purposes. They liked to swallow sand, and this seemed to be natural to them. They devoured both blade and stalk of green Corn, but not the ear, also Straw, Oats and Musk. Above all they ate bread, which was given to them daily, sometimes, if green food were difficult to procure, with Shredded Carrot or Apple (they did not like the fruit itself). They drank water if succulent juicy vegetables were scarce. Sometimes they had twigs of Hawthorn and Common Briar, eating the wood, even if of considerable thickness. Bess died young; Tiney lived to be nine years old; Puss lived to be eleven years and eleven months. None of them had ever seen a Dog until a Spaniel, who had never before seen a Hare, was introduced to them. They all lived together in perfect amity, eating out of the same dish. Cowper's poem entitled "Epitaph to a Hare," beginning:

"Here lies, whom hound did ne'er pursue,"

was written in memory of Tiney.

There are many superstitions about Hares and Rabbits, especially the former, but the Devon and Cornish fishermen will not allow a Rabbit to be mentioned on board ship. If one does so inadvertently they think it best to return immediately lest some dreadful thing happen. The legends about Hares usually show it to be an unlucky animal, yet it was supposed to be a cure for the colic, and Samuel Pepys had a Hare's pad in his possession, which, he said, kept him free from this complaint. The ancient Romans used Hares for the purposes of divination. It is said to be unlucky for a Hare to cross one's path, and if one meets a Hare on setting out for a journey it is a warning to retrace one's steps. In many places in the olden days Hares were supposed to be witches in disguise, and old women changed at night into Hares, thus proving themselves to be witches.

The following story, told to us in the Highlands, is well known in many versions: There was an old woman who was thought to be a witch and change into a Hare every night. Now, it is a well-known fact that the only way to kill a witch is with a silver bullet, so a man took a crooked sixpence and lay in wait for the old woman. He saw a Hare enter her cottage at midnight, and immediately shot it with the sixpence. The next morning the old woman was found dead with the crooked sixpence embedded in her heart.

[*Charles Reid.*

The Stoat in his summer coat of red is every bit as much protected by his colouring as in winter when his fur is white. In the above photograph he is seen setting forth on a prowl with the lust to kill in his heart.

THE STOAT AND THE WEASEL

By ERNEST A. GRAY. M.R.C.V.S.

GANGSTERS of the wild are the Weasel and Stoat, killing ruthlessly and living dangerously. The latter raids nests and slakes his thirst for blood on young partridges or rabbits. The Weasel is the terror of the mouse tribe, and when hunting is not pleasant to encounter. Both assume garments of protective colouring in winter.

THERE are two members of the English countryside inhabitants who can only be described by comparing them to the gunmen of American cities. They are the Stoat and the Weasel ; and, like the gunmen, they have made killing a fine art. A gunman it would seem, is careful of his appearance, and, whatever his other failings, must be allowed one virtue—that of courage. There is not much courage required, perhaps, to put some victim " on the spot," but few will deny that when cornered, our assassin will fight it out grimly, even to death.

So our Stoat, with his red coat, white shirt front, and black-tipped tail, is one of the best-dressed English mammals, and, like his human counterpart, he kills ruthlessly, and yet on occasion shows a pluck which we can only admire. His life is a dangerous one, his ferocity brings down ⌊on him⌋ the wrath of all kinds of animals. The gamekeeper shoots at him on sight, and even the timid rabbit has been known, when with young, to turn on him in the close confines of a warren, and there stifle or kick him to death. Of course, he asks for trouble. He will follow rabbits into their burrows, and even climb trees in search of eggs and young birds. There are times, too, when he will kill and kill unmercifully, striking down a victim by leaping on its back and burying his teeth in its neck, only to slake his thirst with its blood and then pounce on another luckless rambler. In this way he can create enormous damage amongst coveys of young partridge and pheasant. Thus he can never be seen by a gamekeeper but that a charge of buckshot rattles round his ears.

When on his nest-raiding excursions, Master Stoat sometimes makes a mistake, and when a wild animal makes a mistake he generally pays the penalty—rarely is he let off with a caution. And so when the nest he is watching from the fork of a tree happens to be that of a Brown Owl, he is wittingly, hunger-driven, or unwittingly, asking for trouble, for though he may patiently wait the chance to snatch an unfledged bird from beneath its mother's watchful eye, he has to risk attracting the attention of father Brown Owl, who has death-dealing talons and knows well how to use them. A false move and the owl pounces swiftly and surely, striking with his terrible talons, and the relentless grip on the writhing body of the Stoat is only relaxed to allow the raider's corpse to fall to the ground.

The young are born in the spring, five to eight in a litter, and the mother remains

white robe, only the black tail tip remains the same. The French word for Stoat is " Hermine " ; hence the derivative of the word.

The Weasel is a smaller, slimmer animal than the Stoat. His colour scheme is the same—red above, white below—but he lacks the black tip to his tail. It is only seldom that he is seen. He is not such a desperado as the Stoat, and he too has an amazing turn of speed. Stoats like woods to live in, the Weasel prefers open ground, fields and ditches, the reason being that a Weasel's favourite dietary consists largely of rats and mice, and these are not found in any quantity in copses or undergrowth.

When the rats migrate to their winter

Photo : C. W. R. Knight.]   A BABY STOAT.   [Mondiale.

This picture of a young Stoat shows the peculiar scruff on the neck by which the mother carries it. This creature which is valued for its fur, is very destructive and no friend of the farmer, whose poultry yard it is fond of visiting.

attached to her family long after they are able to fend for themselves. Family devotion, indeed, is a second virtue of Stoats. The keeper knows that if he kills a mother, and suspends her body from a tree, setting a trap in the ground below, he is certain to catch one or more of the family, if not all. One by one, the children will seek out their mother's body, and each in turn pay the price of its devotion.

A wary gentleman is this dapper little racketeer, but sometimes in the country, by patiently keeping very quiet, one may be fortunate enough to see him glide across the grass. Quite frequently, too, we may see more than one ; there may be two or three, following each other in single file, like stealthy Indians on the warpath.

An Ermine is a Northern Stoat in winter dress. The red coat is changed for a beautiful

quarters in the farmyard he follows them there, and one may sometimes come across him snugly tucked away beneath a bale of straw or pile of timber. During the winter he levies heavy toll on the rats, and when spring comes round again, and the rats and mice commence nesting in the hedges, he is of greater value still.

As the gunmen of America are tolerated because they keep down one another's numbers, so the weasel must be regarded as a friend for the invaluable aid he renders in keeping down " the small beer " of the world. He is particularly valuable to the poultry farmer. Only seldom will he pick up a stray chick. If he is found nesting near a hen-run, it is a short-sighted policy to kill him. Any damage he may possibly do is as nothing compared with his services rendered in keeping down the rats and mice. A Weasel seldom

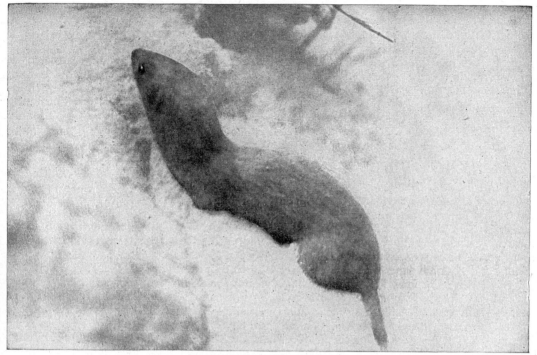

A WINTER PROTECTION.
[W. S. Berridge.

The Weasel is lucky during the cold weather to grow a white coat that gives it not only extra warmth, but added security.   When food is difficult to find it has to be more venturesome, and finds its protective colouring a boon.

THE WEASEL SCENTS FOOD.
[Charles Reid.

The Weasel often tracks down its prey alone, but will join a pack of small killers, especially when there is a food shortage, and from these " fairy hounds," as they are termed by country folk, their quarry have little hope of escape.

kills for blood, it usually devours the animal it kills. It has not the same staying power as the Stoat ; perhaps this is the reason why it lives twices as long as that animal (four years as compared to two). It hunts upon those creatures that do not seek safety in flight ; quite frequently it goes after moles in their runs, and may be caught in the traps intended for them.

A Weasel, indeed, is not quite so un- necessarily offensive as a Stoat, and hence beyond man has few enemies. His chief enemy is the Hawk, sailing over the open ground on which he hunts.

Country folk here and there still speak of the " fairy hounds," and we know that these are packs of Weasels, for they do sometimes hunt in packs, especially when there is food shortage. One is well advised to move out of their path at such times, for, when hunger drives, they are ferocious, fearless buccaneers, and will attack anything large or small which gets in their way. A pack of Weasels is an unpleasant thing to fight, and is not easily beaten off. They are out to kill for food and hunt relentlessly. At the scent of rabbit or hare they will trail doggedly, wearing down their quarry until in exhaustion and fear it lies down and awaits the stealthily and remorselessly approaching executioners.

A grim picture—but, on the other hand, a single Weasel approaching birds, say the foolish Lapwing, provides amusement—though again the end is tragedy. As if aware of the bird's silly inquisitiveness, the Weasel dances and plays antics until attention is attracted, ever creeping nearer and nearer to the birds. He leaps and turns somersaults like any clown until, when he has gauged his spring, he suddenly lands on four feet and with a bound is amongst the audience, and one dies to provide his supper.

A Weasel, like a Stoat, has only one litter a year, usually of four to five young.

While one would hold no brief for the Stoat and Weasel, yet there should be a moment's pause before passing judgment on these furred marauders. Their habits may appear cruel and vicious, yet it must be remembered that they play a vital rôle in Nature's economy. It is only occasionally that the blood lust seizes them ; in their ordinary lives they are of great use. They are handsome, beautiful creatures, as indeed are most of Mother Nature's creatures. Study of them in their natural haunts reveals a passionate joy of life in their tiny souls, and how much more merciful and speedy a death for their prey, to die suddenly beneath their teeth, than slowly and dreadfully in the grip of a steel noose or the remorseless advance of a fatal illness ! Death in the former case is painless.

OUTWITTING THE STOAT.   *[H. Mortimer Batten.*

The Stoat, such a fierce tracker himself, has many enemies on his trail, the trappers who lay bait to entice him to destruction, being the most dreaded. The prowler above, unable to resist the temptation, is heading for disaster.

[*W. S. Berridge.*

The Polecat is a silent stalker, springing suddenly on unwary birds perched on their nests. When he has made a meal of bird-flesh he turns his attention to the eggs. Wherever he goes, he leaves desolation in his trail.

FURRED POLICEMEN

By ERNEST A. GRAY, M.R.C.V.S.

THE woods are full of fierce killers, each pitting their wits and strength against the other in their struggle for supremacy. Many kill for the sake of securing food, but in others the lust for blood is uppermost. A ferocious tribe is described in the following chapter, whose hunting methods are extremely interesting, if not commendable.

ONE of the shibboleths of the day is " The Survival of the Fittest." It implies that only the most powerful and ruthless animals can succeed in the battle of life. But like all similar statements it requires modification. Those who study wild things in their natural haunts know that it is too sweeping a generalisation. Nature is always just. The useless she sweeps out of existence ; but by useless she does not mean, as so many imagine, the weaker. She gives every animal a chance to succeed, no matter how small they may be. To the weaker things she gives methods of protection, long legs for running, and powerful claws to construct dug-outs. And the activities of the stronger she carefully curtails by giving them in due proportion greater and greater difficulties to overcome.

The gentle birds have been taught to build their nests in trees. But it was not long before certain squirrels found it profitable to climb trees, and empty those nests of their eggs. A passer-by strolling through the woods and hearing the uproar overhead as the birds see their tiny families destroyed is apt to shake his head sadly and say, " Oh, well ! a tragedy, no doubt ! But it is the survival of the fittest ! " Only few realise that Nature is not blind, but realises that if unchecked the squirrels would in time wipe out the bird-race ; and therefore she teaches other animals to climb trees, not to prey on defenceless finches and sparrows, but on the red thieves that snatch their young. In this way she wisely ensures an even balance.

In the depths of big woods or forests we may perhaps catch sight of one of these policeman of Nature—a brown weasel-like creature, slipping like a shadow along a bough. We see its brown back, and yellow under-front, and wonder for a moment, perhaps, whether it is a Weasel. But then

223

we realise it is too big for a Weasel, and too small for a Stoat, and that its head is blunter nosed than either of those creatures. It is in fact a Pine Marten.

At one time Pine Martens were common everywhere in big woods, but with the advent of the motor car and arterial roads, they have become more and more scarce. To-day the only places where we are likely to find them in any numbers are the wooded glades of the Welsh and Scottish hills. It is a long-lived creature, its life extending over a period of four to five years. The young are born in the spring of the year, and there may be a family of two or three in the nest.

Squirrel for Dinner.

The Pine Marten's favourite dish is squirrel. I am afraid that on occasion he is a sad rogue and helps himself to an egg or two; but perhaps the birds are willing to pay such a small price for protection from their arch-enemies the squirrels.

Squirrels and Mice make up most of the Marten's dietary; and in a Squirrel's nest he makes his home. The mother lines it with her own fur, with leaves, odd feathers, and even bits of squirrel pelts, or the nest may be made simply in a hollow tree; or if nothing else offers, in a large disused nest. Pine Martens, like most of the tree folk, are very particular as to cleanliness, and they prefer the snug warmth of a tree crutch than the open draughtiness of a nest.

Pine Martens are shy creatures, and avoid human beings and their habitations. They are very difficult to tame. There is a close relative of theirs, however, who is interesting for the following reason.

This relative is the Stone Marten (or Beech Marten) and he has no such dislike for human dwellings, perhaps because he knows from experience what capital nests can be made in them. He often establishes himself in old buildings, granaries, or hobs in walls.

The Stone Marten as House Cat.

The point about this pretty creature is that it is fonder of mice and honey than of squirrels, and would appear to be the Greek " ictis " which did the work of the modern house-cat two thousand years ago.

Another ferocious little beast of the same tribe, who, however, is fond of bird flesh, is the Polecat. He, too, is allied to the Weasel, but is smaller than the Martens who are among the giants of the family. The Marten goes to twenty inches in body length without tail, while the Polecat reaches about seventeen inches only. What he gives in size he makes up for in ferocity. A furtive hunter in blackish-brown fur, underneath rather a yellowish-brown, he lives in a deserted rabbit-warren and feeds on small mammals, reptiles and frogs, eggs and birds.

When the Polecat tackles larger birds, as chance forces a meeting upon him, he has the fight of his life. It is not that he is seeking mature bird flesh for lunch, but that the adult bird surprises him stalking the young one. Should the quarry be young ravens on a rocky ledge in the mountains where the Polecat can in these days only survive, and father is around, the hunter gets short shrift, for a fully grown Raven is a terrible adversary, and with his pick-axe of a beak deals death in a blow to smaller creatures. At night, the real time for the Polecat's safari, the Raven, caught unawares as he perches at his out-post zealously guarding the nest, may suffer overwhelming defeat unless he can deliver a lucky defensive blow which settles the attacker before he can come too closely to grips.

A Slinking Stalker.

The Polecat stalks warily and with admirable precision. As he creeps along a ledge towards a nest containing eggs he will not displace a pebble or a blade of grass. There is not the slightest sound, and the movement is so slow and sure that it is scarcely to be recognised. If the Raven becomes aware of the attacker only as the Polecat springs, the latter's sharp teeth will sink into his neck before he can bring his beak into action, but even then, the talons, equally terrible, get a grip on the lithe body and a bloodthirsty battle ensues. The Raven tries to fly away still gripping his adversary, but the teeth of the tenacious creature are doing their work and eventually the Raven falls dead to the ground and his grip relaxes. In all probability the eggs will be forgotten for a while and the Polecat will call his mate to come and join him in a feast of blood. The pair will suck the corpse dry, leaving the tough flesh alone, for Polecats are delicate as to meat and devour only the tenderest morsels. It is indeed very strange that such ferocity, such bloodlust, should be the striking characteristic of this beautifully built, agile little animal.

Monarch of the mountains

[*Charles Reid.*

The Otter spends most of his time near the edge of the water, occasionally journeying farther afield to hunt for rats or voles, or for another pool where he can fish.   In spite of his partiality to water, he can travel speedily on land.

THE OTTER:

A GAME FIGHTER OF ANCIENT LINEAGE
By R. McLEOD

MANY people imagine the Otter to be almost extinct, but it is often to be seen on the banks of remote streams, its long, lithe body covered with smooth fur and its feet webbed so that it is as much at home in the water as out of it.   It is an expert fisher, and, as we learn in the following chapter, often spends the night on a foraging expedition.

IT is not always appreciated that in these islands there are, apart from species preserved for " sport," considerable numbers of flesh-eating animals, whose whole life is spent in hunting, or in being hunted.

The word " Carnivora " conjures up scenes in tropic jungle or Arctic waste, where the struggle for existence goes on eternally among the creatures of the wild. We seldom indeed associate the word with our own countryside.

Amongst the larger of the creatures that are not nearly so extinct as one might imagine, the Otter claims our attention as a vigorous survival of the beasts of prey that, in ancient days, roamed the forests and marshes of our land. He belongs to the Bear tribe, like the Weasel and Stoat, the Badger and the Polecat, and has a very ancient lineage, for the fossil remains of the forefathers of his race have been found in the latter Tertiary deposits ; that is, before the Great Ice Periods.

But, unlike relatives of the tribe mentioned above, Lutra Vulgaris, to give the Otter his proper high-sounding name, went wet in early days. That is to say he took to the water, and though he has not progressed so far as the Seals, for instance, in this direction, he is a most capable aquatic performer, and has become very much at home in both fresh and salt water, where he hunts and catches his food.

The long, sinuous, fur-clad body ends in a thick, tapering tail, which acts as a powerful rudder, and the whole shape is ideal for rapid movement through water, where this accomplished poacher is as much at home as the fish he hunts. The broad head is flattened from above, the ears are short and rounded, the eyes small and bright. The mouth, well supplied with formidable teeth, gives the Otter the characteristic, relentless expression of the beast of prey. The short powerful legs and the five-toed webbed feet fit him preeminently for the life he has adopted.

But the Otter has not lost his efficiency on land, and in a night, when out on a foraging expedition, will travel up to fifteen miles. A great rover, alert, vigorous and intelligent, he has not one, but several holts, or well-hidden resting-places, which may be ten miles apart, and he will work from one to the other. Further, he is not satisfied with one hunting district, but will pass from one river to another, to lake and down to the sea, where he will be as much at home as in fresh water.

The Otter is a fur-bearing animal. The fur, dusky brown in colour, consists of a soft under-coat of whitish-grey, interspersed with which are longer, thicker and glossier hairs which form the outer coat. Some of the pelts dress up quite nicely and have a quality of their own.

The total length of a full-grown specimen is four feet, but about one-third of this is tail. The weight of a full-grown male may be anything between twenty and thirty pounds ; but heavier specimens have been recorded. The female is slightly smaller than the male.

Although Otters are to be expected wherever there is water to support a good supply of fish, it is the most difficult thing in the world to come upon one at close quarters. Their nocturnal habits, combined with their retiring nature render them fairly invisible to the casual observer. At the mere suspicion of intrusion the Otter effaces himself in a moment. However, on a stretch of water where our compatriot is suspected his peculiar footprints may be traced on the moist bank. There, at sunset, his flute-like note or whistle betrays his presence as he glides into the water for his evening meal.

From the banks of a northern river on the long evenings of June, when it scarcely grows really dark, one can be reasonably sure of seeing the Otter as he marks down his prey.

He slips into the water without a splash, his athletic streamlined body gliding beneath the surface, leaving scarcely a ripple behind. There he swims horizontally and calmly just under water until suddenly he dives, sometimes in a spiral, to reappear with a fish in his powerful jaws. Not always does he get his prey with the first dive, but he is persistent, and it is a smart fish which, once marked down, escapes him. The fish which is secured from below is generally brought to the bank for consumption.

Alas, here, in the case of big fish like Salmon, our doughty hunter falls severely from grace. One good bite from the shoulder suffices him. On a well-preserved Salmon river it is quite common to see fish thus mangled high and dry on the bank, and it is not difficult to imagine the fury of the keeper who stumbles across the practically untouched carcass of a handsome twenty-pounder. We can understand, then, the ruthless war that is waged against the wiliest and most destructive of poachers, for the spawning fish of November and the clean-run spring Salmon are alike hapless victims. The reason for this killing is difficult to understand, except that there is impulse to kill whenever opportunity presents itself.

[H. Mortimer Batten.

THE OTTER STANDS UP.

The Otter, when it chooses, can stand upright, and sometimes when cornered it attacks in this position.

On occasion when pools grow shallow and fish scarcer the Otter does not hesitate to turn to terra-firma for sustenance. Though in the main a fish-eater, Eels, Pike, and other kinds as well as Salmon and Trout being favoured, the Otter does not find other prey amiss, and his range of dishes is a wide one. On the seashore it will readily crush and eat Mussels, knock Limpets off the rocks and swallow them, and when hungry not turn up his nose at a substantial meal of Land Snails, Frogs, Wild Duck, and even Rabbits.

Photo : Ray Palmer]   A USEFUL TAIL.   *[Mondiale.*

The Otter's tail, which is slightly flattened at the end, functions as a kind of rudder that helps it in its graceful swimming movements. After diving for fish, the Otter brings its meal to the bank and consumes it there.

Considerable distances are sometimes covered between the various streams, and the proximity of towns does not alarm him. In recent years an Otter was discovered in one of the city parks of Glasgow ! With a change of habitat a variety is lent to the fish diet, and the epicure who daintily dined on fresh Salmon middle-cut will not disdain a Rat, Vole, or even a Frog.

Lutra does not hibernate. The two or three blind young are born in the depths of winter in a snug underground retreat other than the holt that Mother Otter has cosily lined for a nursery. The Cubs are charming wee mites, and if caught young can actually be tamed. There are records showing where they have grown up into affectionate pets. They are frolicsome fellows, and it is wonderful to see mother and her youngsters at play.

Normally, there is one litter a year of two or three youngsters, which are very helpless at first, and remain blind for a month. The mother is a fond parent, most attentive to her babies. She never leaves them except to make a hasty excursion to get food. When the youngsters can see she takes them out to bask in the sun, and cleans them carefully, then at two months of age she gives them their first swimming lesson. But strangely enough they seem to dislike entering the water, and whimper on the banks, a fact which points to the Otter originally being a land animal and not an aquatic fish-eater. However, mother though affectionate to her babies, is a disciplinarian. She coaxes and encourages, but she also punishes if necessary when teaching them how to seek food and hunt prey, as well as how to behave at meals. For example, they must begin on Eels by the tail, but Trout head first. The lessons continue for a long period until the young Otters in summer are capable of looking after themselves. Later, when hard frosts are experienced and the rivers are frozen over, the Otter will swim under the ice after food if he can find a hole, but generally when the weather becomes too severe he makes his way down to estuaries and the sea, where the salt in the water prevents freezing over.

Naturally such an elusive desperado, whom the ancients looked upon as a fish, offers boundless possibilities for the chase ; and, during the season, in Border districts Otter hunting claims a numerous following. He, or even she, is a game fighter, and many a Hound has to pay dearly for rash temerity. In these enlightened, or rather more humane days, one may deplore certain aspects of the hunt, but the fact that trapping and hunting are required to keep his numbers within bounds proves that even in this industrial mechanical age we have still in our midst a romantic outlaw whose lineage carries the memory back to the days of primeval Britain.

AN APPLE A DAY. [Brit. Instruct. Films.
The Dormouse is not always asleep. When a titbit of food comes his way he is very wide awake indeed.
Though particularly fond of nuts and insects, he nevertheless welcomes a windfall in the form of a large apple.

228

Meal-times are filled with danger for the unsuspecting Mouse. His fondness of cheese often leads him to disaster, as can be seen from the above picture, which has caught the tiny thief a second before the trap acted.

RATS, MICE AND VOLES

By RAY PALMER, F.R.E.S., F.Z.S.

RATS and Mice are by no means universally liked, yet they are interesting little creatures whose habits are worth noting. There are many varieties dealt with below, where the story of the Vole is also related. The sleepy little Dormouse, whose habits, as we learn, are so engaging, and the whole family of nibblers are described in this chapter.

SEVERAL kinds of these rodents are only too well known to farmers, householders and storekeepers all over the country, and the damage they cause is enormous. In the case of Rats the loss caused annually in Great Britain has been estimated at about £66,000,000, while £2,000,000 are spent in keeping them down.

The most curious thing is the great change that has come over the Rat population of the country within the last two hundred years. During the seventeenth century and earlier the great pest in Britain was the Black Rat. This species was prevalent in Europe generally, and constituted a serious menace chiefly on account of its carrying the germs of the plague or " Black Death." The bacillus responsible for this disease is transferred by Fleas. When a Rat dies the Fleas leave the body and seek out another host, and if they should chance to get on to a man instead of another Rat they give him the plague.

Meanwhile the Brown Rat, which flourished in temperate Asia, began to invade Europe from the East. In Western Europe it first appeared about 1716, and was found in England by 1728. This newcomer was a hardier and more adaptable animal, more at home out of doors, fonder of burrowing and a more omnivorous feeder. Thus it had every advantage in the struggle for existence against its smaller and more conservative cousin, and within fifty years it had become the predominant species. The old English Black Rat was gradually squeezed out and became scarcer each year, while its rival increased enormously. By 1850 the Black Rat was on the verge of extinction.

This species has one advantage over its brown relative, however : it is a better climber, more agile and therefore better suited to life on a ship. Owing to this it survived in small numbers in various ports, and has increased somewhat within recent years, due to fresh introductions of the species from abroad.

As is well known the rate of increase of Rats is something tremendous. They begin to breed at the age of four months and at all seasons of the year. There may be five or six litters a year, each consisting of eight to a dozen young. If this increase continued unchecked and all the offspring lived the total in twelve months would be more than eight hundred individuals as descendants of one pair. Fortunately this never actually occurs, for there is great mortality at every stage, and particularly in the young. In view of the enormous damage wrought by these pests, and particularly the part they play in the spread of dangerous diseases, it is obvious that every effort should be made for their reduction.

The House Mouse is very like a Rat in miniature. Like the Rat, it has followed man all over the world and, notwithstanding continual persecution, contrives to exist in undiminished numbers. Its great powers of multiplication, combined with ready adaptability to any kind of diet, account for its prevalence. Although called " House Mouse," this little rodent is even more abundant in outbuildings and farmsteads, and finds a Cornstack an ideal home—until threshing time !

In fields and gardens the place of the House Mouse is taken by a much prettier but equally destructive little creature—the Long-tailed Field Mouse. It is easily recognised by its light-brown colour, with white underparts and feet, and large prominent eyes. This Mouse is particularly troublesome in the garden, eating seeds and bulbs of all kinds, being specially fond of peas. During the winter it becomes more or less inactive, but does not hibernate completely. In the autumn it gathers a supply of seeds, nuts, haws, etc., into some snug retreat, and these provide food during its periods of activity until the spring. Such winter stores of food are sometimes communal, a number of Mice contributing to their formation and then sharing in their consumption as the need for division arises.

When the Mouse nests.

Sometimes the Long-tailed Field Mouse will take up its winter abode in an outhouse, and if stored potatoes are handy will readily utilise these for its food supply. An old bird's nest is frequently used as a feeding place, and such nests may frequently be found containing a quantity of nut and seed shells as a result. Occasionally an old bird's nest is roofed over with moss and used as a permanent residence. The young, however, are born in a globular nest of dry grass, usually underground, and there are several litters during the year.

Closely related to this species is a creature called the Yellow-necked Mouse, which is distinguished by its larger size and an orange stripe across the throat, the latter feature

THE NIBBLER. [*Charles Reid.*]
The Mouse is eternally nibbling at something as it scampers about the woods and fields. When winter draws on it prefers the security of a snug nook inside some house where food is easy to find, if traps and cats can be evaded.

Photo : Eric Hosking]

A GREEDY MARAUDER.

[Mondiale.

The Long-tailed Field Mouse is a destructive intruder in gardens, where it eats seeds and other produce. Though it does not hibernate entirely, it takes long sleeps in winter, after storing up a supply of food for its inactive period.

being very noticeable when compared with the small brown spot on the chest of the common species. Naturalists hold different opinions as to whether this Mouse is really a distinct species or merely a variety of the Common Field Mouse. There is, however, a structural distinction which should be sufficient to give it specific rank ; the tail has thirty joints, instead of only twenty-eight as in its common relative. The Yellow-necked Mouse is also said to be of a fiercer disposition, and easily masters the Common Field Mouse in a fight. It has been found chiefly in the south of England.

There are various local races of Field Mice inhabiting certain islands, which are best regarded as varieties resulting from a long period of isolation. The chief of these races is the Hebridean Field Mouse, with distinct varieties in Bute, Fair Isle and St. Kilda.

OUR third British Mouse is comparatively scarce and little known, and found chiefly in the south of the country. This is the Harvest Mouse, which, with one exception, is the smallest of our native Mammals. Being golden-brown and white underneath, this is really the prettiest and most interesting of our Mice, and is best known on account of its nesting habits, its remarkable nursery having attracted the attention of Gilbert White in the eighteenth century. The nest is a closely-woven, globular structure of fine grass, without any definite entrance. The Mice simply push aside the fibres in any part of the nest

when they wish to leave or enter, and the hole closes up afterwards. The nest is frequently built in a Corn field, being woven to the stems of the Corn about six or eight inches above the ground ; but it may be built on other plants, such as strong grass stems, Knapweed, Thistles or in a low bush.

The Mouse that climbs Corn.

The Harvest Mouse feeds during the daytime, and if in a field of Wheat, Oats or Barley has not far to seek for an abundant supply of food during the late summer. So light is its weight that it can climb up a Wheat stem without bending it. During the earlier part of the year the food is very varied and includes a large proportion of insects. Like the Field Mouse it stores up seeds for winter use in subterranean burrows.

The mother Harvest Mouse is very devoted to her young, this being most noticeable in the case of the late litters which are present in the nests at the time of harvest. Modern reaping machines have doubtless done much to reduce the numbers of this little creature, which seems to have been more common in the old days when the scythe was used. Nowadays the binder comes along drawn by three horses or a tractor and cuts the Corn close to the ground, the straws falling on to a moving canvas which carries them up a narrow space between two revolving canvas belts, after which they are tightly packed together on the tying table, tied with twine, and the sheaf eventually thrown out a long distance from where its contents grew. It is remarkable that young Mice in the nests should survive such treatment, but a great many do. Very often the nest remains intact, bound up in the tightly-tied sheaf, and if the mother has escaped she will before long seek out her young ones and continue to care for them. After cutting, the Corn is left some time in the stook to dry, during which period the young Mice may have time to mature sufficiently to leave the nest. In some cases, however, the whole family gets carried to the stack, where they spend the winter happily, unless disturbed by threshing.

The Dormouse is not a true Mouse, and is popularly supposed to be closely related to the Squirrel, but is really quite distinct from both. It haunts copses and thick hedgerows, where Hazel bushes abound, and is nocturnal in habits, spending the daytime in deep sleep. For sleeping purposes a round nest about three inches across is constructed of dry grass and moss; this is placed in various positions, often high up in the bushes. When empty a small hole is usually visible, but this

Photo : Ray Palmer]   *[Mondiale.*

THE MOUSE'S NEST.

Here is the Dormouse's home, carefully built of twigs, moss and grass, with a circular opening for a doorway.

is closed when the Dormouse is at home. The nursery nest is much larger and made low down near the ground, sometimes even being subterranean.

For nearly half the year the Dormouse is in that deep sleep we call hibernation. Breathing ceases, the heart practically stops beating and the body becomes quite cold; indeed anyone handling a hibernating Dormouse for the first time might easily conclude it was dead. In preparation for its long sleep it eats a lot of food and gets very fat. It also lays up a store of nuts, and on particularly warm evenings may wake up, have a substantial feed, and resume its sleep.

The sleep during the daytime in summer is of course much lighter, and a sleeping Dormouse may sometimes be heard snoring in its nest. If disturbed and made to leave its nest a Dormouse climbs upwards, this being very different from the habits of true Mice, whose instinct is always to make for the ground.

THE Dormouse is a pretty and gentle little animal which readily becomes tame, and thus is a favourite pet for children; it also has the advantage of not possessing an objectionable smell like ordinary Mice. It will eat insects, as well as fruit, seeds and nuts.

Related distantly to the Mice are some small animals called Voles. They differ from Mice in appearance, chiefly by having blunt muzzles, small ears mostly hidden in fur, and comparatively short tails.

The Field Vole is the commonest species, and causes much damage to crops in some districts. This little creature is very different from a Field Mouse in appearance, though generally called the "Short-tailed Field Mouse" by country people. It has a rounder and more stumpy body, no prominent ears and a very short tail only about an inch long.

Sometimes great plagues of Voles occur and cause great devastation to farm crops. Such plagues are undoubtedly in some degree due to the way in which birds and beasts of prey have been practically exterminated in some places by gamekeepers and others. The natural enemies are Owls, the Kestrel, the Stoat and the Weasel, and if these are few in number the Vole population of a district may increase so much that migration is necessary. Such plagues are eventually checked by famine or the ravages of disease, assisted by birds of prey which the abundant food supply has quickly attracted, and so the numbers again drop to normal.

BROWN RAT.

This creature is disliked because of its thieving habits, and many attempts are made to exterminate it.

BLACK RAT.

This Rat is an omnivorous creature. When everything else fails it will even attack and kill its own kin.

A SLEEPY PAIR.

These Dormice are ready for their winter sleep, after accumulating a great deal of fat under their coats.

THE HOUSE MOUSE.

This is the most familiar of the Mouse family—a notorious enemy of the housewife and the Cat!

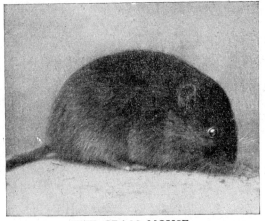

THE GRASS MOUSE.

The short-tailed Field Vole, known also as the Grass Mouse, does very good work in destroying insects.

Photos: W. S. Berridge.

BANK VOLE.

This little creature builds narrow runs in the bank, with plenty of doorways to them for its retreat.

233

The Bank Vole is slightly smaller than the Field Vole and much brighter in colour, being bright chestnut above and white below. It frequents woods and hedge banks rather than open fields, but otherwise its habits are similar. The Bank Vole soon becomes tame in captivity and makes an interesting pet. I once had one that I obtained in a curious manner. Walking along a country lane I saw a cat appear out of the hedge a little way in front. On seeing me the cat stopped still and stared, and I saw that it had something in its mouth, which I took to be a mouse. Seeing the victim was still alive, I decided to try and rescue it, so I shouted and threw my hat at the cat. This had the desired effect, for the cat dropped its prey and ran off. The "mouse" tried to escape, but very feebly, and I easily caught it. To my surprise I found it was a Bank Vole, and as it had no visible injury I took it home. The Vole soon recovered from its shock and ate the food I provided. It soon became tame enough to eat out of my hand, and stayed with me contentedly for several weeks, after which it was allowed to return to its old haunts.

There are several local varieties of Voles, found in the Orkneys, the Hebrides, and Skomer Island.

The remaining species—the Water Vole—is a much larger animal, and often mistaken for a Rat. In fact most country people still call it the "Water Rat," and refuse to be convinced that it is not a Rat or of Rat-like habits. The Water Vole is in fact a creature of most inoffensive habits, and its food is mainly of a vegetarian nature, consisting of the succulent stems of various plants that grow in or near the water. The holes made by this animal in a river bank must be familiar to everyone, also the "plop" with which it dives into the water when alarmed. If one walks quietly, however, it is often possible to watch Water Voles at their various activities undisturbed. Many a time have I watched one of these Voles feeding or cleaning itself only a few yards away, and have remarked how very much it resembled a little Beaver in appearance and habits.

The Shrews bear a superficial resemblance to Mice and Voles, but are in no way related, and so they are dealt with in another section.

Photo : Capt. Knight]   A WATER DWELLER.   *[Mondiale.*

The Water Vole is sometimes mistaken for a Rat, but is of a heavier build and has a rounded instead of a pointed muzzle. It has its haunts by the water-side, feeding mainly on plants, and is an expert swimmer and diver.

[*W. S. Berridge.*

Here is a section of the Mole's underground fortress, planned with great skill by this blind, burrowing creature. It shows the nursery which is made snug with leaves and grass. The young Moles are born naked and pink.

THE MOLE AND ITS RELATIVES

By RAY PALMER, F.R.E.S., F.Z.S.

THE patient creature that spends most of its day underground, blindly burrowing its way to the surface has a curious nature, not at all admired by the farmer to whose land he causes great destruction. His velvet-clad body is greatly prized, and trappers are always on his trail. His story, and that of his relation, the Shrew, is told below.

THE Mole is certainly our most sub-terranean Mammal and is obviously well adapted for the life it leads. The remarkable development of the front feet into great shovel-like paws, together with the powerful though sensitive snout, are splendid equipment for burrowing through the soil. The back feet are comparatively weak, but quite sufficient for speedy progress underground. One of the chief peculiarities is the fur, which is black and velvety, and set vertically in the skin like the pile of velvet. The fur can be stroked in any direction, and thus earth does not cling to it, and the Mole can move backwards if necessary without the discomfort that would be caused by fur which lay in a definite direction.

The Mole lives a life of intense activity, feeds voraciously and fights fiercely. Its principal food consists of Worms, but Leather-jacket Grubs, Slugs and various insects and their Larvæ are also devoured. It is also carnivorous when it gets the chance, and has been known to eat dead Mice and any kind of meat in captivity.

I have several times caught Moles alive and taken them home to observe their habits. It is not easy to do this, because in soft earth the Mole burrows with such wonderful rapidity that it is exceedingly difficult to secure it. The most likely way to catch a Mole is to find one above ground on a hard surface where it cannot dig. The Mole is a fierce animal, however, and needs to be handled with care, as it can give a nasty bite ; but it seems to have no real fear, and will feed directly after capture if a Worm is offered.

On one occasion I found a Mole above ground on a very hot day in late summer after a long spell of drought. This was during a field meeting of the county natural history society and the members stood round and watched the Mole under usually favourable conditions. Thinking it had most likely come above ground in a desperate effort to seek water, a lady member of the party took pity on it and offered it a drink of water in the cup of a vacuum flask. A little water poured on the ground in front of the Mole's nose was eagerly sucked up, and then the Mole rushed about seeking more in a perfect frenzy. The cup of water being placed in front of it, the Mole was perfectly satisfied and drank without hesitation, raising its front paws on the edge and putting its head in the cup as the water got low. It continued drinking for several minutes, and unfortunately no one present had a camera, for it would have been a scene well worth recording. Having drunk as much as it could hold, the Mole turned away, and in a more leisurely manner began seeking for a place to dig. So, having befriended the Mole and perhaps saved its life, we carried it to some soft earth underneath some bushes, where in less than a minute it had disappeared beneath the surface.

An exacting Pet.

The same summer I caught another Mole and took it home. There I placed it in a large case with a good supply of earth, in which it soon made itself invisible. But I soon realised that the feeding of a Mole took more time than I could give to it. I dug for Worms, but they were very scarce in the dry soil and were devoured faster than I could procure them. I therefore had to let the Mole gorge itself on shredded raw meat in order to get time to dig Worms. After two days of this I decided that a Mole was too troublesome a pet, and so it was set at liberty—but not in the garden !

Though the Mole possesses tiny eyes, it is practically blind, and thus seeks its food only by scent and hearing. When a Worm is placed in front of it, the Mole gets very excited, and noses about eagerly until the prey is encountered. The Worm is at once seized in the mouth and then held down by the paws while the Mole feels along with its nose to one end. The Worm is then greedily devoured, the Mole biting away in a quick jerky manner.

When gorged the Mole will kill or disable Worms, and then bury them in the earth until required. It is said that Moles store up quantities of Worms in this way for use during the winter, though the evidence regarding this does not seem very satisfactory.

Moles do not pair, and breeding is promiscuous. The males seek the females in the early spring, and during this process make straight surface runs which throw up the earth in ridges. Similar runs are made at other season when seeking food, but these curve about all over the place, and so are easily distinguished. If two male Moles meet during the breeding season they fight with great ferocity—usually to the death—and these fights take place above ground. It is a curious thing that once a Mole is injured and starts to bleed death seems inevitable.

In making its deeper tunnels the Mole has to get rid of the excavated earth ; it therefore makes a hole to the surface, and through this forces up the soil by means of quick jerks of the head. In this way the familiar " Mole hills " are formed.

Some weeks before the young are due to arrive the female prepares a special nest, over which she throws up a heap larger than the ordinary Mole hill, but smaller than the winter nest. There is only one litter a year, and the young number from two or three to six, four being the average. At first they are entirely naked and red in colour, but they gradually darken, and in about a fortnight are entirely dark grey or lead coloured, with signs of fur. At the end of three weeks they are covered with velvety fur of nearly the normal colour, and the eyes open a few days later.

During the winter the Mole becomes less active, but there is nothing approaching hibernation, and it wakes up every few hours to seek food. In preparation for this period the Mole constructs a special winter dwelling. This is commonly known as the " fortress," and old natural history books contain imaginary drawings and much inaccurate detail regarding the supposed elaborate construction of this domicile. The site is influenced by abundance of food, and most of these so-called fortresses are frequently seen in the open fields.

The Mole's Snuggery.

A nest chamber is first formed and lined with dry grass, and over this the Mole throws up a great heap of earth for protection, making a mound about a yard across and a foot or more in height. Tunnels formed in the mound are solely for the purpose of throwing up the soil during its formation. There is, however, a bolt hole leading downwards

Photo : Ray Palmer] THE MOLE AT WORK. *[Mondiale.*

This industrious little tunneller has a very flexible snout and strong hands, which he uses expertly to turn over the earth. He must have regular meals, for if he goes without food for only a few hours he will die of starvation.

from the nest chamber and curving up to join the main gallery farther away. Passages lead from the fortress in various directions, and along these the Mole travels when seeking food. There is, however, no pre-arranged and complicated plan such as the old books describe and illustrate.

The Mole is very subject to parasites, and these may be found in abundance in the winter nests. They include two kinds of Fleas, one of which is remarkable for its large size, being the largest British species. A curious old superstition is that the paws of a Mole carried in the pocket ward off rheumatism.

Shrews resemble the Mole chiefly in the form of the mouth which opens some way back, behind an extended flexible snout. We have three kinds of Shrews, only one of which is common.

The Common Shrew is more frequently heard than seen, though many people who hear its voice do not recognise it. During a country ramble in the spring we often hear a series of high-pitched squeaks in rapid succession coming from the thick grass of a hedge bank. There is most likely a scuffle in the herbage, but nothing visible. This indicates the presence of Shrews in love-making or rivalry, and if we remain perfectly still they may come out into the open, for their sight is weak. It is surprising how many people are unacquainted with the note of the

Shrew ; some cannot even hear it at all, its high pitch being quite beyond the range of their hearing, and such people are also deaf to the squeak of a Bat. Many of those who do hear it fail to recognise the sound as being made by a Mammal, and attribute it to some insect such as a Cricket or Grasshopper.

The older natural history books refer to this animal as the " Shrew Mouse," and country people often still speak of it in this way. But such a name should not be used, because it is quite incorrect, as the Shrew is not a Mouse and in no way related to it. It is most important that this should be recognised, because the Shrew is an entirely inoffensive and useful little animal, feeding upon insects and other small creatures which might be injurious to the farmer's crops.

A small creature's large diet.

Like the Mole, the Shrew lives a life of intense activity. It has a voracious appetite and is constantly on the hunt for food. If food is not obtainable the Shrew actually starves to death in two or three hours. It is said that it eats twice its own weight of food every day, and in captivity has been known to consume nearly four times its weight in thirty-six hours.

Shrews are more frequently seen dead than alive, being often found lying about on paths and open places in late summer and autumn.

There is still something of a mystery about this autumnal mortality of Shrews, and a number of explanations have been offered, none of which are actually proved correct.

Cats and Dogs often kill Shrews, presumably in mistake for Mice, but do not eat them on account of their strong musky smell ; though Owls, Kestrels, Stoats and Weasels will devour them readily. The fights between rival males may often end fatally, but as these occur in the spring they do not account for the autumn deaths. The bodies found usually show no sign of injury, and evidence seems to point to the probability that the dying-off that takes place at the end of the summer is due to old age. It is thought that the normal life of a Shrew does not exceed twelve or fourteen months.

The young Shrews moult before the winter, and acquire a thicker coat of darker colour. But in the dead Shrews found so abundantly there is no sign of any such change. The fact is that no moult takes place the second autumn, because the Shrew's life has come to an end and there is no use in growing a new coat that it will not live to wear.

Rarer and more local in its distribution is the Lesser Shrew, often called the " Pigmy Shrew." This little creature has the distinction of being the smallest British Mammal.

It usually measures only two-and-a-quarter inches in length, against the Common Shrew's three inches, but there are also structural differences sufficient to give it specific rank. In appearance and habits it is like a smaller edition of the common species, except that it is rather more nocturnal.

The Water Shrew is quite different from both the others in appearance, being much larger and black above with white underparts. It haunts the sides of streams and rivers, seldom being found far from water. It is a beautiful sight to watch a Water Shrew in its native element. As it dives air bubbles cling to the fur and make it appear silvery when submerged, while it seems remarkably buoyant in the water and by reason of the clinging air bubbles the fur never gets really wet. It catches insects both on and below the surface and forages about hunting Caddis Worms, Beetle Larvæ and Water Snails.

Old superstitions credited the Shrew with all sorts of evil influences upon man and beast, and provided a strange and barbarous remedy. A hole was bored in an Ash Tree, and into this a Shrew was thrust alive and plugged up. Thereafter the tree was called a " Shrew Ash," and a twig from this tree was reputed to cure any person or animal who had the misfortune to be " Shrew stricken."

A FURRY SWIMMER.   [W. S. Berridge.

The Water Shrew has a silvery appearance when in the water, which is caused by the air bubbles that show in its fur. Its diet includes insects and small fishes, and it burrows its home in a bank situated by the water-side.

[Charles Reid.

The Wild Cat has been persecuted so much that very few of its kind are left, except in the wilds of Scotland and mountainous parts of Wales, where they are occasionally found. They are very fierce and difficult to approach.

OUR TIGER, THE WILD CAT

By ERNEST A. GRAY, M.R.C.V.S.

A TAME Cat is said to have nine lives, but the Wild Cat appears to have many more, for it is one of the most difficult wild creatures to kill. A fighter of extra-ordinary ferocity, it cannot be induced to relinquish the struggle until it is completely overpowered by its enemy ; but it is seldom brought to bay owing to its hermit-like habits.

ANY one who has had experience of the British Wildcat will not quibble at the title of Tiger—for though a small member of the cat tribe, he does not lack the courage and ferocity attributed to the larger specimens of the jungle. But to see one in the wilds of Britain is a rare event. Blood relative to the magnificent tawny tiger of the Indian jungles, the Northern representative of the cat tribe in our country is somewhat dull in colour, but he is heavier, bigger and stronger than the domestic cat.

Many thousands of years ago our islands were full of most ferocious creatures—mammoths, lions, sabre-toothed tigers, cave bears, wolves and lynx. To-day, all these have disappeared, and only the Wild Cat remains as a forlorn survivor. But it is no mean representative of its savage forbears, and may reach a length of over four feet from nose tip to tail tip. Its markings, too, are suggestive of a tiger. The fur is dull yellowish grey, relieved on the sides and limbs by stripings of a darker hue. A dark line follows the course of the spine along the back, and the tail is marked by nine heavy black rings. This, added to the length of its limbs and the uniform bushy thickness of its tail (the domestic cat's tail tapers towards the tip) makes its distinction easy.

Wild cats to-day are found in only a few parts of Britain. They were never found in Ireland at any time ; and to-day have probably completely vanished from Wales. Our reader, if he wishes to find one, must search the most desolate crags of the Lake district, or hike into the remote Scottish highlands around Inverness-shire. And he is advised, too, to go well armed, to wear thick leather gauntlets and a leather coat buttoned up to the chin, and to carry if not a rifle, a heavy club. The ferocity of the Wild Cat is unbelievable. It is big and ferocious enough to pull down half-grown lambs and fawns,

239

although its usual food consists of hares, rabbits, squirrels, ptarmigan, poultry, indeed any small mammal or bird. Naturally, therefore, it is shot at on sight. Indeed, it is often advisable to do so for self-protection. More than one Wild Cat has attacked a human being without provocation, as the following extract shows :

" There exists at Barmbrough an ancient record commemorating the ferocity of the Wild Cat. The story is that Percival Cresare, a youth of distinguished family was returning to his house from a fair at Doncaster when, as he was passing through a plantation known as Melton Wood, a Wild Cat suddenly leapt from the trees and attacked him. The man sought with his gauntletted hands to grapple with his foe, but the latter's sharp teeth and powerful claws were too much for him. Badly mauled, Cresare endeavoured to escape towards Barmbrough, but the cat pursued him, and compelled him to seek shelter in the porch of the church at Barmbrough. Even here the creature did not relinquish the fight, but inflicted such terrible wounds as to cause the death of young Percival, who, in his last struggle, seems to have crushed the cat with his feet against the wall. In the morning man and cat were found dead in the porch of the church where the weird contest had ended."

This account is well authenticated, and there is no reason to doubt its accuracy.

The lair of the Wild Cat is made in a hollow tree, a crevice in the rocks, or a similar site. Other animals' homes, however, may be requisitioned, such as the deserted lair of a badger (even a wild cat does not deliberately quarrel with sturdy old Brock !) or the nest of a large bird such as a hawk, in which case the owners are bundled out neck and crop !

The young are born early in summer and there are usually five or six in a litter. At first they resemble an ordinary kitten ; but only for a short time. They would seem to imbibe their wildness with the mother's milk. Their fierceness increases with their stature until, when only half grown, they are the personification of ferocity. The young frequently remain with the mother until half-grown. Her milk does not suffice them for long, and soon she is catching rats and mice and small birds for them. Like all wild creatures, the mother is a devoted parent and will die in defence of her young ones.

W. S. Berridge.] A SAVAGE TREE-CLIMBER. [*Mondiale.*

The Wild Cat sometimes makes its lair in the deserted home of a Badger, or in the nest of some large bird, after ousting the rightful owners. Its powerful claws stand it in good stead for tree-climbing as well as fighting.

[*Charles Reid.*

This popular little woodland creature spends most of its time scampering among the branches or building his
" drey " of moss, leaves, bark, and twigs. In this retreat it settles down comfortably for its long winter nap.

THE RED SQUIRREL AND
ITS RELATIVES

By M. H. CRAWFORD

*T*HE *lively little Squirrels make a pretty picture as they scamper along the branches,*
pausing now and again to nibble at a nut or to peer about in search of intruders. They
are friendly creatures, and if orphaned have been known to make a cat their foster-mother,
and to become quite tame.   Their wild home, or " drey," is built high up in the trees.

OUR only true British species of Squirrel
is the Brown (commonly called the
Red) Squirrel, one of the prettiest and
most attractive of all our little wild animals.
The name Red really belongs to the Bohemian
variety, which resembles very much our own
squirrel, but has a bushier tail. The American
Grey Squirrel, at first only a visitor, but
now an inhabitant, is as much at home with
us now as our native species. Whether it is
really ousting the latter from the woods is a
charge not perhaps quite proved. It is much
more friendly and unafraid than our own
Squirrel and, therefore, more often seen.
For the same reason its misdeeds are more
evident.

The Grey Squirrel seems to enjoy man's
society ; in country gardens it may be seen
dancing down the pathway in the early
morning, and every visitor to Kew knows
how friendly it is. But the Red Squirrel
usually keeps to lanes and woods, and its
feeding habits are not so easily observed.

A controversy has raged round the subject
of the Squirrels for a long time, a veritable
battle of the Red and Grey. But whichever
side is taken the general verdict will be that our
parks and countryside would be less interesting
if these cheeky rodents with their perky,
cadging ways were to disappear. None of
our wild animals attracts the children's cries
of delight like the impudent alien Grey
Squirrel, when at near range they watch
his antics with a nut which has been thrown
to him.

Some years back a number of them were
set free in various parts of the country, with
the result that (like the Rabbit in Australia)
they have multiplied and spread afield to
such an extent as to be, it is said, a menace to
mankind in many ways. The American Grey
Squirrel was first liberated in this country in

241

the year 1890, when a number were given their freedom at Woburn Park, Bedfordshire, and at Finnart, Dumbartonshire. Later others were let loose near Malden, in Yorkshire, and in 1905 some of those living at the London Zoological Gardens were allowed to escape from their enclosure. In 1908 a further lot were liberated in Kew Gardens. These " Greys " have multiplied and spread in all directions, and now they are reported to be plentiful as far west as Wales and up north in Durham.

AT one time the British Red was to be found in the Park at Richmond, Kew, Highgate woods and many other places around London, but to-day not one can be seen in these haunts, the Grey invader having usurped these urban retreats. But the Red or Common Squirrel is a true native of the British Isles, and it is not found in any other country. A closely-allied race of very similar appearance, however, inhabits the greater part of Europe, North Africa, and parts of Asia.

The best way to see, intimately and closely, our two English Squirrels—for we must now consider as British the alien Grey as well as the native Red—is to go camping in or near the woods where they live. It is remarkable how little fear they have of us after they have got accustomed to us in the same spot for a few hours. One learns quickly that to be quiet and to move slowly are the best passports to woodland secrets. And it is well worth while to use these passports. Squirrels are our loveliest animal companions, and the Grey especially is very ready to make friends.

Town dwellers are unlikely to realise why the Grey Squirrel has fallen into disfavour in certain circles. Unhappily he is a pushing little fellow, not content to remain tranquilly in those places where he was first released. But he proved to be a great marauder and ranged far afield, deposing the Red Squirrels and robbing, it is said, orchards and gardens. To him is also attributed the habit of biting large holes in growing Apples, Pears, Peaches, Cane Fruits, and Strawberries, tasting here and there and destroying what he does not consume. Bark, bulbs and nuts suffer from his inquisitive nibbling, and not only plant life but nests are visited, and eggs and even young birds devoured, if we are to believe all that his detractors say of him.

In our large town parks he is seen to best advantage. Though never really alarmed when human beings venture near him, he is not always pleased to see them, and at such times he may show his annoyance by making a noise with his claws on the bark of the tree, or by climbing into the topmost branches, peering down through the leaves to see if the intruder is still there. But if a bag of nuts goes with each visit he soon connects the two, and the owner of the nuts is sure of a welcome. The little animal will spring up on the bench and allow himself to be stroked and petted so long as he can get at the nuts. When he tires of eating them he will often go on accepting them, burying them under leaves or otherwise playing with them. When once he accepts you as a friend he becomes quite fearless, and it is indeed a delightful experience to get into such close proximity to him that you can look into his big, clear eyes, touch his furry ears and hold his paws.

Caging the Squirrel.

Both Red and Grey Squirrels make amusing and fascinating pets. There have been discussions and protests about the cruelty of keeping them in small cages with a revolving wheel. To-day such cages are not so often used. It is not pleasant to see the little inmate racing round and round in what appears to be a frantic effort to escape. But perhaps the wheel and cage are no more cruel than any other sort of captivity. Unless a captive Squirrel gets a tremendous amount of exercise, its claws grow so long that the unfortunate little thing can hardly climb or get about. A tragic accident often puts an end to its unnatural way of living, for the claws are apt to get caught in the cage wires or in string, or even in the bark of branches. The moral of all this is that a Squirrel should never be kept in captivity, no matter how large its prison may be. Even when its claws can be kept in normal condition there are difficulties with its food.

It is not very widely known, even amongst animal lovers, that tame Squirrels can be allowed to live in freedom in a house. They will build a nest in some comfortable corner, making themselves at home and providing endless entertainment by their quaint ways. But to their quality of quaintness must be added another, less attractive—that of destructiveness. Of course, they treat a civilised house as they would treat their native woods. They make their nests in places where they will not be disturbed. Such places include recesses behind bookcases, couches and heavy

A FIERCE-LOOKING COWARD

Though the Buzzard presents a fierce enough appearance it is the least daring of its clan. It is so slow on the wing that it cannot even pursue smaller birds, but feeds on mice and creatures that live on the ground.

Photo: C. W. R. Knight.] AN AGILE CLIMBER. [Mondiale.

The Grey Squirrel, imported from America, is popular as a pet in spite of its thieving tendencies. Easy to tame, it makes a fascinating companion. It will build indoors, making itself as much at home as in the tree-tops.

screens which are not likely to be moved for a few days.

It is very surprising how much material a single Squirrel can collect and store within a day or two. They also nibble cushions and chair legs. On the whole, though a Squirrel would be fairly happy if it had the run of a country bungalow, it might be apt, in the end, to tire out the patience of its hosts.

I ONCE heard of an invalid woman who lived in the country, and who had an excellent way of enjoying the quaintness of Squirrels without being troubled by their destructiveness. They were Red Squirrels, and they lived in the trees surrounding her house. She had her sitting-room on the ground floor, and, with the door wide open, spent hours in making their acquaintance. She placed a bird table on the lawn, with food she knew they liked. The table was brought gradually day by day, nearer and nearer to her window. The Squirrels came and helped themselves, gaining confidence at every visit. Finally the table was placed right inside the room. Still they came. At last they were so friendly that if they found the window closed in the morning when they arrived they would tap on it till it was opened. They were always present at meal times and liked to try samples of their hostess's food. If they were not offered the special bit they wanted they just took it. They spent hours racing in and out of her room, and, as there were twenty of them, she had plenty of company. Their antics were as interesting and amusing as those of a family of Tits. In fact their ways were often very bird-like.

Squirrels build huge " dreys " of sticks and other material high up in trees, and here the youngsters are born some time in the early spring. A Cat will mother a baby Squirrel left an orphan, just as it will mother a baby Rat. The small orphan should be placed with the Cat's kittens, advantage being taken of a moment when Puss is away from her family. By the time she has returned the stranger will have rubbed itself against the Kittens and will smell more or less like them, sufficiently so to induce the Cat to accept it.

If no Cat is available a baby Squirrel may be brought up by hand—not an easy task, but it may be carried out with success. The best thing to use is a small paint brush. This should be dipped into warm milk, and the baby should be allowed to suck it. Very soon the little thing will be able to nibble a bit of crust or biscuit. Nuts and grain will afterwards be accepted, but of course the nuts must be shelled. It may be a long time before you can teach the young Squirrel to crack his nuts for himself. A warm nest made of straw and woollen scraps is suitable for a very young Squirrel. When older, it will make its own nest of bits of stick, paper and rags.

Squirrels from different districts have a diversity of tastes. For instance, I think the Surrey Squirrels are inordinately fond of nuts; they will also take cheese greedily, as well as cake and suet.

[Brit. Instruc. Films.

THE SQUIRREL DISPLAYS HIS BUSHY TAIL.
The Squirrel has an amusing way of sitting up on a branch when cracking the nuts of which he is so fond.

In some places you may find Acorns and nuts wedged into holes in trees; probably Squirrels have stuck them there. Sometimes they eat Fungi, and it is said that they will gather it and leave it on twigs to dry. Another article of food is the Fir Cone, preferred when it is green. Beechmast is also much liked. In Fir plantations, damage is sometimes done to the young Firs, as Squirrels are very fond of the small shoots. But it is only in the plantations that a case can be made out against the Squirrel, and in ordinary woodland country the harm they can do is negligible.

[Robert McLeod.

A herd of wild White Cattle with black ears and muzzles is found in Cadzow Forest, Lanarkshire, in Scotland. They make an extremely decorative group among the trees, and are said to be descended from a very ancient race.

WILD CATTLE IN BRITAIN

By RAY PALMER, F.R.E.S., F.Z.S.

THE gentle cow that yields its store of milk for our benefit had ancestors that were by no means so docile. Of great size and ferocity, these creatures fought with all who questioned their liberty, and it took many centuries to tame them. Below, we are told how this happened, and also learn about the cattle that still roam wild in our country.

THE ancestry of most of our domesticated animals lies shrouded in the mists of antiquity, and very little is known with certainty. The Ox was one of the first animals to be subjugated by man, followed somewhat later by the Horse ; thus no truly wild Cattle or Horses now exist which have not at one time in their history undergone at least partial domestication.

Cattle as we know them to-day consist of numerous varieties, the result of selective breeding, but they can be divided into two main types or species—the kinds we are all familiar with on farms in this country, and the humped cattle of the East. The humped Cattle do not concern us, except to mention that they were undoubtedly the first to undergo domestication. Thousands of years ago, when the human inhabitants of Western Europe were naked savages using crude weapons and tools of flint, the highly-civilised Egyptians had tame humped Cattle, which served them as beasts of burden and givers of milk when alive, and provided meat, leather, horn and bone when dead.

The first we hear of wild Cattle in Europe is at a much later period, when the Romans under Julius Cæsar were extending their dominion over the world. In attempting to subdue the Barbarians on the northern borders of their domain, the Roman legions encountered wild cattle in what is now Germany. These Cattle were of gigantic size, and the Bulls exceedingly powerful and ferocious. It is said they could never be tamed, even when taken young, and the Romans greatly feared them. They were certainly captured, however, for during the days of the Roman Empire gigantic Bulls, to which the name of " Urus " was given, were made to provide a spectacle in the arena, where yellow-haired giants from their native land were often put to fight them.

The German name for this ferocious creature was " Aurochs," and it is by this name that it is usually spoken of at the present day.

Coming back to our own country, there is no conclusive evidence of the existence of the wild Aurochs in Britain during the historic period, and though it quite possibly still lingered—particularly in the north—the various references to " forest Bulls " in ancient literature cannot be referred to with certainty.

The last reference we hear to this animal on the Continent is towards the close of the eleventh century, when the First Crusaders encountered the Aurochs in Germany and hunted it both for food and sport.

The great Ox of the Stone Age.

There is plenty of evidence that the Aurochs were abundant in Britain during prehistoric times, and were even contemporary with the palæolithic men of the early Stone Age. At that remote period this country was not an island, but joined to the Continent by a land connection, over which both animals and men could wander freely. The Aurochs had probably come over by this route long before man appeared at all in this part of the world.

Remains of this great Ox, more or less fossilised, have been found in the Fens of Cambridgeshire, the brick-earths of the Thames Valley, and the peat in certain parts of Scotland. Some of the skulls found were transfixed with stone axe heads, fixed immovable in the splintered bone, showing that early man had actually succeeded in slaying this formidable creature with his primitive weapons. Such skulls may be seen in various museums, and an idea of the great size of the animals can be obtained when it is seen that the horns measure nearly four feet across from tip to tip.

As the centuries rolled on successive waves of humanity invaded Britain from the south and east, each new race a little more civilised than the last, and equipped with better weapons, first of polished stone, then of bronze and finally of iron. The Aurochs survived them all, and continued to flourish in the dense forest with which the greater part of the country was then covered. At last came the Celtic and Belgic tribes from Gaul. In their homelands these people had long ago succeeded in domesticating a small breed of Short-horned Cattle, no doubt descended originally from specimens of the Aurochs taken as calves, but greatly modified and reduced in size by a long period of domestication and selection.

These cattle the invaders brought with them

A DARK RACE.   [*Charles Reid.*

The native home of these Cattle, which are now widespread, is in Galloway in the South-west of Scotland. They are noted for the high quality of the beef they produce. A herd of these Black Cattle is seen in the above picture.

A PEACEFUL GATHERING.   [*Charles Reid.*

The domestic Cattle that graze peacefully in the meadows to-day only occasionally show glimpses of their heredity to remind us of their untamed days. They are content and docile, and rarely make use of their horns.

to this country, where they were allowed to roam in herds and many no doubt reverted to a semi-wild state. This breed of Cattle is called the Long-fronted Ox, or Celtic Short-horn, and is known scientifically as *Bos taurus longifrons*. The invading Romans found large herds of these cattle, which provided a supply of meat for the legionaries.

Many of these Celtic Cattle, roaming at large in a country still mostly forest, would escape and never be found. Those that survived the Wolves would interbreed with the wild Aurochs, and thus a race of wild Cattle, intermediate between the two varieties, would be formed. Meanwhile the large native Bulls, by reason of their ferocity and dangerous nature, would be gradually hunted down and killed as the country was opened up, so that in course of time the pure breed of Aurochs ceased to exist, although many herds of their cross-bred descendants remained in a wild state right up to the Norman period, and probably later. A well-known writer in the twelfth century, FitzStephen, writing about the year 1174, states that round about the city of London was an immense forest, the haunt of wild beasts, including Stags, Fallow Deer, Boars and " Forest Bulls."

At this period herds of wild or half-wild Cattle were no doubt abundant all over the country, varying somewhat according to locality and the proportion in which the two original strains had contributed to their formation. Such herds existed during the thirteenth century, and some were by accident or design included in enclosures of forest land made by various noblemen. In this way herds of these Cattle became segregated, and have thus been preserved in a more or less pure condition to the present day.

Some of these park Cattle are therefore the nearest approach to the extinct Aurochs living to-day, though owing to inbreeding and confined range they have decreased greatly in size and become degenerate. Certain of our large and long-horned breeds of Cattle may also be descended more or less directly from the Aurochs, while the small Highland and Welsh Cattle are descendants of the Celtic Short-horn without much admixture. Other breeds are derived from a mixture of these two varieties.

Coming now to the half-wild park Cattle of modern times, about twenty herds were formerly kept at various parks in England and Scotland, but only five have existed within

Photo : M. Wight.]
ANCIENT BRITONS.
[*Mallinson.*

Here is a herd of ancient British Cattle, the only one left in Britain to-day. The herd is found at Dynevor Castle in South Wales, where the Cattle are seen above. They are, of course, a great deal tamer than their wild ancestors.

Photo : Ray Palmer.]
THE WHITE CATTLE OF CHARTLEY PARK.
[*Mondiale.*

The large White Cattle found at Chartley Park, in Staffordshire, are descendants of the Wild Cattle that roamed the forest in the thirteenth century. Though they have long been domesticated, they have many traits of their ancestors.

BEEF IN THE MAKING.   [*Charles Reid.*

This shaggy Highland bull, with its long horns and forbidding countenance, grazes on the mountains of the West Highlands and belongs to a breed that is often called " Kyloes." Very hardy, their flesh makes excellent beef.

recent years. The most famous of these herds is that of Chillingham Castle, Northumberland, the property of the Earl of Tankerville. The park of some seven hundred acres is surrounded by a wall, and was enclosed round about the year 1220. It consists partly of ancient woodland and rough pasture, and formed a portion of the original home, no doubt, of the wild Cattle of earlier times.

A Herd of White Cattle.

The Chillingham Cattle are small in size, with short upturned horns. The hair is rather long and curly, and the colour white all over, with the exception of the brown noses and red tips and insides to the ears. Their present appearance is largely due to selection, however, because records show that at one time black ears were more prevalent than red. Moreover, calves are frequently born coloured—usually red—but these have always been destroyed with the object of keeping the herd white.

These Cattle have quite the habits and characteristics of wild animals. They feed at night, spending the day in sleeping or basking in the sun. The cows hide their calves in the woods for about a fortnight, going to feed them two or three times a day. If anyone approaches a young calf, it lies perfectly still, with its head close to the ground and its ears back, after the manner of a Fawn.

The Cattle are dangerous to approach, and although they at first appear very timorous, are really of a fierce nature. When a stranger appears the whole herd gallops off for about two hundred yards or so, where they face about and proceed to walk back for about half the distance, when they come to a stand and stare at the intruder in a threatening manner. If a movement is made they again gallop off, but for a shorter distance, and come back closer. Each time this manœuvre is repeated they finish up nearer and their behaviour becomes more threatening, so that the stranger usually beats a hasty retreat.

Nowadays visitors are not allowed to enter the park except under special permission, and then they must approach the herd in a cart under the charge of a keeper, as it is not safe to go on foot. The Cattle obtain enough food from the natural grazing during the summer, but in winter hay is taken to them in carts, and it is in these carts that visitors occasionally enter.

In olden days the herd was kept from in-creasing unduly by hunting. A large number of horsemen armed with guns collected in the park, while many other people stood on the walls or climbed into trees. A Bull was then driven off from the herd by the horsemen until he turned at bay and charged his pursuers. Shots were then fired, but were seldom fatal at first, so that the victim became furious and often charged with fatal effect, sometimes as many as thirty shots being fired before the Bull was killed. Within recent times this barbarous sport has been abandoned, and indeed there has been no need to reduce the herd, since disease and other causes have thinned the numbers considerably. At present only forty-four are left.

In 1931 this famous herd was in danger of being broken up owing to the heavy cost of maintenance under modern conditions. The Zoological Society of London came to the rescue, however, and are now responsible for the welfare and upkeep of the herd in its ancient home.

At Cadzow Park in Lanarkshire is another herd very similar in general form to the Cattle of Chillingham, but the ears and muzzles are black, and there is some black hair on the front legs. The herd is a very ancient one, but probably not so pure bred as the more famous one found in Northumberland.

Keeping Black Calves at bay.

Another herd exists at Chartley Park, Staffordshire, and differs greatly from the others. These are large white Cattle with black ears and muzzles, and long, widespreading horns. They are known to be direct descendants of the wild cattle which lived in Needwood Forest at the time of the enclosure of Chartley Park in 1248. They are probably the nearest approach to the original wild Cattle, although the breed is not pure, and a period of domestication is thought to have intervened. Black calves are occasionally produced, and the herd is only kept pure by weeding these out. Indeed if this were not done, it is most probable that black would soon predominate.

We cannot say that these Park Cattle are truly wild, for they are dependent on man's protection for their existence, and some at least of their remote ancestors had undergone complete domestication. But they are nevertheless the nearest approach to really wild Cattle we have left in this country, and as such are of particular interest and value.

Here is a group of West Highland ponies on their native ground in Barra. Very hardy and sure-footed, they are not particularly noted for good looks. The Highland Garron and the Shetland pony are related to this class.

WILD PONIES OF BRITAIN

By RAY PALMER, F.R.E.S., F.Z.S.

THE Horse, we learn below, originally existed in a wild state, and some of its semi-wild relatives remain to-day to remind us of these bygone days. These are found in the Highlands of Scotland, the New Forest, and the Welsh mountains. The author tells of their different characteristics and how they are tamed to obey the will of man.

LIKE most domesticated animals, the exact origin and ancestry of the Horse is doubtful, and it is said that none of the original wild stock, from which our present-day Horses are descended, now exist.

In considering the animal life of the British Isles, however, we come across several races of semi-wild ponies, which, although now under human ownership and control, live a good deal of their lives in a wild natural state, and some of their remote ancestors may indeed have been indigenous.

In certain cave deposits and in the brick-earths in England and Western Europe fossil remains of Horses are abundant, and such remains appear to be identical with the Horse as known to-day, so there is good evidence for saying that the Horse originally existed in a wild state in this country. Such Horses are thought to have been rather small animals of heavy build with large heads. They are known to have been contemporary with the Neolithic men of the later Stone Age, who no

doubt killed them for food ; and certain crude drawings, dating from this period, have been found on pieces of bone and slate from caves inhabited by these early hunters. It has even been suggested that Neolithic man actually succeeded in taming Horses in Western Europe at that remote period.

There is no reason to doubt the possibility of this, because the North American Indians when first discovered were in the Neolithic stage of culture, and readily took to catching and taming Horses after these had been introduced by the Spaniards and run wild.

The Celtic tribes who inhabited Britain at the time of the first Roman expedition in 55 B.C. possessed numerous Horses. Of this we have historical evidence, and there is every reason to suppose that such Horses were derived from native stock, descended no doubt from the Horses of Neolithic times.

The question now arises : Do the Wild Ponies of the present day represent in any degree the Indigenous Horses of Britain ? No simple or certain answer is possible, because all the breeds are now very much mixed, and there is no reliable evidence of their origin. All we can say is that it seems highly probable that these wild Ponies do possess the blood of wild British ancestors dating from prehistoric times, though in a more or less diluted form. They are therefore the nearest approach to the Wild Horse we have left, and as such are interesting.

Our ordinary domesticated Horses have been derived in part from wild European ancestors, but have undergone great modification by mixture with Asiatic and North African breeds. In most of the wild Ponies such cross breeding has also taken place, but to a lesser extent.

The New Forest Ponies are one of the best-known breeds, and they possess many of the characteristics of Wild Horses, being mostly dun in colour, with large heads, long ears and thin legs. They are known to have been in the Forest for many centuries, and are probably descendants of domesticated native Horses of the pre-Roman period. Within recent times attempts have been made to improve the breed by the introduction of Eastern blood, chiefly in the form of Arab Stallions, and thus many varieties are noticeable amongst these ponies. The change has been less marked than would be expected, however, as the native breed seems to assimilate the foreign blood and in a few generations revert to the original type with little apparent alteration.

Although these ponies all have owners, they are practically wild, and many of them live in a state of Nature throughout their entire lives. Most of the mares may live for twenty years or more in the Forest and never know what it is to be shod, harnessed or broken in, and only on very rare occasions are they handled for the purpose of marking.

Rounding up the Wild Ponies.

Pony fairs are held annually at Lyndhurst, Ringwood and other centres. In preparation for these there is a great round-up. Mounted men ride through the forest and collect the Ponies into large herds, which are eventually driven to some place which is more or less enclosed, and where the wild little Horses can be kept under some sort of control. Exciting scenes may be witnessed during this round-up, as the ponies, like the wild animals they are, make every effort to escape, and require

great skill in handling. When at last they are secured the sorting-out process takes place. The Foals are marked, and a number of young ones are selected for sale. Any which are diseased or very old are destroyed and the rest are turned loose again.

These Ponies are very difficult to break-in, after having run wild in the forest for three or four years ; but they are extremely hardy and strong, and most of the work usually done by cart Horses is in the Forest done by these ponies. They are also sold largely for tradesmen's carts, milk floats, and vehicles of a similar nature while some of the better-looking ones may become mounts for children.

The Fly that pesters the Ponies.

New Forest Ponies are infested by a curious parasitic Fly, which is peculiar to the district and is called the Forest Fly. It is a bloodsucker, and crawls about its host after the manner of a Sheep tick, only using its wings to fly from one animal to another. The Ponies are so used to it that they take no notice, but strange Horses brought to the Forest go nearly mad when attacked by this clinging insect that cannot be shaken off. This strange Fly has an extraordinary life history. The egg hatches within the body of the female, only one being produced at a time, and the Larva develops internally. The Fly then deposits, not an egg, but a full-grown Larva, which pupates immediately, and the perfect Fly very soon emerges. A remarkable example of an abbreviated life history.

The moorland Ponies of Dartmoor and Exmoor may be regarded as belonging to one race, which became separated into two through the spread of population in that part of the country. They are still very similar, though with slight differences. The Dartmoor Ponies are larger and slimmer, with larger heads, while those of Exmoor are usually smaller and more thickly set, with a short broad head.

These ponies have certainly been less altered by selective breeding than in the case of the modern New Forest Ponies, and have probably suffered less by the introduction of alien blood than any other, except the Shetland. It has been suggested that they owe their origin to Horses brought over by Phœœcian traders in pre-historic times ; but if a native race of wild Horse existed, there is no need to suggest introduction to explain their origin. The moorland Ponies are of small size, being

Photo : Alfieri.]   THE ROUND-UP.   *[Mondiale.*

The Ponies that run wild in the New Forest are periodically rounded up. Exciting chases take place, and skilful handling is required before the ponies are captured. The young Foals are marked, and some selected for sale.

Photo : Alfieri.]   TAMING THE WILD PONIES.   *[Mondiale.*

Having run wild in the New Forest so long, the ponies find it difficult indeed to settle down to a life of restriction. They are, however, exceedingly strong, and when shod, harnessed and broken-in, able to tackle very heavy work.

253

from twelve to thirteen hands high, the latter being regarded as the limit for a pure-bred pony.

The Welsh Mountain Pony is also an ancient breed, now found in the true semi-wild state chiefly in Breconshire and the Long Mynd Hills of the Shropshire and Montgomery borderland. The Welsh Pony is renowned for its pace, action and stamina, and many of the best Polo Ponies have Welsh blood in them. This Pony has ranged the Welsh mountains since prehistoric times, and is undoubtedly descended from the true native breed. At one time these ponies degenerated greatly, due to only inferior Stallions being left to breed. Since the demand for Pit Ponies has increased their commercial value, however, they have been better looked after and their breeding more carefully watched.

The Dales and Fell Ponies of Northern England are really one breed, and both are descended from the Galloway Pony of the Scottish border region, which is now extinct. These breeds are found ranging the dales and fells of the Lake District, Cumberland, Northumberland, Durham and Yorkshire. They are of a somewhat larger and heavier type than the southern breeds already described, rather resembling small cart Horses.

The Highland Ponies are of three varieties : the Barra Pony, found in certain of the Western Islands, particularly Lewis, is a hardy and sure-footed breed, though not good looking ; the Uist Pony is no doubt of similar origin, but has been improved by the introduction of Arab blood in the past, and is now a first-class riding pony.

The Highland Garron is of larger size, being really a short-legged Horse of great power. It is chiefly used as a pack Horse on rough mountain tracks and for hauling on steep hill roads, for which purpose it has no equal.

Perhaps the best-known of all our native Ponies is the Shetland, famous for its small size. The height of this little Pony varies from nine to ten hands ; the diminutive size no doubt being due to the restricted range and privation to which the breed has been subject in its native islands. The Shetland is probably the purest of all our breeds of Ponies, because no other blood can be introduced without increasing the size, and smallness has been prized as the chief characteristic.

Although Shetlands have great popularity as children's Ponies, it is for use as Pit Ponies in the mines throughout the country that most of them are used, their small size and great strength and endurance making them particularly suitable for this class of work.

SHETLAND PONIES. [*Mondiale.*
The shaggy little Shetland pony is a hardy creature, well adapted to the stormy conditions of its bleak home. The thick, woolly coat which it grows in autumn protects it from the cold. Above is seen a group of mares and foals.

[Charles Reid.

In their wild moorland home the Deer roam at peace until the stalkers come on the trail. They are keenly alert, however, to the presence of danger, and their speed and subtlety often help them to make good their escape.

OUR GRACEFUL DEER

By EVAN STRONG

THE monarch of the mountain, glen, and the wild forest in spite of its graceful appearance is not popular because of the damage it wreaks on young trees, of which it consumes large quantities. The huntsman who finds that this subtle adversary yields him keen sport, has no fault to find with the Deer. Formerly kings followed the chase in pursuit of this swift creature, which, as we learn below, can travel as far as fifty miles at a time.

OUR most majestic animal still lives on in the wilder parts of Britain, thanks to our joy of the hunt. Were it not for the extension of Deer forests, especially in the northern parts of Scotland, the noble Red Deer would to-day be extinct, at any rate in the wild state. So, too, that other beautiful native Deer, the Roe, owes its continued existence and freedom to the same spirit of the people. But both have had to alter their mode of living somewhat, with marked results in the case of the red Deer, for they are forest dwellers, and the development of population and needs of cultivation have everywhere reduced the woodland area. This process had advanced so far at the beginning of the last century that very few Deer forests remained. For instance in 1812 there were only five Deer forests proper left in Scotland.

The Red and Roe may be termed British Deer. The Fallow, seen mostly in our parks, is an immigrant from Mediterranean lands.

The word Deer was originally the name of one of the two British species, but to-day it covers the whole family of Cervidæ, which is distributed all over Europe, and is found also in Asia, North African lands and in America. They are all forest dwellers, and are considerably affected in stature when driven out into moorland and highland. Bones of prehistoric Deer found in the peat bogs of Scotland reveal that the ancient Red Deer (Cervus elaphus) was a very much larger creature than his descendants of to-day. He had unlimited woodlands to roam and feed in, however.

The Red Deer, standing forty-two to fifty-two inches at the shoulder, is an aristocrat amongst the Mammalian fauna of these islands, even though he is smaller in bone and antler than his early ancestors. Stag is the name given to the male. Strong of wind and fleet, he will lead a hunt twenty to thirty miles and defend himself vigorously when brought to bay. The splendid antlers which give

255

him such a proud aspect when caught sight of on a hill crest, are used for fighting other males, and in defence, but usually the Stag relies on his fleetness to escape enemies. It is a question whether really the antlers are grown as weapons or are merely especially masculine features, for some Stags fight with hooves and teeth, and it is an extraordinary fact that the Stags which fight with their hooves are occasionally the victors in fights with rivals who are equipped with antlers.

The Deer's birth certificate.

The antlers of the Deer help us to recognise age, and each part is especially named. In the first year mere knobs appear at the top of the brow, being outgrowths from the forehead or frontal bones ; and these remain throughout life. The following year the main shaft, known as the beam, appears. And then each succeeding year there appear a brow point, or brow tine, the bez tine, trez tine, or royal, and the branched summit, the crown or surroyal. A " Full antler " shows brow, bez (or bay), trez (or tray) and three points on top, but a fine head may show more than a dozen points.

After the Rutting season in September or October, the antlers are shed, the older animals dropping theirs first. A few days later growth recommences. This new horn is covered with a thick protective velvet which prevents injury to the joint which is as yet soft and tender. The young growing horns are very sensitive and the Deer becomes quiet and reserved, for he seeks to avoid knocking his still soft antlers against obstacles which would cause hurt. It takes about twelve weeks for the horns to grow fully again and harden, when the animals rub them against the trees to get rid of the velvet. Since the weight of the antlers is about from ten to fifteen pounds, it needs a sturdy neck to support them. Except in the case of Reindeer, only the males have antlers.

There is some controversy as to what becomes of the old horns. We rarely find them, because they are dropped in out-of-the-way places, and in preserves keepers collect them to make knife handles and such like. But for the greater part the dropped antlers are eaten by the Deer themselves. Observation has proved this : both Stags and Hinds showing a liking for them.

The Red Deer may be over six feet long, a noble, graceful fellow, holding his head up royally. In weight he will be about thirty stone, and yet he can run swiftly for fifty miles at a stretch when pressed. A great jumper, too, he can clear a fence seven feet high, or a chasm twenty feet across. He is a good swimmer and a bonny fighter.

In summer his coat is a reddish-brown, short and glossy, and in winter greyish-brown, long and rough. The calves are born about May or June, there being generally only one and rarely two, which remain hidden in the bracken until capable of looking after themselves. They are, however, lively and delightful little creatures with spotted coats (until the following spring) and like all young animals seeming to find life a fine game to be fully enjoyed.

We usually associate the Red Deer with the mountains and moorlands, but, as before mentioned, it was originally a creature of the forest. He is very fond of the leaves of trees, especially Beech, Alder, Hazel, but frequently has to be content with heather tops and even grass. The family travels widely and will invade fields and orchards, where Cabbages, Carrots, Potatoes, Turnips, young and ripe Corn, as well as Apples and Acorns will be eaten and destroyed. Indeed the Red Deer is a careless feeder and will do a lot of damage. When at the seashore Deer will go down and lick the salt off the rocks.

To observe them one must be a patient and hardy watcher, for they are very keen to the presence of danger, and very subtle in their ways of avoiding it. At the first alarm the Hinds let out their call of Bru-ach, bidding the Calves to lie quietly hidden. The Stag destroys his scent by crossing and recrossing streams, and when cornered seeks a rock to fight back to. It is a fine spectacle to watch the movements of the wild Deer, and the actions of a number of Hinds as yet unwarned of a possible enemy. They possess wonderful sight and have an exceptional sense of smell. As soon as they become suspicious they are alert, the startled herd streaming away across the mountainside like the wind at a spanking pace, even over the roughest ground.

Canute, and the Forest Law.

The Red Deer and his relations have from the earliest days provided royal sport, and therefore have always been more or less " preserved." It was Canute who, in the first year of his reign, that is 1018, preserved forests and chases, and that same year his council,

MONARCH OF THE FOREST.   [*Central News.*

The graceful Red Stag is an aristocratic-looking creature, with noble antlers which he uses in fighting other males,
or in defence against human enemies. His speed and strength of wind aid him to make his escape when pursued.

257

Photo: Hedda Walther.] A NOBLE HEAD. *[Mondiale.*

The antlers of the Deer, as we are told in this chapter, help us to recognise the age of the animal. These are shed every year, and replaced by new growths. Only the males possess antlers, except in the case of the Reindeer.

A LONG-DISTANCE RUNNER. *[Charles Reid.*

Deer are renowned for their agility and great powers of endurance. They are splendid jumpers—the Red Deer especially, which can clear a fence seven feet in height. It can also run as much as fifty miles at a stretch.

at Winchester, is supposed to have passed his forest law code, which subsequent kings confirmed and developed to regulate ownership, and the management of vert and venison. These early laws were administered by a " swainmote," composed of verderers and foresters, offices which have continued to exist up to this day. The king's nobles, and the church, held special forest jurisdictions which were most oppressive, and offences against forest laws, even of mere trespass by cattle, were very severely punished. In Norman times the lawyers made the pretence that all game belonged to the king.

King John had eighteen forests, thirteen chases, and seven hundred and eighty-one parks. A chase was open woodland, and not subject to the ordinary forest law ; a park was an enclosed chase on land belonging to the proprietor. Another term, a purlieu, referred to an addition made to an old forest.

There were seven hundred parks in England before the Civil War, but there are only about three hundred now, and of these only about fifty contain Red Deer. After the middle of the eighteenth century, when Stag hunting gave way to Fox hunting, Deer were kept mainly for breeding and ornament in

enclosed parks. However, Stag hunting still lives on the moors of Somerset and Devon, but in Scotland the sport is Deer stalking. Beyond the Tweed there are about 2,000,000 acres of Deer forests, or Deer lands. In 1812 there were only five such forests, but in 1905 the number rose to one hundred and thirty. The change is due to the sport of Deer stalking which grew rapidly in favour during the nineteenth century. Many complaints have been heard that this development of the sport encroached on the homesteads and cultivated lands of crofters and small agriculturists, turning families adrift from the land and driving many overseas, in search of new lands where they might settle and build up new homes. This is not quite accurate. It was more likely the development of sheep farming which brought about the altered conditions of the Highlands.

Most Deer are polygamous, the males fighting for the possession of females, and not satisfied with one mate. With the Roe-Deer it is different. More than one Buck and a Doe together will be rarely seen. They are not found in herds, and the male and female remain attached to one another for life. The Buck is pugnacious, however, during the breeding season.

The Roe Deer is a small forest species of Deer seldom found in the higher and bare Highlands, where the Red Deer roams. About two feet three inches high at the shoulder, it is of a shiny tawny brown in summer, but dull and unkempt in winter. The hair is longer than is common to most Deer, and the tail is short, while the antlers, particular to the male, and about nine inches long, are erect, round horns, with a rough surface and furrowed. Mature animals have two or three tines, sharply pointed, as are the tips of the antlers. They form a serious weapon and can inflict a nasty wound. The Roe Deer (the male is a Roebuck) is very agile and sure-footed, capable of making great leaps, in which respect it is something like the Goat and the Chamois, and as wild as the latter. Its food is the tender shoots of trees and bushes, and its flesh is excellent, better than that of the Red Deer, though not equal in quality to that of the Fallow Deer.

This last is not a British animal really ; it was brought here from the Mediterranean and has flourished in parks. It is only about three feet high at the shoulder, but is a graceful creature, which adds much to the beauty of our woods and parklands. Though timid, it has become accustomed to man, and will allow approach so long as no violent or sudden movements are made. Indeed in the parks they will themselves follow motor-cars in anticipation of tit-bits.

In summer the Fallow Deer has a reddish-brown coat and white spots, with tail black above and white below. In winter the spots are fewer and the coat generally duller. But there are many varieties of colour amongst them. Only the Bucks have antlers with two tines somewhat apart, the horns eventually expanding in a shovel or palmate form. The first year the males have no antlers, which appear only the second year. The breeding season is about October, and there is a single Fawn—rarely two.

The Deer are amongst the proudest of our native animals, with powers which all must appreciate. That our land would be a much poorer place if the march of civilisation meant their extermination except in rail-guarded parks, anyone who has descried a sentinel Stag in the Highlands will readily agree.

IN THE DEER-PARK. [W. S. Berridge.

The Fallow Deer wears a white-spotted coat in summer, which grows duller when winter approaches. It is a very graceful addition to deer-parks, and is also greatly valued because of the excellent flavour of its flesh.

[W. S. Berridge.

Schools of Black-fish or Pilot Whales, have frequently been driven ashore at the Shetland Islands, where over a thousand have been killed in two hours. These Whales, which are black, are sometimes known as Ca'aing Whales.

WHALES, SEALS, AND OTHERS

By JAMES HORNELL, F.L.S., F.R.A.I.

THE great sea-monsters that occasionally visit our coasts are all the more intriguing because we are so seldom able to examine them at close quarters. Here, however, their characteristics are explained to us, and the enthralling mysteries of the deep are revealed. The story of how daring men set forth in whalers to secure monsters would fit into any fairy-tale, and of how Dolphins disport themselves in the water, can be read below.

TO the Basques of a thousand years ago belongs the credit of first venturing to sea in pursuit of those leviathans of ocean, the Great Whalebone, Baleen Whales, usually called Right Whales, because whalermen in the old days esteemed no other Whales worth pursuit—all others were "wrong," or worthless creatures—though they must surely have excepted the Sperm Whale from this wholesale condemnation.

Probably the method of whaling practised at first was akin to that surviving in the Faroes and Orkneys. There a school of the Ca'aing Whale, best-known of the Whales frequenting the British coast, is sometimes driven into shallow water by an excited crowd of fishermen who, in their small open boats, form a seaward cordon round the terrified Whales, cutting them off from escape. Then a shouting mob, wild with the lust for killing, dash among them, slaughtering the stranded creatures by the score.

As with kingdoms, so with whaling; the fall of one dynasty was but the birth of another. When the Basques passed out of view as Whalers, British, Dutch and French seamen took their place, pushing their fleets of Whaling ships far within the Arctic Circle in pursuit of the huge Greenland Whale, a veritable mountain of flesh, ranging in length from fifty to sixty feet. This, too, is a Whalebone species, for its mouth, instead of being armed with teeth, has the entrance to its gullet guarded by a movable barrier of closely-set, flexible plates and filaments of Whalebone for the purpose of straining out the tiny creatures forming its food.

In pursuit of these monsters, the old whalers, armed with nothing better than hand-thrown harpoons and lances, faced incredible danger when attacking their formidable foe. The hardships and perils of their life were terrible, but these were willingly endured, for they were lured on both by the hunter's instinct and by the hope of rich reward. Most famous of the earlier Arctic whalers were the Dutch who based their whaling fleet on Spitzbergen, where at one time (about 1680) they employed 260 ships and about 14,000 men! The English whalers worked mainly to the westward, chiefly in Davis Strait and Baffin Bay, west of Greenland.

The daring sport of Whaling.

With the passing of Dutch whaling supremacy, the British became masters of the industry, nearly every port on the East Coast of England and Scotland sending hardy crews to the north to bring back oil for the lighting of the lamps of Europe. Another fleet of whalers sailed out of London during the last quarter of the eighteenth century to exploit the vast whaling riches of the South Sea, as reported by Cook, Vancouver and other of the famous explorers who, at this time, were writing their names across the face of the Pacific Ocean.

The quarry of these Pacific whalers was the Sperm Whale or Cachalot, a vindictive creature of huge size and strength, with jaws of stupendous power, armed with great ivory teeth, pointed and terrible. Around this species centre most of the tales of foolhardy, desperate courage and hairbreadth escapes— yes, and of awful tragedy as well—that thrill the blood when reading old-time stories of whaling. With one flick of the mighty tail a whaleboat could be reduced in a second to a mass of splintered matchwood and struggling men, bleeding and mangled; or the terrible jaws might crush the boat as a nut beneath a hammer blow. Truly the courage of mere men in attacking a living tornado of seventy feet of muscle and bone with puny harpoons and lances must be counted among the most courageous deeds in the history of mankind; and yet to these hardy seamen this was but the routine of the day's work!

The Arctic Whale fishery continued to give employment to whalers from Dundee and other East coast ports during the greater part of the nineteenth century, but to-day this has passed into the hands of the Norwegians, who also virtually monopolise the exceedingly valuable fishery in Antarctic seas, developed entirely within the present century. This latter fishery is now the most prolific whale fishery in the world, and contributes a greater amount of oil and other Whale products than the combined totals from all other parts of the world. Unlike the fisheries of olden times, this newcomer depends mainly upon the Humpback, Fin Whale and Blue Whale. Comparatively few Right Whales and Sperm Whales are caught, though these are hunted with eagerness when the rare occasion offers, owing to the high value of their products.

That Whales are not fishes, even though whalermen persist in so terming them, need not be stressed. Everybody now knows that they are warm-blooded animals, breathing by means of lungs and not by gills, and that they suckle their young in quite human fashion. Before birth some show traces of hair on the skin, but adults have perfectly smooth hides. Unlike fishes, which use their fins and body movements for swimming and their tail as a rudder, Whales rely almost entirely upon their powerful tail to propel them through the water, using their flippers to maintain balance. In further contrast to fishes, the tail lobes or flukes of a Whale are set horizontally instead of vertically. Fore-limbs, the flippers, only are present, the hand encased in a fleshy fingerless glove of skin. Nearly all the best-known species, with the exception probably of the Greenland Whale have been recorded from British waters, the rarer from individuals cast up on shore.

As a group Whales are divided into the Whalebone Whales and the Toothed Whales. Of the former the most valuable are the Greenland Whale, the Biscayan Right Whale or Nordkaper, the Humpback, and the various kinds of Rorquals or Fin Whales. These have two blow-holes at the top of the head, the equivalent of nostrils, for the spouting of a Whale is really the violent expulsion of air from its lungs after it has had to hold its breath for long minutes whilst swimming under the surface of the water; the warm, moist vapour condenses into spray as it rises in the chilly Arctic air and gives the impression to the watcher that the Whale is spouting water.

The Giant of the Deep.

Longest of all Whales is the gigantic Blue Whale or Sibbald's Rorqual, said to reach one hundred feet in length. Professor D'Arcy Thompson has calculated that the weight of such a monster would reach the almost incredible figure of six hundred tons!

Of the Toothed Whales, their names are legion. Foremost is the ponderous Sperm Whale or Cachalot, made familiar to us by

Photo : J. S. Hodgson.] BRINGING HOME THE CATCH. [Mondiale.
Here is a Whaler, after its voyage in the North, returning to harbour bearing the spoils of the expedition. The
dead Whales are blown up with air to keep them afloat, so that their great weight will not interfere with the boat.

Frank Bullen's charming tales. Among other peculiarities it is distinguished by the enormous expansion of its forehead into a huge cask filled with coarse fat and blubber, saturated with the oily fluid called spermaceti; from this is obtained the much-valued sperm oil, esteemed for the lubrication of small and delicate machinery, as it does not readily go rancid or gummy.

Other British Toothed Whales include the Bottle-nose; the Fighting Grampus or Orca, often called with truth " The Killer " ; the White Whale or Beluga ; the Narwhal ; the Ca'aing or Pilot Whale ; the Porpoise and several species of Dolphin. All these are equipped with but a single blow-hole, operated at the creature's will by a tight-fitting valve in the skin, usually horse-shoe shaped.

A terrifying Fiend.

Most beautiful of all is the Orca or Killer Whale, a very fiend incarnate. It is everybody's enemy, happy only when persecuting its own kind. Porpoises and Whales flee for their lives when they sense its approach ; even the Sperm Whale is terrified at the onslaught of a band of these unholy brutes ; for, like Wolves, the Orcas hunt in packs.

This terrible beast, which ranges up to thirty feet in length, is the veritable tyrant of the sea ; even the largest Whale often succumbs to its attack, so swift and lithe are its movements, so sharp the teeth that tear and slash away great gobbets from poor Leviathan fighting hopelessly his last battle against these fierce sea-tigers. Orcas are a pest also on Sealing grounds, snapping up the unwary Pups'; even the powerful Sea Lion hastily retreats ashore rather than encounter an Orca in the sea.

The Narwhal is a true Sea-unicorn, remarkable for the long, straight tusk of spirally-twisted ivory projecting from the upper jaw of the male. In reality this is one of a pair of eye-teeth, its companion remaining rudimentary ; in rare instances this second tooth develops into a replica of the first. What the use of this long head-spear is has occasioned controversy. Sowerby suggested that it may be used to spear fish with, as he found a large Skate in the stomach of one, but this has been encountered by the pertinent remark that if this be so, the female will fare badly, as she is destitute of this weapon. Others have thought that it is used to keep ice-holes open in winter. A third theory is that it is used

A DROWSY SEAL.   [W. S. Berridge.
The Common Seal, found round British coasts, is perfectly adapted for water-life, but likes to spend some time ashore or to bask on the rocks. It has a very plaintive cry, and baby Seals bleat after the style of lambs.

THE FISHERMAN'S ENEMY—AND FRIEND.   [*W. S. Berridge.*

The Porpoise, which is really a miniature Whale, is so destructive to smaller fish that it has a great many enemies, though the fisherman is sometimes pleased to see that it herds shoals of fish into the bay in which he is fishing.

to dig Shell-fish from the sand, as these figure in its dietary. A more probable explanation seems to be that this tusk is of secondary sexual character, employed by the males in defence of the females and their young.

The Narwhal tusk has value as ivory and as a curiosity. Various quaint stories centre round it, and one of these attributes to it the virtue of warding off the evil eye. Confident in this belief a petty Indian Rajah some years ago stockaded his palace all round with a fence of these tusks.

Unlike the rest of their kind, the general grey colouring of the skin is mottled and spotted with black. They travel in great herds and are very active and sportive creatures, gambolling together with obvious enjoyment of the game.

Another frolicsome and docile cetacean is the White Whale or Beluga, in spite of its seemingly unwieldy bulk of sixteen feet when fully grown. On two occasions, in 1877 and 1878, the old Westminster Aquarium had one in its Whale tank. Frank Buckland in his usual chatty style tells the story of the arrival of the second one at the end of an eventful five-weeks' journey from Canada.

It lay on its stomach in a huge box packed round with seaweed, and Buckland's delight was great when he saw the valve of its blow-hole working regularly. "It looked," he says, "just like a gigantic white human baby with white lips (the blow-hole), snoring in its sleep." It weighed a ton and a half—its box must have been a gigantic structure !

The Dolphins' Appetite.

Commonest of all the tribe in British waters are the Porpoises and Common Dolphins. The differences between them relate chiefly to the form of the teeth, sharp in the Dolphins, flattened in the Porpoise, and in the form of the head—rounded in the Porpoise, beaked or sharp-pointed in the Dolphins. Both are Whales in miniature, for Dolphins average only six to eight feet in length and Porpoises from four to five feet. Both feed upon fishes, and in our own seas Porpoises in particular are terribly destructive to Herrings, Pilchards and Mackerel. Their ravages among Sardines at times are so enormous that the French Government has had on occasion to send gunboats to shoot and chase them away. On the other hand they are sometimes useful to fishermen by herding shoals of fish into bays, where gill and seine nets reap a rich harvest.

From very early times the playfulness of both these handsome creatures, leaping, cavorting and gambolling like Kittens or Lambkins at play, has appealed to the imagination and artistry of ancient Greece. To the Greeks the Dolphin was the embodiment of gracefulness; it appears on their coins, their vases and their sculptures; they harnessed Dolphins to the car of Amphitrite, and they were sacred creatures to Apollo.

How the Whale feeds.

Varied and often curious is the diet of the various kinds of Whales. In the Baleen group, where teeth are replaced by a Whalebone sieve, vast shoals of small, soft creatures, such as tiny Shrimps and soft-shelled Sea Butterflies (Pteropods) form the food of the Greenland Whale, his cousin the Biscayan Right Whale and also the Humpback Whale. These Whales feed by swimming openmouthed, backwards and forwards through shoals of these little creatures until appetite is satisfied or the supply exhausted. The smaller Rorquals prefer Cuttlefish, varied by Herrings, Pilchards and other small fish.

The Toothed Whales mostly feed upon fishes and some have specialised tastes, requiring some particular food. The greatest of the tribe, the Sperm Whale, appeases his appetite on Cuttlefish and Squid whenever possible. He searches them out, often at great depths, and species otherwise rare or even unknown have been extracted from his stomach. The Bottlenose also loves Cuttlefish, and shares the Chinaman's appreciation of the Sea Cucumber, the Trepang and Bêche-de-mer of commerce.

The smaller kinds of the Toothed Whales are mostly declared enemies of all fishes. The ruthlessness of the Orca has been mentioned. The White Whale feeds on Cod and Salmon; the Narwhal on fish, Crustaceans, Shellfish and Cuttles; the Dolphin on Flying fish, Sardines and indeed all the smaller shoaling fishes; the Porpoise largely on Herrings, Mackerel, Plaice and Salmon.

With the exception of the Orca, Whales are of great profit to mankind, so much so that man has pursued them for centuries with such intensity and ever-increasing efficiency of weapons, that several species have been exterminated, or so thinned in numbers as to be rarely seen. Everywhere the story is the same—rapid decrease and increasing difficulty in catching sufficient numbers to be remunerative. To-day the whaling industry is highly specialised. It is profitable only in floating factories and a fleet of steam whale-catchers be sent to the ends of the earth, to the confines of the dreary wastes of the Antarctic. There the catchers attack the Whales with great harpoons shot from a small cannon mounted in the bows. When the carcases are delivered to the floating factory (or, less frequently, to a shore factory) the blubber is peeled off by special apparatus and rendered down by heat into oil. The best of the flesh is made into meal suitable as cattle food, the rest of the carcase into fertiliser. The Sperm Whale is by far the most valuable, for from it, in addition to a quantity of ordinary oil, much meal and fertiliser, we obtain spermaceti, ambergris and tooth ivory. Ambergris is a curious greyish solid found occasionally in the intestine of this Whale and believed to be a secretion induced by the irritation set up by the undigested horny beaks of the Cuttlefish forming this Whale's food. Lumps of it are sometimes found washed up on shore, rich jetsam from the broken-up bodies of dead Whales. It is invaluable in fixing perfumes and commands a very high price, as no substitute has been invented or found.

With the possible exception of the great Greenland Whale—the true Polar Whale— nearly all the well-known species are to be reckoned either as regular or as occasional members of the British fauna, those that are not common being known from individuals which have been stranded alive on our beaches or upon occasion thrown ashore dead.

The fiercest Whale.

The largest of this jetsam of the sea are usually Finner Whales or Rorquals, easily recognised by the way that the skin of the throat is wrinkled into long pleats and grooves. The sharp-toothed Orca or Killer is another common kind that is sometimes stranded on our shores. This, the fiercest as well as the most beautiful of our Whales, has the belly and throat white in colour, contrasting sharply with the glossy black of the back; a large and conspicuous white patch behind the eye is characteristic.

The dorsal fin is unusually long, sometimes nearly equal in length to one-fifth that of the entire animal. Were it not that the Loch

A SEA-MONSTER YAWNS.   [*Mondiale.*

The Sea-Elephant has a very peculiar profile, its pronounced nose being of an especially curious appearance. This giant of the sea measures about twenty feet when full grown, and is nearly the same width round about.

Ness "Monster" shows no inclination to spout, the long fin seen in some photographs would suggest the presence of a small Killer in the loch.

Although the chief centre of the whaling fishery is now situated in the Antarctic seas, the industry still survives in the Shetlands and the Hebrides; the catches include a large variety of species. Two kinds of Rorquals head the list, the Finner or Blue Whale accounting for more than fifty per cent. of the total catch, with Rudolphi's Rorqual contributing about twenty-five per cent. The balance is made up of Humpbacks, Bottle-noses, Sperm Whales and Biscayan Right Whales, all of trading value to the whaler.

Three families of Seals.

Seals, in the wider sense of the term, include three distinct families—the Eared Seals (Sea Lions and Fur Seals), the Walruses, and the True Seals. From the form and arrangement of their teeth and other anatomical characters, it is clear that the ancestors of all were carnivorous land animals that forsook Mother Earth for Father Neptune, tempted by promise of easily-caught food or of refuge from enemies much stronger than themselves.

Unlike the Whale, the tail of a Seal is short and degenerate; what seems to be the tail in the Common Seal is just the hind legs stretched out straight and joined together as far down as the heels by a webbing of skin, an arrangement ideal for swimming, but a grave handicap on land. Conversely, in the other groups, the hind legs, although altered also into paddle-shaped flippers, are more free and flexible and enable their owners to hobble along more or less swiftly.

Once when wandering alone on a sunlit sandy beach in the Galapagos, on turning the corner of a sandhill, I blundered almost on top of a great Sea Lion, huge as a small Elephant. The sandy hollow where he lay was the cosiest nook about; the great beast was snoozing like a Cat in the sunshine, and when he wakened up in a flurry I doubt which of us was the more astonished. I wanted to take his photograph, but he refused. Off he galloped towards the sea in a wild, lolloping, clumsy scurry.

Sea Lions and Walruses have much in common; both are huge and friendly, except when in fear for their young or when attacked. Of the two the Sea Lion is the more intelligent and tamable. It has an almost human

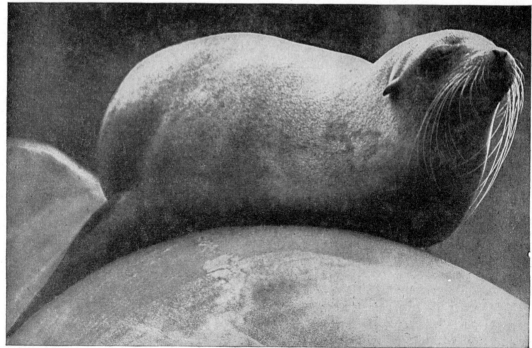

Photo: H. Bastin.]   THE REST-HOUR.   [Mondiale.

The Sea-Lion is usually very cautious, but this bewhiskered monster has given way to the gentle influence of sleep. Some herds place a sentinel to guard over them and to raise the alarm signal, which they do very effectively.

A VIGOROUS SWIMMER.

The Elephant Seal is an alarming monster to encounter in the water, as can be imagined from the above picture, which shows it slashing the spray as it turns. The layer of fat under its skin yields about 200 gallons of oil.

faculty of understanding what its trainer wishes to be done ; it will fetch and carry on dry land like a Retriever, sit up and beg like a Terrier, and even perform the circus tricks of jumping or stumbling through a hoop and going up and down a ladder. It lives mainly upon fish, and its presence is a sure sign of an abundance of fish in the sea around.

THE Walrus, on the contrary, is a ground feeder, routing about on the sea-bottom for Cockles, Clams and other burrowing Shell-fish, digging them out of the sand and gravel with the two great curved tusks that sprout from the upper jaw. Another use they have is to help the Walrus to climb on to the ice. It is a gregarious creature, loving to drowse and sleep in herds on the ice or on some lonely beach, packed together like sardines in a tin, heads and tails resting against or upon one another and snoring in great comfort. All appear to sleep, but guard is kept, though reluctantly. One Walrus will raise his head and give a listless but vigilant look around ; if satisfied, he turns to his relief, snoring along-side, and calls him with a grunt and a dig in the ribs with his tusks ; the other wakes up sleepily and takes over guard before re-peating this strange changing of the guard.

In the early part of last century immense herds of Walruses were to be found wherever there was open water among the ice-floes of the Arctic from Greenland to Spitzbergen and thence to Bering Strait and the Alaskan Islands. From the latter region the tusks of as many as 12,000 Walruses were landed annually at San Francisco between 1870 and 1890, and these were but the smaller part of the total destroyed merely for the hide and the tusks. To-day their numbers are so reduced that they are no longer worth hunting on a large scale. Although an Arctic animal, occasional stragglers have wandered south to the Scottish coasts.

The True Seals, with hind legs useless for walking or crawling, have a nearly world-wide range outside of the tropics. Two species regularly visit our coasts, the Common Seal and the Grey Seal. In these beautiful animals, so sleek and well groomed, so soft eyed and gentle, we have the prototype of the mermaid of legend and myth. When one was captured in olden times, its human relationship was often assumed. Of all the stories that have come down to us, one of the most remarkable is the account of the taking of one in Suffolk in the reign of Henry II. It was believed to be either a man bewitched or else an evil spirit that had entered into the body of a drowned sailor. Believing it to be silent from evil intent, its captors tortured it to make it speak. Failing in this, they carried it to the church and held it up to worship Christ and the Madonna. But as it showed no reverence, it was adjudged not to be human, and this was fortunate, for now it was taken back to the castle and given a meal of fish. The tale has a happy ending, for it is related that it escaped and returned to the sea.

The Common Seal is an animal of great intelligence and docility, and of the many stories of its domesticity the following is typical. Caught while young, one became so tame that when called from a distance, even when gambolling in the sea, it would answer with a plaintive cry, swim ashore and wriggle its ungainly way over stones and grass to its owner's house.

An occasional visitor to our shores is the pretty little Ringed Seal, not unlike the Common Seal, but smaller and spotted on the back with oval, roundish rings. Its skin provides the Eskimos with breeches and jumpers, and its flesh with a much-valued food supply, although that of old males has a disgusting odour. The Eskimos may even have borrowed the plan of their beehive-shaped " igloos " from that of the ice-covered shelters constructed by this Seal.

All Seals have great staying power under water. Their nostrils are controlled by powerful closing muscles which function like the horn nose-clips of Arab pearl-divers ; with breathing thus arrested mechanically, they are able to remain submerged for periods ranging from ten minutes to half an hour, or even more, according to age and species.

The breeding season of the Common Seal is in June ; at this time a considerable number continue to seek out lonely caves on the rock-girt coasts of Cornwall and south-west Wales. Others favour grottos and sheltered ledges at the base of the cliffs of Caithness and Sutherland or of those of the Hebridean Isles. There the young are born, to be nursed and tended by the parents in very human fashion. Usually but one is brought forth at a birth, two being comparatively rare. While suckling the Pup, the mother, normally so gentle and timid, repels fiercely any intruder into the family circle ; in such an emergency she calls her mate to her assistance in barking tones very different from the usual plaintive cry. The Pups are pretty little creatures, pure white or grey at birth, and covered with soft wool which, however, is shed after a few days.

Grey Seals breed during October and November ; their usual haunts in Britain are the Hebrides, though pairs and small colonies are sometimes seen on the east coast of Scotland, with an outlying colony at the Farne Islands, off the Northumberland coast. Unlike the Common Seal, they hold aloof from mankind, and can seldom be domesticated. In intelligence they are also markedly inferior, a difference accounted for by the smallness of the brain as compared with the other species.

Fishermen abhor them, for they are inveterate raiders ; not content with pursuing the Salmon—their favourite prey—they steal all the goodly fish meshed in the nets of the Salmon fishers set off the coast or in the estuaries, leaving only the heads for the fishermen. Often the nets themselves are broken through and badly torn by the depredators, powerful creatures that sometimes grow to a length of eight feet.

Economically the carcases of Seals are of little use ; the flesh has a rank, fishy taste, and is of no value, save as meal for cattle and poultry ; unfortunately our people are not yet fully awake to the profit to be gained by a systematic utilisation of such material.

Seals have few enemies in these seas other than man. Elsewhere their great foe is the ferocious Orca, the Killer Whale. Off the Seal " Rookeries," where Seals congregate during the breeding season, the Killer is usually to be found on the look-out for stray Cubs that wander away from their mothers' apron-strings. As showing the immense havoc these great brutes may inflict, the stomach of a large Orca was found to contain the remains of thirteen Porpoises and fourteen Seals.

On certain parts of the Scottish Coast, Seals, which a few years ago abounded, are being driven to the seclusion of the unfrequented rocks of the more northern islands, for Salmon fishers, on account of the great damage they do to their stake-nets, wage deadly feud against the Seals. An old Seal will become so cunning and so impudent that he will actually take the Salmon out of the nets, despite the efforts of the fishermen. Sometimes at high-water, and when the river is in flood, a Seal will pursue Salmon relentlessly right into the fresh water channels.

Photo : W. S. Berridge.]   [Mondiale.

When the female Grass Snake has deposited her eggs, which might number anything up to four dozen, their size increases because of the moisture they absorb. Here are some youngsters escaping from their shells.

BRITISH REPTILES

By PERCY W. HORN

THERE are not many varieties of Snakes to be found in our country, for which we have reason to be thankful, and those we are likely to encounter are not very alarming. The Grass Snake and Adder are mentioned below, and the story of how these wriggling creatures go about their daily lives is explained in an interesting manner. After reading it, our slight disgust of anything " snakey " is likely to give way to admiration.

THE mere mention of a Snake is apt to cause a shudder, but the nervous country-lover need not be unduly alarmed, for of the two kinds likely to be met with on a ramble, the Grass Snake, the commoner of the two, is quite harmless. It is widely distributed, and always found in the vicinity of water, but it is curious to note that it is sometimes absent from localities where the conditions are apparently ideal for its existence. Recently we were discussing this point with reference to a certain area in Norfolk which looked the very spot for snakes, and it transpired that the district in question was completely surrounded with a wide belt of dry, sandy heaths. The conclusion arrived at was that the dry belt, being deficient in snake-food, was an effective barrier to the overflow from the snake population outside.

The Grass Snake is not readily observed in the wild state ; you will seldom catch it asleep. The usual indication of its presence is a rustling in the hedge bottom and a brief glimpse of a whip-like tail disappearing down a convenient hole. The Grass Snake is plentiful in the county of Essex, even on the outskirts of London, and many a fine example have we scooped out of the water when on pond-dipping and angling excursions. It swims well on the surface with a graceful, undulating movement, its head held just above the surface, and on occasion will submerge and explore the bottom in search of food.

The colour of the Grass Snake varies considerably. Some individuals are almost black, but the usual type is of a grey-green colour similar to that of a young ash sapling, with an underlying series of black spots running down the body, more distinct on the sides, which are pale yellow. The underparts are leaden black. Behind the head, which is black, is a very conspicuous yellow collar. This should be particularly noted as it is the chief external character which distinguishes the harmless Grass Snake from the poisonous Adder.

Grass Snakes grow to a fair size, especially

the females, which are the stouter. One, which we kept for four years, measured four inches over the yard, but the average length, irrespective of sex, is nearer two feet. A snake's eyes are like a fish's. They have no eyelids. The eyes are protected by skin which extends in a continuous layer over the whole of the body, including the eyes.

In its wild state the Grass Snake feeds on frogs, toads, newts, and possibly it may include young birds and mice in its dietary.

Do Snakes eat birds ?

The big snake mentioned above would also take live fish, but all attempts to entice it with a young sparrow were failures. However, it is not safe to dogmatise from observations on captive animals. The late Abel Chapman in his delightful "Wild Spain" instances the Colubrines as devouring young birds, and a friend who is a competent naturalist assured us that he had once taken fledgling skylarks from the interior of a big Grass Snake. It must be remembered, too, that animals in captivity often change their habits. We once kept a Perch which lived in harmony with a small Minnow.

Snakes have been stigmatised as being "cold and clammy." This is partly imaginary. The Snake is certainly cold-blooded, but its skin is quite as dry as that of a human being

Twice or thrice each season, and perhaps more often when at liberty, with no restrictions on its diet, the snake discards his old coat. The portion shed is the thin, whitish layer which overlies the epidermis. The same thing happens with human beings, but the process is constant and so gradual that it is hardly noticed. For some days previous to sloughing there is a marked dulling of the snake's colours, and the eyes lose their brightness. The creature wanders around, poking into corners and rubbing its head on any rough surfaces. If offered food it will either refuse to look at it or make a few half-hearted shots which invariably miss the mark. As a matter of fact, it is more or less blind. The skin over the lidless eyes is becoming loose and opaque. After a while the snake manages to fray the skin round the lips. It redoubles its efforts and the skin comes right away from the head in two ragged flaps. When once the head is free the remainder of the shedding process is easy work and the snake finally rubs himself clear of the entire skin, leaving it in one piece, usually turned inside out. The

Photo : Ray Palmer.]　　　　　　　　　THE GRASS SNAKE'S SNOOZE.　　　　　　　　　[Mondiale.
Here is the female Grass Snake curled up in a complicated fashion. It is usually the largest and heaviest member of the family. In autumn it retires to some safe shelter in the woods to pass most of the winter in sleep.

Photo: *K. Stülcken.*]   READY FOR FOOD.   [*Mondiale.*

The Grass Snake has the power of contorting its body into many queer shapes. Above, it is ready to attack some unseen prey, which it will swallow whole. Its bottom jaw has elastic qualities that enable it to stretch its mouth.

discarded skin is worth examination. If it could be tenderly filled out, the flimsy transparent envelope would be an exact replica of the creature itself. Every surface detail stands out in sharp relief, the beautiful pattern of the dorsal surface, the big transverse underplates, and, most fascinating of all, the portions which formerly covered the eyes. These portions resemble tiny lenses or watch glasses. The new coat is much brighter in colour than the old one, and the snake usually celebrates the occasion by indulging in a hearty meal.

How is it that a Snake can crawl so quickly? A glance at the skeleton would enlighten us. A Snake's skeleton is practically all ribs and backbone. It reminds one forcibly of a long-legged centipede. There is no rigid pelvic girdle, as in birds and mammals, to interfere with lateral movement and hamper its flexibility. Every vertebra, except those of the tail, carries a pair of ribs, attached loosely so that they can be moved to and fro. The free ends of the ribs are attached by connective tissue to one of the big scales of the belly, of which there is one to each pair of ribs.

When the snake wishes to crawl it sends a wave-like movement down the ribs, which in turn is communicated to the scales. The edges of these catch up in any roughnesses of the ground, and the Snake is thus propelled forwards. Movement is also assisted by leverage of the tail, and the friction gained by the lateral, undulating movements of the supple body. Thus the Snake can get along very nicely without the aid of legs. It can climb walls and trees, providing the surfaces are rough, but place it on a smooth table, and it can make very little progress.

One of the greatest drawbacks to the keeping of Snakes is their horrible method of feeding. It will not, as a rule, take dead food, and it cannot be educated to eat bread and milk. If the creatures are to be kept, live frogs are the most convenient food, and incidentally we would warn prospective snake-keepers that the food bill is likely to be a heavy one. The big pensioner previously mentioned, fed, on the average, three times a fortnight and took three or four large frogs at a meal.

Snakes swallow their prey whole. When we compare the slim proportions of a two-foot Snake with the portly form of a Frog it seems incredible, almost as incredible as a small boy swallowing a water melon. But the Snake has considerable advantages over the small boy. In the first instance, its mouth is so constructed as to accommodate objects twice or thrice the diameter of its body. The lower jawbone, instead of being in one rigid piece, as in the boy's, is made up of two halves loosely joined together at the point of the chin by an elastic ligament. At the points where they articulate with the upper jaw, more loose connections are to be observed. The bones in the roof of the mouth are also joined together in precisely the same manner.

Duel between Snake and Frog.

We will describe what happens when a Frog is dropped into the vivarium. It may temporarily escape notice, but the Snake seems to sense its presence. The head is raised inquiringly, the cleft tongue flickers in and out and the beady eyes glisten. Immediately the Frog makes the slightest movement the Snake darts its head forwards and seizes it, and its doom is sealed, even if it is caught by the tip of the leg. Its frantic struggles are useless: the smoothness of the skin is of no avail.

There is no escape, for the interior of the Snake's mouth is armed both at top and bottom with an array of fine sharp teeth which point backwards. The Snake merely has to hang on. We find similar teeth in the predatory fishes, notably the Pike. After struggling fruitlessly for a while, the Frog lies still. Now we have a good opportunity to observe the wonderful mechanism of the mouth in action. One side retains its original hold, but the other begins an insidious creeping movement, working its way slowly up the leg until it gets a fresh grip nearer the body.

The head then turns a trifle, and the other half of the mouth releases and also creeps forwards to a fresh position. And so the action continues until the whole leg is engulfed. When the Snake reaches the Frog's body its progress it interrupted by the free hind leg which then stands out at right angles from the gape, in a very awkward position. Any other creature would be beaten, but not so the Snake. It literally dislocates its jaws. The elastic connections stretch to their utmost, the widely-separated bones take all manner of angles and work independently of each other, and the distended mouth loses all semblance of its original shape as it forces the Frog's leg into line with the body and continues to creep inexorably upwards. After a brief rest the Snake continues, and soon all

that we can see of the unfortunate Frog is its head, front legs and the tip of the hind leg protruding from the Grass Snake's mouth.

Finally the Frog disappears entirely, its progress down the gullet being indicated by a huge lump over which the Snake's skin is stretched to the utmost. The Snake yawns, rubs its mouth free from any adhering particles of grass or litter and, if satiated, settles down quietly to sleep off its big meal. It may occur to some that the Snake is liable to choke when negotiating a big Frog. Nature has provided against this happening. The circulation of the Snake's blood is very feeble and sluggish. That is why it is " cold-blooded." It requires far less air than the higher animals, and can also retain a large amount of air in its lung. In addition, the end of the windpipe opens out at the front of the mouth, not the rear, and can actually be protruded if necessary, as when the Snake is swallowing a large object.

Grass Snakes soon adapt themselves to captivity and become quite tame and familiar with their keepers. Freshly-caught specimens, however, should be handled at arm's length, as they have an objectionable habit of ejecting an evil-smelling fluid from two glands at the root of the tail when alarmed. It appears to be their only weapon of offence. They will hiss in the most threatening manner, but we have never known this reptile to bite.

How to cage the Snake.

The cage should be fitted up as described for the Frog, but it should be larger and placed in a sunny position, as snakes delight to bask. They are fond of bathing and climbing, too, and a few rough boughs will enable them to display their proportions and also assist them in the trying period of sloughing. Feeding has already been mentioned, but we would add that it is essential to give Snakes, and all animals which hibernate, plenty of food in the autumn, so as to build up a reserve of energy for the winter. Snakes should be watched when feeding, otherwise there may be trouble if two Snakes seize upon the same Frog, particularly if one is much smaller than the other.

There is no difficulty in keeping Snakes over the winter. Ours usually hibernate, or partially hibernate, in a litter of hay and dry leaves under the tray at the bottom of the vivarium. A similar arrangement could be fixed up with a flat tile or a few dry turfs. On

Photo : K. Stülcken.] A GRACEFUL SWIMMER. [*Mondiale.*

The Grass Snake likes plenty of moisture, and is a good swimmer and diver. It makes a graceful picture as it skims through the water, but any frog lingering nearby does not pause to admire it before dashing to safety!

Photo : K. Stülcken.] CAST-OFF CLOTHING. [*Mondiale.*

Before pairing, the male Vipers slough their skins and reveal themselves in brilliant colours : whitish-green, bluish-white, yellowish-white, black metallic and glittering zig-zag bands. *L.*, the sloughed skin ; *R.*, the vigorous male.

Photo : Ray Palmer.]　　　　　　THE MALE ADDER.　　　　　　　　[*Mondiale.*

The Adder, or Viper, is usually found on sandy heaths or dry moors, where it loves to bask in the sun. It is stouter than the Grass Snake, but its body is not as long. It feeds mainly on small mammals.

Photo : Farnsworth.]　　　　　　A COLOURFUL VIPER.　　　　　　　　[*Mallinson.*

The Viper, with its decorative markings, is seen hunting in the long grass for a meal. In autumn it retires for a long rest to some dry and secluded nook. Its young are from six to eight inches long when born.

several occasions our captives have laid eggs, twenty to thirty in number. They are about the size of those of a Blackbird, dirty white in colour, with a tough, leathery skin. We have never succeeded in hatching them. In a wild state the Grass Snake lays the eggs in dung heaps and melon beds where there is a constant gentle heat and plenty of moisture, so possibly our substitute—grass clippings—was not sufficiently mature to supply the requirements necessary for successful incubation.

In contradiction to the Grass Snake, the Adder is usually found in dry places, such as sandy heaths, overgrown chalk quarries and open moors. We understand that it is plentiful in Devon, and have found it in Hants, Kent and on certain Essex commons. Formerly they were more plentiful in the neighbourhood of London, but of late years they appear to have decreased in numbers. No doubt the growth of the town has had its usual effect but we are inclined, in some cases, to ascribe the decrease to the periodical fires which have been so prevalent of late on our open spaces, and which must destroy countless numbers of ground animals.

When the Adder is Lazy.

The best time for observing Adders in the wild state is early April, when they are warming their sluggish blood after their long absence from the sun's rays. They are then more reluctant to move.

To the experienced eye the Adder is readily distinguished from the Grass Snake. Its body is very much stouter, lacking the beautiful taper, and the yellow neck patches are absent. However, when in doubt it is not advisable to take risks, for, as in the Grass Snake, the colours are variable. The usual type has a ground colour of dark-reddish brown, but some examples, generally males, are of a beautiful silver or pinkish grey. Along the back is a line of black blotches joined together to form a zig-zag pattern. Near the head the line ceases abruptly, and on the head itself we get the inverted " V " and dark marks which are popularly supposed to represent a skull and crossbones.

The Adder never attains the length of the Grass Snake. Twenty inches is a fair length, and any Adder longer than two feet may be considered to be a very big one indeed. We are informed that the food of the Adder consists of Lizards and Mice. Personally we have never been fortunate enough to see one feed.

Young Adders are hatched internally and produced alive.

The flickering, black appendage which Snakes protrude so freely is a harmless, sensitive tongue and not, as is commonly imagined, a deadly " sting." The poison apparatus is in the roof of the mouth and not exposed except when in action. It consists of two poison glands near the angles of the gape, a pair of tubes or canals to conduct the venom, and two long, sharp, hollow teeth inside the fore part of the upper jaw.

Examining deadly Fangs.

It is a risky business to examine the fangs of a live Adder, so we will assume that we have a dead one handy. When the mouth is opened no teeth will be seen, but if a match stick is rubbed gently along the roof of the mouth and sides of the jaws we shall soon detect the presence of numbers of tiny teeth, both at top and bottom. These are not poisonous, but are used for the purpose of holding the prey. The poison fangs lie folded backwards, like the blade of a penknife, along the roof of the mouth and are hidden in folds of the pink skin, but they can be located and prised up carefully with a needle.

They are quite insignificant weapons, having the appearance of delicate, curved fish bones scarcely more than one eighth of an inch in length, but they function as the hypodermic needle with which the Snake injects its poison. In life the raising of the fangs is brought about by an ingenious arrangement of bones and muscles which act as levers, and the mechanism cannot be worked properly until the Snake opens its mouth.

When the Snake is roused.

It is popularly supposed that a Snake is unable to strike when its body is extended. It can, however, regain its position so quickly that it would be unwise to experiment in this direction. We have seen an Adder deliver a double knock on a walking stick, and the blows were felt almost simultaneously. Usually, when irritated, the Adder draws back into a compact heap so as to get the necessary purchase and leverage for its muscular body. The mouth is opened and fangs erected after the strike has started, and the action is of the nature of a blow rather than a bite.

Adder " bites " are seldom fatal to human beings, though dogs and cattle will sometimes succumb. As in the case of bee stings, a lot depends on the condition of the person bitten and the location of the bite. The late Mr. Leslie Hocking, who was bitten at Danbury by a small red Viper one foot in length, stated that it caused him little inconvenience.

Bitten by an Adder.

On the other hand, the late Mr. Fred Cooper, the well-known fish-stuffer, had a less happy experience when Adder-hunting on the clay banks near Hadleigh, Essex. He was bitten on the hand, collapsed into complete insensibility, and had to be carried home. Two days later he was sufficiently recovered to return and capture his enemy together with six others.

Mr. Cooper's experience, together with our own with Honey Bees, leads us to believe that in such cases the venom is injected into one of the larger blood vessels, and not into the capillaries. The usual symptoms of Adder bite are, burning pain at the place of injection, local swelling, which gradually extends up the bitten limb to the body, accompanied by fainting, headaches and vomiting. The action of the heart may become irregular, and there is a purple and yellow discoloration of the limb, extending to the body. The effects may last a few days or a fortnight.

The action of the poison is very rapid, but it may be partially neutralised by scarifying the wound and applying permanganate of potash.

Adders are most unsatisfactory " pets." Apart from the risk involved in keeping them, their intractable nature precludes the opportunities of interesting observation as afforded by the docile Grass Snake. They cannot be handled except in very cold weather or under the influence of chloroform. In cold weather they hide away out of sight, and when enlivened by the sun they are perpetually endeavouring to escape. They refuse all food, lose their plumpness and ultimately die at the end of the summer.

They vary greatly in temperament. Some are merely sullen, others the reverse. We had one, a fine grey male, one summer when the weather was exceptionally hot, and it could not be equalled as an example of sheer malignant ferocity. Our reptiles usually become reconciled to the attentions of visitors and realise the futility of striking against the hard glass ; but this particular example would assume the striking position at the least provocation and quiver all over like a coiled spring, with suppressed rage. A tap on the case invariably brought a lightning response, and one was indeed thankful for the intervening glass. He died in September, his spirit remaining unbroken till the end. His companion, a small darkbrown specimen, never attempted to strike, and was handled on several occasions.

Photo: K. Stülcken.]   *[Mondiale.*

THE SNAKE'S HEAD-ARMOUR.

This close-up shows the head-armour of a Grass Snake. The small, overlapping scales act as shields to protect it.

During the ten years in which we have kept Adders we have never known one to take food, though they drink occasionally. We have tried Mice, Lizards and young birds. The mice were far more attractive to juvenile visitors than the Adders. They made themselves comfortable nests and lived quite happily. One was observed performing its toilet within three inches of an Adder's nose, and another, a Field Vole, added injury to insult by making a meal off the dead body of one of its grim companions. Adders cast their skins in captivity, but not so frequently as the Grass Snake, owing to the fact that they do not take the nourishment necessary for their full growth and development.

[Robert McLeod.

The Common Frog, having successfully reached maturity after its transition period as a Tadpole, is an ungainly creature ready to indulge in the hopping exercises at which it is so expert. It is especially frisky in rainy weather.

FROGS AND TOADS

By PERCY W. HORN

THE curious little creature that hops about our ponds and fields has a story behind it that reads almost like a fairy tale. Before it reaches maturity it goes through many processes that make us marvel at the ways of Nature. From a mass of jelly to a full-grown Frog seems a miraculous development. The author explains how this happens.

OF a certainty the Frog was born under an unlucky star. Observe him as he sits quietly in the shade of a dock leaf. Squat and ungainly, with his humped back and his prominent eyes staring fixedly upwards, he is indeed grotesque. Nobody admires him, and he is regarded with aversion, except by humorists, who from the time of Æsop to Twain have found in him a convenient butt for ridicule. For him and his kindred, life is one long period of persecution. We know of nothing which eats the spawn, except perhaps the domestic Duck with its wonderful sieve-bill, but farmers sometimes object to its presence in the ponds, averring that the glutinous mass deters the cattle from drinking, and in some parts it is customary to anticipate the nuisance by introducing a Pike for the express purpose of devouring the happy nuptial couples. The Tadpole stage is an exceptionally critical period for the Frog. Fish look upon Tadpoles as special tit-bits (a hint for readers who keep tropical fish), and the larvæ of the various aquatic insects harass and slay them with all manner of horrible devices. When mature, they constitute the chief food of the Grass Snake, and their grisly remains are to be found among the cast pellets which litter the ground beneath roosting places of Heron and Little Owl. From time immemorial they have been subjected to unmentionable cruelties at the hands of the small boy, and, in their thousands, they are stock subjects for the biologist and vivisectionist. The marvel is that the Frog survives, and is so common.

Take a good look at this quaint creature. He has several obvious peculiarities, for instance the ugly hump. If we examine his skeleton we find that the hip bones are not fused together into one solid mass, as in

279

human beings, but are long and slender, attached only at the extreme ends, forming a triangle, of which the hump part is the base, the apex pointing backwards and down, towards the rear. At the apex, well under the body, the muscular legs are attached. The result of this peculiar arrangement is that the Frog, when in a resting position, is always poised or set in readiness for a sudden spring.

Again, note the skin—always shiny and moist. There is a reason for this familiar characteristic. Just below the surface are numerous tiny blood vessels to which air penetrates, thus assisting the lungs in their function of blood purification. If the skin should dry it becomes impervious to air, hence the Frog is provided with perspiratory glands which continually secrete moisture. In addition, Frogs and Toads carry a reserve supply of water, which they will eject if roughly handled. This sudden ejection is somewhat disconcerting, but the liquid is in no way offensive and is very important to them. If, after compelling a Frog to empty his reservoir, we place him overnight in a dry cardboard box before he has had time to take in a further supply, he will be found dead in the morning.

Children invariably desire to know the

Ray Palmer.]   THE VOCALIST.   [Mondiale.

The green edible Frog displays his musical abilities during the spawning season, when the vocal sacs, which are situated below his ears, are brought into full use.

reason why a Frog's throat is in a state of perpetual motion. As mentioned, the skin plays an important part, but main respiration is carried on by the lungs. In the higher animals air is inhaled by the expansion of the chest cavity, effected by movements of ribs and the muscular partition or diaphragm, which separates chest from stomach. In view of the fact that the Frog's "ribs" are merely tiny projections of the vertebræ, and the diaphragm is absent, it follows that it cannot inhale as we do. Nature has got over this difficulty by modifying his capacious mouth into an air pump, of which the tongue with its massive base muscles constitutes the piston, the nostrils functioning as valves. When the mass of muscle is depressed air rushes through the nostrils into the vacuum thus formed. The interior apertures of the nostril passages are then closed with the tip of the tongue, and the muscles are raised, thus compressing the air, which is pumped or gulped down to the lungs. (The return journey or exhalation, it may be remarked, is brought about by the muscular compression of the flanks.) It is the operation of the throat mechanism that gives rise to the familiar throat palpitation. We have not tried the experiment, but, theoretically speaking, if we were to force a Frog's mouth open and keep it open, he would die—from lack of air !

While on the subject of the Frog's tongue, there is another matter worthy of note. If we examine its tongue we find that its attachment is at the front of the mouth, the free end lying back towards the gullet, in contradiction to the generality of tongues. It is broad, fleshy, and coated with an adhesive substance, and is used for the purpose of catching small insects. When the Frog sees a desirable fly he crawls within range, the tongue is flipped out and over with an audible click, and the insect disappears as if by magic. In fact, the tongue functions as a "fly swatter," only in this particular instance the fly adheres to the "swatter." The action, which is extremely rapid, is best observed in the Toad, and anyone who has witnessed this fascinating operation will readily understand why our forefathers believed that the Toad "spat fire."

The life history of the Frog has always exercised a fascination over the minds of naturalists and has been put forward as one of the arguments in favour of the Evolution theory. This subject is beyond the scope of this article, but it is interesting to note that, up to a certain point, the life history of the Frog is the life history of the higher vertebrates, Man included. We all start from one common point—the egg-cell. This divides and sub-divides, gradually forming the embryo. The embryos are almost identical, even to the possession of gill-slits. The similarity is continued into the Tadpole stage, the only difference being that the " tadpole " of the higher animals is still being nourished and protected within the egg shell or body of the parent, when the Frog Tadpole is out in the world getting its own living. Here the similarity gradually ends, and the paths diverge. The Frog develops into a highly-specialised animal, but he does not advance quite so far along the path of evolution as the human being !

DURING the winter Frogs hibernate in the mud at the bottom of ponds, emerging in February for the purpose of propagation. Their conspicuous love-making and the resultant spawn and hordes of wriggling Tadpoles are too well-known to be described here. A female will deposit up to 4000 eggs at a time. A brief word or two concerning the rearing may induce readers to collect spawn and make their own observations in an aquarium. For this purpose an old, well-established tank, the greener the better, with plenty of growing plants, is recommended, care being taken to exclude the larvæ of aquatic insects.

The true egg is the black speck. The globe of clear jelly, a protective envelope rather than a yolk, is a most convenient medium through which to note the growth of the embryo. The Tadpole takes no food for the first day or two—in fact, it has no mouth —but when it becomes a free swimmer and loses its external gills it soon begins to nibble at the green stuff, and rapidly brings the tank into crystal-clear condition. Hind legs appear at the age of six weeks, when a piece of cooked meat should be provided, otherwise lack of animal food will stunt the growth and retard development. The gradual formation of internal lungs is indicated when the front legs appear and the Tadpole loses its plump form and becomes angular, when the animal will cease to feed and will be noticed endeavouring to leave the water. At this stage floating slabs of cork should be provided. Young Frogs may be removed and fed on

Photo: Ray Palmer.]　　　　　　　　　[Mondiale.
THE FROG IN ACTION.
The Frog is well adapted to life in the water, but has many enemies who are eager to snatch at his body.

the tiny black flies which breed in rotting fruit, but it is a bothersome business, and we have found that they invariably die when cold weather sets in, so it is best to give them their liberty.

Two species of Frogs only are found in our isles : the Common Frog, referred to above, and the Edible or Water Frog. This second kind rarely leaves the water, and is to be found only in Cambridgeshire and Norfolk. During the spawning season it utters a loud noise, and for this reason is ironically called the " Cambridgeshire Nightingale." In many parts of Europe the flesh, or rather the legs, of this Frog is eaten, and in Paris alone up to about 100,000 francs is spent annually on this delicacy by diners of epicurean tastes.

The life history, structure and habits of the Toad are somewhat similar to those of the Frog. It spawns later, usually in April, and the eggs, instead of being deposited in a shapeless mass are laid in a double string festooned from plant to plant. Toad Tadpoles are black, in contrast with the greyish progeny of the Frog, and incidentally we would remark that we have found them distasteful to fishes in an aquarium. They complete their metamorphoses and leave the water in August and September on damp,

Photo : *Albert Leon.*]   FROG-LAND.   [*Mondiale.*

In some marsh-lands communities of Frogs can be seen playing themselves in the water where myriads of Tadpoles may be fighting their way to development.   They spend the winter in the mud at the bottom of the pond.

Photo: K. Stülcken.] THE TOAD'S DEVELOPMENT. [Mondiale.

The small black eggs of the Toad are embedded in a jelly-like substance to which the larvæ cling when hatched. Eating their way out, they develop into small, tailless Toads. Above, they are seen emerging from their covering.

Photo: K. Stülcken.] THE TADPOLES SHOW THEIR TAILS. [Mondiale.

After twelve days the Tadpoles of the Common Toad are strong enough to propel themselves through the water by their tails, and enter into many conflicts. They show gill tufts, but the mouth has developed into a sucking organ.

rainy evenings. Myriads of tiny Toads, less in size than a man's little finger-nail, may sometimes be seen hopping and scrambling across the roads and bare spaces, and it is quite within the bounds of possibility that the visitation of the Egyptian plague of "frogs" was nothing more than one of these annual migrations on an abnormal scale.

How the Toad protects itself.

The appearance of the Toad is well known to most of us, but many people still confuse him with his relative. The Frog has a smooth, shiny skin usually much lighter in colour than that of the Toad, which is rough and blackish and covered on the upper surfaces with distinctive warts or tubercles. These tubercles are organs of defence. They secrete an alkaline fluid which has a faint smell and an unpleasant taste, as many an inexperienced dog has discovered to his obvious discomfort. As far back as 1852 two French scientists demonstrated the poisonous character of this secretion which caused paralysis and death when injected into the blood of small birds. The secretion, however, is no protection against the Grass Snake. On three separate occasions we have made freshly-caught Essex Grass Snakes disgorge large Toads. Shakespeare's statement anent the Toad being ugly and "venomous," though doubtless written under a misconception, is not without foundation, but the secretion is the poor old fellow's sole means of defence, and is used only under the greatest provocation. Many other Batrachians, notably the warningly-coloured Spotted Salamander, are possessed of similar means of protection, and it is always advisable to take the safe precaution of cleansing the hands after handling Newts and Toads.

Toads are most useful creatures in garden or greenhouse. The problem is to induce them to stop at home. They are of retiring and sedentary habits, but very discriminating in their choice of residence. Moreover, they can, if necessary, climb and burrow, and it is not safe to assume them to be secure within the confines of a wall or fence. The best plan is to construct a number of small caves in the damp, shady corners and allow them to select their own retiring places. They will utilise the crevices in ornamental rockwork, but such is their individual perversity that they are more likely to make their abode beneath boxes of seedlings and other incon-

Photo : K. Stülcken.]   TOAD TADPOLES.   [*Mondiale.*

The black Tadpoles of the Common Toad often leave the water on damp evenings, scrambling about on land, eager to explore an unknown world. In five years they attain maturity : the full space of the Toad's life is unknown.

A FULL-GROWN TOAD.

[*Charles Reid.*

Here is a mature male Toad. Its colour varies, depending upon the soil of its surroundings. Its tints cleverly blend with the earth, so that it easily passes unseen. Unlike the Frog, it has no musical ability—except croaking.

venient places. The domestic cat, that bugbear of naturalists, will leave them severely alone after the first encounter, and they will soon settle down, providing no Hedgehog is kept in the garden. Mr. Prickles disdains to eat the Toad's body, but is always ready to satisfy himself with a meal off the limbs.

How the Toad spends his evening.

In the evening the Toad leaves his retreat and walks abroad in search of food. Inanimate objects are ignored, though it is possible to fool him with a piece of rag attached to a fine thread, when his astonishment is ludicrous to witness. He has a quaint air of alertness. All small moving objects which come within a distance of two feet are intently scrutinised and patiently stalked. If the prospective victim halts, the Toad halts, too, and the luckless Wood Louse or Beetle is temporarily safe. At the least sign of movement friend Toad resumes his approach until he arrives within effective shooting range, which is about two inches. A sudden forward jerk of the body, a pinkish flash, not unlike a flash of fire, as the adhesive tongue is flicked out and over, and there is a startling vacancy. The Toad gulps, blinks, wipes the sides of his mouth

clumsily with his forelegs and proceeds with the good work.

We have only two faults to find with the Toad, and one of these is merely a matter of circumstance. If Bees are kept he will soon discover the source of food and take up position beneath the stool of the hive in order to snap up the laden bees which have missed the alighting board and fallen into the entangling herbage below. The remedy is to keep the ground free from herbage. He is fond of the useful Earthworm, too, stuffing himself to repletion when they come up after dark; but perhaps we can forgive this iniquity in view of the enormous quantity of insect pests, winged and larval, which he destroys.

On account of their retiring habits and their peculiarly effective means of defence, Toads often live to a ripe old age. Specimens kept in captivity are apt to escape or meet with a violent end just when they are approaching the patriarchial stage, but we have several personal records up to six years, the latter age being attained by one of the big Continental varieties, a fine fellow which was stolen by a lady admirer. A better opportunity is afforded by the pensioners in the garden. We had one, recognisable by a deformity or injury to the foot, which lived for eighteen years in a London garden.

The Toad is an amusing and intelligent fellow and much more amenable to close confinement than the Frog, but we dislike the idea of keeping him in captivity, much preferring to see him take his evening constitutional on the garden paths. If he must be kept indoors, as in public institutions, we would advise a roomy metal and glass case, the bottom covered with a two-inch layer of clean fresh earth, overlaid with slabs of turf. A shallow bath must be provided, and the Toad will most likely make his lair beneath it.

He will be dependent on charity, and, as he has a healthy appetite, the question of food supply will need consideration. The best and cleanest method is to remove him daily and feed him on the floor. He will soon recognise his keeper and evince keen interest in things in general, in this respect showing far more intelligence than the Frog. If time is a consideration, big Earthworms are a convenient food, particularly if the large Italian variety of Toad is kept. Our own

examples, too numerous to be dealt with individually, are provided with a smooth, shallow dish which is kept replenished with a supply of " gentles " or maggots of the Blue Bottle Fly (*not* the smaller tough, shiny larvæ of the brilliant green Lucilius) and Frogs, Toads and Lizards can help themselves.

Surplus Maggots are allowed to pupate and are placed in a tin with a perforated lid, which is then stood in a corner of the vivarium. By regulating the contents it is possible to maintain a regular supply of flies, and, when once the idea " catches on," it is quite amusing to see the circle of prospective diners watching patiently day by day for the newly-hatched flies to crawl forth.

Occasionally, too, we empty the contents of a balloon fly trap (after shaking it violently) into the case. The bath should be renewed now and again and the earth replaced with fresh when foul or wet. Frogs and Toads are best kept apart, and the big Italian should be kept with his own kind. We had one pugnacious example who would even butt his keeper, and we have a suspicion that he was concerned in the mysterious disappearance of several small Lizards.

Photo: Eric J. Hosking.]　　　　　　　　　　LEAP-FROG.　　　　　　　　　　[*Mondiale.*

Here are two high-spirited Toads in playful mood. After their evening hunt for food, during which they travel a considerable distance, they are always eager to hurry back to their watery home, or to their " form " in the fields.

Photo : Ray Palmer].   *[Mondiale.*

Here is the Common Lizard, surrounded by her young. They start life about an inch long, but later grow to a length of six or seven inches. They take no food for some days after birth, and then begin to seek it for themselves.

OUR BRITISH LIZARDS

By RAY PALMER, F.R.E.S., F.Z.S.

LIZARDS are sun-worshippers, and are therefore rarely seen in our comparatively chilly country. Those that do make their homes in Britain retire to some warm nook in winter and emerge when a ray of sun invites them to come out and bask. These elusive creatures are dealt with below, as are also the Slow-worms, a species of legless Lizards.

IN a comparatively cold country such as ours reptiles are not much in evidence, and the majority of people seldom notice them. It is in warmer lands that reptiles are really at home, and no visitor to southern Europe can help noticing the numerous Lizards that abound everywhere, basking in the sun, running up walls, and darting about in all directions.

Our native reptiles, however, are few in number, and consist of three kinds of Snakes and three (possibly four) kinds of Lizards. The Lizards in particular are very elusive, and exceedingly difficult to approach or observe in their wild state. As you walk across a sandy common among the gorse and bracken, or over some heather-clad moor, a sudden rustle attracts your attention, and if you are very quick you may catch sight of the end of a snake-like tail just as it disappears into the herbage. That is all most people ever see of

Lizards in England, owing to their extreme alertness and activity and the type of country they frequent.

Lizards are most likely to be observed in the heat of summer, as, although particularly active in hot weather, they like to lie and bask in the sun, and may sometimes be approached when thus engaged. They are more active in warm weather because they are " cold blooded " ; that means that they have no means of regulating the temperature of their bodies as in the case of " warm-blooded " animals, and thus the body is at the same temperature as its surroundings, and vitality increases with heat.

During the winter Lizards hibernate, and usually spend cold spells at other times in a state of inactivity. This is not invariably the case, though, and on one occasion I caught a Lizard in March on a common that was still partly covered with snow. Cold is not the only reason for Lizards spending the winter in sleep; it is a question of food supply. They feed entirely on insects and other small creatures which are not to be found in winter. Insect-eating birds get over this difficulty either by migrating or by changing their diet. Lizards can do neither of these things, so they find a snug retreat and go to sleep until the spring sunshine calls them forth again to feast on a fresh brood of insect prey.

The Common Lizard is more or less abundant all over the country. It is five or six inches long and usually light-brown in colour, with a bronze tinge. There is a dark

at my headquarters I borrowed a large glass jam jar, lined it with moss and placed my captive therein. As I was returning home the following day I knew it would not have to undergo such close confinement for long, so I supplied some insect food and tied the jar over with muslin.

Imagine my surprise when, on inspecting the jar the next morning, I found not only my female Lizard—looking smaller and more sprightly—but five little black baby Lizards, climbing very actively about the moss. I knew now the reason for her inactivity of the day before and her reluctance to abandon her sun bath on the hot stone. The sun had

Photo : Ray Palmer.]   THE SAND LIZARD.   [Mondiale.

This Lizard, which is superior in size to the Common Lizard, lays from five to twelve eggs, which it covers with leaves or sand before leaving them to incubate. It spends the winter underground in a dormant state.

line down the centre of the back, and another on each side edged with white, or yellowish. It is sometimes called the Viviparous Lizard, because it does not lay eggs in the traditional reptilian manner, but produces living young, the eggs being retained by the female until their development is complete.

An interesting example of this occurred some years ago when I was on a holiday in Devonshire. On a hot day in late June I came across a Lizard lying on a stone basking in the sun. Much to my surprise it did not dart away at my approach, but allowed me to approach quite near and then only moved slowly a few inches. Of course I did not miss such an excellent opportunity of catching a lizard to photograph, and on arrival

done its work, nevertheless, and the world was richer by five tiny black morsels of reptilian activity.

One of the illustrations shows this Lizard mother with four of her babies. The fifth objected to being photographed and made a dash for liberty at the critical moment. I fed the baby lizards on green-fly as being the most convenient food obtainable in quantity. On this diet they continued to thrive for several weeks, after which the whole family was released, to enjoy, I hope a happy existence some two hundred miles from their birthplace.

When attempting to catch a lizard never take hold of the tail, or you will find that you have caught the tail only and lost the

Photo: Eric J. Hosking.] AN AGILE CLIMBER. [Mondiale.

The Common Lizard is a nimble climber, putting its long, delicate limbs to good use. A pursuer who tries to catch it by the tail is disappointed, for the Lizard's tail is so brittle that it easily breaks off, and through time grows again.

Lizard. I remember my amazement as a schoolboy when this first happened to me. I had been chasing Lizards among the heather and bilberry of a north-country moor, but they had been too quick for me. The next Lizard was in more open ground, and I grabbed at it just before it reached cover. My fingers naturally closed on the tail, the rest of the creature being already out of sight ; but the lizard stiffened momentarily, gave a sharp jerk and was gone ! I was left staring in bewilderment and horror at the severed tail which I still held ; for not only had it come off in such a weird and unexpected manner, but it now moved, and jerked about from side to side, as if possessed of independent life.

I dropped the tail when my surprise was over and looked round for the poor Lizard, but of course it was not to be found. The tail continued to move vigorously for some time and I carried it away to watch it more closely. The movements grew less after a time, and then it moved only when it was touched ; before the day was finished all movement had ceased — the tail was dead.

But I need not have pitied the Lizard or been horrified at the severed tail, for this is merely a strange method of defence with which Nature has endowed the Lizard. It may be called an emergency measure, by means of which the Lizard can save its life at the expense of its tail. Lizards have many enemies which seek to devour them, and if some bird or beast of prey seizes the tail, as must often be the case, this organ can be severed easily without endangering the owner's life. Being parted from the body, the tail becomes active on its own account, and thus distracts the attention of its captor, while the Lizard quietly makes its escape—and immediately sets to work to provide itself with a new tail.

In some cases a mere injury to the tail which does not actually sever it will have the effect of starting the growing process, the result being that the Lizard eventually has a forked tail, caused by a smaller appendage growing out from the seat of the old wound.

The Sand Lizard is a larger and less common species, being practically confined to the southern counties of England, where it is very local. It is more spotted and more strikingly marked than the common species, and reaches a length of from seven to nine inches. The male often shows a good deal of green on the sides of the body. One specimen was caught after an exciting chase on a Surrey

Photo : Karl Stülcken.]   THE LIZARD'S SUN-BATH.   *[Mondiale.*

The young Common Lizard is fond of the heat, and likes to disport himself on a sunny rock. His vitality increases with the warmth of his surroundings. Because of the cold and the lack of food in winter he retires to sleep.

Photo : K. Stülcken.] FEMALE SLOW WORM. [Mondiale.

The Slow Worm's litter of from six to twelve young look like glittering silver needles about two inches long. Their colour changes to bronze as they mature. They are quite independent, and soon begin to find food on their own.

heath, during which it was caught and lost again on two or three occasions, but fortunately without injury to its magnificent tail. I happened to be collecting Dragonflies at the time, and just managed to secure the Sand Lizard only by making good use of my insect net, which I found a most excellent implement for the purpose.

THE Sand Lizard is oviparous, that is to say, it lays eggs in the usual reptilian fashion, depositing them in sand and leaving them to hatch in the warmth of the sun. The eggs are soft, with a leathery skin, and yellowish at first, but darken as they mature. This Lizard has a very wild nature and does not take kindly to captivity. At first it rushes madly about its cage and will escape if there is the slightest chance ; but when it finds that escape is impossible it is liable to pine and refuse food and will die if not soon released.

Our third Lizard is often not recognised as such, and is indeed a creature which suffers from misleading and erroneous names. Known as the Slow Worm or Blind Worm, it is certainly neither blind nor slow, and to call it a " worm " is a gross insult. The scientific name—*Anguis fragilis*—is not much better, for it means " brittle snake," and it is not a Snake at all ; it is a legless Lizard ! The chief external feature in which it differs from a Snake is in the possession of eyelids. A Snake has no eyelids, and so its immovable eye has always a fixed stare.

The remote ancestors of our modern Slow Worm undoubtedly possessed legs, as its internal structure shows. There are indeed certain foreign Lizards which are half-way between the completely legless condition of the Slow Worm and a true Lizard. Their bodies have developed the snake-like form, but they are still in the possession of legs, although these are greatly reduced in size and power.

The Slow Worm is probably more abundant than the Common Lizard, and it is a great pity to see how often this harmless and beautiful creature is mistaken for a Snake by ignorant people and immediately killed. Indeed in some parts of the country it is known by the rather curious name of " deaf adder," but the reason for such a title is difficult to suggest.

The principal food of this legless Lizard consists of small Slugs, of which it is very fond, but it will also eat Earthworms and small insects. It is easy to keep in confinement, and seems quite tame from the first. Like other reptiles, the Slow Worm changes its skin at intervals throughout its life, the old outer skin being cast off in the form of a " slough." The young are born alive, as in the case of the Common Lizard, and at first are of a pale silvery colour with a black line down the back. As they mature, the colour gradually changes to bronze brown.

The Worm leaves its tail behind.

Like other Lizards, the Slow Worm readily parts company with its tail when captured, and the severed tail has independent movement for a time, as already described. Before the new tail has grown the Slow Worm looks very peculiar. The new tail is usually shorter and blunter than the original one.

Slow Worms are particularly fond of stone quarries and similar places, where they hide in crevices under and between the stones. A good way of finding them in such situations is to poke a thin flexible stick into the interstices between the stones, when the reptiles will be driven out into the open.

These three species are the only Lizards which are natives of Britain, but in the Channel Islands two other kinds occur, though both are of Continental origin. The Green Lizard is very much larger than our English Sand Lizard and averages fifteen inches in length. It is a very handsome creature and a great favourite with reptile fanciers, as it makes an excellent and most attractive pet and does not take long to become quite tame.

The Green Lizard has been recorded from various localities in England, and it has undoubtedly been found in an apparently wild state. In the eighteenth century Gilbert White recorded it from Farnham in Surrey, and there have been many records since. It seems most probable, however, that the authentic specimens of this species found here have been escapes from captivity, while others were mistaken records referring to greenish specimens of the Sand Lizard.

The Wall Lizard, another European species, occurs in the Channel Isles, and has been recorded from this country also ; but there is no definite reason to suppose that it is any more a native British species than the Green Lizard, and it has undoubtedly been introduced in a somewhat similar way.

Photo : Eric J. Hosking.]   THE GARDENER'S FRIEND.   *[Mondiale.*

The Slow Worm casts off its skin sometimes as often as four times a year to make room for its growing body. It is fond of a meal of slugs, and is a great aid to the gardener, though he often fails to appreciate its good points.

Photo : Ernst Krause.]   [Mondiale.
When winter approaches the Snail is ensured of a safe retreat where it can hibernate in peace. The Vine Snail,
above, seals its shell opening with a lime cover and, safely enclosed, goes to sleep anywhere suitable.

SNAILS AND THEIR WAYS

By RAY PALMER, F.R.E.S., F.Z.S.

*THE queer little gentleman who carries his home on his back is another of Nature's
marvels. He has sixty-eight cousins on land and many more in the water, each
with their own peculiarities. Some carry their eyes before them ; others, we are told,
were included in the diet of the Romans, and others possess over fourteen thousand teeth.*

WALKING one evening in the dark
along a country road I had my first
introduction to the study of Snails in
a curious manner. At the side of the road
was a piece of rough ground more or less
covered with tangled vegetation of all sorts ;
beyond this was the hedge bank, and between
the two a deep ditch. Nettles, Thistles and
Knapweed were the predominating plants
on this roadside waste.

Looking ahead along the road, my attention was attracted by a weird phenomenon
—a moving light appeared to come from the
ditch and shine on the adjacent vegetation,
flashing about in various directions. The
slight mist of a damp autumn night intensified
the strange appearance, which was rendered
all the more curious by the fact that I could
not see the actual source of the light, but
only its reflection on the vegetation and
the surrounding mist.

As I approached cautiously, however, I got
evidence that the strange light was not of

supernatural origin ! I heard a human voice
make an exclamation—the words uttered are
not printable in polite literature—but I
gathered that they were directed at the Nettles,
from amongst which the voice issued. A
head and shoulders appeared in the dim
light, and then a human form raised itself
out of the ditch and stood rubbing a nettled
hand that held a bicycle lamp.

Perceiving the presence of a stranger, a
young man hastily scrambled out of the
ditch on to the roadway and murmured a
somewhat sheepish, " Good-evening," as I
came up. But my curiosity had been aroused,
and I was not to be put off like that ; so I
stopped and inquired politely what he was
doing, grovelling about at night in a wet
ditch amongst the Nettles.

The reply certainly amazed me. " I am
looking for Snails," he said.

" Whatever for ? " I asked.

" Well," he replied, " you'll probably think
me mad, but I'm a conchologist." I had

little idea then what a conchologist was, but I did not wish to show my ignorance, and concluded it was a person who studied Snails.

"But I can find plenty of Snails in my garden during the daytime," I said, "without coming out on a foggy night and squatting amongst stinging Nettles in a ditch."

Then it was the conchologist proceeded to enlighten me. Common Snails could, of course, be found anywhere, but did I know there were sixty-eight Land Snails to be found in this county alone, as well as over forty water snails and mussels, while the British list totalled about a hundred and thirty species. Most of the land Snails were nocturnal in habits, and in some cases it was easier to find them abroad at night than search for their hiding-places during the day. He had been seeking further specimens of a particular rarity he had found near the same place a few days ago, but, I gathered, without success.

As I showed a certain amount of interest, I was eventually invited to visit this young man's home and see his collection of shells; so one evening a few days later I went. He showed me drawers full of specimens, the smaller ones neatly mounted on cards, the larger ones lying on cotton-wool in glass

Photo: W. S. Berridge.] [Mondiale.

THE COMMON SNAIL.

This creature's activities begin at dusk. Like most snails it hides away in seclusion during the daytime.

topped boxes, and all labelled with Latin names. Meanwhile the shell collector discoursed about *Paludinidæ, Limnæidæ, Helicidæ*, and so on, getting particularly enthusiastic about some aquatic species named *Planorbis*, and some extremely minute Land Snails called *Vertigo*. Among other things, I learned that Slugs have a rudimentary shell, though in most cases this is internal. In this way I was first introduced to the study of Snails, and have retained an interest in them ever since, though the collecting of their empty shells never appealed to me.

The food of the Romans.

Our largest British land Snail is commonly known as the "Roman Snail." Whether this title is justified or not it is difficult to say; it was certainly used as an article of diet by the Romans in their native land, and is to-day the edible Snail of Europe. Tradition has it that this Snail is not a true native of Britain, but was introduced by the Romans. It may well be true that these Snails were brought here from the Continent by the Romans and by other people since, and it is a fact that many of the localities where they are common are known to have been Roman settlements. Nevertheless we have no evidence for saying that it did not exist in this country before any such possible introductions, and conchologists now maintain that it is an indigenous species, because its shells have been found in geological formations laid down long before the Roman period.

The large shell of this Snail is yellowish white, with brown bands, which vary greatly in colour and extent. In many shells the bands are so faint as to be hardly noticeable, while I have occasionally found specimens which appeared dark brown all over, owing to the coalescence of the bands which were much darker than usual. The body of the Snail is pale yellowish.

Like others of its race, this Snail feeds on the leaves of various plants, most of which are not to be found in winter. On the approach of autumn, therefore, it burrows into the ground, making a chamber which it lines with dead leaves and earth, cemented together with slime which dries into a kind of mortar. Having done this it secretes from its body a substance that resembles liquid plaster of Paris, and with this closes the mouth of the shell. This material hardens into a calcareous cement, which forms a thick lid, giving a sure protection against cold and enemies.

The Snail then withdraws far into its shell, leaving a space between its body and the lid. This space contains several layers of a fine membrane, produced from slime, which gives additional protection to the enclosed mollusc. On the return of spring the snail is able to dissolve the lid of its shell and so come out to resume activity.

The mouth of a snail is very curious. It consists of a pair of arched jaws of a horny nature, and a kind of ribbon-like tongue armed with teeth, which works against the jaw with a rasping action. The tongue-like organ is called the " radula," and the teeth it carries are very numerous, being arranged in a series of transverse rows, each with over a hundred teeth. In the Common Garden Snail there are 135 rows, each containing 105 teeth, which gives a total of 14,175.

With this ribbon of teeth the mollusc rasps off particles of the vegetable matter on which it feeds. The action can best be seen by watching a water snail on the glass of an aquarium where there is a slight growth of green confervæ; the mouth opens, the tongue scrapes the glass and the mouth closes again, the process going on with great regularity. As the front rows of teeth get worn away the radula is pushed forward by growth from behind and a fresh lot of teeth come into action.

Many kinds of Snails are hermaphrodites, that is to say the sexes are not separate as in the higher animals, but both male and female organs exist in the same individual, as is usually the case in plants. Pairing takes place, nevertheless, and both Snails lay eggs. The eggs are joined together in a cluster and buried in a small hole in the ground excavated by the mollusc with its foot.

The Snail that carries its eyes.

The tentacles of Land Snails are interesting, because the eyes are carried at their tips; but they are also extremely sensitive organs of touch, and sight is undoubtedly of a very rudimentary nature. If we watch a Snail gradually extending its tentacles we can see that in doing so they are turned inside out, and the eye does not appear until the tentacle is fully extended. Touch one of the tentacles and it instantly disappears, being drawn outside in, just like the finger of a glove, into a cavity which is situated in the head.

Photo : Ray Palmer.]   *[Mondiale.*

ROMAN SNAIL.
This Snail, said to have been utilised as food by the Romans, is the largest of British land snails.

Water Snails are perhaps more interesting than those of terrestrial habits. The most completely aquatic is the River Snail which can breathe water by means of gills like a fish. This is a large Snail with a shell about one-and-a-quarter inches long; in colour it is greenish with brown spiral bands. The members of this family are unique among fresh-water Snails in possessing a horny lid which closes the shell when the animal has withdrawn inside. This lid, which is called an " operculum," is attached to the upper part of the Snail's foot and lies back behind the shell when the animal is extended.

Another remarkable thing about the River Snail is that the eggs hatch internally and the young are thus produced alive; they appear a few at a time, and some attain quite a large size before leaving the parent. The River Snail is found in canals and sluggish rivers, also in lakes and reservoirs, but is rather local in distribution.

All the rest of our fresh-water Snails belong to a single family—*Limnæidæ*—and resemble the Land Snails in breathing air by means of lungs. They can remain below for a very long time, but periodically have to come to the surface for a fresh supply of air, in spite of the fact that they also possess gills which enable them to obtain some air from the water. Evidently the aquatic method of respiration is not so efficient in these snails as in the River Snail and its relatives, and so they cannot get on for long without atmospheric air. When a Pond Snail needs air it climbs or floats to the surface ; on arrival there it opens a hole on one side of the body behind the head. This is the entrance to the lung, and through it the air supply is replenished.

One of the commonest and, at the same time, the largest of our Pond Snails is often called the " Freshwater Whelk." It has a long, pointed shell from one-and-a-half to two inches in length, and is plentiful in many ponds and ditches, and in the Fenland dykes. The eggs are laid in long, jelly-like masses on the stems and leaves of water plants.

The Aquatic Snails of the genus *Planorbis* are particularly interesting, and can always be identified by their flat, coiled shells. They vary greatly in size, from an inch or more across down to about one-eighth of an inch. The largest kinds are called " Ramshorn Snails," and are special favourites with people who keep aquariums. In an aquarium tank they eat confervæ off the glass, thus helping to keep it clear, and also act as scavengers by devouring both animal and vegetable refuse.

One small Pond Snail—*Limnæa truncatula*—is of particular interest to sheep farmers, and is the indirect cause of much trouble and loss. This Snail acts as the first host of a parasitic flat-worm known as the Liver Fluke, which passes the greater part of its life in the liver of the sheep. Eggs of the fluke pass out of the sheep, and some of them may find their way to a pond where the animals drink. A few weeks after reaching

Photo : Albert Leon.]   *[Mondiale.*

THE SNAIL'S ASCENT.

Some Snails carry their eyes at the tips of their tentacles and can withdraw these peculiar headlights at will.

the water each egg hatches into a little creature that swims about until it finds a Snail. It then bores its way into the Snail's respiratory cavity, where it undergoes a series of transformations. The Fluke eventually leaves the Snail and swims about for a time, later leaving the water and climbing up a grass stem. Here it encloses itself in a case and waits ; sooner or later a Sheep comes along and eats it, when the case is dissolved and the Fluke emerges in the sheep's stomach to complete its strange life history.

Slugs are similar in all respects to Snails, except that in most cases they possess no visible shells. They all have a more or less rudimentary shell however ; in the majority of Slugs this consists of a hard plate beneath the mantle protecting the vital parts. Slugs' chief method of defence is their slime, which they can exude in great quantities. The large Black Slug (*Arion ater*) is one of the best known, but many of the smaller kinds can do great damage to cultivated plants, as every gardener knows to his cost.

The most interesting Slugs are those belonging to the genus *Testacella*, often called " Snail-Slugs." In these the shell is external, but very small, and carried on the tail-end of the body. Testacella differs from all other Land Molluscs in being entirely carnivorous. It is very savage in its pursuit of prey, which it hunts at night, following worms into their subterranean tunnels and attacking them ferociously.

The Slug possesses a formidable array of curved teeth with barbed ends, and with these the unfortunate victim is gradually drawn into the mouth and devoured alive. The small shell at the rear end no doubt serves to protect the Slug from attack when it is pursuing its prey underground.

Photo : Albert Leon.] [Mondiale.

The Queen of the Red Ants is seen here with one of her worker-minors, surrounded with eggs. These minors are the slaves of the ant-hill, looking after the ever-increasing nursery being the main purpose of their lives.

THE ANT

By GOMER WILLIAMS, B.A. (Oxon.)

IT is surprising to find that such small creatures as the Ants have reasoning powers and organising capacities that would not disgrace a human. In this chapter we are shown their well-planned kingdom where milkmaids, statesmen, architects, nursemaids, and many other workers strive with success to keep this miniature world together.

WHEN Nature created the Ant, it fashioned a pigmy, but endowed it with the qualities of a giant. She worked with economy, as usual, and gave the little creature a body exactly fitted for the purposes of its existence ; but smiling, possibly, at the stark utilitarianism of the result, she took counsel with herself and said, " What is this I have made ? I must do better." Having created Man and endowed him with intelligence, Nature gave the tiny Ant something very like it—instinct, which is developed to a remarkable degree.

And so it is that the ways and habits of this Ant, which so strangely, so startlingly, resemble those of Man, have become the subject of much scientific observation and investigation. Much has been observed, yet there is still very much to be learnt. The virtues of the Ant are comparable with those of Man, and, strange to say, so are its vices. So proficient are these little creatures in the technique of living in a community, so far-seeing in their

provision for the continuity of their orderly life, that Solomon advised Man to take lessons from them.

So many others examples of the diligence and wisdom of the Ant have been brought to light that one is tempted to ask : " Where exactly does the wisdom of the Ant stop short of human intelligence ? " As there are thirty known species of British Ants, it is obvious that they cannot all be dealt with, but they differ from one another so minutely both in form and in habits that in dealing with one we are, generally speaking, dealing with them all. Almost everyone has been stung once by an Ant, and few desire to repeat the experience. It is the little Red Ant which gives you such a rude awakening when you are enjoying a comfortable snooze in the open air on the roof of his abode. When you realise what a perfectly planned home you are, in your ignorance, threatening with utter destruction, you can readily sympathise with the little fellow's anger. But how does he hurt you ?

There are still many people who think that the Ant bites. So he does, but it is not that which hurts you. He punctures your skin with his powerful mandibles, but you would hardly feel that. But when he injects into the holes he has made in your skin a few drops of formic acid, which he carries in a tiny pocket near his waistband, then you come to regard him as a spiteful little creature.

The Ant's honeycomb eyes.

The only other things of especial interest and importance in the body of the Ant are its eyes and its antennæ. The eyes of the Red Ant look just like a network of lenses—rather like a honeycomb, in fact. These eyes or " ocelli " are immovable, but the lenses, acting as a number of eyes, enable the Ant to look in many directions. But they cannot alter the form of these lenses so as to adapt the sight to meet the object of vision as we do, and in consequence they cannot very well see objects near to them. This is where the antennæ come in.

These long, very sensitive feelers, more sensitive than the whiskers of a cat, make up for the deficiency of the eyes. Living as they do the greater part of their lives in the dark, it is natural that they should come to rely more and more on their feelers, and thus it is that Ants are losing gradually their sense of sight.

But how does this interesting little creature come into existence, and how does he grow up into such a model citizen ? Every Ant community consists of four classes of citizens, each of which has its appropriate function. There are the workers-minor, the workers-major, the Queen and males. The workers-major and workers-minor are really un-developed females who rarely, and only in case of dire necessity, lay eggs, but in other respects they are the most important people in the colony.

The workers-minor do all the hard work of the colony, and it is due to their untiring labour that we see such wonderful architec-ture, such wonderful tidiness in the Ants' home. They provide all the food for the colony, they nurse and educate the young in all the stages of their development with exemplary devotion, they help to defend their homes against enemies, whether they be Ants of another colony or other enemies, the names of which are legion. And when Ants fight they display a courage and a reck-

lessness of danger which beggars description. No intruder is too large for a single Ant to attack at sight.

It has never been unmistakably discovered what the duties of the workers-major are, but from the fact that they are always the first to rush to the summit of the nest when the alarm-signal is given, it is surmised that they are merely Soldier-Ants, and take no visible part in the domestic economy of the colony. In size they are a trifle larger than the workers-minor, which are the smallest members of the species.

Just as in the case of Bees, there is only one Queen to each colony. She is much larger than all the other inhabitants, and is dis-tinguished by brighter colouring.

Once the colony has been formed, her sole duty is the laying of eggs. This she does at a tremendous rate—many thousands in twenty-four hours. She has the power, which is unique in Nature, of determining the sex and nature of the egg she will lay, and this in strict keeping with the economic require-ments of the colony. Thus if more workers-minor are required, she lays more worker-minor eggs. This is the reason, to a very large extent, why an Ant-community is so perfect in its organisation, so exquisitely balanced, and suffers so little from waste.

Where the Queen reigns supreme.

The constitution of an Ants' domain is very like our own—a limited monarchy. The Queen keeps together the state and serves as an incentive to a patriotism, which is seldom equalled and never surpassed by human beings. The Princesses, that is, all the brightly-coloured females with gay wings and mantles, on reaching the age of maturity quit the nest, as the constitution does not permit of more than one full-grown female. It is highly amusing to see the excitement of the whole community when the Princesses leave. They are accompanied to the exit by the workers-major and minor, who seem at once distressed at their departure, and yet deter-mined to be loyal to their own Queen. " We are very sorry to lose you, but we are afraid you have to go," they seem to say.

Strange as it may seem, the gentlemen of the community are the least important of all. They are very short-lived, and seldom survive more than one winter, whereas a Queen will often live for fifteen years, and the average life of a worker is about seven

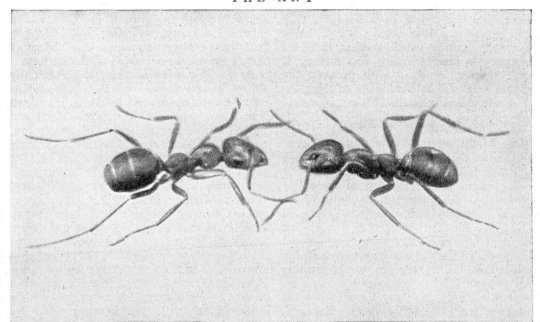

Photo : H. Bastin.] THE LATEST NEWS. [*Mondiale.*

Two Ants are seen above exchanging confidences by means of their antennæ. They have not much time to waste in gossip, however, for they are busy workers, ruling their underground colony with amazing dexterity.

Photo : H. Bastin. STRANGE PETS. [*Mondiale.*

This young collector is seen feeding captive Ants with a little honey inserted into the opening of the glass house where his pets are kept. The opening is closed with a cotton-wool plug and the Ants left to enjoy their meal.

years. Like the drones in a Bee-hive, they are a lazy lot and do no work ; it is probably their very laziness which renders them an easy prey to their enemies, thus making it much simpler for Nature to preserve the economic balance by getting rid of the comparatively useless members of the community.

The Queen eats her Wings.

One of the most peculiar and significant features in the nature of male and female Ants is that they have wings until they decide to shed them in the interests of the whole community. When the Ants swarm and have chosen the site for their colony, the Queen is settled in and then proceeds to bite off her wings. If she does this reluctantly or too slowly, the workers take a hand and help her to bite them off, so keen are they on making sure of their Queen. The males follow suit. After this the Royal Lady never leaves the nest, but proceeds to lay eggs against time, for the Ant-instinct is that there is safety in numbers.

Soon the abdomen of the Queen will take on the appearance of an inflated bladder, and it becomes so distended with eggs that it is quite transparent. The nice white little egg under the fostering care of the Queen soon becomes a nasty, wriggling little Maggot, and then the workers-minor take charge of it and store it in a portion of the nursery.

As if fully aware that Maggots are unsightly things, it soon wraps itself in a silken waistcoat or cocoon, but not before it has grown into a fat, strong Maggot, carefully fed and nursed by the workers and carried daily into the light to obtain the full benefit of the sun's strength and growth-provoking qualities. For three weeks it lies asleep in its cocoon, still assiduously attended by the workers and taken out into the sun. And then it emerges, not without a struggle and not without much help from the nurses—a changed being.

But this is a miracle ! Other insects change in this way from the grub to the chrysalis, to the insect—but not as the Ant to the fully-developed insect, complete in every particular save one—experience. He is not yet fit to be a citizen, to take his place in the complex life of the colony, to give and receive the hard buffets of life, and to pull his weight in the interests of all.

He must go to school, and to school he goes usually on the next floor above the nursery. There he is taught all the duties of his state ;

THE ANTS ACT AS GRAVE-DIGGERS.   [*Brit. Instruct. Films.*

The wisdom and forethought of these industrious creatures often puts man to shame. Realising that this dead Mouse was a nuisance they have, with painstaking thoroughness, set about the business of burying it.

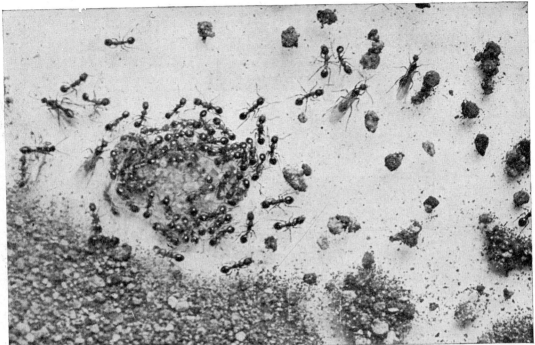

Photo : M. H. Crawford.] SOME BUSY WORKERS. [Mondiale.
Here is a glimpse of a community of busy workers showing winged ants, workers, and pupæ. Each ant knows his own duty. Some are architects, statesmen, or housemaids, but all have learned to work peaceably together.

if he is a worker-minor, as in fact he is, he learns in turn the jobs of scavenger, pantry-boy, housemaid, nursemaid, architect, soldier, and many others of which we know nothing. But his most important job, however, will be to join the workers in their ceaseless search for food and to discriminate, ever so carefully, between the elements of danger and safety.

Preserving the Race.

Nothing is more wonderful in the habits of the Ant than its instinct for race-preservation, which it shows so markedly in the care of the young of the species. One cannot help being struck when watching an Ant-migration, or when they are changing from one nest to another, by the loving care with which the eggs and young larvæ are moved to their new home. Next to the Queen, who has a stout bodyguard, they are more zealously watched and attended than any others.

It is on such an occasion also that one begins to realise the enormous population of an Ant colony and to what extent this is swollen by the number of boarders, vassals, pets and other camp-followers attached to the community. It is extremely difficult to believe that Ants keep pets, but such is the case.

There are certain tiny insects which please them by the aroma they diffuse or by the cheerful noise they make. They are fed and housed by the Ants, much as our pets are treated by us.

It is almost more incredible still that Ants should keep cows, which they actually milk ; but in every nest there are many of these. We all know well the objectionable little green-fly, called the Aphis, which plays such havoc with our choicest rose-blooms, smearing the leaves with a sticky mess like the trail of a Snail. It is just this secretion of the Green fly, called "honey-dew," which the Ant loves so much. He will capture with infinite guile these Aphides and put them into cells from which they cannot get out, but into which an Ant can squirm his lithe little body. He then taps the cow's stomach gently with his antennæ until she gives her milk, which oozes out from the end of her two short antennæ.

Ants love this honey-dew so much that they will collect as many eggs of the Aphis as they can, store them carefully for the winter and, when they have hatched out, place them back on the bush so that they can grow into fine healthy cows, when they are again recaptured and brought into captivity. Before such prudent provision for the future the efforts of other animals below the status of Man pale into insignificance. Yet in the case of many foreign Ants in climates warmer than ours we find them using this amazing instinct in far more wonderful ways.

The community dwelling where all these extraordinary things take place is interesting to study. But how can it be done except by keeping Ants ourselves? This we can do in the following way, which I have found best for the purpose of observation. Obtain a bell-jar from a chemist— a medium-sized one is best—and stand it on a water-tight tray in about half an inch of water. Ants will not cross water. Next, find in your garden an Ant's nest — a Red Ants' nest for preference —and with a trowel dig up the earth of the nest until the bell-jar is about half full. Carefully search for the Queen — she is unmistakable—and, when you have found her, place her in the jar on the earth. Next select about fifty to one hundred Ants and a good number of eggs; collect them in a bottle and empty them into the bell-jar. Place the bell-jar well out of the sun, in a darkish corner, cover the bell-jar with a cloth, and go to bed —or at any rate go away for a few hours and await results.

When next you visit your formicarium, take a magnifying glass with you, and by its aid you will see that a wonderful transformation has taken place. At the very least you will see work being done by workers that will surpass your wildest dreams for speed and precision. In all probability, if you have had the patience to wait long enough, you will see a palace with the Queen-Ant comfortably housed in a wide and deep apartment at the bottom of the jar and a network of cells all around it in which the Ants live.

THE ANT'S HOME.   [*Charles Reid.*

Inside this mound lies a busy little kingdom, carefully planned with winding galleries, nurseries, and a palace.

On the next floor above there will be what looks like a spacious hall, extending the whole width of the bell-jar, with beautiful pillars supporting the roof. Above this will come the nursery-gallery with more cells, and, above this, a wide passage with many small passages leading to the air above. All this will be clearly outlined against the sides of the bell-jar, as if a section had been cut through the next; though, of course, details may vary considerably.

If you desire to keep your Ants' colony you must feed them, giving honey, honey and again honey; they never tire of it. Of course, you must introduce some Greenfly, if not for the pleasure of the Ants, at least for the fun you will get in seeing them being milked. Honey placed all round a match stick on the top of the earth is as good a way as any of serving their dinner. Invent ingenious devices and place them between the Ants and their food, and you will get an object lesson in the ingenuity of these little wonders. Your ingenuity will have to be of a very ingenious kind to outwit them. Hang a lump of sugar over the cope of the jar on the end of a string and watch the excitement, the curiosity, the daring. You will never keep them from that sugar. They will overcome all difficulties to reach it.

Drop a Beetle or some deadly enemy like a Spider into the jar and you will see war— red war—and courage that would win a V.C. a hundred times a minute. Watch them carrying loads ten times as heavy as themselves—observe how they carry burdens over obstacles, how they engineer tunnels, assist one another in a hundred ways. Mark their conferences when facing a difficulty; note the method they apply, each doing his bit, and you can never doubt that they have formed a deliberate plan. Is it instinct, or more?

Here is a Wasp's nest opened to show the cells, some containing grubs that are reared from the juices extracted from insects. As many as ten thousand eggs may be laid in one nest throughout a summer.

BEES AND WASPS

By M. H. CRAWFORD

*O*F *all the creatures of the wilds, the Bees are the most worthy of our admiration.
Their life is one long working-day, and their energies are not expended aimlessly,
for the result of their labours is the honey that holds in its flavour all the delicate sweetness
of the flowers. Below, we are taken into their hive of industry, and shown how they work.*

WHO first brought Bees into England? Nobody seems to know. It is popularly supposed that the Romans were responsible, but there are evidences that Bees were hived and extensively kept long before the Romans arrived. Pliny gives an account of the voyages of Pytheas, which took place three hundred years before the invasions of the Romans, and he records that Pytheas found that the inhabitants of Britain brewed a drink made from wheat and honey.

In the Saga of the ancient Bards and Druids we get some hints of the activities of the Bee-keeping Briton. In these old songs the Britain of those days had earned the name of the Isle of Honey, for the great forests abounded with wild Bees. Virgil wrote of Bees being kept in hives made of wattled osier, and no doubt the hives of our ancestors were also basket-like affairs of osier. They must certainly have been extremely awkward to

handle, and the arrival of the old straw skep would be a decided step forward.

Till the time of the Norman Conquest honey was the only sweetening agent of the people, and it was the foundation of the drinks made by them. During the Anglo-Saxon period the universal drink was mead, made with honey, and probably flavoured in various ways. Honey was at that time the great industry of the country, and, until about three hundred years ago, it was used much as we use sugar at the present time. Even as late as the seventeenth century there were bee-keepers renowned for their excellent brews of mead.

At the head of the " Social " Bees stands the Honey-Bee. An ordinary, well-stocked hive contains an enormous population, consisting of workers, drones and one queen. The workers are undeveloped female Bees who do all the work of the hive, and the drones are stingless male Bees. Drones are necessary for the purpose of fertilising the queen Bees, but they are useful for this purpose only. They lead a gay, care-free life all the summer, for which they pay with their lives in the autumn, when the work of the hive comes to a standstill and they are no longer needed.

Only the queen and her army of workers live through the winter. When cold weather commences the workers bite off the wings of the drones and leave them to starve; in fact, they are previously subjected to a term of imprisonment in the hive, where they are kept without food, so that when brought into the open air they are weak and incapable of offering any resistance. This is one of the ways by which a Bee community is preserved and carried on. There would be no wisdom in keeping in the hive during the winter a host of hungry insects who would have no work to do the following spring. Besides, the Bees are only torpid in winter; they do not actually hibernate; and they need food. This means that a large store of honey must be laid up, sufficient to feed the queen and her thousands of workers. To clear the way for the great awakening in spring all the drones, therefore, as well as surplus stores of eggs and larvæ, are destroyed.

Photo : M. H. Crawford.]   [Mondiale.

A DROWSY BEE.
Sleep has overcome the Bee after gathering its store of nectar. Its closed jaws hold it firmly to its resting-place.

As the honey flow from the flowers gradually diminishes, so the work in the hive gradually lessens, until it stops altogether. During the winter, in mild days, one may often see a few Bees flying about, but they are not working, and after a short flight they all go back to the hive.

The queen and her army of helpers work incredibly hard. To the workers, at least, it is difficult to deny a sort of intelligence. The queen seems to be guided in all her actions by the workers; she may, for instance, make the mistake of laying two eggs in one cell, or she may want to leave her egg-laying and go and kill the " princesses," still in their cells. But workers are always at hand; the extra egg is at once removed and destroyed, and the young " princesses " are carefully guarded.

The Bee's first duties.

When a worker Bee first emerges from its pupa case it is occupied for a short time in tending the young larvæ; but when its wings and legs are strong enough it leaves the hive and flies off in search of nectar, pollen and a resinous substance called propolis, which it collects from sticky buds and the bark of trees. This is an invaluable aid to the Bees in stopping up small holes and chinks in the hive.

The work of the queen consists of egg-laying. She has no respite from this except during a swarm, or when, for a brief period, she is allowed to get at the young princesses and kill them. A good queen is able to lay from two to three thousand eggs per day (about one hundred every hour), and this goes on all through the busy season, when summer days are longest and when there is plenty of honey to be gathered.

When the queen is too old to lay more eggs the workers surround her and gently but decisively crush her to death. She is literally suffocated by one immense caress, and her reign is at an end.

A swarm of Bees will frequently settle down in an unusual situation. The roof of a shed or of a house is sometimes chosen. In one ancient house Bees were known to have been living in the walls for three hundred years. In another case Bees took possession of the space between the ceiling and the floor; they came in through a ventilator. But their quarters were too cramped, and they overflowed into a bedroom. They considered this bedroom as their own, and greatly

Photo : O. G. Pike.]　　　　THE QUEEN'S COURT.　　　　[Mondiale.

The Queen Bee, whose task it is to lay about one hundred eggs every hour, is seen in the hive, surrounded by her retainers. The duty of these workers is to look after the eggs and see that everything goes smoothly in the hive.

305

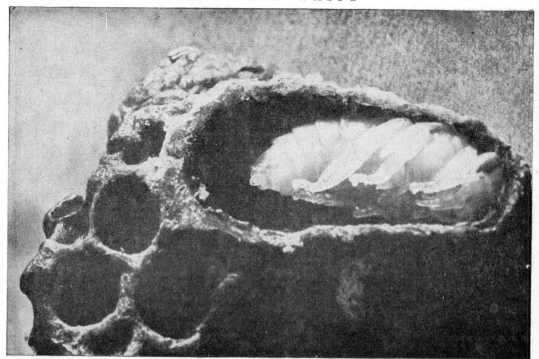

Photo : Alex. Stöcker.] A YOUNG QUEEN. [Mondiale.

This view of the Royal Cell shows the " Princess " in her cradle. The pupa, carefully guarded by the worker bees, will one day take on the onerous duties of a Queen Bee, when she will have to lay about three thousand eggs a day.

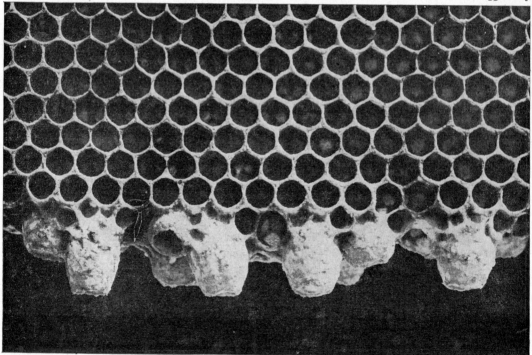

Photo : Alex. Stöcker.] THE ROYAL CELL. [Mondiale.

Here is another view of the royal breeding cells where future Queens are reared. It is at the edge of the comb where the honey is stored. Note how every section has been perfectly formed by the industrious workers.

SPRING IN THE ORCHARD
The Kent Cherry Orchards present a dazzling picture in springtime. The ornamental trees are of value even after their fruit-bearing is over, for the wood is of great value to joiners and cabinetmakers.

resented the presence of the lawful occupier. They were a particularly vicious crowd, and months elapsed before they could be evicted. Another swarm took possession of a church roof, but as they caused no annoyance they were left undisturbed.

Unfortunately for their peace they were attacked by the dread Isle of Wight Disease. The parson's peace of mind also suffered. He was preaching one day when a cascade of sick Bees descended on his head and began to crawl over him. He left the pulpit in a great hurry. For a few days afterwards the sexton spent his time sweeping up the dying Bees. The swarm was completely wiped out.

How Humble-Bees are useful.

From an economic point of view Humble-Bees come next to Hive Bees. They are valuable to both gardener and farmer. They give us no honey, but, in company with all members of the Bee family, they assist in the fertilisation of flowers. The strongly-built Bumble-Bees, with their long tongues, are specially useful. There are two chief groups : those which nest underground and those which nest above ground, commonly known as Carder Bees. Both have " social " instincts, but those nesting underground have larger communities, and will sting more readily than the others.

It is sometimes asserted that Humble-Bees do not sting. This is a fallacy, and anyone who explores the subterranean dwelling of a Humble-Bee must exercise discretion. Only the young Queen Bees live through the winter ; the workers and males all die. In the spring the queen looks out for a suitable nursery. A mouse hole is a desirable residence ; even a bird's nest has been utilised. A small batch of workers (small female Bees) is first reared, and these afterwards do all the work of the community, the queen devoting herself to egg-laying. A fact worth noting—and not yet satisfactorily explained—is that the workers become fertile in cases of necessity and are able to carry on the family life when the queen has died or has been killed.

Generally speaking, the nest of an underground Humble-Bee may contain three or four hundred individuals. Those Humble-Bees nesting on the surface of the ground, however, rarely have nests which contain more than a hundred or so.

The Common Wasp is much more in evidence than any other Bee or Wasp, and

Photo : Ray Palmer.]   [Mondiale.

A BUSY MONARCH.
The Queen Humble-Bee, who devotes herself solely to egg-laying, is the only one of the community to survive through the rigours of the winter season.

therefore it bears the blame for many of the sins committed by its relatives as well as its own sins. To most people this is an utterly useless and annoying insect, and one that should be destroyed without mercy. One hears a gardener boasting how many Queen Wasps he has destroyed every spring ! The autumn madness of the Wasp is always remembered against it, and few stop to consider that during the greater part of the summer the Wasp is an insect-feeder. The larvæ, unlike the larvæ of Bees, are fed with insect food ; Caterpillars, Flies and Beetles in various forms of preparation are fed to the hungry grubs.

During the summer five to ten thousand eggs may be laid in a single nest, and each grub must be reared on juices derived from insects or grubs. The whole of the Fly or Caterpillar is not used, and this means that literally millions of tiny insects and larvæ are killed every summer for the nursery larders of the Common Wasp. This is going on through May, June, July, August, and often takes place during September and on into October.

At the end of the summer when insects are not so abundant the Queen Wasp lays fewer eggs ; the labours of the workers gradually come to an end. Finally, the nest is deserted, the queen hibernates in some quiet spot, and the drones and workers take a holiday. It is the one holiday of their lives, and they make the most of it. All are seized with a terrific hunger, and they go to butchers' shops, fruit orchards and jam pots. Nothing to do and plenty to eat! They get demoralised and vicious (as we call it). But these orgies are short; chilly nights and over-eating kill off the revellers. It is these autumn orgies which have given the Wasps their bad name.

IT was once recorded that a certain district had destroyed 240 Queen Wasps one spring-time. Each of those queens would have laid an average of twenty thousand eggs, and there would have been four or five million grubs to feed. One grub would probably be able to account for a dozen small insects in its larval career, so that means that about 50,000,000 Greenfly, small Flies and Caterpillars were left alive in that enterprising district!

Probably the inhabitants did their best, with sprays and washes and grease-bands, to fight the pests. But they would not accomplish so much as the Wasps would have accomplished. One often sees Worker Wasps among fruit trees in spring. They are busy catching insects which have come to lay their eggs on some part of the trees.

Another interesting thing about the Common Wasp is the way it makes the paper for its house. On sunny spring days anyone may watch the Queen Wasps collecting material. An oak fence is a favourite source of supply. They tear off, with their powerful jaws, tiny scraps of wood, mix them with gummy saliva into a sort of pulp, and with this pulp build up the walls of their houses and make the egg cells.

Ground Wasps, including the Common species, often appropriate deserted burrows made by mice or moles. Bush and Tree Wasps build in the open air, but their nests are almost as difficult to find as those of the Ground Wasps; the " paper " is of a whitish-grey colour, and the small roundish nests, under twigs and amongst leaves, are not at all easy to detect.

Ground Wasps are very much like the rest of the family. They are strictly underground dwellers. The queen, who has hibernated through the winter, makes the foundation of the nest, using the root of a tree or plant on which to construct the footstalk. Four or five inverted cells, under a small canopy, depend from this footstalk. In each cell she lays an egg, glued safely to the top. Each comb in the nest is horizontal and held to the one above it by means of short " ropes " made of pulp. The cells all open downwards, and the larvæ are upside down all their lives. The whole life of egg, larva and pupa occupies about three or four weeks.

It is not always a dangerous matter to destroy the nest of the Common Wasp. Even when it has been dug up the Wasps do not always sting. I heard once of a large nest which was dug up and one of the combs, about nine inches long, was thrown out on the ground. The Wasps crowded over it, but they were not angry. The piece of comb was placed in a box and covered with glass, leaving a hole as entrance and exit. The wasps settled down happily. They built a beautiful shell-pattern paper roof over the comb, fed the grubs, and carried on their daily life till the autumn.

By the way, it was rather curious to see the troops of strange Wasps which quickly swooped down upon the shattered nest and carried away the dislodged grubs and pupæ. No doubt they fed them to their own familiar.

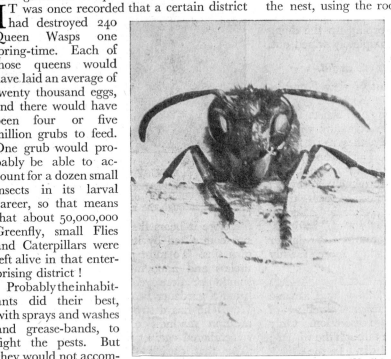

Photo : M. H. Crawford.]   *[Mondiale.*

WORKER WASP EMERGING FROM NEST.
The Common Wasp brings up her young charges exclusively on animal food, though she herself has a preference for the sweet juices of plants and flowers.

Photo : O. G. Pike.] A DIVIDED KINGDOM. [Mondiale.

Wherever the Queen Bee goes the rest must follow. Above, a divided swarm is seen in an orchard. The Queen first settled on the branch where the small cluster is, then changed her mind and moved farther off.

There are two native Tree Wasps. They make their nurseries in shrubs and trees. They are not very common. But their nests are worth looking for; they make good additions to one's cabinet of curios. Size varies; sometimes nests are found as large as a turnip, but I have not seen one larger than a small apple. They seem to disintegrate very quickly when left outside all the winter. Excess of damp and rough winds contribute to their final ruin. Even a nest which has been taken during the summer will hardly keep very well unless placed in an airtight case; the paper becomes more and more brittle, until a slight touch is sufficient to destroy it.

Bush Wasps are not so irritable as Ground Wasps. I have watched a Bush Wasp building her nest in a shed—a very unusual place, by the way. She was absorbed in her work and took no notice of the people who were constantly opening and shutting the shed door. When the door was closed she discovered a space at the top between the door and the framework, and became quite expert in flying straight in through this crack, twisting her little body sideways in her flight.

Finding a Hornet's nest.

To discover a Hornet's nest is always an interesting and very rare event. The Hornet is reddish-brown and yellow, and at least an inch long. Ordinary Wasps are black and yellow. The nest is often built in a hollow tree, and the queen, as usual, builds the footstalk and the small envelope for the first few cells. If the position is well protected from wind and rain the workers do not subsequently make a very large cap or envelope for the nest as it enlarges; more cells are, of course, added, but the wasps build no more of the outer covering than is necessary.

I have a Hornet's nest in a log of wood. A hole had been made in the log to tempt a pair of Tits to build a nest there. But a Queen Hornet got in before the Tits had made up their mind, and she began building at once. She worked industriously and was constantly seen going in and out. Then one morning her dead body was found below the nest. It was one of those unexplained tragedies so common in the lives of the little outdoor folk.

The difference in the behaviour of Bees and Wasps at the end of summer is very marked, but, at the same time, quite natural.

The Worker Bees pull carefully out of their cells the pale, immature grubs and throw them out of the hive. Worker Wasps will pull them out and eat them. But, then, Bees are not carnivorous. Also the Worker Bee has a store of food in the hive; the Worker Wasp has no store, and her best policy is to eat when food comes along.

The Potter Wasp makes an interesting little home and is solitary in its ways. The nest is shaped like a jar and is made of clay pellets. The Wasp hangs her egg by a silken thread from the cell roof. Food is provided in the form of paralysed Caterpillars which are placed so that the newly-hatched grub can just reach them and feed on them.

To examine the egg, larva and pupa of a Common Wasp the nest should be located during the summer and dug up about the end of August. Many small enemies take possession of a Wasps' nest when the workers desert it, and it is soon destroyed. The pupæ are, perhaps, the strangest occupants of the deserted home.

I have examined a pupa which was obviously almost ready to emerge as a mature insect; it was almost colourless, and its limbs and antennæ were folded close to its body. There was a film over the large eyes. The head protruded beyond the surface of the comb, and the size and shape of this head made the covering dome shaped.

The Larva, before pupating, had spun for itself a cocoon of fine white silk, closing up the bottom of the cell, where its head rested, with an extra thick wad. This wad, as well as the curved shape of the pupa, prevented it from falling out head first. Next in interest to the pupa was a fat, whitish-yellow grub in the same comb, still very much alive. Under the magnifying glass its head could be seen constantly moving, almost revolving, and its jaws opened and shut with mechanical regularity.

Interesting also in the same comb were some small, opalescent eggs. A cell never contained more than a single egg, and it was always high up in one corner, pointing slightly downwards and outwards from the centre of the comb. The eggs are fastened with a kind of cement to the cell walls, and it is hardly possible to detach an egg without breaking it.

The combs of a Common Wasp are smaller than those of a Hornet, and the cell walls of a Hornet's cell are of a more gluey consistency.

Photo : H. Bastin.]   [*Mondiale.*

The dainty, gossamer web that hangs, dew-spangled, in the garden, glittering as it sways in the breeze, illustrates the perfect workmanship of the Garden Spider. Lace-makers have tried laboriously to copy his wheel-like web.

BRITISH SPIDERS

By K. STÜLCKEN

WHO has not admired the fairy-like loveliness of a glistening web on a dewy morning and marvelled at the skill of the spinner ? The story of this family of weavers is told here, where we learn of Spiders that carry air-bubbles, and others that bear their family wherever they go. The real story of the fly and the silken parlour is also told.

THERE is no denying that Spiders are ferocious in their habits. The males fight each other, and the females, which are as a rule larger and stronger, frequently make a meal of the father of their young. It is not this characteristic, however, which is responsible for aversion to Spiders, particularly of the housewife, but a scarcely reasonable fear of the venomous nature of Spiders, and a natural disgust because they are creepy, crawly things, and cobwebs. We have no dangerous Spiders in this country ; but, of course, to a degree, Spiders are venomous, for they undoubtedly secrete a poison which paralyses their victims, enabling them to suck out the blood while it is still fluid. If they killed outright they would not be able to feed over long periods on the blood of flies or other insects caught in their snares.

Stories of Spiders are numerous and go back a long way. Country folk are sure that from the habits of the Spider one can foretell the coming weather. Early writers have said that the instinct of the Spider is so sure that the manner of web-weaving is a certain indication of approaching weather. For instance, a web spun when windy or rainy weather is not far off will have its radiating threads spun much shorter than they would be if fine weather were to be expected. When the Spiders busy themselves repairing their webs fair weather may be anticipated— but this cannot be claimed for all Spiders— for the Spider generally is too provident of his silk to weave unnecessarily. Then, again, it may be taken that the night will be calm and clear if Spiders are seen working on their webs between six and seven o'clock in the evening.

In olden times Spiders were supposed to have curative value in certain complaints, if utilised in several ways, both weird and wonderful. In 1736, the author of a work entitled " A Natural History of Spiders and

Other Curious Insects," expressed the hope that his work would be "no less agreeable than useful to the public in the cure of intermitting fevers," and later on asserts that he had cured children of agues by hanging a spider in a box about their necks on a string reaching almost to the pit of the stomach.

How Webs eased Pain.

Medical men as late as the opening of the nineteenth century employed Spiders and webs in cases of pain and fever. Dr. Watson, in his "Lectures on the Principles and Practise of Physic," dealing with ague and cures effected by agents operating through strong mental emotion on the nervous system, wrote of the "swallowing of a Spider gently bruised and wrapped up in a raisin, or spread upon bread and butter," and "keeping a Spider suspended from the patient's neck in a nutshell till it dies," as occasioning such disgust and horror by which cures were effected.

As a styptic the cobweb is used by country people to this day, and I well remember a farm hand who had cut himself badly and was bleeding profusely going into the cow byre to find cobwebs, which he applied to the wound. But I have never personally checked the curative value of this treatment.

Photo : M. H. Crawford.]   [Mondiale.
THE SPIDER'S SNUGGERY.
Here is the nest where the Garden Spider rears her young and keeps them secure until they reach maturity.

Of British Spiders, apart from the House Spider, T. Civilis, and his four-inch brother, *Tegenaria parietina*, who for all his fine name is an ugly brute, the easiest to study is perhaps the Cross or Garden Spider, which becomes active in autumn. For one reason, the young Spiders of this family remain for a week in the nest before dispersing, which they do only when able to fend for themselves. The nest in which they congregate will, on being shaken, send out a rain of tiny spots, which are the scores of frightened babies dropping down the line which they have spun. When all is quiet again they return to their snuggery.

As soon as the young Spiders are able to catch food for themselves, they set about constructing snares for the capture of insects. Of these snares there are various kinds. But to remain with the particular kind, we find that the Spider first selects a suitable spot for building, and having decided that here she will sojourn a while, she lets herself drop with all eight legs outspread, while a line of silk issues from her spinnerets. She does not reach ground, but just before stops and turning makes her way up the anchored lines, now spinning a second thread which she draws out with her two back legs.

Having done this she rests a while until the breeze wafts a loop of silk on to a twig or the like and is held fast. The base of the snare is laid. Additional strengthening lines are added, thread after thread is drawn out from the spinnerets and fixed in place until the web is finely and surely completed, and the worker is satisfied with her labours. The parlour is now ready for the fly to enter, and the host, making no attempt to encourage visitors, rests until a meal presents itself.

The Spider captures a Prisoner.

As soon as an insect becomes entangled in the snare, out rushes the Spider, binds it up a secure prisoner, and then gives it a bite, injecting a tiny drop of poison, not to kill, but to paralyse, so that the blood may be drained at will.

The spinning glands of the Spider are in the abdomen, there being two, three or four pairs of spinnerets. These are jointed, and vary in length and form. In some genera the spinnerets are cylindrical, the upper pair being very long and having free motion ; the others are short and cylindrical or conical. The tips and lower surfaces of these spinnerets are furnished with numerous minute tubes through which the silk issues.

Actually the silk is a viscid fluid secreted from glands in the abdomen connected with the spinnerets by small ducts. This fluid hardens into the silk we know immediately on being exposed to the air. The silken strands are hollow and full of sticky liquid which renews the cohesive properties of the surface when damaged.

When the web is torn the Garden Spider does very little repair work, but later on she will gather the silk threads, eat them up and then respin. The Angular Epeira remakes her web almost every evening, but the Banded and Silky Epeira will not trouble to renew their snares until they are absolutely torn to rags. All varieties of Spiders make nests.

A Home of Silk and Air.

The Water Spider, an air-breathing creature, works on a water plant below the surface, where it forms a bell of silk consisting of closely-woven threads. This bell it fills with air, coming to the surface and then diving with an air-bubble entangled in the hairs of its body. When it comes up for air after a period hunting food below surface, or working on its nest, the Water Spider raises its abdomen and then jerks it down suddenly with an air bubble between its hind legs. Swimming below its nest it releases the bubble which floats gently up into the silken bell, which is gradually filled up by repeated efforts of this nature.

The Wolf Spiders are vagabonds, constructing no snares, and carrying their eggs and afterwards the young about on their bodies. Very rapid movers, they hunt their prey keenly, killing one to pass on to another victim, darting this way and that in their greediness. It is said that a Wolf Spider will sometimes allow itself to be carried into the air by a large fly it has attacked rather than let go of its prey. And not only in hunting are they ferocious—the female will fight desperately for the protection of her cocoon, and, if deprived of it, she will, it is said, go into hiding and die.

It may be surprising to many to learn that Spiders are not insects, the latter being defined as creatures with a special kind of breathing apparatus called tracheæ, and three pairs of legs. A Spider possesses four pairs of legs, however, and the breathing apparatus is a simple but very wonderful arrangement.

Photo : Karl Stülcken.]   [Mondiale.
THE WATER SPIDER.
By carrying a bubble of air entangled in the hairs of its legs this spider can hunt for food below the surface.

On the low side of the abdomen are the breathing holes like gills, which communicate in turn with the tracheæ or air-tubes. Inserted in the envelope of the gill is to be found a tough ligament which, passing upwards, is attached to the membranous covering of the heart. The dilation and contraction of the heart causes the gill to open and close, alternately filling it and emptying it of air.

The Spider's Trap-Door.

There are so many kinds of Spiders, that it is impossible to deal with them fully here, so only a few of the especially interesting forms can be touched on. The Trap-door Spider is one that deserves attention, if only on account of the peculiarity of his home, which he prepares by digging a cylindrical hole in the ground. This hole he lines with silk, and, attaching a hinged lid over the hole, he is safe from disturbance, or even notice unless he chooses to emerge into the open. Then there are the representatives of the Thomisidæ family, the legs of which are so jointed as to spread out straight from the body, enabling the creature to move freely in any direction forwards, backwards and sideways. It has a crab-like appearance, owing to this peculiarity and the shortness as compared with

Photo : Karl Stülcken.] A PROTECTING WEB. [Mondiale.

The Spider can spin not only an alluring " parlour " to which she entices visitors, but also a cloak of defence for her own benefit. This female Spider has spun her web to protect her head and ward off the attacks of her enemies.

Photo : Paul Unger.] BUILDING SILKEN HOMES. [Mondiale.

Here is a colony of Water Spiders constructing their curious bell-like chamber of silk beneath the surface of the water. The Spiders carry air-bubbles from the surface down to these bells and inflate them with air.

A GAME FIGHTER.

[*Mondiale.*

The Wolf Spider, which carries its eggs in a large pocket attached to its body, is a keen fighter of the " never say die " type. Even when a large fly carries it into the air, it will not give up the struggle but hangs on grimly.

breadth of the body. The Drassidæ construct silken cells in which to hide themselves in leaves and crevices. Sometimes a cell open at both ends is formed on a leaf doubled and fastened together by silk threads, on the underside of an arched roof to protect the den.

Various attempts have been made to utilise the silk of the Spider in the manner of the product of the Silk Worm, but never with commercial success. As far back as the early part of the eighteenth century stockings were made of Spider Silk, but there were, and are, many reasons which make the production of silk from Spider cocoons impracticable. The Silkworm's thread is four times as strong, while the process of manufacture of Spider silk is difficult and expensive. Again, Spiders cannot be farmed, for they fight too freely, the stronger killing and eating the smaller in captivity. There is one especial use, however, for the Spider's very fine thread, and this is in the micrometer eye-pieces of telescopes where intersecting lines of extreme fineness are required. For this purpose the exceptionally fine silk of the web is valuable.

If the reader will collect and preserve Spiders for study, he must first take a little practice in careful observation of their habits, for they are not so easily caught. If one be seen lying in wait upon some part of its snare in a bush, the chances of catching it depend on the calculation as to whether it will drop on the approach of the hand, or retreat suddenly to its hiding place. Take, for example, the Agelene Labyrinthica, which watches at the entrance of its silken tunnel ; it will be noticed that it escapes with the greatest ease, and on retreating into its tube it escapes through it, but never returns to the front entrance.

Most Spiders can be caught in pill boxes, the open box being placed under the Spider and raised quickly, then on with the lid before the captive has time to escape. Another good reason for the pill box method of capture is that the creature may then be studied alive, by substituting a glass top lid for the ordinary cardboard one. Open-mouth bottles of spirit may be carried also for the capture of Spiders required for close study and collection. A camel-hair brush wetted in the spirit is useful in getting smaller Spiders running on the ground or hiding in crevices where otherwise they would be awkward to take.

Photo : Ernst Krause.] A JEALOUS MOTHER. *[Mondiale.*

The Wolf Spider, complete with its store of eggs, does not seem to be hindered by this burden, for it moves rapidly, and has a habit of pouncing suddenly on its prey. It fights desperately also in defence of its cocoon.

Photo: K. Stülcken.]   [Mondiale.

The larva's life-duty is to eat and grow as fast as it can so that it can finally emerge, after passing through many stages of development, as a brilliant dragonfly. Above, it has discarded its hull, which has become too tight.

STORY OF THE DRAGONFLY

By RAY PALMER, F.R.E.S., F.Z.S.

ONE of the strangest biographies ever recorded is that of the Dragonfly. It begins life in the water, where it spends its time feeding so that it can go through the physical changes necessary for its development. When it finally discards its last garment it takes to the air, a graceful, gauzy-winged creature, with only a few days at most to live.

THE Dragonfly is an insect that has captured the popular imagination, as can be seen by the frequency with which it figures in literature and decorative design. Its beauty and grace have inspired poets and artists, while preachers have used its marvellous and spectacular transformation as a parable of the future life.

An ugly and sluggish creature, dwelling in the mud and slime of some stagnant pond, becomes transformed with amazing suddenness into a glorious winged being of the air and sunshine—no longer condemned to a squalid and restricted existence in the murky depths, but free to traverse the country far and wide on its gauzy wings and revel in life under entirely new conditions. The wonder and beauty of such a metamorphosis make an unforgettable impression on anyone who beholds it.

There are some forty species of Dragonflies to be found in Britain, and they vary greatly in appearance and habits. It will therefore be best to follow the life history of a typical species, and we choose the large Green-spotted Dragonfly which is one of the commonest kinds in many parts of the country. Its scientific name is *Æschna cyanea*.

If we watch carefully by some pond in late summer, when the water has sunk somewhat below its normal level, one of these large Dragonflies may be seen to alight on the wet mud around the edge. The long, thin abdomen is then arched and the end thrust into the mud, withdrawn, and again inserted in another place. This goes on for some time without the insect moving from the spot, then it changes its position and repeats the process elsewhere. Here we are observing the very start of a new generation, for the Dragonfly we have been watching is a female laying eggs.

Sometimes the eggs are inserted in the stems of aquatic plants, other kinds of Dragonflies merely drop their eggs into the water at random, but the species we are describing seems to prefer to deposit them in the mud.

In due course the pond fills up, and the eggs, being now well under water, hatch. But the tiny creatures that emerge from the egg shells are not in the least like Dragonflies. There are no clearly defined Larva and Pupa stages, as in the case of Butterflies or Beetles, and so the creature that hatches from a Dragonfly's egg is called a *Nymph* or *Naiad*.

The Nymph that lives by preying.

At first it is exceedingly small, as the egg from which it emerges is less than an eighth of an inch in length. Its form is seen better when it grows larger, and is depicted in one of the illustrations, which conveys a better idea of its appearance than any description. The colour varies somewhat according to age, but in this species is always some shade of brown, usually closely resembling the mud of the pond in which the Nymph lies half buried. Its movements are sluggish, and it lies in wait for prey, snapping at any small creatures that pass by. This it is enabled to do by reason of an extraordinary apparatus it possesses for the purpose.

What is really the lower lip in such insects as Grasshoppers, in the Dragonfly Nymph has been specialised in a wonderful manner to form a long, jointed arm, flattened at the end into a broad, triangular plate, and furnished with a pair of formidable jaws or pincers. When not in use this curious organ lies folded up underneath the head, covering the mouth and lower part of the face, and for this reason is called the " mask."

On the approach of any small moving object the Nymph shoots out its mask and the pincers on the end seize the prey and draw it back to the mouth. A Dragonfly Nymph has a voracious appetite and will snap at almost anything. If an inanimate object is seized, or a hard insect such a Beetle, it is released at once ; but should the captive be a Worm, Tadpole or soft-bodied Larva, the case is very different. The unfortunate creature has no hope of escape from those powerful jaws. The Nymph holds its struggling victim with the mask, much as we hold food in our hand, and calmly munches away until it is all devoured, or hunger is finally satisfied.

At first only very small prey is captured, such as Daphnia and Cyclops, but as the

Nymph grows it attacks larger and larger creatures, until when full grown it is a match for any of the smaller denizens of the pond. Cannibalism is not uncommon, at least in captivity, and small Nymphs in an aquarium are very liable to get devoured by their larger relatives.

Unlike Water Beetles and many other pond dwellers, the Dragonfly Nymph is completely aquatic and does not have to come to the surface for air. It obtains its supply of oxygen from the water, and in a rather curious manner. If the tail-end of the Nymph is examined, it will be seen that it has five short spines at the extremity, three being much longer than the others. These spines can be spread wide apart or closed together to a point, and their function is to protect small openings at the end of the abdomen. Water is sucked through these openings into an abdominal cavity which is lined with a complicated system of air tubes. In some mysterious way the Nymph extracts air from the water, after the manner of a fish, and the water is then expelled and a fresh lot taken in. This goes on regularly all the time, so that the Nymph may be said to breathe water through its tail.

We have said that the Nymph is sluggish, and such is its usual habit. It can move quickly if necessary, however, as is the case when escaping from an enemy or on the rare occasions when hunger makes it attempt pursuit of prospective prey. The Nymph swims, if swimming it can be called, in a truly remarkable way, which is simply an exaggeration of its normal breathing action. Water is drawn into the abdomen and ejected with considerable force, thus propelling the creature forward after the manner of a rocket. This is done a number of times in succession, so that the insect shoots forward in a series of jerks ; but it soon tires from this exertion, and cannot sustain the effort for long.

The Nymph changes its garments.

As the Nymph grows it changes its skin at intervals, because the skin is not subject to growth once it has hardened ; thus it soon becomes too tight for its owner, and is shed like a suit of clothes. The complete skin is cast in a piece, even the claws of the legs and the covering of the eyes coming away intact. Growth is therefore not gradual as in the higher animals, but proceeds in a series of sudden stages. When the Nymph is about

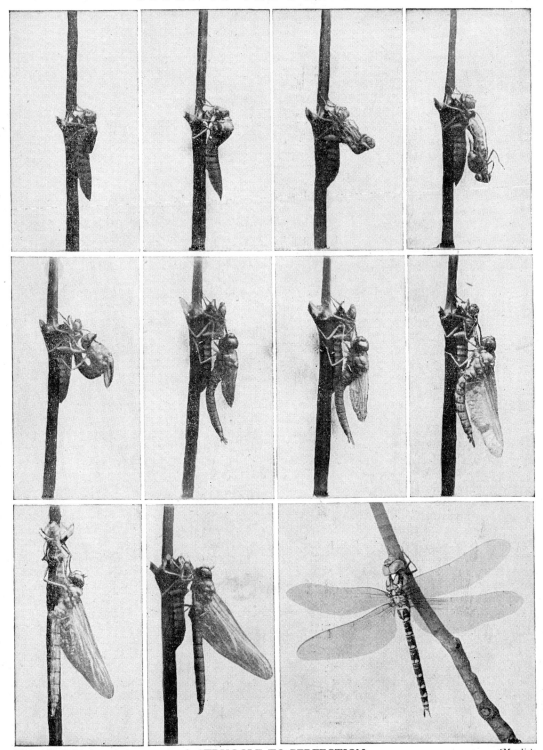

Photos : Ray Palmer.] A STRUGGLE TO PERFECTION. [Mondiale.

When beginning its final journey to perfection the Dragonfly Nymph clings tightly to a suitable stem and, as seen in this series of pictures, goes through many extraordinary contortions before emerging a perfect insect.

319

half grown, rudimentary wings begin to appear on the thorax, and increase in size with each change of skin.

As maturity approaches, the Nymph becomes more active ; she spends less time wallowing in the mud, and wanders at large over the bottom, climbs about the water plants and occasionally swims a short distance. The length of time spent in the water varies somewhat according to the food supply, but in the larger Dragonflies is never less than two years and more often three. Towards the end of this period a gradual change in the respiratory organs takes place, and the aerial breathing system of the Dragonfly is formed under the skin of the Nymph ; but for a long time the spiracles or breathing pores are closed, and the Nymph continues to breathe water in the usual way. Later on some of the spiracles become open and capable of functioning, particularly the four large ones in the thorax ; thus the Nymph, which hitherto derived the whole of its air supply from the water, can now, if it chooses, breathe atmospheric air as well.

It is this physical change, no doubt, that causes an alteration in habits, because the insect which previously lived in the mud now spends most of its time near the surface and frequently comes right out on to the floating leaves of water plants, or climbs up a reed stem and rests with its head and thorax out of the water, thus being able to breathe in two ways at the same time. It seems possible that the aquatic method of respiration becomes less efficient as the time for emergence approaches, because Nymphs kept under observation in the aquarium resorted to the aerial method with increasing frequency as time went on. Indeed, Nymphs may frequently be found quite out of the water some days before they are ready to change ; they return after a time, as though they were making a preliminary exploration of the world above.

Anyone who has had some experience of rearing Dragonflies can tell by looking at the eyes of a Nymph when it is nearly ready to emerge. A few hours before the great event, the eyes, which had previously appeared dull and opaque, become brilliant and translucent ; this is attributed to the eyes of the perfect insect within having already acquired a great deal of their brilliance, and pressing against the outer skin.

At last the day arrives for the final great metamorphosis, one of the most spectacular transformations in the insect world. It will be best to describe this as actually observed in the case of the specimen from which the photographs were taken.

I had been keeping a number of Nymphs in my aquarium with the object of watching and photographing their transformations, but several had escaped me by more or less completing their emergence when I was not present. One morning I noticed a Nymph resting half in the water and half out on a dead stem I had placed there for the purpose, and on looking at its face I saw that its eyes were brilliant. I knew what to expect, and so photographed it in position through the glass side of the aquarium. It remained like this all morning, and at 12.30 had not moved. Looking at it ten minutes later I saw the Nymph had climbed farther up the stem and was resting several inches above the water, in a position it had possibly reached several times before.

This time some impulse urged it onward, and instead of returning to the water as on former occasions, it climbed rapidly higher and higher, seeming possessed of a feverish energy. The supreme moment of its life had come ; it had left the water for ever. The insect can have no conscious knowledge of what is about to happen to it ; yet, guided by the mysterious thing we call " instinct," it follows a similar course to what its ancestors have done from remote ages to the present day. Higher and higher it climbs, until it finds a suitable spot where it can get a good grip and is free from all obstruction.

The specimen under observation chose a place where several branching flower stems of the water plantain had been broken off, nearly two feet above the water. Having fixed its claws in firmly it remained motionless, allowing the water to drain off its wet body and its skin to dry. So still did it remain that it appeared lifeless, and indeed this may be termed " the death of the Nymph "—for as such its existence had come to an end. On more than one occasion I have found Nymphs at this stage and thought they were dead, on finding that they made no movement when touched. It is no doubt during this resting period that the Nymphal skin becomes separated from that of the Dragonfly within, and it is probably insensible to touch ;

AN INSECT AEROPLANE. [E.N.A.

A Dragonfly—the veritable aeroplane of the insect world—is seen whirling through the air, carrying as passenger a Nymph that is clinging to its back. So expert is it on the wing that it is believed that it can even fly backwards.

the eyes also have lost all their brilliance and look dead and lifeless.

This state of inactivity does not last long, however. After a few minutes the Nymph seems ill at ease and begins to move its body about in a strange manner, while muscular movements seem to be going on within. The result is that the skin splits and almost imperceptibly a slit opens along the thorax, stretching from the wing cases to the head, and through this slit can be seen the yellowish-green body of the Dragonfly.

The insect continues its muscular efforts, in response to which the slit rapidly expands, until the whole of the top part of the thorax is seen protruding. As it comes out the body seems to swell and so further enlarge the aperture, while at the same time another slit forms cross-ways above the eyes. For the next few minutes progress was very rapid, and quick plate changing was necessary to catch the various stages. It will be noticed that the first eight photographs after the emergence started were taken with only intervals of one or two minutes between each.

Through the newly-formed slit the head began to appear, swelling larger and larger as it came. A minute later and the head was free, and the insect straining backwards to drag the first pair of legs from their sheaths, the claws of the latter still retaining their firm grip on the stem although they were now only empty cases. In another minute the second pair of legs were half withdrawn.

In the illustration some white threads will be noticed stretching from the sides of the insect's thorax during the early stages of the emergence. These are the linings of the four great air tubes of the thorax, which remain attached to the old skin and are drawn out from the spiracles.

The efforts of the Dragonfly to free itself were very apparent at this stage; it could be seen straining backwards with all its might, occasionally relaxing and renewing its efforts with a jerk. As the third pair of legs come away the insect leans so far backwards that it hangs head downwards, and four of the photographs show this curious attitude. The white threads had now broken off and were left attached to the case, the Dragonfly remaining suspended only by the end of its abdomen.

At last the legs were all free and the insect hung swaying gently and exercising its legs by working them to and fro, stretching them out and drawing them in again. After a short time the legs were drawn up close to the body and all movement ceased. During this resting stage the legs are no doubt hardening and gaining strength and the body developing energy for the gymnastic feat that is to come. The head and thorax swell greatly at this stage, and looking at the large head of the Dragonfly it seems incredible that it should have come out of the small head of the Nymphal case only a few minutes ago.

The resting stage in this case lasted twenty-two minutes, and throughout this time it was necessary to keep a close watch so as not to miss the wonderful reversing action, which is over in an instant. The Dragonfly began to move its legs again, and then by a sudden and violent exertion swung itself up and gripped its old case, as shewn in the photograph taken at 1.42 p.m.; in a second the abdomen was withdrawn and the insect clinging by its legs only. The Dragonfly was now free, but very different from what it would shortly become; its whole body was pale-green without any markings, and looked wet and limp, but the wings had already begun to grow.

Wing development took place very rapidly, and they had attained their full size in twenty-three minutes, but were still soft and limp and of an opaque yellowish colour. The expansion of the wings in this remarkable manner is no doubt due to the injection of fluid into them along the veins.

While the wings were developing the abdomen was held in a curve, but as soon as the wings had attained their full size the body was straightened and became longer and thinner, after the discharge of a quantity of fluid. Actual development was now complete, but the new-born Dragonfly had to wait a long time for the drying and hardening process to take place before it could fly. In the photograph taken at 2.50 p.m. the body was straightened out and had begun to darken, the wings were also transparent, but still held together over the back in a position never assumed by these Dragonflies once their wings are dry.

After a little while the insect became active, climbing about the stem and occasionally fluttering its wings, but not until 4 p.m. did it spread out its wings into the normal attitude. Even now it lacks all the brilliant colouring that is typical of its species, and the wings have a glassy appearance. Dragonflies at this stage are spoken of as " immature," and the full colouring does not appear until they have been several weeks on the wing and gradually darkens with age.

Before long the Dragonfly will turn its attention to feeding, and thus it becomes a terror to the smaller insects on which it preys. It was the Dragon of the pond during its Nymphal life, and now it is a Dragon of the air. One of these great creatures swooping down on a May-Fly or Caddis Fly must indeed seem a terrific monster from which escape is impossible. Dragonflies are marvellously expert on the wing, and it is said they can even fly backwards. It is a beautiful sight to watch one of these magnificent insects sailing to and fro on rigid wings over the sunlit surface of some reed-fringed pool. Now and then it will dart aside, with surprising agility, to pounce on some luckless insect, only to resume its course up and down the pond, devouring its victim in mid-air.

Perhaps the Dragonfly we are watching is not engaged in feeding; if so it is probably a male on the look-out for a mate. Presently he espies a female and darts at her, but she flies away at tremendous speed, with her lover in pursuit. We hear the rustle of their wings many times as they clash together and finally the male succeeds in seizing the lady round the neck, with a special pair of claspers at the end of his long body, and the pair then fly off quietly together, tandem fashion, to complete their union elsewhere. Such is the Dragonfly's strange method of love-making.

Now we have completed the cycle of the Dragonfly's life story, for the female will soon deposit her eggs in the mud at the pond's edge as already described, and so we have come round to the point from which we started.

In conclusion it should be mentioned that Dragonflies are perfectly harmless, so far as human beings are concerned, and the popular notion that they sting is entirely without foundation. Though often called " horse stingers " by country folk, who have seen them flying round horses and cattle, the application of such a name is most unjust, for all they are doing is feeding on the flies that are tormenting the animals; thus, far from being harmful to either animal or man, Dragonflies are actually beneficial.

Pond-snails display beautiful shells of various designs. When the snail dies, the shell sinks to the bottom of the pond, where a large collection has accumulated. The unique photograph above shows a snail swimming.

LIFE IN POND, STREAM, AND COUNTRYSIDE

By A. McCLAY

IN one small pond or stream there can be found congregated together myriads of small creatures of varying species, each struggling bravely for existence. There are Frogs and Fish, Bugs and Fleas, Newts, and the larvæ of many insects. There are also pond-dwellers invisible to the eye, and tiny masses of jelly that are each human entities.

THE drama of Life is played on many stages, on land and in sea. Every pond, stream, lake and river, mountain, moor and fen, is an isolated territory inhabited by a community of living plants and animals, which form very intimate relationships.

The existence of the community depends on what is called the Balance of Nature, and to preserve the various species for the ultimate good of the whole Nature works through the factors of climatic changes, drought, carnivorous and herbivorous enemies, and disease. While Nature is prolific, unrestrained reproduction rarely, if ever, occurs. Fecundity is held in check under ordinary conditions ; but if the delicate adjustment of factors is in any way disturbed, it is an indication of climatic change, or, more frequently, the unwise intervention of man.

The alarming increase of Rabbits in Australia, of the Gipsy Moth which destroys forest trees in North America, the American Water Weed invading the rivers of Western Europe, or the extensive conquests of the Prickly Pear in Australia are a few familiar instances of the results of introducing species into new countries where they are not controlled by the ordinary checks occurring in their native localities.

There is a wonderful wealth of animal forms in the British Isles. However small a pond may be, it holds many surprising secrets. Skaters and Whirligigs play about on the surface ; Bugs and Beetles, Fishes and Amphibians swim in the depths below, and the bottom is the home of the Water Scorpion and numerous other creatures. It is a mysterious world that lies at the bottom of still water. We have many interesting fishes in our ponds and streams ; Frogs, Toads and Newts, with exceptionally instructive life histories, that inhabit both land and water ; and

THE POOL.   [Will F. Taylor.

The quiet surface of this drowsy-looking pool belies the activity that is hidden underneath. Countless little
creatures inhabit this watery kingdom, and many a battle for supremacy is fought in its subterranean depths.

on land reptiles and other vertebrates—or backboned animals—together with an almost countless number of invertebrates, such as insects, spiders, snails, earthworms, etc., etc.

Spring in the pond.

Ponds and streams are rapidly repeopled with life in spring. In a few weeks myriads of larvæ of Gnats, Caddis Flies, Dragon-flies, May-flies, Water Beetles, and other aquatic insects are to be found in them. The eggs of frogs, toads and newts are hatching ; and water fleas, water mites, cyclops and other quaint and minute creatures are to be discovered, as well as many forms of life not so well known.

Some of the most perfect forms of beauty are invisible to the naked eye—desmids and diatoms, for example. We know about 2000 species of desmids and some 10,000 of diatoms, any one of which far excels man's finest handiwork. Diatoms have shells of exquisite patterns although the largest of them is no more than a fiftieth of an inch in diameter. The Foraminiferæ, about the size of a pin head, have built up the chalk of the earth. They form their shells, beautifully fretted and chased in an endless variety of designs, of carbonate of lime secreted from salt and fresh water. The shell sinks to the bottom when the creature dies. Some Pond Snails have shells of great beauty and delicacy, with regular and accurate spirals. *Planorbis* is a genus with a considerable variety among its species. Its spirals are left-handed " sinistral," following a direction opposite to that of a clock hand. The genus *Limnæ* also has many variants, but the shells have a " dextral " or right-handed whorl. Then there are the Amoebæ, real entities in the animal world although they are mere specks of jelly never more than about a hundredth of an inch across ; vorticella, shaped like a bell ; paramecium, shaped like a slipper ; tardigrada, like a bear ; stentor, like a trumpet ; trachelocera, like a swan ; hydra, a creature with an uncanny power of recovering from injury ; and so forth.

How the Water Flea breathes.

The curious little Water Flea is a crustacean, like the Lobster and Crayfish, but belonging to the sub-class *Branchipoda* or gill-footed crustaceans, because the breathing organs are attached to the limbs. There are several British species, of which *Daphnia pulex* is the commonest. Unlike the Crayfish or Lobster, the segments or joints are inside, not outside, the body, which is enclosed in a reddish-brown transparent double shell or " carapace."

The eye is set in the middle of the forehead, and as the frontal portion of the head is transparent, the creature can see forward in all directions. There are from four to six pairs of feet, which are not used for locomotion but for laving currents of water, carrying food particles on to the tissues when the valves are open. The animal swims with a jumping motion by strokes of its antennæ.

The female, which is larger and more abundant, carries her eggs about with her in a space between her body and the shell. They are of two kinds. The small and thin-skinned eggs develop without fertilisation and produce males ; the large variety are thrown off after being fertilised and can resist dryness without any injury. They produce females. The largest species of Water Flea is about one-tenth of an inch in length.

The Bug that skates.

The Pond-skater is a water bug belonging to the *Gerridæ*, of which we have ten species. A common one is *Gerris najas*. The legs and lower part of the insect are covered with a velvety pile which is impervious to water, and it lives by sucking the juices of dead and dying insects on the surface of the water. It moves about rapidly in a series of glides using the intermediate pair of legs for that purpose, the hind pair being used to steer the course and the first pair to secure food. To the naturalist the *Gerridæ* are remarkable insects, because in most of the species three forms occur : wingless, with abbreviated wings, and with fully developed wings. The Sea-skaters belong to the genus *Halobates*. They are almost the only insects of which we know that can live entirely upon the surface of the ocean, often hundreds of miles from land.

But of all the creatures that rise from the depths of pond, stream or river, the May-flies have always held human interest. They appear in multitudes with unfailing regularity in late May or early June, are seen for two or three days and then disappear until the following year. The phenomenon is well known to fishermen—and fishes. The nymph stage is passed in water and lasts two or more years. Then the fragile flies emerge, chiefly towards evening, but only to live a brief span of a few hours, in the course of which, if they escape their many enemies, they mate, lay eggs and

Photo: E. Pedder.]   [Mallinson.

THE MATURE MAY-FLY.

The May-fly, often believed to live for a day only, spends two years in the grub and pupa stages in the pond

[Ray Palmer.

SHELLS OF FRESHWATER SNAILS.

At the bottom of the pond lie brightly-coloured and delicately-fashioned snails, a variety of which is seen above.

[Brit. Instruct. Films.

A ONE-EYED POND DWELLER.

Another of the quaint creatures to be seen in ponds is the Cyclops. The female with egg sacs is seen above.

Photo: K. Stülcken.]   [Mondiale.

THE LARVA'S RUDDERS.

This picture of the Larva of the Dragon-fly shows the odd three-part rudder appendages used in locomotion.

die. Hence they are called *Ephemeroptera*, or Day-flies. There are about forty British species. A common one is *Ephemera dancia*. *Ephemera vulgata*, a large species, is to be found on running water only.

The female is larger and stronger. The male is distinguished by his large eyes, about twice the size of the female's. Neither are capable of taking food, for the mouth parts are func‑tionless. Eggs are deposited in plate-like discs, from 700 to 800 at a time, and scatter as they sink in the water.

The larva of the common May-fly is car‑nivorous. It makes a U-shaped burrow in the mud and causes a current of water to flow through it by a motion of the feathery out‑growths which act as its gills. In due time the nymph comes to the surface, its skin splits, and the insect rises into the air. This is the sub-imago stage, unique among insects, and is known to anglers by the name of the " Green Drake."

But it is not yet a perfect insect. After settling upon some support and resting awhile, it sheds its skin for the second time, when the true *imago* or fully developed insect (the angler's " Grey Drake ") emerges and flies away to find a mate or, more likely, immedi‑ately fall a prey to its enemies. Although so delicate, these insects go back to the earliest times, well-preserved forms being found in the Devonian and Carboniferous rocks.

Coming to the vertebrates, or animals with backbones, we have the fishes, which have been fashioned by a series of gradual improve‑ments to dwell in water. As we all know, they breathe by gills which, in most cases, are protected and hidden by a shield-like cover called the operculum. Water is taken in through the lips, passed over the gills, which absorb the oxygen dissolved in it, and then sent out through the openings behind the opercula. I can do no more here than only mention a very few of our familiar pond and river fishes.

The common Carp is a handsome fish that can live out of water for some hours and may attain a great age. Anglers speak of it as the " fresh-water fox " because it is cunning enough to withstand their lures and resist their efforts to catch it.

The Perch is probably the handsomest of all our fresh-water fish. Its red fins, deep green back paling to greenish-yellow lower down in the body, with dark, broad trans‑verse bands, make it easily recognisable.

The Pike has been very aptly named the " water wolf."

The Roach is related to the Carp. It has a greenish-brown back with silvery sides and belly, and red fins.

The three-spined Stickleback is particularly interesting. The outstanding point of interest in this fish is the strong paternal instinct of the male. His care for his young has already been described in this volume.

Parents who desert their Young.

Other fish show no interest whatever in their young ; once the eggs are laid the parents swim away. To balance this exposure to great danger enormous clutches of eggs have to be laid. The Tench lays as many as 300,000 eggs ; the Pike may be responsible for a million eggs at a time ; a Cod may produce over six millions, and a Turbot as many as nine millions.

The olive-green Tench is a very hardy, but sluggish fish, with quite small scales. It buries itself in mud during the winter months and remains there in a drowsy state.

Vertebrated gill-breathing animals are always aquatic, but the converse, that lung-breathing vertebrates are always terrestrial, is not true. Amphibians—the word signifies double life—have lungs and can live on land as well as in water. They represent the transition from aquatic to terrestrial life, but almost all have remained within easy reach of the water.

There are two species of frogs—the Common Frog and the Edible Frog. The life history of frogs is interesting because the young are so very different from the adults. They issue from eggs as Tadpoles, which are practically fish. Then they breathe as fishes do, by means of gills. Later, they change again and develop lungs and limbs, leaving the water for land, but their skins are always soft and moist and capable of absorbing oxygen from the air.

Fishes are cold-blooded, possess a heart with two chambers, and breathe by means of gills. Amphibians and reptiles are also cold-blooded, but the heart has three cham‑bers and respiration is carried on through their lungs. Birds and mammals have four chambered hearts, and a further great difference from all other vertebrates is that they are warm-blooded or " stenothermal." Their body temperature does not change with that of the surrounding medium.

[*Dorien Leigh Ltd.*

The beautiful Monarch Butterfly and a gauzy-winged Dragonfly make the same toadstool their resting-place. The Monarch has migratory habits : though at times found in the South of England, is most common in North America.

OUR BUTTERFLIES

By EVAN STRONG

NO princess is more beautifully and colourfully garbed than the " floating flowers " that brighten up a summer day with their gay flutterings. The variety of hues and patterns that decorate their garments dazzle the eyes and put the paint-box to scorn. Yet, before they can achieve this brilliance they have to undergo a long period of struggle.

AS soon as the days of persuasive warmth and sunlight arrive, all those insects which during the winter have been dormant and hidden away out of sight, appear again in swarms of new life. Bees flock to the flowers, and not only the sophisticated Hive Bees, dupes of mankind's passion for sweetness, but many untrammelled wildlings whose nests and dormitories are in subterranean burrows or hollowed stems. Beetles, like sparkling gems, scurry across the footpaths or sun themselves at points of vantage on the adjacent herbage. The first Butterflies to appear—the Brimstones and Tortoiseshells—are old stagers who, since their autumnal diversions, have lodged in the chinks and crannies of decaying tree trunks, or among the rafters of barns and outhouses. And though some of them may show signs of wear and tear, they hurry to the nuptial revels which are already in progress where the Buckthorn Bushes are bursting into leaf and beds of Stinging Nettle shooting. But the Black and White Butterflies—those mis-

creants of the cabbage garden—are the truer portents of the resurrection which takes place in every corner of the countryside. They are spick and span as a pierrot troupe celebrating the initial day of its season, having just escaped the mottled chrysalis skins which swathed their budding infancy. So, too, with the Dragonflies, those tyrants of the shimmering air. They, in truth, are children of the sun, for not one of them is seen while summer tarries.

The marvellous birth of the Butterfly has often been described and pictured. The history of the Peacock Butterfly is fascinating. The fully evolved creature is richly coloured, with decorations on all four wings, resembling the display feathers of a Peacock, while undersides are dully coloured, so that the effect of the closing and opening of the wings is striking.

The Peacock Butterfly seeks a nettle-bed when egg-laying time comes. Its inborn instinct guides it to the plant that offers suitable food for the future larvæ. Large

328

numbers of minute eggs, delicately ribbed and fluted, are laid. They are olive green, making them inconspicuous against the green background of nettle leaf. To escape from the egg the larvæ bite their way through the shells. Very tiny beings, they nevertheless clearly show the rings of their bodies and the feathery hairs adorning them. In colour they are black and the surface of their firm skin is glossy. From now on their life is one long meal, interrupted only by the periodical moults. The outermost covering of the larva's body does not expand and so when it becomes too tight it is cast off, a looser and larger covering having already been formed beneath it. The Caterpillar then proceeds to eat and grow again, to fit its new cuticle. This occurs several times before the larva reaches its full size.

The head of the Caterpillar bears groups of simple eye-spots on each side, a pair of short feelers, and several mouth-parts, including a pair of strong jaws suitable for biting plants. Behind the mouth there is a tiny opening from which comes liquid silk from the silk-glands. This fluid immediately solidifies in the air, forming a silken thread that can be manipulated by movements of the larva's head. The three rings behind the head each bear a

READY FOR FLIGHT.
The Swallowtail Butterfly is seen drying its beautiful wings in the sunshine before taking off on its flight.

pair of jointed and clawed legs, which correspond to the three pairs of legs of the adult insect, while farther along the body other appendages are seen, four pairs of stumpy "pro-legs" on successive rings and a fifth pair, the claspers, especially placed for gripping on the last segment.

The Caterpillar uses its silk to make a lifeline, and also its cocoon for the pupa stage of its development. If its food-plant is shaken, or if a questing bird comes too close, it drops from the leaf it has been nibbling. Before it falls it attaches a thread of silk, from which it can dangle until it is safe to climb up again.

At the last moult its skin cracks open and is worked off down to the tail, gradually displaying the pupa. Attached to the plant by its own silk it hangs head downwards.

The Life of the Pupa.

The pupa is at first quite soft, but it soon hardens. Its skin is semi-transparent and through it can be seen long feelers, small wings, and other structures that suggest the form of the adult insect that will later appear. The pupa of the Peacock Butterfly varies in colour and is usually well hidden on the under sides of leaves in a nettle-bed. Within it, a great change, known as the *metamorphosis*, takes place. The larval organs are transformed into new ones suitable for the life of the adult insect. A biting and crawling caterpillar becomes, after pupation, a sucking and flying Butterfly.

When the Butterfly is ready to emerge, the pupa-skin breaks open and the winged insect draws itself carefully out of the hull. It is limp and damp, with small crumpled wings.

The eggs of the "White Butterflies" (*Pieridæ*) have a characteristic sugar-loaf form, and are laid on cruciferous plants, including the cultivated varieties of cabbage. Those of the "Tortoiseshells" (*Numphalidæ*) are squat and dumpy by comparison, and will be found on Stinging Nettles and other economically worthless vegetation. So, too, with caterpillars and chrysalides. Those of the quaint little Central European "Map Butterfly" (*Araschnia levana*) obviously conform to the same "type" as our British "Peacocks" and "Red Admirals." Again, in the "Swallowtail" (or "Dove-tail") family, the caterpillar may always be recognised by the retractile scent organ behind its head, and the chrysalis by its twin projecting "nose-horn." Similarly, in the "perfect" or winged state, details of habit or preference often betray family re-lationship ; as, for example, when we see Burnet Moths (*Zygænidæ*) of divers species instinctively flocking to the flower-heads of thistles and scabious, while avoiding the spacious umbels of carrot and fennel, whereon Soldier and Sailor Beetles gather in crowds.

How the Butterfly attains Perfection.

It is when we watch the transformations of the Butterfly that we realise the wonder of its life story. The various stages are many, as noted above, and then we come to the insect as it escapes, perfect, from the chrysalis. As it creeps out with some effort from the hull in which so much change has taken place, dragging its soft damp body with wings all crumpled and as yet helpless, one can hardly realise that in a few moments it will be the brilliant dilettante of the flower world. But in the sunlight the soft wings begin quickly to fill out with the life fluid, straighten and expand. The tiny creature trembles a moment as if afraid of the new element into which it must launch itself, then with a final flutter it is in the air, a beautiful thing, worthy of all Nature's efforts to produce it.

The sense organs are important to all forms of life. We classify them as sight, hearing, touch, taste and smell. The Butterflies which subsist on flower nectar are guided to their food by the organs of sight and smell. It is the bright colours of the flowers that mainly attract them, and if you observe closely you will find that they go to the blossoms and pass over the sombre-toned foliage.

These are the days of joyous flitting and love-making. After mating the female's interest changes, the leaves of plants have now an attraction for her, for she must find a place to lay her eggs.

It is the sense organs which draw the Butterfly to the right place. Take the peculiarity of the Cabbage White Butterflies which lay their eggs on cabbage leaves—and also other similar leaves which contain juices having a definite smell. Here, experiment has revealed, it is not the mustard oil, as the juice is called, in itself which attracts the Butterfly, but the smell ; for if some of the oil is rubbed on plants which are not the natural food of the kind, the female Butterfly will be deceived and lay her eggs on these false plants.

On the other hand, while the smell sense of the Butterfly is highly developed, the eyes are comparatively simple. Instead, for example

Photo : Ray Palmer.] [*Mondiale.*
GREEN HAIRSTREAK BUTTERFLY.
A series of white dots decorates the wings of the Green Hairstreak, which resembles the leaves of its perch.

of being formed of one adjustable lens, the Butterfly's eye has a large number of lenses, each lens fixed on the top of a crystal cone wider above than below. The picture seen is not one whole, but made up of all the sections registered by the various lenses.

Coming back to the Cabbage Butterflies, we find that the eggs are laid on the underside of the leaves. After the female butterfly's visit a tiny patch of yellow eggs will be found, which on the tenth day are hatched out, the young grubs having shiny black heads. They are very hungry, but before starting to devour the cabbage leaves they first consume the shells from which they have escaped. After feeding ravenously they get too big for their skins, when they stop feeding while their skins split and the grub crawls out. As soon as the new skin is dry, they recommence their unending meal until they again need a larger skin, when the same process is repeated. The grub's body is made up of various rings on most of which are two tiny breathing holes, one on each side. There are two kinds of legs : six proper just behind the black head, and several false legs underneath the rings of the body. Birds dislike them, more is the pity, for otherwise perhaps a real garden pest would be kept within

Photo : Winifred Williams.] THE ADMIRAL TAKES NOURISHMENT. [Mallinson.

The Red Admiral, with its arresting garb of black and scarlet, is conspicuously lovely as it flits about the garden, stopping here and there to suck the potent nectar from the flowers till it becomes too listless for further flight. It stays there in a drugged attitude till it gathers sufficient energy to move off to another flower.

Photo : Ray Palmer.] THE LARGEST BUTTERFLY. [Mondiale.

The Swallow-tail, the largest of British butterflies, has wings ornamented with black, blue, and red, making a very decorative effect. It is a rare species, found only in a few districts in Norfolk and Cambridgeshire. The eggs are laid on the leaves of the milk-parsley on which the caterpillars feed when they emerge.

Photo: Karl Stülcken.] [Mondiale.

THE BUTTERFLY'S NEST.

The Peacock Butterfly deposits its olive-green eggs on nettle-leaves, where they generally remain unnoticed.

Photo: Karl Stülcken.] [Mondiale.

THE GROWING BUTTERFLY.

In the initial phase of the pupa stage the Caterpillar industriously spins an anchorage upon the leaf stem.

Photo: Karl Stülcken.] [Mondiale.

A WINTER RETREAT.

The Caterpillar attaches itself to a twig and spins a cocoon in which it pupates and spends the winter.

Photo: M. H. Crawford.] [Mondiale.

FULL-GROWN PEACOCK BUTTERFLY.

The Butterfly has now emerged in all its fresh beauty. On each of the velvety wings is a " peacock's eye."

bounds. After the various changes of skin the caterpillar seeks a favoured spot where it spins silken threads from a tube under its mouth. With these threads it makes a kind of carpet with a little pad at the bottom for its tail, and a rope with which to anchor and bind itself to the object to which it has attached itself. After this effort the caterpillar rests for a couple of days while the body grows shorter and thicker, and then the skin behind the head splits open, and very gingerly as it wriggles its tail, the old skin comes off backwards. It is a new kind of creature now. The caterpillar shape is lost in the queer marks and ridges which appear on the body, and the form of wings can be seen. The whole body is covered with a shiny liquid which very quickly dries into a hard shell to protect the delicate creature within ; it is now a pupa and appears to have gone to sleep. During this sleep extraordinary changes take place, the results of which are to be seen two or three weeks later when it is observed again. The hard case has burst and hangs empty, but nearby trembles a Butterfly with small white wings which expand for flight, on a thin hairy body and head with two big eyes, two feelers and six long legs. It cannot eat cabbage, for it has no mouth. Instead there is a long tube curled up like a watch spring, and with this it sucks honey from the flowers. Soon it flies away to find a mate, then lays eggs and restarts the whole process over again. And so this wonderful series of transformations goes on eternally.

The Butterflies of the various hibernating species, the Sulphur or Brimstone, for instance, will appear frequently on warm sunny days in early spring. A Large White may also be seen occasionally. The small garden White may not disappear from the air before Nov-

Photo: Alexander Barns.]   [Mondiale.

A NEWCOMER.

This new species of Butterfly of the order Chaxaraxes has beautiful wings, and makes a decorative picture.

ember, and will reappear in March and April. The joys of spring would not be complete were it not for the appearance of the Butterflies. Cold winds keep them in hiding, but as the sun becomes more powerful Tortoiseshell and Peacock emerge. Brimstone and Peacock are aged fellows from last year, but at the end of April the new Butterflies are on the wing. In the country lanes, for example, the dainty Orange-tip is found, an extremely delicate creature whose days are comparatively short and do not extend to the late summer months.

The Small Tortoiseshell is the most common of the hibernating species; on the other hand, the Large Tortoiseshell is rare. The former, it would seem, is a very light sleeper, for members of his family may be seen flitting about on any sunny winter day. In the middle of April if the sun approves, the White Cabbage Butterflies show up, and then follow Red Admirals, the Peacock (not too early), the large Skipper, the Clouded Yellow, and so on. But not until July do we get a real profusion of Butterflies. This is the real Butterfly season, and not only do the fine flying regulars play in the sun then, but sometimes May and June Butterflies, like the pearl bordered Fritillaries, will join in the merry dance. It is said of these last that they have two broods, the second appearing as late as July.

The dingy Skippers are woodland Butterflies, and frequent the copse grasses and flowers. A rare woodland Butterfly is the Wood White, of feeble flight, the smallest of six species of the White Butterflies.

Though June is not the true Butterfly month, numerous kinds come out then, including the Meadow Browns, Red Admirals, large Skippers and Common Blues. Of the smaller insects the Blues form a delightful group ; the Clifden Blue, a favourite with some people, the Azure or Holly Blue, Silver Spotted Blue, Chalkhill Blue, etc. Common Blue flash out in thousands during June and again in much larger broods in August or September. As the month proceeds and merges into July the more resplendent flyers appear one after the other, gorgeous fellows like the magnificent Purple Emperor, the elegant White Admiral, and those strikingly marked Fritillaries, the Light Brown, Silver Washed and Dark Green. These too, for the most part, will be found in wooded areas along with the various *Vanessæ*.

Some favourite Butterflies.

Every hunter of Butterflies has his favourite. There are some who especially admire the Clouded Yellow because of its fine colouring and assured flight, possibly because he is one of the last of the season, but almost every one will be enthusiastic over the Purple Emperor, undoubtedly the noblest of our British Butterflies, with powerful wings which give it confident flight. Its colouring is splendid, and with the spots it affects places it in the van. Empresses are rarely seen, strangely enough.

The Purple Emperor likes to hover high above the tops of the oak-trees, and as he darts about in strong flight, forces one's attention.

Nevertheless, he does not seem to be so well recognised as those larger Fritillaries which country folk call Copse Butterflies, and the Peacock, called Harvest Butterfly. If you really wish to attract an Emperor to a spot so that he may be studied, a piece of high meat will do the job. Red Admirals and Small Tortoiseshells may be similarly attracted by a concoction of rum, beer and sugar, and known as " Sugar."

As the Emperor favours the oak, though the caterpillar feeds on the Sallow, the White Admiral shows a preference for Hazel. The latter is a very graceful fellow, especially in flight. The Purple Hairstreak also frequents the tops of oaks, where he and his kind hover in scores. His wife has a little purple about her wings, but is not so deeply blue.

In open spaces such as commons and by the woods, the Marble White will be found in July, as well as generally the Grayling, Peacock and Large Tortoiseshell. The following month brings the Speckled Wall, Wood Argus and Painted Lady to the front, and then the Butterflies begin to decline. With the cool autumn winds most of them disappear and very soon all have ended their short gay life, or gone to sleep during the winter months.

THE CABBAGE BUTTERFLY.   [*Brit. Instruct. Films.*

The Large White, or Cabbage Butterfly, which deposits its large batches of eggs on a cabbage leaf, is one of our most familiar Butterflies. The Caterpillars that hatch from the eggs in about seven days feed on the leaf.

H. Bastin.]
[Mondiale.

This Hawk-Moth is sipping nectar from the blossoms of the honeysuckle. The Hawk-Moth family is a large one, containing some sixty species. Ten only of these are found in Britain, and some of these ten are rare.

SOME BRITISH MOTHS

By M. H. CRAWFORD

THE moths and butterflies of Britain would require many volumes to treat them individually and adequately, there are so many hundreds of species. Here the author tells the story of the moth's metamorphosis and of some of the types of moths we see about us.

TWILIGHT-LOVING Moths are, of course, less familiar to us than sun-loving Butterflies. To study their ways in the dusk is not an easy matter, but it is well worth doing. It is a hobby which increases in fascination as each June comes round. There are Moths to be seen all the year round, but June is the most wonderful month for Moths.

Variations in colour, size and shape of the eggs are endless. There is the almost invisible egg of the little White-shouldered Moth. Compare this with the large, brownish-speckled egg of the Oak Eggar or the greenish-white egg of the Drinker. The eggs of the White Shoulder, when freshly laid, have the appearance of a very tiny mound of dust. In colour, also, there are surprising differences. Those of the Common Magpie are yellow or pale-green, covered with minute indentations. The pale-yellow eggs of the Yellow-horn seem to glow with light ; the thin shell is very finely ribbed. Those of the Vapourer

are pale buff, ringed and spotted. Those of the Ghost Moth are black and shiny. Many are green ; for instance, the August Thorn, the Least Grass Emerald, the Dotted-border Umber. The rose-pink eggs of the Bordered Beauty are strikingly pretty. We come across a very unusual shape in those of the Straw Belle. Still more curious are the eggs laid by the Scalloped Oak ; these resemble very small bricks, whitish in colour with dark specks. Eggs of the Feathered Thorn, deposited very evenly and neatly on twigs of Oak and Thorn in November, have, when empty, the exact appearance of a minute Wasp's comb. Eggs of the Red Underwing are of a rich purple shade with yellow at the top. Generally speaking, Moths' eggs may be divided into two classes : upright and flat. In the flat egg the micropyle—the opening through which the egg is fertilised—is at one end ; in the upright egg the micropyle is at the top, or on that side which lies parallel to the leaf or other object on which it is laid.

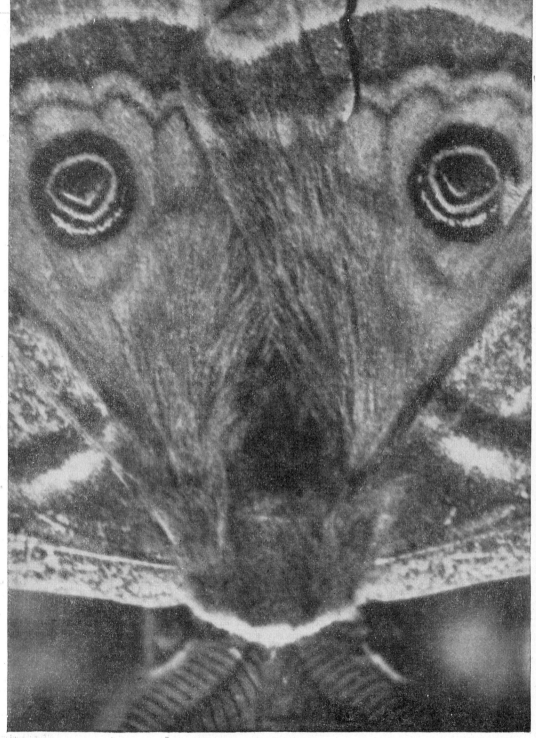

Karl Stülcken.] WHAT IS THIS FACE? [*Mondiale.*

Moths are often endowed with strange markings. Some are given by Nature as camouflage and others as protective or warning colorations. The Emperor Moth has two "eyes" on its wings to frighten its enemies.

The Magpie Moth is one of the few species which fly during the day, and its eggs are very easily obtained for examination. It may be followed about as it flits from place to place, laying an egg here and an egg there. Eggs laid in the garden on Currant and Gooseberry Bushes are often larger than those laid in the open country on Blackthorn; such eggs are probably laid by Moths bred from caterpillars which have fed on the same fruit bushes. Magpies do not always wander far from the place of birth; they are very fragile insects.

Another common, garden-bred Moth is the Lackey, which lays its eggs in August round twigs of Apple, **Pear, or Bramble.** They do not hatch out till spring and are easily seen. They are pale stone in colour, and are so firmly glued together that it is usually simpler to re-move the whole brace-let of them than to detach a single egg.

The thickness of the shell varies a good deal. The eggs laid by the plump, wingless, spider - like Winter Moths have very strong shells, proof against insecticides and sprays. They are exceedingly small, pale-green at first, growing darker as the Larva inside develops. The green eggs of the Lappet Moth have also very strong and tough shells.

Usually eggs are laid on or near food plants of the Larvæ, but there are exceptions to this rule, and sometimes the subsequent needs of the Larvæ seem to receive no atten-tion. One day in August I found a branch of yellow Broom literally covered with the white, pearl-like, ribbed eggs of the Large Yellow Underwing. When the Larvæ hatched they would all have to descend and make their way to low-growing garden plants or vegetables. These eggs were exposed to the full glare of the sun and to the keen eyes of the numerous Blue Tits, but they were,

apparently, quite safe from both sun and birds.

Very different was the method adopted by a Browntail Moth for the safety of her eggs; she wrapped them up in a thick case composed of the woolly hair from her own body. It is not easy to catch her doing this, as she seems to prefer night for the operation. Equally careful to hide its eggs is the Dark Tussock Moth. The eggs are sticky and shiny, plas-tered all over with short, dark hairs from the Moth's thorax and legs. A batch of these eggs looks exactly like a scrap of dark fur.

The pale, yellow eggs of the Angle-shades Moth are usually laid on Nettle or Groundsel, but this Moth will lay them anywhere. She always seems anxious to get her duties over as quickly as possible so that she may enjoy a little life in garden and field before her strength and vivacity pass away. Once her eggs are laid, she un-curls her long pro-boscis and is ready for a feast at the nearest suitable flower before resuming her care-free existence.

A magnifying glass is necessary to examine the eggs, but the Caterpillars are always so large that we may dispense with such extra aid. As soon as they escape from the shell growth is extremely rapid, and continues rapid for a few hours.

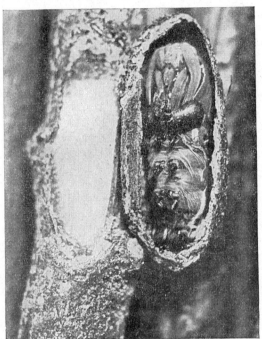

Photo: Karl Stülcken.]   *[Mondia'e.*

A SLEEPING BEAUTY.

The Puss Moth has spun its cocoon, slept while Nature worked a miracle in it, and now is in the pupal state.

For purposes of study and examination, it is wise to hatch Caterpillars in captivity. The food question is not then so difficult. Later on the Larvæ will probably eat nothing except the leaves on which they have been reared. When very young they generally do not object to a change-over from one food to another.

Several times I have proved this. For instance, a large family of handsome Cinna-bars were feeding inside a rosette of Ragwort leaves; some were placed in a tin box and

Photo: H. Bastin.] FROM WHITE TO BLACK. [Mondiale.
The above collection of specimens of the Buff Ermine Moth show the changes brought about by in-breeding in captivity. In ten generations the white, or buff, has turned almost to black. This is known as melanism.

A GAY FLUTTERER

The brilliantly coloured Emperor Moth is found most often near heather, as it is fond of the caterpillar that feeds on this plant. The male is of a much brighter hue than the female, but both have " eye-spots."

carried home, together with a few leaves. A few days later they wanted fresh food and were provided with Groundsel (which, of course, is closely related to Ragwort). They all refused to touch it. Some were full grown and ready to pupate, but the others died. The same thing is true of the Common Tiger Moth Caterpillars ; when very young they will eat almost anything, but maturity makes them conservative in their tastes, and if they are then deprived of their accustomed food they will wander about, hungry and disconsolate, till at last they shrivel up and die.

A colourful Caterpillar.

One of the most beautiful Caterpillars I know is the Larva of the Emperor Moth. It is not at all rare, and will feed happily in the garden on Raspberry Bushes. The Moth comes out in the early summer, about May, laying the eggs on Blackthorn, Beech, Heather, Bramble and Apple, so that by July and August the Caterpillars are large enough to be easily found. Their colour is green, of a peculiarly brilliant shade, with black velvet bands. There are seven pink, hairy tubercles and bright orange breathing-holes, or spiracles. Sometimes the tubercles are bright-yellow instead of pink.

A very common but interesting Caterpillar, found all over Europe and doing a great amount of harm, is the Larva of the Lackey Moth. It takes its name from the red, blue and yellow marks on its back. The Caterpillars make a web of silk, and live and feed underneath this till nearly full grown. The whole life history of this Moth may be followed out in almost any garden.

All the Hawk Moth Larvæ are deeply interesting. Those of the Poplar Hawk are green, dotted with light-yellow, and marked along the sides with seven oblique yellow lines. The large green eggs are laid on leaves of Poplar, Sallow and the garden Lauristinus, and the Caterpillars, when they hatch out, are easy to rear. A life history of this common and beautiful Moth is worth having. The real difficulty comes at the end, when the Moths themselves appear. They are very heavy, and the walls of the breeding box should be made rough, with little projections, so that the insects may get a good foothold, otherwise they will fall and injure the undeveloped wings.

It sometimes happens that eggs kept in captivity hatch before the food leaves are ready. In this case one has to resort to all sorts of measures to keep the tiny things alive. Chopped-up, unopened leaf-buds provide a food which is often accepted. Or twigs may be peeled and then scraped ; it is the scrapings, of course, which the Caterpillars may eat.

Caterpillars are often found crawling on the ground, when it is impossible to discover their food plant. There are a few plants which are acceptable to a wide variety of Larvæ, and it is a good plan, when breeding Moths, to have some of these plants growing in one's garden. Here is a short list :

The Common Knotgrass, a weed with pinkish flowers, growing in most gardens.

Bird's-foot Trefoil, with clambering stem and deep-yellow pea flowers in August.

Ground Ivy, with strong scent and creeping, kidney-shaped leaves.

Dock. The best species is the broad-leaved.

Clover, white and purple.

Borage. A few seeds will keep up a supply of leaves all the year round.

Leaves of Plum, Sallow and Blackthorn.

The entomological world of wonders may be delightfully entered by making a collection of Chrysalides. Summer is the best time to make a start, and the hobby or pastime or study (for it is all these and more besides) can be carried on through the autumn and winter. By that time the birds, with their keen eyesight, have found and devoured all the exposed Pupæ, but they cannot very well reach the buried Moth Pupæ. All the mechanical aids required are a small garden trowel and a box containing some damp moss.

A beautiful Pest.

The first Pupa you find may be in your vegetable garden. It may be that of the Common—all too common !—Cabbage Moth. The Moths themselves sometimes blunder into the house and are recognised as garden pests, killed and forgotten. But they have, nevertheless, great beauty. Keep the shiny brown Chrysalides on slightly damp moss or earth in the tin box, and you will be astonished at the rich, browny-gold colourings of wing and body in the newly-emerged Moths.

One August evening a Swallowtail Moth was found clinging to a Cabbage leaf in the rain. It was rescued and taken indoors.

H. Bastin.]   *[Mondiale.*
THE WHITE PLUME MOTH.
This moth was photographed through the window-pane on which it was sitting. The photo is enlarged.

H. Bastin.]   *[Mondiale.*
"MOTHER SHIPTON'S LIKENESS."
A common moth which has markings on each wing (seen best sideways) much resembling an old crone.

W. Williams.]   THE TIGER MOTH.   *[Mallinson.*
Moths have often received names from their markings. The Tiger Moth is vivid in colouring and easily seen.

Ray Palmer.]   THE DEATH'S HEAD.   *[Mondiale.*
One of the Hawk-Moth family, the Death's Head has markings like a skull on its back. The above is a male.

H. Bastin.]   ERMINE MOTH.   *[Mondiale.*
Again the markings suggest the name. White, with dashes of black, give the appearance of ermine fur.

H. Bastin.]   TAPESTRY MOTH.   *[Mondiale.*
This gentleman is not appreciated in the home. His mate is less welcome, for she is the clothes moth.

Warmth revived it, and by next morning six eggs were laid, and the Moth, with dried wings, was resting comfortably in a corner of the box. At dusk she flew away, leaving her eggs behind. They all hatched out, lived on Honeysuckle leaves, and grew to about an inch long.

A few weeks later they fell asleep, for it is their habit to hibernate during the winter. They were green, darkish, streaked, with several tiny ridges and spots. They were exactly like small twigs. They stood upright, with heads erect, and tiny projecting feet that resembled minute leaf-buds. In this position they went to sleep. Sometimes they awoke and moved, but they were all connected together in a mass of silken threads.

In daylight these threads were hardly visible, but at night the light of a lantern revealed a most amazing sight. In the long beam of light one saw that the Caterpillars were enclosed in a globe of grey, sheeny, silk tissue. The bright light disturbed them, and they swayed about gently, but they made no attempt to crawl away. When spring came they all left their silken balloon during the day, returning to it at night. Then they moulted and separated from each other.

When about three inches long they pupated. That was in April. The cocoons were like sheaths of grey silk, suspended from twigs and covered with odds and ends of leaves and Spiders' webs. A magnifying glass showed how all this rubbish had been woven into a sort of felt. I happened to be on the spot when one of the Moths actually emerged. Quite suddenly it broke open the tight pupa case and stuck out its head and enormous eyes.

As quickly as possible it extricated itself from the case and climbed upwards, body suspended, so that the short, crumpled, damp wings hung clear. Very gradually these dried and expanded. They were pale sulphur-yellow, crossed by distinct lines of greenish-olive. The pointed tip on each hind wing was like a tiny Swallow's tail, and justified the Moth's popular name.

Rearing Moths is much more than a mere holiday pastime. I prefer rather to call it a most fascinating entomological study, with endless opportunities for original research.

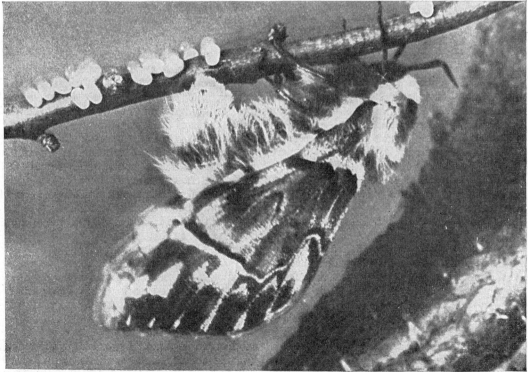

E. Krause.]
[Mondiale.

THE MOTH LAYS EGGS.

The male moth does not live long after mating. The more powerful female, however, busily concerns herself with the laying of eggs. These she deposits in such a place that the young caterpillars will have food at hand.

[*Mondiale.*

The thrill of watching the loaded fishing-boats return to harbour is almost as great as taking part in the fray oneself. Nets, containing a rich store of Pollack, are here seen drawn from the ocean's depths.

SOME MEMORIES OF FISH

By LEO WALMSLEY

MY first interest in living fish was predatory. In front of the little East Coast village where I spent my boyhood, long, curving reefs, called Scaurs, reach out to sea. They are bare at ebb tide ; but at their seaward ends are deep weedy channels, with the water in them crystal clear in calm weather. My fishing gear was a stick, a piece of grocer's string and a ha'penny hook, my bait the soft body of a Limpet snicked from the scaur top, and my chief quarry was fish the village boys called Pennocks, which are Billets when half-grown, Coal-Fish or Saith when they reach maturity.

They were elegant little fish with grey-blue backs and silvery bellies which flashed in the sunlight when they turned. They hung together in small shoals, but, unlike the " mass-produced " Herring, in whose vast shoals each fish is alike in age and size, there would be little Pennocks and big Pennocks, and always one who'd be boss and bully to the rest.

They were pernickety, too. My favourite spot was where there was a gap in the even line of the scaur, making an extra deep pool with a sandy bottom, fringed, like a grove in a wood, with a tall growth of oar-weed. There wouldn't be a fish in sight when I started, but I'd let my bait hover gently close to the dark fronds of weed, and suddenly see the nose of a Pennock just showing ; and then my job was to lure the whole shoal out, so that they'd show clear against the sand. Then they'd swim round and round the bait, pretending not to look at it, until one of them, usually the smallest in the shoal, would approach cheekily, touch it with its nose then wuffle it, and finally give it a bite ; and as soon as this happened they'd all rush for it, and I'd try to move it so that the biggest one, the bully, would get a fair bite and be caught. When a Pennock *was* caught the rest usually darted back to the weed, and it might take me a long time to lure them out again.

There were other fish, of course. Once on that patch of sand I saw a large Flounder, just the colour of the sand itself, and dead still but for its gently-vibrating gill covers. My line was not weighted, for Pennocks never feed on the bottom, and as luck would have it the Pennocks had never been so hungry and reckless. I wanted to drop my bait close by the Flounder's mouth, but before it sank half-way down, one of those wretched Pennocks would seize it, and I'd have to waste precious minutes taking it off, and re-baiting, and all the time I was expecting the Flounder to move away. At last, in desperation, I tied my pocket knife to the line just above the hook, and after several attempts I managed to get the bait absolutely touching the Flounder's snout. What I feared then was that my line would not be strong enough to hold such a monster. It was a needless fear, for although it could have swallowed the hooked bait without more exertion than the opening of its jaws, and a slight suck in, the Flounder completely ignored it as though it had been a pebble, and it remained lying there until the tide flowed, and I was compelled to shift.

Capturing a Conger.

The behaviour of another fish was very different. That time, a hot calm day in the summer holidays, there were about half a dozen of us boys fishing in the same place. Suddenly a great Conger swam leisurely out of the weed. One of the boys shouted in terror, but I whispered hoarsely to him to keep quiet, and I jerked my bait right in the Conger's path. I didn't see it open its mouth. I just saw my bait disappear, and felt a slight tug ; and the Conger moved on to the next boy's bait, and the next, and the next, until it got the lot, when it swam slowly out of sight. And it was not until then that I could really believe that it had taken not only my own bait and the others, but the hooks, too — every one of them.

As I grew older my interest in fish did not cease to be predatory, yet it became more philosophic. There were fish that you could not catch with a hook, or were of no use for food or sport. But some of them, like the Wrasses, were lovely as Butterflies to look at, and some had the most fascinating habits. At very low water " springs " in March or April there were places where I could always find a Lumpsucker, a queer, ugly fish with a thick body covered with spiny lumps like the skin of some prehistoric Lizard. It was always the male I'd find, stuck on to the rock with his peculiar ventral sucking disc at the mouth of a little cave under the scaur,

and effectively blocking it. Stuck to the ceiling of the cave would be a thick mass of eggs, which he was guarding, and would continue to guard until they were hatched.

Often, at a very low tide, I'd find one actually stranded at his cave mouth, almost dying, and I'd lift him into a pool and give him a breather ; but as soon as he recovered he'd make valiant efforts to get back to his eggs. Not once did I find a female ; and I have reason to think that she was the chief enemy he had to guard against, for it is a peculiar habit of the females of many species of fish to devour their own eggs, or to wait for the hatchment and devour the fry as they are hatched.

The habits of the Worm Pipe-Fish showed a less cynical attitude on the mother's part. These fish I usually found under a stone in a weedy pool. Lifting such a stone, my attention would be attracted by what might have been mistaken for a piece of cord weed, had it not moved jerkily about, as though deliberately attracting notice. That would be mother, whom I can best describe as looking like a stiffish Worm, with a tail and a tiny, vibrating dorsal fin and a head terminating in a long snout. I'd find father if I looked closely. He'd be twisted in among the weed, keeping absolutely still, and, I am convinced, doing his best to *look* like a piece of weed. But he went one better than father Lumpsucker. The eggs, very big and heavy, were actually cemented to his body, forming an effective and perilous sheet anchor. I have no doubt that mother's conspicuous movements were deliberately designed to attract the attention of possible enemies away from him and his precious burden.

Father rears the Family.

This habit of the male taking charge of the eggs appears to be fairly common among sea fish, and is even more romantic in the case of the fifteen-spined Stickle-back, which, like the Pipe-Fish, I found in weedy pools, although not under stones. Here the male actually builds a nest of scraps of weed ; really a tunnel, in which the female is almost entirely hidden when the eggs are being laid. While this is happening, he watches her very closely, and when finished he takes no chances, but peremptorily drives her off, fertilises the eggs, and takes up his duties as watcher and protector ; for again the female herself is the chief peril. He will,

THE SILVER POLLACK.   [Mondiale.

The Silver Pollack, often mistaken for the Hake, which it resembles in many ways, is a popular food-fish, greatly sought after by fishermen. It is caught mainly in the Channel and on the Irish and Scottish coasts.

THE JUMBO HADDOCK.   [Mondiale.

Here is another fish that finds its way on to many tables. Known by the peculiar name of Jumbo Haddock, it is also sometimes called the Scottish Hake, as it is a frequent visitor to the shores of Scotland.

Photo: H. Stokes.] THE CURIOUS CAT-FISH. [Mondiale.

This queer fish has no scales on its bony skin. It is a member of a family of over a thousand species. They are very rarely found in salt water, but mainly in rivers where the climate is temperate.

Photo: W. S. Berridge.] THE MACKEREL. [Mondiale.

Shoals of Mackerel find their way into the fishermen's nets on the East coast of Britain, and eventually to the table. They are covered with small scales, being silvery underneath, and are sometimes as long as eighteen inches.

Photo: W. S. Berridge.] THE WHITING. [Mondiale.

The Whiting, another marine food-fish, is related to the Cod family. It weighs about a pound and a half, and is abundant in shallow water round our coasts, extending also into the Mediterranean.

Photo: W. S. Berridge.] THE HERRING. [Mondiale.

Herring, found in shoals near the surface of the water, are caught in drift nets, and sold fresh or smoked. The eggs are deposited on weeds in shallow water and they hatch out in a few weeks.

in addition, fight pugnaciously any other creature that may approach, no matter what his size, and I have watched one chivy a large shore Crab, and effectively drive it off.

There is an excitement in finding fish like these—in watching them during the all too brief period allowed by the tide—that transcends the excitement of angling. The surprising thing is the immense number and variety of fish you can find on an average British shore when your eyes become practised. Nearly all fish have some means of camouflage, either directly visual, or of habit. They may be coloured in exact imitation of the weed in which they usually live. They may be marked with curious bands or blotches which mask the form of their bodies and render them almost invisible on any background, so long as they remain still. This keeping still, often spoken of as " shamming death," is an essential condition of successful camouflage. The eye perceives movement outside the field of its focus ; and it is doubtful whether the eyes of fish (which, after all, constitute the chief enemies of fish) are capable of sharp focus, as we know it. Salmon, Trout, Cod, Mackerel, almost any *hunting* fish, will snap at a *moving* artificial bait, even at a bare hook, whereas they will not cast a glance at it if it is perfectly stationary.

How the Angler Fish fishes.

The classic example of " marine " camouflage is that of the Angler Fish—a brutal-looking creature with a broad, flat head out of all proportion to its quite slender body ; and with a sinister mouth full of teeth as sharp as razor blades. Projecting from the head is a movable spine ending in a little feathery filament ; and when the fish is " fishing," the whole head and body is buried in the sand, but with the spine erect, and the filament exposed. Whether this actually fulfils the purpose of a bait, as many observers think, is, in my opinion, doubtful. In the many specimens I have examined I have never found one with the filament missing, or even damaged ; and, unless the taste or " scent " of it was such that it had no interest for big and equally voracious fish, it would be strange if it was not frequently snapped. More likely it functions as a special sensory organ. Certainly a small fish or Crab has but to graze it, and the hidden Angler springs up with its mouth agape, and its surprised victim is engulfed.

Perhaps most exciting and fascinating of all my youthful experiences with fish was in summer when the Herring Fry came in to our bay. Their presence first was shown by flocks of Gulls screaming wildly over a dark patch—like the shadow of a cloud—on the calm water far out at sea. Towards evening, however, the shoals would move in towards the land, and wherever you stood along the scaurs you'd see that the water was an almost solid mass of tiny Herring, each fish a darting, quivering bar of silver. Keeping them in perpetual motion, driving them relentlessly in to still shallower water, were other fish—Billet, Mackerel, Cod, Whiting, Plaice, Dabs, even Dog-Fish and Congers ; and you'd see where these hunters were at work by the Fry rising to the surface, making a sound like spattering rain, and perhaps you'd see the dorsal fin of a great Cod rising clear out of the water as it rushed in pursuit. Later, when darkness fell, the hunters would lose all caution and go mad in their pursuit of the Fry ; and what increased the excitement of it all was that the scene would be illuminated, for each moving fish stirred up the phosphorescent organisms in the water, so that you could imagine a miniature submarine volcanic eruption was in progress.

Ironically, it was futile to attempt to fish under these conditions, for the big fish, once they had got a portion of the shoal trapped between two converging scaurs, could literally browse on the Fry, and it was too much to expect them to trouble with an ordinary dead bait. Yet, standing bare-legged in the water in the thick of a shoal, with the Fry tickling me like Flies, I have had Billet and Cod bump into me, and caught them with my bare hands, and I remember once seeing a big Cod shoot out of the water on to the dry scaur, and lay there flapping, spitting Fry from its mouth until I killed it.

The Herring's Enemies.

Nothing could show more forcefully the intense struggle for existence that goes on among fish and other creatures of the sea than the life history of the Herring, of which their summer slaughter is but a phase. From the first moment of their hatchment (actually before, for the Spawn itself forms the diet of many fish) the Fry are relentlessly preyed upon. The miracle is that any one of them should survive to reach maturity, and so carry on the race, and incidentally supply

346

mankind with an abundance of food. Not only are the shoals of Fry decimated by fish and Gulls, Seals, and Dolphins ; with certain conditions of tide and weather they may be stranded on the shore, and I remember once when the whole shore of our bay was strewn with them, so that from the cliff top it appeared as though there had been a heavy fall of snow. Every rock pool, every hollow in the scaurs, were literally full of dead or dying fish, and the farmers took cartloads of them away for manure.

It saddened me, that, I remember. Those little fish looked so beautiful alive, with their silver bellies, and bright eyes, and delicate, vibrating fins. I thought that no matter how clever a human craftsman was, he could never fashion anything so perfect as one of these creatures of which billions were dead and swiftly rotting. Even the little scales which stuck to your hand if you touched one were marvellously formed, and had the translucent tints of an opal.

One evening, not so long ago, I was sitting with my fisherman friend, Marney Lunn, on the cliff that overlooks our bay. The tide was high, so that all the scaurs were hidden. The sea was calm, and far out we could discern the buoys of a long line we had set, and were to haul in the morning.

"It's a queer thing," Marney remarked suddenly in his slow, thoughtful way. "It's a very queer thing. But I've been fishing in that bay nearly all my life, and I know no

more really what's going on at the bottom of it than what's going on in the moon. That's the queerest thing about fish. You know they're there, of course, but you only see them properly when you catch them and take them out of where they live. You don't know *really* why you can catch Whiting and Plaice one day and not the next. You don't know how they spend their time, whether they go to sleep or not, what they do in rough weather, and you never know quite what sort of bait they like best, or whether they ever feel hungry like *we* do. You'd have to *be* a fish to know how they really feel about everything. Being under water must be like being in another world."

This I believe is true. We know a great deal about the nature and habits of fish. We know, for example, that the Common Eel of our shores and streams is hatched in the Western Atlantic, and that, in the fulfilment of its destiny, it retraces thats tupendous and perilous voyage to the place of its birth, to breed and die. Yet of the exact mechanism of this instinct, the driving and guiding forces at work, we know nothing that is not conjecture. Herein perhaps lies the true fascination of fish. Unlike terrestrial animals with which we share a common element, subject to the same conditions of atmospheric pressure, of light and dark, heat and cold, fish live in an element which by the simple fact that man cannot breathe in it, is as remote from his perceptions as the stars.

IN THE TROUT-STREAM.   [*Brit. Instruct. Films.*
The Trout, our commonest fresh-water fish, affords good sport to the angler. Found in all inland waters, it frequents the shallower streams during the spawning season. Its weight varies from half a pound to two pounds.

Photo : H. Stokes.] [Mondiale.

The Pike, most ferocious and largest of fresh-water fish, will even attack bathers on occasion. It eats many kinds of fish, and also includes Water-Hens in its diet. Pike have been known to weigh as much as fifty pounds.

BRITISH FRESH-WATER FISH

By D. THURSBY-PELHAM

THE lives of fresh-water fish are better known to us than those of the monsters that dwell in the deep. Yet there are many little-known facts about them explained below. There are fish in our streams that are expert nest-builders, others that look like snakes, some whose skins are said to cure ailments, and yet more that can be fed on bread and milk.

THE study of fresh-water fish has this advantage over that of their brothers in the sea, in that we can watch what they do and how they live for, at any rate, a part of their lives. There are very few places in the British Isles where we cannot see them, even if it is only in a pool by a brickyard, where the clay has been dug out. It is nearly true to say that wherever weeds and water insects can live, there fish will be found. It is only where chemicals and the overflow of factories kill all vegetable and animal life that they will be absent.

The lives of the different kinds of fish are as varied as those of human beings : there are the adventurers, who travel thousands of miles, and the stay-at-homes ; those who take care of their young—very much in the minority, sad to say—and those who leave them to chance ; lazy fish, fierce fish, greedy fish. All are interesting to watch.

Although all the fish that are spoken of here pass part of their lives in British waters,

some migrate to the sea at certain seasons, either for feeding or spawning.

At the bottom of the scale come the Lampreys. They are so unlike fish that at first sight they might be mistaken for Snakes, since they have no side fins, and long eel-shaped bodies. Instead of having jaws, the mouth ends in a round, toothed, sucking disc, into which fits the tongue, also furnished with teeth. With this disc the Lamprey fastens itself on to other fish and scrapes off the flesh with the tongue. So tightly do they cling that they are carried great distances by Salmon, and even by ships. If unable to find such means of transport when travelling up a river which is too rapid for them to swim against, they can be seen making a series of darts forward, and attaching themselves to a stone between each jump. Three kinds are to be found in these islands : Sea, River, and Brook Lampreys. It is on the Sea Lamprey that King Henry I. fed so greedily that " he died of a surfeit."

The breeding habits of all three are the same. In the early spring the male moves upstream and starts to prepare a nest, choosing a spot where the stream is rapid, just above a ripple. He clears away the stones from the sandy bottom and builds them up round the sides, the female joins him and gives a helping hand, or rather mouth, in shifting the larger stones. When all is in readiness the female fixes herself head down to a stone, the male twists himself partly round her body, and eggs and milt are then mixed together.

Builders that Die from Exhaustion.

The eggs are sticky, and after they are laid, both parents stir up the sand so that particles cling to them and weight them to the bottom. They then move the stones at the head of the nest so that sand is washed down by the current to cover them over. Several nests are made in this way, and when all the eggs are laid the parents are utterly exhausted and die of their exertions.

The eggs hatch out into tiny creatures half an inch long, called " Prides," quite unlike their parents, as they have an upper and lower jaw. Each makes a tube in the sand, where they live with their heads ready to pop out to catch the minute animals that float past in the water. Here they remain for three or four years, when they change into the form of the adult and take to a fish diet. The Sea Lampreys then go out to sea, where they stay for three or four years feeding all the while and growing to between two and three feet in length and between two and three pounds in weight. Then back they come to the rivers to spawn and die.

The River and Brook Lampreys are smaller and probably do not leave fresh water.

Eels, though quite unrelated to Lampreys, have the same snake-like shape, but their heads are normal with ordinary jaws. The story of their lives is quite different. It is one of the most wonderful tales of animal life that has ever been revealed, and for this we have to thank Dr. J. Schmidt, the great Danish scientist who has lately died, and his helpers, for their untiring work and many voyages. The story, however, is given in the chapter on Eels elsewhere in this book.

The remainder of the migrating fish belong to the great Salmon family, and its near cousins. The Salmon has been described in another chapter. Sea Trout, or Sewen as they are called in Wales, lead very much the same life as Salmon, with the following differences : When they reach the Smolt stage about April or May they go down to the river, but instead of swimming out to sea they wander up and down the estuaries for a few months and come back to the river or lake for the winter, where they feed. As a rule they do not spawn this season, though a few do so. Both Kelts and Clean Fish return to the open sea in March, where they stay till they re-enter the rivers in July and spawn in the autumn or winter. They can withstand the

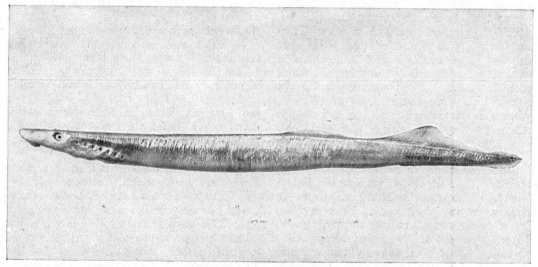

THE RIVER LAMPREY.

Lampreys, found in all temperate waters, have a habit of clinging to rocks and fishes by their mouths. The above type, which ascends the rivers for spawning purposes, is captured mainly for use as bait to catch sea fish.

H. Bastin.]   THE FOOD OF THE MONKS.   [Mondiale.

The Carp, which can live a long time out of water, is not a native of this country, but was introduced from Turkey some five hundred years ago.   It was formerly kept in ponds near monasteries for the use of monks.

effects of spawning better than Salmon, as it is not uncommon to find fish that have nine spawning marks on their scales.

The Little Smelt or Sparling is another of the Salmon tribe who spend their early life in the rivers and go out to the estuaries to feed. They travel up in large shoals to spawn, and crowd together so thickly that every stick and stone will be covered with eggs in the place they select.

The Shads are more nearly related to Herrings than to Salmon, and are very like them in appearance. They are found only in these islands in the Severn and the Shannon, which they ascend to spawn in May. They make no preparations for their eggs, but can be heard making quite a noise when spawning, by vigorously thrashing the water with their tails. The young remain in the river till they are about fifteen months old, when they go down to the sea, and do not return till they are three or four years old.

How the Salmon hides its Eggs.

Several members of the Salmon tribe pass their lives in fresh water, such as the Brown Trout, which can be found all over the country in any clear stream, river or lake, but they will not breed in stagnant water. Like their relatives, the Sea Trout, they make a " Redd " on gravelly bottoms and cover the eggs with a deep layer of gravel. Their food consists of insects, Shrimps, Worms, Minnows, etc., and even of each other. Large

Trout are regular cannibals, and chase and eat many of their young. During the season, when the May Fly hatch out in the chalky streams and rivers, they can be watched leaping up and gorging themselves till they can eat no more.

Although all Brown Trout are of the same species, they vary greatly in colour according to the place in which they live. The inhabitants of the peaty streams are much darker than their fellows of the clear chalk rivers. They differ also in size ; the dwellers in the small mountain streams rarely are heavier than a quarter of a pound, while in the large lakes they may grow to thirty pounds.

In habits and appearance Char are very like Trout, but are purely lake dwellers.

The Whitefish or Coregonids, such as Vendace, Pollan, Powan, Schelly and Gwyniad again are lake fish. The only exception is the Grayling, which inhabits many of the rivers where Trout are found from the Dee to the Itchen ; but not all Trout streams suit the Grayling.

There are many different members of the Carp family (Cyprionids) in this country. The Carp itself is not a native, but was introduced probably from Turkey some 500 years ago. This would seem incredible when one reflects on the length of time taken for the journey in these days ; but Carp can live a long time out of water. Indeed, in Holland they hang them up in nets in damp moss for weeks and feed them on bread and milk out of a spoon ! In the time of the monasteries they were cultivated in England, and still are on the Continent. They live in slow-flowing rivers, canals and ponds, where they grow to a great size, even up to thirty to forty pounds, and attain to still bigger dimensions in Germany where they are fed.

Wintering in the Mud.

They browse on vegetable matter, but also eat Worms, Snails and Insects. During the winter they bury themselves in the mud and eat nothing. There are no fish more difficult to catch ; they ignore the bait of the angler, and elude nets by burrowing under or leaping over them. The eggs are laid in May or June among weeds to which they adhere. Often three or four males attend the spawning female and become very lively, leaping out of the water.

There are many legends of the immense age to which they are said to live. How true these tales may be it is not possible to tell, but as legend often has a foundation, in fact it is likely that they *do* live a long time. Many observers have seen the curious phenomenon of Carp being attacked by male Frogs, who fix themselves on their heads and press their feet so firmly on to the eyes as to cause blindness.

The Tench, Roach, White Bream, Bream, and Rudd live in much the same waters as the Carp, and spawn in the late spring or early summer. As a rule they live the same placid life. The most interesting of these fish is the Tench, which gets its odd name of the " Doctor " from an old superstition that the slime on their skins cured many ailments both in men and in fish. It was said in particular that the Pike would not eat them, but would rub up against them to cure a wound. Alas, there is little foundation for the belief in the Pike's gratitude, since they will readily take them when offered as bait ! The idea probably arose from the undoubted fact that numbers of fish have been seen rubbing themselves against the Tench time after time, but why they do it we know not. Like Carp, they can live a long time out of water, and have often been found buried in the mud of ponds that dried up in the summer. Their winter sleep is so sound that they will not wake up till repeatedly hit with a stick.

The little Bitterling, which are only three inches long, have the most curious spawning habit of all the Carp family. They wear a dull-grey dress most of the year, but in the courting season the male gets a bright violet, red, and green suit, and the female grows out a long, tube-like oviduct. This she inserts into the shells of Freshwater Mussels and lays her eggs, where they are protected till the young hatch out. At the same time the Mussel sends out clouds of her minute young, which attach themselves to the skin of the Bitterling, burrow into the skin and there remain till they are old enough to fend for themselves.

The other members of the Carp tribe live in rivers. Barbels, so called from the barbs or beards which hang from their lower lips, are found only in the Thames, Trent, and some Yorkshire rivers. The distribution of Gudgeon, Chub, Dace and Bleak is limited to rivers south of the Firth of Forth ; they are not found in Devon, Cornwall or the west of Wales.

The little Minnows seem to be able to live anywhere, but prefer clear streams. They move about in shoals, always following their leader. They are inquisitive, and if a net is put down the leader will investigate, and soon be followed up by the rest so that the whole shoal can be scooped out. They spawn in May and June, gathering together in numbers in the shallows. The eggs are sticky and become fixed to the stones on the bottom. When spawning is finished the males lie together in a great heap, which may easily be mistaken for a mass of weed. After resting like this for a few days, they resume their usual busy life.

Loach are small fish nearly related to the Carp, and are present in small, clear streams. They live under the stones during the day and feed at night. Many readers will remember the delightful account in R. D. Blackmore's *Lorna Doone* of the boy wading downstream, turning over the stones and spearing the Loach as they swiftly darted out.

The Cod's large Appetite.

Only one member of the Cod family, the Burbot, lives in our English rivers, and it is confined to the east side of England. Though it often weighs sixty pounds in Alaska, here it rarely exceeds three pounds. They are greedy fish and take immense numbers of fish eggs, and will eat fish half as big as themselves.

Two kinds of Perch are common—the Perch and the Ruffe or Pope. They inhabit

Ray Palmer.]   THE RETIRING LOACH.   [Mondiale

Loach, found in small, clear streams, come out from their hiding-place under a stone at night to search for food.   They are small fish, nearly related to the Carp.   They can be caught by using the art of " guddling.'

A NEST-BUILDING FISH.   [W. S. Berridge.

The Stickleback, found in many ponds and ditches, builds a real nest of roots and stalks.   It is the male of this species that stays at home and looks after the eggs, afterwards tending the young Fry with great attention.

lakes, rivers or ponds where there are deep pools in which they pass the winter. Moving about in shoals, they are a terror to small fish which they chase and eat. In the spring they move to reedy shallows. The eggs are banded together and the female rubs against a reed till the end of the Roe is attached to it. She then moves forward and twists about till all the eggs have come out in a long string, which floats upwards in the water till they hatch.

The ferocious Pike are the largest of the purely fresh-water fish, and have been known to grow to four and five feet long, with a weight of forty to fifty pounds or more. They are found in all parts of the country, in still or running water, lakes and pools. They will attack anything and have even been known to bite bathers! They eat any fish, and even Water-Hens. It is by no means uncommon to catch a Pike and to find another one inside him nearly as big as himself. Unlike most fish, each male chooses a female in the autumn, and the pair live together in deep water till the spring, when they find a quiet backwater or ditch where the eggs are laid. From babyhood they live solitary lives, each little fish defending its own little pool from other baby Pike, just as the adult will kill or drive away its fellows from its own particular haunt.

Our two smallest fish, less than four inches long, are the Bullhead, or Miller's Thumb, and the Sticklebacks. The Bullhead pairs with a mate, and they make a hollow nest under a stone. The eggs are stuck to the underside of this roof, and for a month the father guards them jealously from intruders.

Sticklebacks, which may be found in shoals in ditches and small ponds, make far more elaborate preparations. In the spring the male finds a suitable spot for a nest. First he collects his building materials of roots and stalks and then builds up a real nest, binding the pieces together to form a little barrel with a hole at the top, an inch across, by means of a sticky substance from his kidneys. When it is finished he looks about for a wife, and swims about her or pushes her into the nest with his sharp spines.

When the female has laid her eggs she makes another hole and swims away; he then enters and fertilises the eggs and goes off again for other wives till the nest is filled with eggs. Fierce battles will take place when two Sticklebacks want the same lady! The work is not over when the eggs are laid; the father guards the nest and even aerates the water by vibrating his fins. When the young are hatched he removes the top of the nest, but keeps the Fry in the cradle till they can fend for themselves; any over-adventurous child who tries to leave too soon is caught in his mouth and put back again!

Photo: Ray Palmer.]   **THE COLOURFUL PERCH.**   *[Mondiale.*

Perch spend the winter in deep pools in lakes or rivers, proving fierce enemies to the smaller fish on which they prey. In the spring they move away to the shallows, where, among the reeds, their eggs are deposited.

The Red Mullet, so bright and attractive in the water, loses all its gay colouring when dead. Its suit of scarlet and gold is very elegant when the fish is alive, but when dead it looks ordinary and drab.

OUR COASTAL FINNY LIFE

By JAMES HORNELL, F.L.S., F.R.A.I.

THERE is no lack of variety in the large family that inhabits our coastal waters. Fish of all hues and shapes, fierce and inoffensive, grotesque and colourful, are to be found there, dodging the fisherman's nets and the jaws of their pursuers ; fish with dangerous tails armed with dagger-like spines, Sea-Horses, and other amazing creatures.

NO story is more delightful, more full of absorbing interest and variety, than that of the complicated lives and strange habits of the fishes that people the seas round our coasts, and afford restful sport to thousands of eager anglers who patiently whip the waters of our lakes and rivers. Apart from the interest in life given by a nodding acquaintance with some of the more striking incidents in their life histories, it behoves us to know something of the habits of those that make frequent appearance on our tables and supply us with the most tasty and nutritious of our animal foods.

Much has been written in fulsome praise of the wonderful beauty and gorgeous colouring of the finny mannikins of tropical seas, of the bizarre and often grotesque forms that they often assume, and of the surprisingly curious habits characterising many of them. Too frequently is it assumed that the denizens of our home waters are dull and drab in colour and of little interest by comparison.

Such a sweeping generalisation is far from being true. In our own seas we have fishes that can hold their own with many of the famed beauty queens of the Tropics. What, for instance, is more glorious than a scarlet Butterfly Gurnard volplaning through the water with outstretched, translucent wings, tinged with alternating wavy bands of scarlet and blue ? The Red Mullet and the Weever look pallid and unattractive on the fishmonger's slab, for their brightest colours fade in death ; but see them alive, the Weever darting eagerly after his prey and the Red Mullet combing the sand for food, and it is difficult to realise that they are the same fishes. In life the Red Mullet wears a slashed costume of scarlet and gold, while the Weever has one striped with narrow, slanting lines of brown, gold and pale-blue.

If the elegance of refined colouring and of graceful form be preferred, none can excel the beautifully-tapered torpedo shape of the Mackerel, the back a vivid lustrous blue shot with green, the belly pearly white, flashing with opalescent blushes of rainbow hues, and the sides finely marbled with broad, sinuous bands of dark colour ; or the Garfish, long and narrow like the scabbard of a sword, beautifully enamelled a brilliant malachite green above, plated with silver beneath.

The queerest Sea-Creatures.

But if the grotesque be required, that veritable Falstaff of the seas, the strange Lumpsucker, warted and mountainous in shape, is hard to beat ; the Fishing-Frog or Angler-Fish, its mouth extending cavern-like across the monstrous width of its flattened body, is the most fearsome-looking of its kind, and then the solemn little Sea-horse, ridiculous caricature of its land namesake, what more curious form could be imagined ?

In taking up the study of fishes, it is necessary to sort them into groups. These may follow lines of bodily structure whereby in the first instance all our familiar fishes are divided by the Zoologist into those with a cartilaginous or gristly skeleton, like the Dogfishes, Sharks, and Rays, and those where it is hard and bony, a division which includes the majority of our prime quality food fishes, such as the Sole, Cod, Herring and Mackerel. Or they may be classed from the practical fishery standpoint according as they live on or near the bottom and are captured by the trawl or by bottom lines, or swim in large shoals in the upper waters, like the Herring and the Mackerel, in search of their food supplies ; these latter are usually caught by floating nets and by trawling.

Of bottom-living fishes, Plaice and Sole, lumped together with Turbot and Brill as flat-fishes, have many habits in common. They love to lurk on sandy ground, their bodies concealed by a film of sand ; only an inconspicuous snout and two rounded eyeballs, easily mistaken for small pebbles, peep out. Everything about them has become adapted to their chosen habitat. When born out of a tiny floating egg, Larval Soles and Plaice, and Turbots, too, have an elongated body like that of ordinary-shaped fishes, such as the Cod and the Haddock, which, because of their almost cylindrical bodies, we class as " round fish." Like all round fish, the eyes of the little Larvæ are placed symmetrically one on each side of the head.

Before long the tiny creatures tire of a roving life. They want to rest ; the soft-surfaced sand will surely make a luxurious resting-place for their tired fins. But the shape of their body requires effort to maintain it from being rolled about by the current that sways the seaweed fronds to and fro so gracefully, so the little fish pancakes out and gets a firmer grip of the ground. This has the advantage, too, of making it less conspicuous.

Little by little the new conditions of life involve other changes. At this stage the little Flatfish is a delicious tit-bit to all the hungry small fishes and Crabs that scour the sands in search of food ; to guard as quickly as possible against this danger, microscopic brown and yellow dots of colour begin to be sprinkled over the upper side, and eventually the skin coloration exactly matches that of the surrounding sand ; if the sand be light in tint, the yellow dots expand ; if dark, the brown show up more conspicuously.

Simultaneously the bones of the skull begin to twist round in such a way as to compel the eye on the lower side to migrate to the upper or coloured side. For the remainder of its existence the Flatfish rests on one side —the right in the case of the Plaice, the left in that of the Turbot. Even when swimming it maintains this lop-sided attitude.

How the Plaice preserves its safety.

When the fully-formed Sole or Plaice lands on the sandy bottom after a swimming excursion, a few powerful flicks of the fins that fringe the body suffice to send clouds of sand upwards into the water, to settle back in a few seconds upon the upper surface of the now motionless fish, further concealing it from preying eyes.

The Ray family, which includes the Skates, have bodies as greatly flattened as those of the true Flatfishes, but here the flattening is caused by the body merging into the side fins, which broaden out into powerful and muscular wings. The Rays lie upon their bellies, and so their mouth is on the underside and not placed sideways as in the Plaice. Here, too, the colouring of the upper side usually tones with the tints of the ground where the fish lies, but several species glory in bright and gaudy hues.

These are mostly large and powerful fishes ; for them colour camouflage for protection is not necessary, neither is it of assistance when stalking their prey, for their food usually consists of Shellfish and Worms. Unlike their relatives the Sharks, the teeth of Rays are

Photo : W. S. Berridge.]   THE SMALL SPOTTED DOGFISH.   *[Mondiale.*

The Dogfish is a species of small shark of from three to five feet long. Some produce their young alive, others from eggs. The rough shagreen skin of some species is used for polishing wood ; some are sold as rock salmon.

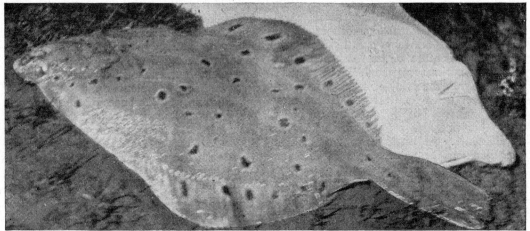

Photo : W. S. Berridge.]   A WARY FLAT-FISH.   *[Mondiale.*

The Plaice likes to lurk at the bottom of the water on sandy ground where it is easily concealed. To escape further from its enemies, it flicks up clouds of sand with its fins and these settle back on top of it.

Photo : W. S. Berridge.]   A TAILED FISH.   *[Mondiale.*

The Skate is provided with a long tail which it finds useful in warding off undesirable intruders in the water. It has a triangular snout, its mouth and nostrils being on the underside. Its length is up to four feet.

not fitted for offence ; in many species they form a mosaic of flat-topped pavement teeth suitable only for crushing the shells of the Molluscs on which they feed.

Mostly they are inoffensive fishes so far as man and other fishes are concerned, but certain among them—the Sting-Rays—have powerful and dangerous tail whips armed with one or even a couple of long, dagger-shaped spines, having an ugly row of backwardly-curved teeth along both edges. Woe betide the swimmer or diver who falls foul of one of these fearsome brutes. Lashing out with its tail, the toothed edge of the spine is capable of cutting a man's leg to the bone, and even comparatively slight wounds are apt to fester if there be delay in cleansing and sterilising them.

IN Ceylon terrible wounds have been inflicted on pearl divers in this way ; but the giant Ox-Ray, a fish with a width across the wings of eighteen to twenty feet, is dreaded most of all. The divers declare that it endeavours with devilish persistency to blanket any man it comes across, interposing the immense spread of its great, flapping wings between him and God's daylight till he drowns. The Ox-Ray ranges all tropical oceans and has been recorded even in British waters. Plagued by annoying parasites, it attempts to free itself by hurtling its vast bulk out of the water to a height of ten or a dozen feet or even more, to fall back with a mighty thud and splash—a sight familiar to those who often voyage through the Red Sea and Indian Ocean.

Most curious of the Ray family is the strange Torpedo Ray. In its tissues Nature, ages ago, evolved a type of electric cell that functions as efficiently as any small-powered, human-made battery. Even little fellows with a body disc less than the palm of the hand are able to give a smart shock if touched with the hand. Those full-grown can give a discharge so strong as to numb the arm to the shoulder. This remarkable power is used by the Torpedo both defensively and as a means of numbing its prey. Lying in wait on the muddy bottom where it makes its home, the approach of a Grey Mullet, its favourite victim, literally galvanises it into activity. Darting upwards, it hurls itself against the unfortunate fish, numbing it with an electric shock so intense that it finds it impossible to struggle or make any effort to escape. In a few moments it has disappeared down the Torpedo's throat.

The Fishing-Frog or Angler-Fish is another bottom-loving fish, not unlike the Torpedo Ray in outline, and with the same habit of lying inert in the mud. Too lazy and sluggish to hunt for its food, it has devised an artful

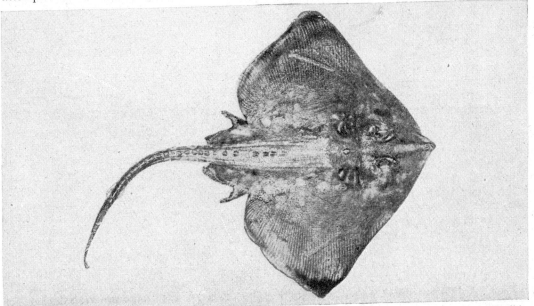

Photo : H. Stokes.]　　　　A STRANGE FISH.　　　　[*Mondiale.*

There are many peculiar members of the Ray family, mostly powerful fish. Their bodies are flat, their fins broadening out into muscular wings. Some have tail-whips with dagger-like spines that make dangerous weapons.

Photo : H. Stokes. [Mondiale.

AN ARTFUL DODGER.

The John Dory is a very stealthy stalker of prey, appearing so benevolently among the little fishes that they do not suspect his sinister intention of feeding on them. He, himself, is valued as a table-fish.

plan of luring smaller fish within easy snapping distance. The spiny rays of the dorsal fin have become free and the foremost one, hinged at its base, has developed into a veritable fishing rod, tipped by a fragment of skin representing the bait. Concealed in the mud, all that other fishes notice is the fluttering little rag bait at the end of the rod, which is raised ever and anon in the fashion of an angler casting his line. Nothing suggests danger, but woe to the fish that gives way to its curiosity ! Great goggle eyes have followed its movements, and just as the fish is investigating the bait, an earthquake, or rather mudquake, occurs, an enormous gape opens and the too-curious visitor disappears from sight.

Life in the sea is a continuous struggle for food and existence. Some fishes, like the Bonito and the Tunny, depend for success in the chase upon their speed. Many, less agile, stalk their prey. Of these is the John Dory. Good to eat and comely to look upon, this handsome, solemn-eyed creature moves so gently and quietly about his quest for food that the little fishes on which he feeds feel little alarm at his approach. The Dory appears so benevolent, so like a pious old vestryman, that surely no guile can lurk in his brain. But, alas ! even amongst the fishes outward appearances are often deceptive.

Watch him sidling towards that Goby fossicking among the weeds for his dinner. Nothing happens for quite a long time, the Goby merely moving quietly away every time the Dory comes near. At last any vague fears that the Goby had are lulled and vigilance is relaxed. The Dory sees and seizes the opportunity. The colour bands on his sides intensify and darken, the dorsal fin goes up—it had lain folded down till now—then a swift swoop, a huge telescopic mouth is thrust forward—the Goby disappears, and the Dory gives a satisfied gulp.

When Conger-Eel and Octopus fight.

In the combination of intelligence and great muscular power the Conger-Eel has few equals. Its appetite is tremendous, and its growth is correspondingly rapid. Lurking by day in crevices among the rocks, it becomes active at the approach of night, scouring the bottom for its prey. All kinds of fish appear equally welcome, nothing comes amiss, but the soft-fleshed, tasty Octopus is its favourite tit-bit, and a fight between the two is as exciting as one between a Mongoose and a Snake, and invariably ends with the disappearance of the Octopus. Even the Lobster sometimes falls a prey to the Conger's consuming hunger, and it is not an uncommon thing to find this fish in a Lobster-pot.

The muscularity of its tail is enormous. Instances are known where a Conger, having been thrown alive into a boat, has felt with the tip of its tail around till it touched the gunwale. Instantly a grip was taken, and in another moment the fish had hurled his body overboard. Hence it is the custom of some fishermen, not only to bludgeon the fish, but also to give it a smart blow at the root of the tail. Again, when a Conger is caught in a Lobster-pot, it sometimes effects its escape by thrusting its tail between the willow rods, forcing them sufficiently apart to allow the body to wriggle through backwards to freedom.

A Vegetarian Fish.

Very few fishes are vegetarian in diet, and none has developed a taste for the luxuriant masses of brown weeds that drape our rocks between tide-marks. The Grey Mullets are the most important of those that seldom touch animal food ; their small mouths are specially well adapted to browse on the velvety growth of the smaller seaweeds that are found on rocks and harbour piling ; the green varieties are their especial favourites.

The breeding and spawning habits of fishes are as varied as their devices for catching their prey. A few species, chiefly those of the Shark family, bring forth their young alive, sending them out into the world able to fend for themselves from the very moment of their birth. All other fishes are born from eggs, but whereas those of most fishes are produced either in considerable or in vast abundance, and are, individually, generally minute in size, those of the Dogfishes, Rays and Skates are of a fairly large size and are laid singly, enclosed in a large, horny case.

The " Sea-Purses," common on our beaches after storms, are the empty egg-capsules of the Skate, rectangular, flattened cases about two and a half inches long, with a short spike or horn projecting from each corner. Those of the Dogfish are amber-brown, smaller and more slender, and the horns seen in the Sea-purses of the Skate are here changed into coiling tendrils. The mother fish in the act of extruding the egg whirls round and round some chosen fronds of seaweed at lightning speed, intent upon entangling the tendrils amongst them to the end that the egg-case may be anchored securely and so defy the danger of being washed away by the waves or the strong under-currents.

So transparent is the Dogfish egg-case that the development of the little fish may easily be followed if one of these eggs be kept under observation in a small aquarium. It is wonderfully interesting to see how the yolk sac, at first many times bigger than the little fish itself, gradually diminishes as the contents are used up, until the day when the last atom of yolk is exhausted—the signal to the baby Dogfish that it must force open the valve at one end of the case and seek a living by its own unaided efforts.

Sharks, Dogfishes and all the Ray family pair after the fashion of land animals, but among other fishes the usual custom of the females is to shed their eggs freely into the water, where they are fertilised by milt from the males, shed simultaneously in the same place. Fertilisation is terribly haphazard, but so enormous is the number of eggs laid, and so profuse the milt, that few remain unfertilised. After this the eggs float at the mercy of the currents, drifting hither and thither.

While the Embryo is developing, vast numbers are destroyed by those fishes which, like the Herring, subsist upon the microscopical floating life of the sea—Plankton, as it is called by biologists. At last the time comes when the Larval fish bursts its prison walls and begins its free life. Beset by a host of enemies, instinct comes to its aid, for most Larval fishes at this stage shape a course for the shallows found close to the land, where they seek safety by concealing themselves among the weeds and rock crevices.

Where Fish lay their Eggs.

Contrary to the general belief, comparatively few fishes deposit their eggs upon the sea-bottom. The only one of importance with this habit is the Herring. Certain places in the North Sea are its favourite spawning grounds, and great controversy rages as to the amount of harm alleged to be caused by steam-trawling in these areas. In spite, however, of the intensive use of this method of fishing, the shoals of Herrings do not seem to suffer appreciably from this cause ; the quality and abundance of the food supply are much more important factors.

The ugly Lumpsucker also deposits its eggs on the bottom in large purplish masses, usually in clefts or at the foot of rocks where a curtain of weed affords a certain amount of concealment. So abundant are the Lump-

Photo : W. S. Berridge.] A POPULAR CATCH. [Mondiale.
The Whiting, a marine food-fish, is related to the Cod family. It is an extremely popular item as a table-dish.

A USEFUL FISH. [Mondiale.
The Cod is rated very highly as a food-fish, and also for the medicinal value of the oil procured from its liver.

Photo : W. S. Berridge.] THE RED GURNARD. [Mondiale.
This fish, found chiefly near the coast, looks like a butterfly when its finger-like rays are in motion.

ANOTHER FOOD-FISH. [Mondiale.
The Hake, found chiefly in the waters of the North Atlantic, is caught by night, chiefly in pilchard nets.

suckers in northern localities that these egg-masses are salted down and made into an inferior kind of caviare.

Other fishes that attach their eggs to rocks and boulders are the Blennies and the Gobies. Usually the eggs are deposited in a closely-set, even layer. Blenny eggs are round and about the size of small pin-heads. Those of the Gobies are spindle-shaped, and as the capsule is transparent, the growth of the Larval fish may be watched through all its stages. When the contents of the yolk sac have at last been absorbed, the fish begins to wriggle violently within its prison. At last the membrane splits and the little fellow emerges, tail-first. Sometimes the effort is too great at the first attempt ; the prisoner has to rest awhile, often with half of its body still within the capsule. A few seconds suffice for recovery, and then with a few more wriggles the little fish swims away.

NONE of these fishes keep regular watch over their eggs, though the beginning of the habit appears to be present for the males are often seen hovering about. True nest-building fishes are rare in British waters. These include several of the brightly-coloured Wrasses, sometimes called Rockfishes, and the two Sticklebacks, the big fellow with fifteen spines that lives in the sea and the little three-spined one of our streams and ponds. The nests of these three kinds of fishes show an interesting gradation in the mechani-cal skill of the makers. The Wrasses are content to gather a large quantity of fine seaweeds, usually the soft red kinds, and to pile this in a rocky crevice. The large, amber-coloured eggs are loosely scattered through the tangle, and the male fish stands by, defensive, until the Fry emerge.

The fifteen-spined Stickleback has a higher ideal of architecture. Usually it will use for the foundation and walls a tuft of rooted seaweed which is shaped into a round or pear-shaped mass about the size of the closed fist, the whole bound together with a tangle of strong mucilaginous threads. If unable to find a tuft of suitable size or position, the fish will collect fragments of weed fronds and work them into the required shape with thread from its own body, just as a Silk Worm Caterpillar forms its cocoon. Still more elaborate is the nest of the three-spined Stickle-back, woven by the male from fragments of water-weed fibres held together by gluey threads after the fashion of his marine cousin. The nest, about an inch in diameter, has a cavity in the centre about the size of a Hazel nut for the reception of the eggs.

Even more watchful of the safety of the developing young are the members of the quaint group of Pipefishes and Sea Horses. A nest is not safe enough for them. Father again is to the fore, for the females of these families consider they have done their full and entire duty by producing the eggs. It

THE LEMON SOLE. [*Mondiale.*

The Lemon Sole, inferior in flavour to the ordinary Sole, is yet as popular for fishermen, who fish for it in trawlers. It is not allied to the true Sole, its name being a corruption of the French for dab—*limande*

Photo : Ray Palmer.] THE ACROBATIC ELVER. [Mondiale.

The young Eel, which is born in the sea, struggles back towards the river till it finds a spot where it can procure suitable food. When grown to maturity it journeys downstream, back to the sea.

is he who takes charge of them as soon as they are laid, by cementing them in an even layer to the underside of his body. Some species. have folds of skin along the sides which, like the flaps of a coat, fold over and protect the eggs.

In the Sea Horse the edges of these flaps are joined together to form a real incubatory pouch. On one occasion I was so lucky as to watch the opening of one of these pouches and the emergence of over two hundred tiny baby Sea Horses, exact miniatures of the parent, each barely three-sixteenths of an inch in length. Solemn little mites, they seemed to feel their helplessness more than other fry ; they were reluctant to leave father, keeping close to him for some days in a little shoal.

Why the males alone of these fishes display solicitude for the safety of eggs and young, while the females go gadding about, is a problem that awaits solution.

The majority of sea-fishes die when transferred to fresh water. Of the exceptions the most notable is the Salmon. This handsome fish, born in our rivers, wends its way after a time to the sea, where it remains till sexually mature. The urge to propagate its kind then takes supreme possession of its actions, and instinct urges it to enter a river mouth and to ascend the stream until it finds a reach where the water purls gently over a clean gravel bed. Rapids and waterfalls deter it not. It threads its way through boiling whirlpools and leaps the falls time and again

till it succeeds at last or dies in the attempt. Once past these obstructions, the female Salmon prepares to spawn. Choosing a clean stretch of gravel, she ploughs a furrow in it and there lays her eggs, careful at the same time not to disturb the eggs laid by others of her kind. Over these the male sheds his milt, fertilising them. Thereafter the hungry parents are free to return to the sea, where ample food awaits them. If they survive, they return the following year to the same river and raise a fresh brood. This habit of migrating from sea to river for spawning is common to a few other fishes ; among them are the Hilsa of India and the Shad of North America, both near relatives of the Herring.

When the Eel travels inland.

The Fresh-water Eel reverses this habit. Born in the open sea, far from land, the young make their way in countless millions towards the mouths of our rivers, which they ascend in order to reach all the suitable waters where food can be found. Here they remain and grow to maturity until the sexual urge comes upon them. When this happens they begin to move downstream towards the sea. No impediment daunts them, and it is marvellous what obstacles they overcome in their long and weary journey to the spawning region thousands of miles from England.

Fishes which never quit the sea have also their special seasonal migrations. Like the modern tourists, they love to move in great companies, but their tours are either group honeymoons or migrations in search of pastures new, where food is to be had in abundance. If the migrating fishes be small, like the Herring and the Sardine, the larger fishes follow in their wake, cutting off stragglers and harrying the main bodies.

The flesh of different fishes varies very greatly in quality. The so-called "White Fish" which comprises practically all non-oily fishes with white flesh, such as the Sole, Plaice, Whiting, Cod, and Skate, is the most valuable and nutritious of our animal foods because of its easy digestibility. Fishes with much oil in their tissues, as the Herring, Sardine, Mackerel, Salmon and Eel, are even more nutritious, but the presence of the oil, which saturates them, gives a richness when cooked that renders them less easy for the invalid to digest. For the man in health who takes plenty of exercise or performs manual labour, however, the Herring is *par excellence* the finest food to be used as a regular item in his dietary. It has the added advantage of being the cheapest fish within our reach. Certain little Water Fleas, Copepods, as they are called, form the favourite food of the Herring, and as these minute creatures feed upon microscopic plant life exceedingly rich in vitamins, so the cycle runs on into the Herring, while at the breakfast-table the fish yields these vitamins in turn in rich abundance to those who appreciate the tastiness and value of the Herring as a food-fish.

Let us remember, too, that in helping ourselves to health by eating Herrings, we are aiding one of the greatest of British fishing industries and helping indirectly to keep in being a hardy, courageous and simple-minded class of men ; their work is hard ; danger from gales and tempest, from fog and blinding storms of driving rain are often their lot, and, as we know, without their help in the terrible submarine menace of the Great War, the task of the Navy would have been immeasurably more difficult than it was.

To give an adequate idea of the vast extent of the fishing industry is exceedingly difficult ; arrays of enormous rows of figures convey their import but vaguely to the mind. So, when we learn that the average catch of bottom-fish averages 550,000 tons per annum, and that of Herrings—a branch of the industry sadly crippled by the post-war falling-off in demand from Russia and the Baltic countries—still exceeds 120,000 tons, all we can grasp is that catches are on an enormous scale.

Most of the bottom fish are caught by steam-trawling, with line-fishing coming a long way behind. The Herring and its relatives swim high and are taken in drift nets, which are walls of netting, buoyed along the upper margin in order to float them vertically in the water. According to the height in the sea at which the shoals are believed to be swimming, so are the nets carefully adjusted.

THE HALIBUT.
The largest of the flat-fish family is found on the northern shores of Britain. At one time this fish, which is still popular as a table-dish, was eaten on holy days. It sometimes reaches the length of eight feet.

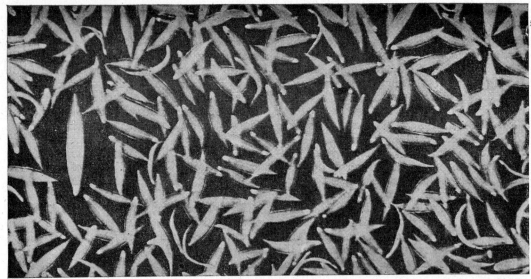

Photo: James Hornell.]   [Mondiale.

This amazing picture shows a few specimens out of several hundred eel-fry that were caught in the Western Atlantic. These tiny, animated needles develop snake-like bodies ultimately and grow to a length of nearly four feet.

THE MARVELLOUS LIFE-STORY OF THE EEL

By JAMES HORNELL, F.L.S., F.R.A.I.

THE Eel has a romantic life, swooping in first of all from its nursery in mid-ocean to mature in the river, and then making its way back to brave the dangers of the deep. These journeys are fraught with many difficulties, as the author tells below, and the wriggling little Elvers and snake-like Eels experience many thrilling encounters.

FOURTEEN years ago the Danish zoologist, Dr. Johannes Schmidt, returned from that historic voyage of the schooner *Dana*, which resulted in the discovery of the breeding-grounds of the Eel. By wonderful good fortune I happened to pass through Copenhagen in August of that year (1920), and although the amazing story had not been communicated to the world at large, Dr. Schmidt generously gave me a peep behind the scenes. Never was I more astonished than when he held up in triumph a bottle containing eight hundred Larval Eels, each about an inch long, all taken in one haul of the net in the Sargasso Sea area, away to the east of the Bahamas. But this is anticipating, and the epic of the Eel must begin nearer home.

As contrasted with the fierce Conger Eel and the snake-like Murreys that spend their lives in the sea, the Common Eel of our ponds and rivers is usually called the Fresh-water Eel. This is really a misnomer, for the Eel is born in the sea and dies in the sea; its life in fresh water is merely an interlude in the play.

As we know it, this fish varies considerably in colour. The smaller ones, the "snigs" of the North of England, are dark olive-brown on the back, and golden-yellow on the belly. Large ones caught in the autumn when migrating seawards are lighter coloured on the back, while the yellow of the belly has changed to a silvery white. Naturalists formerly considered these to be distinct species; to-day it is recognised that the many species into which the Eels of Europe were once divided must be reduced to a single one. Similarly the Eels of North America are all referable to another but different species.

How and where the multitudes of Eels that swarm in rivers and lakes reproduce, and how their numbers are replenished year by year, have been amongst Nature's most mysterious and most closely-guarded secrets from the beginnings of history. All that the early naturalists recognised was that little creatures about two inches long and as thick as a darning needle, generally called Elvers in England, appeared in myriads during the spring months in river estuaries, earlier in those of the west coast, later in those on the east, and that these made their way up streams and grew eventually into ordinary Eels.

Besides this, those who gave the matter any thought, perceiving that large Eels never ascend rivers, whereas large numbers are known to descend to the sea every autumn and winter, concluded that Eels must breed but once in their lifetime, and do this somewhere in the sea. Country folk thought otherwise; they settled the matter offhand by declaring that the Elvers grew from horsehair. The dark coloured Elvers thronging together in dense and wriggling masses in their eager rush upstream, jostling, surging and inextricably mixed together, certainly do look like a tangle of black horsehair, and so the countrymen decided that as they look like horsehair they must certainly be of horsehair origin—how or why was not worth troubling about!

The yellow-bellied Eels that grow from the little Elvers remain in this bright livery for very long periods; the average for the females, which are larger than the males, is about seven-and-a-half years, whereas the males are ready for betrothal—I purposely avoid terming it "wedding," for that would be premature—at an age varying from five-and-a-half to seven-and-a-half years. Should any obstacle prevent the Eel from setting out on its journey to the sea, it may live many years longer; some have been credited with reaching the ripe old age of twenty years— the reward of a celibate existence, free from the consuming flame of any love-episode.

How are these ages ascertained? By counting the annual rings of growth on the the scales. Contrary to common belief, Eels are not scaleless; scales do exist, but so small, so tenuous, and so buried in the slime-covered skin that they cannot be seen by the naked eye, nor felt by touch. These scales continue to grow with the passage of the years. During the warm months each year when food is abundant, a broad, clear band is added at the outer margin, whereas in winter when the fish is torpid and more concerned to find a comfortable hole in a bank than to search in ice-cold water for a meal, the growth of the scale is all but arrested, a very narrow, darkish band marking this time of stationary growth.

Every autumn a contingent, consisting approximately of between one-sixth and one-eighth of the total number of Eels in any river or lake, approach maturity and feel the intense and irresistible urge to proceed downstream to the sea, with the object of

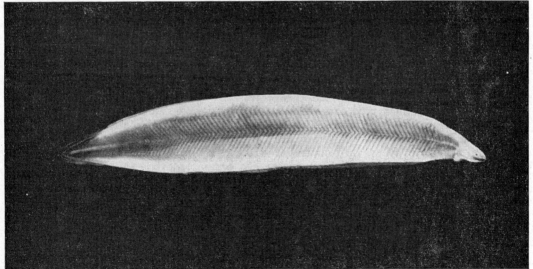

AN UNDEVELOPED EEL.
The life-story of the Eel still remains something of a mystery. Larval Eels, such as that seen above, are found mainly in deep sea waters, where it is evident that Eels breed. At a later stage, they journey toward the coast.

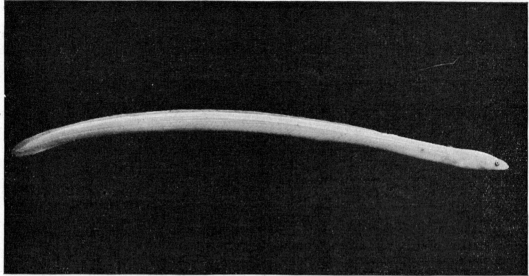

Photo: H. Stokes.]
THE ELVER'S ORIGIN.
[*Mondiale.*

The young members of the Eel fry are called Elvers. Shoals of these dark-coloured wriggling creatures make their way in masses upstream. The country folk, in bygone days, declared that these Elvers grew from horse-hair

breeding. They cease to feed, and so far as we know take no food during the long, drawn-out journey to the spawning-ground, living meanwhile upon the accumulated fat in their tissues, for at this time they are so loaded with it that in the great Eel-preserving factory at Comacchio, near Venice, an immense quantity of oil drips from them when roasted preparatory to being pickled in vinegar and spices for the German market. Few are the obstacles able to check their downward career. If they live in a pond without outlet, they have been known to make their way over damp grass for considerable distances in search of a stream.

Once the sea be gained, those Eels that hail from British waters disappear immediately from human ken. None has ever been found in the small-meshed nets used for catching Shrimps and Sprats; none ever enters a Lobster or a Prawn-pot. Only in the Baltic has it been possible to follow their course for some part of their journey, for innumerable Eel-weirs are worked on the coasts of that sea, enabling marking experiments to be carried out. In this way it has been found that Eels from Baltic rivers travel towards the North Sea at an average speed of about nine miles in a day. Thence their course is known only by passing to the other end of the life-cycle and deducing the ultimate goal of the breeding Eel to be in that locality where the youngest Eel-Larvæ are found.

Strangely enough no one has ever captured an Eel, either male or female, with the reproductive organs ripe for spawning. The sexes have no outward distinguishing marks, and males were not even recognised by dissection till 1873. It is now known that full-grown males are smaller than females, and that they have an inclination to linger in estuaries and the brackish reaches of rivers, whereas the females prefer a fresh-water home. The female also comes later to maturity, due probably to her need to store up a greater food reserve in her body against the time when the developing of her eggs makes call upon her strength. This, however, is just beginning when she sets out on her journey seawards.

The location of the spawning grounds and the history of the young fish from the egg upwards were among the great unsolved problems of animal life at the beginning of the present century, although in 1896 two Italian zoologists, Grassi and Calandruccio, had been able to prove that a little fish, going by the name of *Leptocephalus brevirostris*, and found in the Strait of Messina, was in reality not a separate species, but a Larva that changed little by little into the Elver of the Common Eel. This was a notable discovery, not so much as a fact standing alone, but because it gave a starting-point from which to work forwards. No further advance was made till May, 1904, when Dr. Schmidt was led by chance to tackle the problem. At that time he was engaged on other investigations promoted by the International Council for the Study of the Sea. In the little *Thor*, a vessel lent by the Danish Government, Dr. Schmidt was one night towing a fine-meshed trawl-net, specially designed to capture young fishes near the surface of the sea. In one of the hauls was a fairly large fish Larva, recognised at once as the little creature that the two Italians had discovered to be a stage in the life-story of the Eel. This epoch-making find occurred west of the Faroe Islands. It was followed soon after by the capture of a second specimen of this Lepto-cephalid Larva—the name now given to the creature —by the Irish Fishery Cruiser, the S.S. *Helga*.

How Eels help Industry.

In Denmark the Eel fishery is a specially important industry, so the Scientific Council, which directs these matters, arranged for the Danes to take charge of the work of carrying this investigation of the life-history of the Eel to a conclusion. Little did Dr. Schmidt dream of the long and weary chase to which he was committed ; little did he think, as he himself has said, that it would be sixteen years before he could settle the main facts—even then several more years were to elapse before it was possible to fit all the facts into a coherent scheme and to find satisfactory answers to certain minor puzzles that cropped up from time to time to complicate the original problem. Even to this day the eggs and the spawning fish have not been obtained in spite of concentrated effort ; but this is a matter of such minor importance that Dr. Schmidt has now turned his attention to solving the problem of the breeding-places of the several species of Eels living in the Western Pacific and the seas around India.

Where Eels breed.

To return to our Larval Eels. The two found in 1904 were caught in places where the depth of the sea is about five hundred fathoms. On the hypothesis that in this depth might be found the breeding-places of the Eel, intensive work was carried out during the succeeding year along a broad belt of sea reaching from the Faroes to Brittany ; sure enough more Larvæ were found, all to the west of the five-hundred fathom line, but no smaller sizes were found than in 1904. This result proved two facts : that all Western European Eels come from

the Atlantic and that the breeding-place is not in shallow water.

And so the story was gradually built up in face of endless difficulties and disappointments. The *Thor* was found too small for the prolonged work far out in the Atlantic that was now seen to be necessary ; no other vessel was available. The best that was possible was to interest the skippers of vessels plying to and from the West Indies to make occasional hauls with nets provided for the purpose. Let it be said to the credit of the Danish mercantile marine, such good work was done that the material so provided enabled a notable advance to be made. Partly from collections made in this way, and partly from other sources, it was possible for Schmidt to say definitely in 1912 that the spawning-grounds of the European Eel lay far away to the westward in the North Atlantic.

In the following year he obtained the use of a small schooner, the *Margrethe*, and extended his research to the West Indies, obtaining large quantities of Larvæ of different sizes, but eventually losing his ship on the rocks of one of the islands. Fortunately the valuable collections were saved.

How the Eel knows its Home.

The chase was now getting hot. It was clear that, whereas the Eel Larvæ increased in number from east to west, in size they increased in the opposite direction—west to east. The most astonishing fact of all was that some Larvæ of the European Eel were found in a locality comparatively close to the American coast—only nine degrees farther east than New York—and others not far to the north of the outer West Indies. Almost as strange and even more perplexing was it to find in some hauls a mixture of the Larvæ of both the European and the American Eel. These, by the way, are recognised in the adult fish by a difference in the number of the vertebræ in the backbone, and in the larvæ by a difference in the number of the bands of muscles between head and tail.

Although Denmark was neutral during the war, the submarine activities of the Germans eventually cut off the supplies collected by Danish merchant steamers, and it was not until 1920 that Dr. Schmidt was enabled to obtain a vessel, the *Dana*, to take him to the spot where he now felt sure he would solve the main problem. No longer was he working in the dark ; as a consequence, the collections made in 1920 and succeeding years have enabled him to prove that the breeding-place of the European Eel is in deep water to the north-east and north of the West Indies, or, to be precise, to comprise the area lying between 22° and 30° North latitude and about 48° and 65° West longitude. He also found that the breeding-place of the American Eel lay immediately to the west of this locality, and in part overlapped it. In quite a number of hauls the Larvæ of both species were represented. How tremendous was the labour entailed in this investigation may be imagined from the fact that the muscle-segments of every one of the seven thousand Larvæ caught during the 1920 expedition had to be counted under the microscope before the identity of each could be ascertained. And these seg-

deep water in the region of the Sargasso Sea, beginning in early spring and lasting well into summer, and that they must die thereafter. The earliest Larval stage taken was just a quarter of an inch in length. At this size and till the little fishes gain a further half-inch in length, they live far down in the depths, and the net has to be towed between one hundred and one hundred and fifty fathoms to catch them. With greater increase in size they move nearer to the surface, favouring for the most part a depth of twelve to twenty-five fathoms.

No sooner do they reach this horizon than they begin to travel away from their birthplace and to head in the direction of Europe. The journey is slow. In their first summer they are all found in the Western Atlantic ;

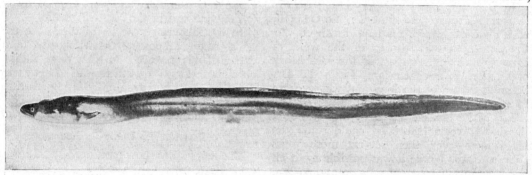

THE FULL-GROWN EEL.   [*Mondiale.*

Having attained maturity the Eel is now ready for adventure in mid-ocean. It may attain an age of twenty years if it can escape the many obstacles that threaten its life. Those that avoid the journey to the sea are safest.

ment or muscle bands vary from 104 to 120 in each Larva !

The gathering together of the ends of the scattered threads, and the untying of the many hard-tied knots in this tangled puzzle of marine life took several years longer. In all it has occupied the major part of twenty years in Dr. Schmidt's life to elucidate the main problem, and to explain away the fresh difficulties that arose from time to time as the work progressed. For instance, if the spawning-grounds of the European and the American Eels overlap, how is it that the young fishes know unerringly which is the right direction to take in order to reach their respective homes ? How long does it take the young of the European Eel to journey to the British coast, and what becomes of the old Eels after spawning ?

To put the answers and main facts into the proverbial nutshell : Schmidt found that the spawning of the old Eels takes place in

in the second they reach mid-Atlantic, doubled in size and now fully two inches in length ; in the third summer, having attained their full Larval size of three inches, they are found in the vicinity of the steep seaward edge of the wide submarine plateau marked out by the hundred-fathom line off the west coast of Ireland. All this time they retain the same appearance—a long, ribbon-shaped body, pellucidly transparent, tapered to a point at each end, for the head is absurdly small compared with the depth of the body. Tiny as it is, the head has jaws armed with sharp teeth, well adapted to seize the microscopic life on which it feeds voraciously.

The route taken coincides with that of the Gulf Stream. There can be no doubt that its steady flow towards the north-east is of the greatest help to the little creatures in their long and arduous journey. All the time they swim steadily onwards, ever heading directly towards Europe, impelled by an instinct that eludes our probing. Millions perish by the way, but none stray to waters other than those around Europe and North Africa.

A different instinct possesses the Larvæ of the American Eel. Instead of following the Gulf Stream, they strike to the north-west, heading straight for the coast line of the United States. In this was one of the greatest puzzles that cropped up unexpectedly in the course of the investigations. Even yet it is only partially solved by the explanation that the change to the Elver stage is reached at the end of a single year in the case of the American Larva, whereas that of its European cousin lasts nearly three years. A single year of life is far too short to enable one of these little creatures to reach Europe, so a nearer home has to be sought, and that means America. But this rather begs the question, for why should the immature life of one kind be three years, and that of the other only one?

When the Larval Eel becomes an Elver.

When the European Eel Larvæ reach the coastal waters of Europe in their third summer they begin to change gradually into the Elver stage. Till this is complete they cease to feed. The Larval teeth drop out, the body shrinks and narrows, and the broad leaf-shape, so characteristic hitherto, is transformed into a thin, needle-like creature of considerably shorter length. It is now a true Elver, and untold billions and trillions of these tiny wriggling, worm-like fishes swarm into the estuaries of all the rivers of Western Europe. Ireland receives the earliest of the invading hosts which arrive there between October and December. In January and February they are swarming into the Bristol Channel. They make a tasty dish when fried, and vast numbers meet their untimely end in this inglorious manner. So rich is the catch of Elvers in the Severn that Germany began the import of large quantities before the war to stock such of her rivers and ponds as did not receive a sufficient natural supply, for we have to remember that the Eel is a keen rival of the sausage for the favour of the German people.

Like the adult Salmon, the little Elvers are able to surmount any reasonable obstacle to their passage up rivers. In reaches where the current is strong they swim along alert to take advantage of every eddy and stretch of slack water. Rapids are passed by short rushes from stone to stone exactly as infantry are trained to advance under fire. When a waterfall interposes, they make use of the damp mosses draping the sides, wriggling into the dripping vegetation, they pass from stalk to stalk, leaf to leaf, in an endless procession like an army of Ants on a foraging expedition. Even lock-gates are sometimes surmounted ; every inequality in the woodwork is availed of, and if some die in the attempt this but makes it easier for their comrades to ascend, for their dead bodies form useful ladders.

Helping the Elver on its Way.

In localities where Eel-culture is carried on, the ascent of the Eel Fry over weirs is sometimes assisted by placing coarse ropes made of twisted straw in grooves cut in the masonry. Up these the Elvers crawl in such masses that at a distance the rope looks like a black oak log.

The greatest and most famous of Eel farms is that carried on in the lagoons around Comacchio, an ancient town southward of Venice. Here live a self-contained community of fishermen who cultivate their shallow waters as methodically as the farmer tills his fields. These are descendants of Roman subjects evicted from their homes in the fifth century by a flood of Barbarians from the north. They sought refuge in the bosom of an immense marsh, which their industry has transformed through the centuries into a gigantic system of Eel ponds without rival in the vastness of their extent and in the richness of their produce. The industry is a communal one, owned and worked by the people themselves. The lagoons, stocked in spring with Elvers, are fished between October and December by trapping the mature Eels as they attempt to force their way to the sea.

Catching Eels by the Ton.

Large catches are made only on moonless or overcast nights. When a storm from seaward coincides with one of these black nights, the quantity of Eels that accumulates in these labyrinths is sometimes so enormous that they become choked with a solid mass of struggling, gasping fishes. After one such memorable night, over three hundred tons of Eels were taken from the traps. Quantities so vast are inconvenient to handle, so, whenever the men find the fish arriving too quickly, they light bonfires at the inner ends of the passages, and this has the desired effect of checking the migration temporarily.

Photo : James Hornell.]   THE EEL-FARM.   *[Mondiale.*

In some places Eel-catching stations, at an outlet towards the sea, are built to trap the mature Eels on their journey to the ocean. Tons of Eels make their way into the traps, and are taken possession of by the fishermen.

Pho o: James Hornell.]   THE DEATH-TRAP.   *[Mondiale.*

This view of the Eel-farm shows in the centre between the locks the place where the fish are caught. On the right may be seen the building where large catches are stored. Here many captive Eels end their days.